Boater's Guide to
Lake Powell

Featuring Hiking, Camping, Geology, History & Archaeology

5th Edition

Michael R. Kelsey

Kelsey Publishing
456 E. 100 N.
Provo, Utah, USA, 84606-3208
Tele & Fax 801-373-3327
Email Addresses--one of these should work:
kelsey@canyoneering.com
mrkelsey@veracity.com

For Canyoneering Information on the Colorado Plateau, Contact:
kelseyguidebooks.com
This website is linked to **canyoneering.com**
Guidebook Updates - Canyon Conditions
Weather Forecasts - Desert Ecology
Open Forums - Canyoneering Techniques
Gear & Book Reviews

Other websites which may have updated information
on canyons or hikes in this book or others are:
americansouthwest.net
canyoneeringUSA.com
canyoneering.net
climb-utah.com
toddshikingguide.com
Or Google any canyon by name and see what happens

D0199309

5th Edition, March, 2008
4th Edition, September, 2001
2nd Updated Edition, August, 1996
Updated Edition, November, 1991
First Edition, March, 1989
Copyright 2008 Michael R. Kelsey All Rights Reserved
Library of Congress Catalog Card Number 2007905476
ISBN 0-944510-24-8
New ISBN# 978-0-944510-24-7

Primary Distributor All of Michael R. Kelsey's books are sold by this distributor. A list of Kelsey's titles is in the back of this book.

Brigham Distribution, 156 South, 800 West, Suite D, Brigham City, Utah, 84302, Tele. 435-723-6611, Fax 435-723-6644, Email brigdist@sisna.com.

Most of Kelsey's books are sold by these distributors.
Alpenbooks, 4206 Chennault Beach Road, Suite B1, Mukilteo, Washington, USA, 98275, Website alpenbooks.com, Email cserve@alpenbooks.com, Tele. 425-493-6380, or 800-290-9898.
Books West, 11111 East, 53rd Avenue, Suite A Colorado, USA, 80239-2133, Tele. 303-449-5995, or 800-378-4188, Fax 303-449-5951, Website bookswest.net.
Liberty Mountain, 4375 W. 1980 S., Suite 100, Salt Lake City, Utah, 84104, Tele. 800-578-2705 or 801-954-0741, Fax 801-954-0766, Website libertymountain.com, Email sales@libertymountain.com.
Treasure Chest Books, 451 N. Bonita Avenue, Tucson, Arizona, USA, 85745, Tele. 520-623-9558, or 800-969-9558, Website treasurechestbooks.com, Email info@rionuevo.com.

Some of Kelsey's books are sold by the following distributors.
Anderson News, 1709 North, East Street, Flagstaff, Arizona, USA, 86004, Tele. 928-774-6171, Fax 928-779-1958.
Canyonlands Publications, 4860 North, Ken Morey Drive, Bellemont, Arizona, USA, 86015, Tele. 928-779-3888, or 800-283-1983, Fax 928-779-3778, Email info@clpbooks.net.
High Peak Books, Box 703, Wilson, Wyoming, USA, 83014, Tele. 307-739-0147.
Rincon Publishing, 1913 North Skyline Drive, Orem, Utah, 84097, Tele. 801-377-7657, Fax 801-356-2733, RinconPub@UtahTrails.com.
Recreational Equipment, Inc. (R.E.I.), 1700 45th Street East, Sumner, Washington, USA, 98390, Website rei.com, Mail Orders Tele. 800-426-4840 (or check at any of their local stores).
Online--Internet: amazon.com; adventuroustravelers.com; btol.com (Baker-Taylor); Ingrams.com; Bdaltons.com; borders.com (teamed with amazon.com).

For the **UK and Europe**, and the rest of the world contact: **Cordee,** 3a De Montfort Street, Leicester, England, UK, LE1 7HD, Website cordee.co.uk, Tele. Inter+44-116-254-3579, Fax Inter+44-116-247-1176.
For **Australia** and **New Zealand: Macstyle Media,** 20-22 Station Street, Sandringham, Victoria, Australia, 3191, Website macstyle.com.au, Email macstyle@netspace.net.au, Tele. Inter+61-39-521-6585, Fax Inter+61-39-521-0664.

Printed by Press Media, 1601 West, 820 North, Provo, Utah 84601.
All fotos by the author, unless otherwise stated.
All maps, charts, and cross sections drawn by the author.

Front Cover

Front Cover Fotos
1. Fotogenic Slot, Labyrinth Canyon
2. Alcove Cave, South Fork of Iceberg Canyon
3. Warm Springs Canyon Overhung Campsite
4. Rainbow Bridge, From the East Side

Back Cover

Back Cover Fotos
5. Star-shaped Metate, Bowns Canyon Cave
6. Narrow Inlet to Labyrinth Canyon
7. Rafters, Clearwater Campsite, Cataract Canyon
8. Aerial Foto of Gregory Butte, Looking East
9. Anasazi Ruins, Bowdie Canyon
10. Deep Narrows, West Canyon

Table of Contents

Acknowledgments

There have been dozens of people contributing information leading to the writing of this book but the following people were most helpful. Several people worked for the National Park Service. They were archaeologist Chris Kincaid, who read part of the rough draft and made helpful suggestions. Paul Zaenger and Chuck Wood were helpful concerning hiking places and water quality. Ross Rice informed the author of the wild horse roundup in Bowns Canyon. Jim Holland, Vic Viera, Kate Cannon and Karen Whitney reviewed the original rough draft.

There were older stockmen in the local communities who helped to locate and gave a history on some of the old cattle trails in the area. They include Riter Ekker of Hanksville; Leo Wilson and Vernon Griffin of Escalante; hunting guide and former BLM ranger Carl Mahon, and John Scorup and Melvin Dalton of Monticello; Clarence Rogers of Blanding; and Edith Clinger of Orem.

In addition, the author spoke with two aging Navajo men about trails located on Navajo Nation lands. They were Kee B. Tso, who lived near the Kaibito Chapter House, and the late Owen Yazzie who lived just southeast of the butte named Leche-E Rock. Yazzie worked as a member of one of the Civilian Conservation Corps (CCC) crews which built trails in Navajo Canyon in the mid-1930's.

Stan Jones of Page, correlated some information with the author, and his map of Lake Powell got the author started. There was no personal communication with C. Gregory Crampton of St. George, but his published research from the University of Utah in the late 1950's and early 1960's, was most helpful in locating many old stock trails and gave a history of Glen Canyon before the coming of Lake Powell.

There were several employees of ARAMARK (formerly ARA Leisures, the concessionaire on Lake Powell) who looked at original rough draft. They were Steve Ward and Dave Neuburger. Also Carol Bierhaus of Dangling Rope Marina was most helpful. The author also spoke to several hikers who volunteered information. They were Byron Lemay, Herb Taylor and Nat Smale

In 2007, and for the 5th Edition of this book, Kevin B. Schneider & Julia Drugatz of the NPS in Page, spent time updating the author on marinas and policies regarding GCNRA. Val Dalton, a rancher from Monticello, Utah, Robert Redd, formerly of Monticello, and Sue Bellagamba of the Moab office of The Nature Concervancy, updated the author on the grazing situation, grazing permits, history of the Dugout Ranch, etc. east of Lake Powell.

My mother Venetta B. Kelsey, was instrumental in proof reading the earlier editions and watching after the business while I was out boating, hiking and having fun on the lake. Reaola Kelsey Holm also helped in proof reading the original manuscript.

The Author

The author, who was born in 1943, experienced his earliest years of life in eastern Utah's Uinta Basin, first on a farm east of Myton, then in or near Roosevelt. In 1954, the family moved to Provo and he attended Provo High School and later Brigham Young University, where he earned a B.S. degree in Sociology. Shortly thereafter, he discovered that was the wrong subject, so he attended the University of Utah, where he received his Master of Science degree in Geography (minoring in Geology), finishing classes in June, 1970.

It was then real life began, for on June 9, 1970, he put a pack on his back and started traveling for the first time. Since then he has seen 223 countries, republics, islands, or island groups. All this wandering has resulted in self-publishing 16 books. Here are his books listed in the order they were first published: *Climber's and Hiker's Guide to the World's Mountains & Volcanos (4th Edition); Utah Mountaineering Guide (3rd Edition); China on Your Own, and the Hiking Guide to China's Nine Sacred Mountains (3rd Ed.)* **Out of Print***; Canyon Hiking Guide to the Colorado Plateau (5th Edition); Hiking and Exploring Utah's San Rafael Swell (3rd Edition); Hiking and Exploring Utah's Henry Mountains and Robbers Roost (Revised Edition)* **Temporarily Out of Print***; Hiking and Exploring the Paria River (4th Edition); Hiking and Climbing in the Great Basin National Park (Wheeler Peak, Nevada)* **Out of Print***; Boater's Guide to Lake Powell (5th Edition); Climbing and Exploring Utah's Mt. Timpanogos; River Guide to Canyonlands National Park & Vicinity (***Temporarily Out of Print***); Hiking, Biking and Exploring Canyonlands National Park & Vicinity (***Temporarily Out of Print***); The Story of Black Rock, Utah; Hiking, Climbing and Exploring Western Utah's Jack Watson's Ibex Country; and Technical Slot Canyon Guide to the Colorado Plateau (2nd Edition comes out in the summer of 2008).*

He has also helped his mother Venetta Bond Kelsey write and publish a book about the one-horse town she was born & raised in, **Life on the Black Rock Desert--A History of Clear Lake, Utah** *(***Temporarily Out of Print***).*

Metric Conversion Table

1 Centimeter = 0.39 Inch	1 Mile = 1.609 Kilometers	1 Ounce = 28.35 Grams
1 Inch = 2.54 Centimeters	100 Miles = 161 Kilometers	1 Pound = 453 Grams
1 Meter = 39.37 Inches	100 Kilometers = 62.1 miles	1 Quart (US) = 0.946 Liter
1 Foot = 0.3048 Meter/30.5 Cms	1 Liter = 1.056 Quarts (US)	1 Gallon (US) = 3.785 Liters
1 Kilometer = 0.621 Mile	1 Kilogram = 2.205 Pounds	1 Acre = 0.405 Hectare
1 Nautical Mile = 1.852 Kms	1 Metric Ton = 1000 Kgs	1 Hectare = 2.471 Acres
1 Kilometer = 3281 Feet	1 Mile = 1609 Meters	0.1 Mile = 161 Meters
1 Cubic/Liter = 61 Cubic/Inches	50 C/L = 3050 C/I	100 C/L = 6100 C/I

Meters to Feet (Meters x 3.2808 = Feet)

100 m = 328 ft.	2500 m = 8202 ft.	5000 m = 16404 ft.	7500 m = 24606 ft.
500 m = 1640 ft.	3000 m = 9842 ft.	5500 m = 18044 ft.	8000 m = 26246 ft.
1000 m = 3281 ft.	3500 m = 11483 ft.	6000 m = 19686 ft.	8500 m = 27887 ft.
1500 m = 4921 ft.	4000 m = 13124 ft.	6500 m = 21325 ft.	9000 m = 29525 ft.
2000 m = 6562 ft.	4500 m = 14764 ft.	7000 m = 22966 ft.	8848 m = 20029 ft.

Feet to Meters (Feet ÷ 3.2808 = Meters)

1000 ft. = 305 m	9000 ft. = 2743 m	16000 ft. = 4877 m	23000 ft. = 7010 m
2000 ft. = 610 m	10000 ft. = 3048 m	17000 ft. = 5182 m	24000 ft. = 7315 m
3000 ft. = 914 m	11000 ft. = 3353 m	18000 ft. = 5486 m	25000 ft. = 7620 m
4000 ft. = 1219 m	12000 ft. = 3658 m	19000 ft. = 5791 m	26000 ft. = 7925 m
5000 ft. = 1524 m	13000 ft. = 3962 m	20000 ft. = 6096 m	27000 ft. = 8230 m
6000 ft. = 1829 m	14000 ft. = 4268 m	21000 ft. = 6401 m	28000 ft. = 8535 m
7000 ft. = 2134 m	15000 ft. = 4572 m	22000 ft. = 6706 m	29000 ft. = 8839 m
8000 ft. = 2438 m			30000 ft. = 9144 m

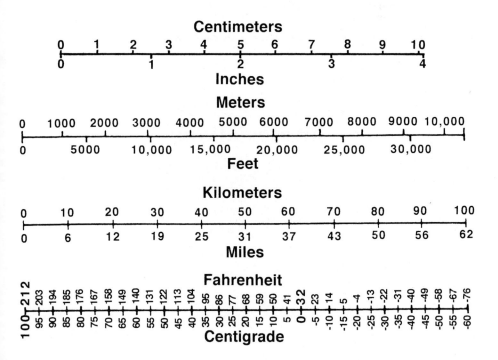

Centimeters / Inches

Meters / Feet

Kilometers / Miles

Fahrenheit / Centigrade

Map Symbols

Building, Ranch or Cabin.............	▫	Trail...............................	------
Possible Lakeside Campsite.........	▲	Route--No Trail....................	••••••••
Campsite (Road Access).............	⌂	Peak and Prominent Ridge.......	⌇
Campground (Developed)............	⋀	Flowing Stream or Creek.........	⌇
Visitor Center (NPS)...................	⌂	Dry Creek Bed....................	⌇
Landing Strip or Airport................	✈	Waterfall or Dryfall...............	⌇
State, US Highway................	�995 ⑧89	Canyon Rim, Escarpment........	⌇
Road (Maintained)...............	▬ ▬ ▬	Lake or Colorado River.........	⌇
Road (4WD or HCV).............	**4WD HCV**	Mine, Quarry, Adit, Prospect.........	⬝↗
Mile Post Markers..............	548 549	Spring...............................	o
Geology Cross Section........	⬝⬝⬝⬝	Pass................................	)(
Buoys--Miles(Kilometers)...M76(K122)	⬟	Natural Bridge, Arch or Cave.........	⌒
Petroglyphs & Pictographs........	⦿PIC ⦿PET	Elevation in Meters....................	1128

,

Abbreviations

Canyon	C.	Campgrounds	CG.
Lake	L.	Campsites	CS.
River	R.	Mine	M.
Creek	Ck.	Four Wheel Drive	4WD
Peak	Pk.	Two Wheel Drive	2WD
Waterfall, Dryfall or Formation	F.	High Clearance Vehicle	HCV
Kilometer(s)	km, kms	Spring	Sp.
Sandstone	SS.	High Water Mark	HWM

Glen Canyon National Recreation Area	GCNRA
United States Geological Survey	USGS
National Park Service	NPS
Bureau of Land Management	BLM
Miles (Kilometers) uplake from Glen Canyon Dam	M171 (K274)
Miles (Kilometers) uplake from the mouth of the San Juan River	M54 (K86)
Elevation of Lake Powell at the High Water Mark (HWM)	1128 meters (3700 feet)
Civilian Conservation Corps	Triple C's or CCC's
July 4, 2007-Water Level 1100.70 meters/3611.19 feet	7/4/2007-WL1100.70m/3611.19'

Part I--Introduction & History

For several years the author thought about writing some kind of guide book to Lake Powell but it wasn't until he saw the visitation chart showing nearly 3 million people visited the Glen Canyon National Recreation Area in 1987, that the idea was seriously considered. It seemed odd that an area so popular would be without a guide book of any kind.

The only problem was, he had never been in a small boat in his life. This was the biggest challenge of the entire summer of 1988; going out on the second largest man-made lake in the United States alone with new and untried equipment.

It was decided to buy an inflatable boat (rubber raft) because; it could be used later for river running, it would be very light weight, no trailer would be involved, and storage would be easier. His under-powered but highly economical 1981, 52hp VW Rabbit Diesel was instrumental in making the decision to buy an inflatable.

To go with the raft, a small 4hp outboard motor was bought, and a small frame was built to make the motor mount more rigid. At times the speed of movement was sheer agony, but the 4hp did well, and the author did most of the foot work for this book in a 3 month period, during the spring and early summer of 1988. Another month of foot work was completed in the fall of 1988. That winter he bought a small aluminum boat & trailer and a 10hp outboard, and did more foot work in 1990. In 1991, he spent nearly another month on the lake preparing for the 1st Updated Edition. May and June of 1996, he was on the lake for another three weeks preparing for the 2nd Updated version. For the 4th Edition, he spent 36 days on the water during March, April and May, 2001.

During July, August, September and October of 2007, he spent another 31 days on the water and visiting almost every canyon on the lake (plus 2 aerial picture taking trips covering all the lake). This time it was to checkout campsites at low lake levels, and to refoto everything with a digital camera. By that time he had a 90hp, 2002 VW Golf Diesel TDI, plus a 25hp outboard motor and a slightly heavier riveted aluminum boat--that soon starting leaking like a sieve because of the pounding of Lake Powell's wind & boater created waves.

The original idea for this book was that of a hiking guide only, since that's the author's specialty. But once on the lake for the first time, it was evident that more was needed. First of all, some sections of the lake have no camping places whatsoever. The already-available written material didn't cover camping very well so it became necessary to include some kind of guide for that. As it turns out, the camping guide part of this book won't be as good as hoped, because some of the author's travels were when the lake was near the high water mark (HWM). That was during the mid to late 1980's after big time rains & snowpack of the early 1980's. When the lake is low, some campsite locations change completely. After that first summer, the lake level has been going down steadily.

Since there were a number of Anasazi ruins in the canyons and below the lake, it was necessary to include something about these ancient inhabitants. Many years after the Anasazi left this canyon country, in came fur trappers and explorers, then miners and cattlemen. Each of these groups left a mark on Glen Canyon, so it was thought something should be said about each, and their history. The last subject to be included was some kind of discussion on the unique geology of the canyon, which is after all, the main reason everybody wants to visit this lake. It's the scenery! Without doubt, **Lake Powell is the most-scenic & fotogenic lake in the world!**

The First Occupants

We know little about the first peoples who lived in the side-canyons along the Colorado River. Studies made of the bottom layers of caves in the region reveal there were mammoth, bison, sloth, and camel inhabiting this region about 13,000 years ago. In **Cowboy Cave**, between Lake Powell and the Henry Mountains, dung from the above listed animals was found. **Bechan Cave** in **Bowns Canyon** revealed similar findings. Most researchers believe the reason these animals disappeared on this continent was over-hunting by man. The most recent studies indicate man first appeared in North America about 14,000 years ago and proceeded to kill off all the large mammals in the next 3000 years or so.

In Cowboy Cave, the earliest sign of human existence (charcoal) was concluded to be about 8900 years old. In another layer, some clay figurines were found and dated to about 6700 to 6400 years ago. In each layer of that cave more evidence was found of human habitation, up until nearly the present.

Some of the more recent settlers to these canyons have been called the **Anasazi**. This is a Navajo word meaning, **The Ancient Ones**. They may have been in the canyons about 2000 years ago, but little is known of the earliest groups. The people we know so much about today are the ones who lived in the Four Corners area from about 900 AD until about 1300 AD. It's this last group of people who built the cliff dwellings seen in many of the canyons leading to Lake Powell.

The Anasazi have been divided into several groups. The ones who occupied the area north of the San Juan River but east of the Colorado River, were the **Mesa Verde Anasazi** with the heart of their civilization at Mesa Verde in southwest Colorado. South of the San Juan and east of the Colorado was inhabited by what we call the **Kayenta Anasazi**. In areas west of the Colorado River and south of the Aquarius Plateau were the **Virgin Anasazi**; and west of the river and north of the Boulder Mountains were, for the most part, the **Fremont Indians**, a totally different linguistic group of people.

The **Anasazi**, whose ancestors are now believed to be the **Pueblo Indians** of the southwest, developed into an agrarian society. They grew corn, beans and squash, and ate wild fruits. They had domesticated turkeys and made permanent homes. They also did some hunting. The earliest Anasazi made baskets, but had no pottery. Later they made fine pottery, some of which has been found in the former occupied areas.

The **Fremonts**, who may have been the forefathers of today's **Utes & Piutes**, were hunters and gatherers. However, they borrowed ideas from the Anasazi, including some agriculture, but it was used very little. The Fremonts left behind much less that is visible today than did the mostly-cliffdwelling Anasazi. Both groups however did engage in rock art. They both made pictographs (painted images) and petroglyphs (pecked onto the rock) and some of these are visible in almost every canyon. Pictographs and especially petroglyphs, are almost always found on south facing boulders or walls, with lots of desert varnish; or in the case of pictographs, in caves or in protected places under overhangs.

Most of the cliff dwellings studied in this area date from about 1150 AD to 1300 AD. There is little or nothing dated from after that period until more recently when Navajos, Piutes and Utes were in the same area. Why the Anasazi left is still a mystery but prominent ideas are; there was a long drought, or there was fighting with some hostile tribe. The author bought these ideas, until he saw Lake Canyon and the remains of Lake Pagahrit.

Briefly, the little Lake Pagahrit at the head of Lake Canyon was in an unused area until the whiteman came with his herds of cattle. Cattle were first introduced there in the 1880's, then in the mid-1890's there was a sustained drought which forced many of the big cattle operators to leave the area. After a few years of overgrazing and trail making, the land couldn't handle it any longer. After 3 days of heavy rains, Lake Pagahrit burst it's natural dam on November 3, 1915. That resulted in the downcutting of the soil seen in the lower canyon today, and the lowering of the water table.

With lots of Anasazi people in these canyons, the same erosional patterns could surely have taken place, with all the trails, disturbed ground, etc. Once erosion got started, it would have down-cut during periods of flash flooding to the point that water couldn't be used for irrigation and the water table would have been much lower. This, along with the cutting down of all trees in the area for firewood, would mean they had to abandon the canyons. There are also other theories as to why they left.

The Spaniards and Trappers

During the years after about 1300 AD, not much is known of the Glen Canyon country until the Spaniards came in 1776, a void of almost 500 years. Surely there were occupants, but they were likely nomadic, and left little or nothing but foot prints in the sand.

Some researchers believe the Navajo came into the region very late in time, about 1500 AD. The **Navajo** people are part of the **Athabascan** language group and are not related to the Hopi or other Pueblo Indians of the American southwest. They migrated south from the Yukon region where others of the same tribe still reside (the Athabascan Tribe of the Yukon Territory). Navajos were in the canyon country mostly to the south of the San Juan River at the time the Spaniards first arrived.

A new era came to Glen Canyon with the **Dominguez & Escalante Party**. They were Catholic priests out looking for a new route to California from their home base in Santa Fe, New Mexico. They went north through western Colorado, west through Utah's Uinta Basin to Utah Lake near Provo, then south to about Cedar City, approximately along the present-day I-15 Highway route. Because of various reasons, they decided to head back home rather than complete the journey to California. Rather than backtrack, it was decided to look for a new shortcut route, so they headed east across southern Utah.

They eventually ended up at the mouth of the **Paria River**, which in recent years has been known as **Lee's Ferry**. From there they headed northeast and eventually crossed the Colorado River at a place called, the **Crossing of the Fathers**, now under the waters of Padre Bay. That was on November 7, 1776. They then headed south and east back to Santa Fe. Read more details of this crossing in the section with **Maps 38 & 38A**.

These 2 priests and their expedition were the first white men to see the Colorado and the Glen Canyon area. Half a century later, and about the same time Mexico became independent (1821), a Mexican named Antonio Armijo took a trading party of 31 men across the Colorado at the Crossing of the Fathers, and later returned from California the same way. These people called the crossing, **El Vado de Los Padres**. But the country was so rugged and wild, another easier route was eventually opened further north near Moab, Utah. After that, the crossing became lost and was not re-discovered until Jacob Hamblin used it in 1858. It was also observed by the Powell Expeditions of 1869 and 1871.

In the 1820's and 1830's, the **Old Spanish Trail** crossed the Colorado River near what would later be Moab; then to the Green River where Green River town is today. From there it headed west, but north of the San Rafael Swell, up over Salina Canyon, and on southwest to California.

After the Spaniards and Mexicans left the region, there were a few solitary travelers in the canyon, mostly trappers. Little if any is known of these men, but one apparently put his graffiti on the walls of the lower Green River and in Cataract Canyon of the Colorado. That was **Denis Julien**, a French Canadian-born fur trapper, who must have passed that way by boat in 1836.

The Mormons

The next reported time any white man crossed the Colorado at the Crossing of the Fathers, was on November 8, 1858. That was when **Jacob Hamblin** and 10 companions headed south to Hopi Land to preach to the Indians. On a subsequent trip, their luck ran out and one Mormon was killed near Moenkopi as the group rode toward the Colorado River. All in all, Hamblin and other missionaries made many trips across the river at this old Spanish crossing, which in Hamblin's day was referred to as the **Ute Ford or Ute Crossing**.

In the mid and late 1860's, there were many crossings of the Colorado, mainly by Navajos, who raided Mormon settlements and drove cattle back across the river. Indians all over Utah were more or less at war with the Mormons for a time in the 1860's. The reason for the conflict was pretty simple, the Mormons were taking over the hunting grounds of the Indians.

All this fighting led to a war between the Navajo Nation and the United States. Kit Carson was sent to Arizona in 1863 with orders to destroy all Navajo crops and livestock. Their hogans were destroyed, fields burned, and they were hunted down with many being killed by the US Cavalry. Finally the majority of the Navajos, about 8,000, walked to, and were incarcerated at Fort Sumner in eastern New Mexico from 1864 through 1868. In Navajo history, the journey to and from Ft. Sumner is known as **The Long Walk**. Those who refused to be exiled, hid out in lonely canyons, or mixed with the Piutes. During this time period the Mormons withdrew from outlying areas, but the Navajos still raided and took cattle east across the Colorado along the Crossing of the Fathers route.

All traffic stopped using the Crossing of the Fathers route in the period after 1872-73. This was because of the opening of **Lee's Ferry** at the mouth of the Paria River by **John D. Lee**. John D. was sent to this lonely outpost by the Mormon Church because Federal lawmen were pursuing him for polygamy and his involvement in the **Mountain Meadows Massacre**, which left 120 members of a Missouri wagon train dead. Read more about this event in another book by the author, *Hiking and Exploring the Paria River.*

Lee and part of his family arrived at the Colorado River on December 23, 1871, and first used one of John W. Powell's boats as a ferry on January 18, 1872, to help some Navajos across the river. Later, a real ferry boat was built by a man named Heath, and was first launched on January 11, 1873. After the building of this ferry, the Crossing of the Fathers or Ute Ford was used no more.

Another group of Mormons was called in 1879 from the southern Utah communities of Parowan, Paragonah and Cedar City, to colonize the San Juan River Valley in the area that is known today as Bluff, Utah. They could have used John D. Lee's boat at Lee's Ferry, or they could have headed north to Green River, then south to Moab, and on to the San Juan, but they chose to try a new shorter route in-

8

Anasazi and Fremont Indian Groups

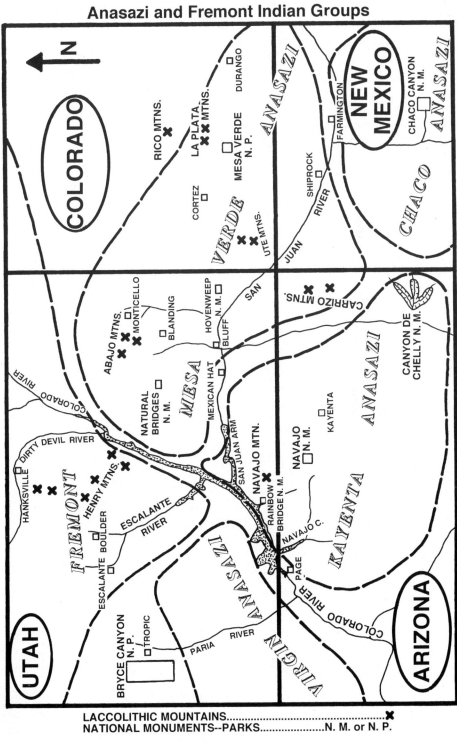

LACCOLITHIC MOUNTAINS..✗
NATIONAL MONUMENTS--PARKS....................N. M. or N. P.

stead. This is what we now call the **Hole-in-the-Rock Trail**. They thought they could get there in 6 weeks--but it took 6 months. This was called the **San Juan Mission Party**, otherwise known as the **Hole-in-the-Rock Expedition**. Read more details under **Map 20**.

River Exploration and John Wesley Powell
On May 24, 1869, John W. Powell and nine other men got off the train in Green River, Wyoming, jumped into 4 little rowboats and started one of the epic journeys of all time, a boat trip down the uncharted Green & Colorado Rivers. This was the first time it had been done. Others had seen parts of the river canyon, but Powell and his men saw it all. Actually, while in the Grand Canyon, three of his men abandoned the expedition, and while walking north to Kanab, were killed by Shivwits Indians.

A second journey by Powell resumed in May of 1871. The second trip was better organized and more for scientific study than the first, which was more a test of survival. This trip ended at Lee's Ferry, and Powell spent nearly a year doing survey work in southern Utah. Finally, they resumed the river expedition again at Lee's Ferry, and went as far as Kanab Creek in the middle of the Grand Canyon, then it was abandoned.

Because of his exploits on the Colorado, and other survey work in the region, the one-armed John W. Powell ended up as head of the USGS, and the lake behind Glen Canyon Dam was named in his honor. Years after his expeditions, he published his report originally titled, *Canyons of the Colorado*. Later printings of the same book were called, *The Exploration of the Colorado River and it's Canyons*. This one is still in print and is based mostly on his first trip down the Colorado.

On Powell's second expedition was a young man named **Frederick S. Dellenbaugh**. He kept a good diary which he later published. It's titled, **A Canyon Voyage**. In the various sections of this book are quotations from both of these men's diaries.

History of the Cattle Industry of Southeastern Utah
The history of raising and herding cattle in the canyons leading to the Colorado River and to present-day Lake Powell, largely began with the early settlements founded by the Mormons. On the west side of the river it took until the 1880's before any one even got close to the river and the almost impenetrable canyons. **Hanksville** was first settled in 1882, but most of those people were farmers, with cattle ranching mostly a sideline. It must have been sometime in the late 1880's before they really got down into the canyons. By that time some ranches were being developed in the Henry Mountains south of Hanksville and others in the Robbers Roost country east of town. It was only then the lower winter ranges were fully utilized.

In 1887, Wise Cooper, John King and Mack Webb of the Fillmore area, took a herd of cattle to the east side of Boulder Mountain for the summer. Later on, they moved cattle down into the lower canyon country near the Colorado River to winter. This was likely the first time cattle had ranged so near the river on the west side. A little southeast of Boulder Mountain is the ranching community of **Boulder**. It was first settled by Amasa Lyman and his family in 1889. These original settlers were farmers.

Slowly but surely, others migrated into the region and settled places like **Escalante** (late 1870's) and Kanab, but these people were mostly farmers too and it took a while before they built up large herds of cattle. Also, in the beginning there was trouble with the various Indian tribes stealing their livestock, so this factor kept herds close to home. It appears to have been in the 1890's and near the turn of the century before Glen Canyon was really used much as a winter grazing area for cattle on the west bank.

The east side of the Colorado River has quite a different history. All this country was later to become **San Juan County**, a region almost forgotten by Brigham Young in his early colonizing efforts. The **Moab** region, or **Spanish Valley**, was first settled (or rather, attempted to be settled) by what was called the **Elk Mountain Mission** in 1855. They were Mormons sent there by the Church (in Utah, the Church, spelled with a capital C, always refers to the Mormon or LDS Church). But it wasn't long afterwards that 2 members of the group were killed and 3 others wounded by Indians. The settlement and fort were abandoned and the land returned to its rightful owners.

It wasn't until the late 1870's that whites again attempted to settle this forgotten corner of the Utah Territory. These were scattered farmers and ranchers who generally speaking didn't have successful beginnings. One farmer was **Peter Shirts** who first tilled soil along the Paria River in the mid-1860's, later to build a cabin on lower Montezuma Creek south of the Abajo Mountains near the San Juan River.

There were others in the Moab area and to the south of the La Sal Mountains. These included the Maxwells, Rays and McCartys in 1877. At about this same time, there were several individuals from the settlements of Mount Pleasant, Salina, and Manti areas of central Utah, who took small herds of cattle and built homes at what would later be called La Sal and Coyote, just south of the La Sal Mountains. They wintered their cattle close to the Colorado in what is today **Canyonlands National Park**, just northeast of the north end of Lake Powell.

The first successful effort to colonize any part of San Juan County by the Mormon Church was with the San Juan Mission, otherwise known as the **Hole-in-the-Rock Expedition**. This group from the Cedar City and Parowan areas arrived on the San Juan River at Bluff in April of 1880. They had begun with 1000 head of livestock, but fewer than that ended up at Bluff. However, they did stop at **Lake Pagahrit** in upper **Lake Canyon** along the way to rest their animals and found it to be an excellent pasture. From that time on, the Bluff Mormons always had cattle grazing the Pagahrit country. Read the full story of their incredible journey under **Map 20**.

At about the same time Bluff was first settled (1880), a man named Wilson brought in a number of cattle to Recapture Creek, due south of the Abajo Mountains and near the San Juan River. According to Day's thesis, his cattle soon spread over a large area, then in the early 1880's, he sold all or most of his stock to the LC or **Lacy Cattle Company**. The Lacy outfit ran stock from the area of Monticello south to the San Juan River. Later, the Lacy Company sold most of its holdings in the late 1890's to people outside the state, but many cattle were stolen by their own rustlin' wranglers.

The author believes this may be the Wilson who first ran livestock in the Wilson Mesa area, which includes Gray Mesa, Wilson Creek (originally called Sunshine Canyon), Cottonwood and Iceberg Canyons (for many years before Lake Powell days this drainage was called Wilson Canyon), and The Rincon. If indeed it's the same Wilson who left his name on so many geographic areas, it is perhaps he who first began to build some of the livestock trails down into the slickrock canyons between the Colorado and San Juan Rivers. According to old timer Clarence Rogers of Blanding, Wilson had a number of horses on Gray Mesa in the mid-1880's to about 1890, then he left the country.

During the same time period Bluff had its beginnings, a man from western Colorado named Joshua (Spud) Hudson discovered the Blue Mountains (now generally known as the Abajo Mtns.), which he said was virgin cattle country. He put stock there for the first time in 1880. This also appears to be the first time any non-Mormon attempted to settle the region.

In 1883, a large outfit known as the **Kansas and New Mexico Land & Cattle Company**, owned by 2 English brothers named Harold and Ted Carlisle, began operations in southeastern Utah. They bought out the Hudson interests, and later became one of the biggest cattle companies in the United States. It appears they never did make it to the canyons close to the Colorado River, but instead ran cattle in the Abajo Mountains during the summer, and between the Abajos and the La Sal Mountains in winter. Their company headquarters was just north of present-day Monticello, at a place called Double Cabin. Later the ranch headquarters was called Carlisle. They ran cattle until about 1898, then the drought forced them into selling most of their stock. When they sold the cattle, sheep were brought in in their place. The Carlisle Ranch was sold to a group of Mormons, including some of the Redds, in 1911. From that point on, **Charley Redd** and some of his kinfolk, and others, ran cattle in the former Carlisle and Lacy or L. C. Cattle Company ranges.

In February of 1884, a big flood came down Cottonwood Canyon and nearly wiped out the town of Bluff. As a result of plentiful rainfall that spring, a man from New Mexico brought a large flock of sheep into the country and grazed them in the vicinity of Bluff. The Mormons became worried for fear their own livestock wouldn't have enough grass to eat, so they banned together and bought the entire flock. This community effort was known as the **San Juan Co-op**, which also ran the only store in town at that time. Later writers have called this the **Bluff Pool**.

In 1885, Charles H. Ogden and Jim Blood, who represented investors from Pittsburg, arrived in the Moab and La Sal region of San Juan County. They bought out all or most of the small cattle ranchers to form the **Pittsburg Cattle Company**. They wintered stock to the west in the lower canyons leading into the Colorado River just northeast of the upper end of present-day Lake Powell. This is the east part of what is now Canyonlands National Park. The Pittsburg outfit lasted until just after 1900, when 3 men; Cunningham, Carpenter and Prewer bought them out. Still later, these 3 sold out to the **La Sal Livestock Company**. This cattle company still exits today, but it's had many different owners over the years.

In 1885, a number of small cattlemen moved into the Indian Creek area, which drains the north slopes of the Abajo Mtns. Today, this area belongs to one big outfit known as The Dugout, or **Dugout Ranch**. It got its name because some of the first settlers lived in dugouts. It's located northwest of Newspaper Rock and along the road leading to The Needles District of Canyonlands National Park. These stockmen used the Abajo Mountains as their summer range, and the canyons closer to Cataract Canyon of the Colorado as winter range. The first to settle Indian Creek was D. M. Cooper and Mel Turner.

In 1887, John E. Brown settled in the same area and planted an orchard and began to raise hay. He was the first of the cattlemen in San Juan County to use hay or alfalfa for winter feed. In 1895, the **Indian Creek Cattle Company** at **Dugout Ranch**, was bought by David Goudelock and others. He lived there until 1918. It's believed by present-day cowboys, that Goudelock was the one who built many of the stock trails in the region just east of Cataract Canyon at or near the upper end of Lake Powell.

On the other side of the mountain at Bluff, things weren't going so well. The Mormons were basically farmers, and they had hoped to create diversion dams and canals to divert water from the San Juan River to irrigate their farms. But this proved more difficult than they had imagined. The San Juan was prone to huge floods at times and very low water at other times. It also had a wide sandy bottom which made it difficult to get river water out and onto their fields. Also, the spring flood of 1884 down Cottonwood Canyon had wiped out many of their ditches and roads. In 1885, and on the verge of failure, they decided to expand and get into the cattle business. At that time, they were surrounded by an estimated 50,000 head of cattle belonging to Gentile outfits (non-Mormons) in San Juan County. Thus began a new era in the history of Bluff. In a year's time it changed from a struggling farm village to a cooperative livestock enterprise, which made Bluff one of the richest towns in America, per capita.

The person who began to implement this change was Francis A. Hammond, who was appointed president of the Mormon San Juan Stake in 1885. According to Charles Peterson's story, *San Juan in Controversy*; he [Hammond] was elected to the San Juan county court in the August election of 1885, thus giving him an important political position several months before he left his home in Huntsville [in northern Utah].

After several months of planning, Hammond and the Mormons put together what was later known as the Bluff Pool (sometimes called the **Mormon Pool**) on January 16, 1886 (According to L. H. Redd, in those days they just called it the **San Juan Co-op**). And since they grazed on the Elk Ridge to the north during the summer season, the livestock end of the business was called the **Elk Cattle Company**.

This group put out an invitation to other Mormons, *to come immediately and help us stock up the range.* They also made friends with the Piute Indians who had camps high in the Abajo Mountains, which they claimed as exclusively theirs. This alignment effectively kept the Gentile outfits off the west slope of the Abajos, an area usually known as **Elk Ridge** or the **Elk Mountains**, an important summer range. The Mormons also filed for water rights and crossings, and used the Indians to their advantage. From that time on, until the Bluff Pool sold most of their stock to **Al & Jim Scorup** in 1898, they ran cattle in the area east of the Colorado, north of the San Juan, and west and southwest of the Abajos.

In 1888, the last of the large cattle companies arrived in San Juan County. A herd of 2000 Texas Longhorns under the foremanship of John Crosby, ended up in the southern end of Comb Wash (south of the Abajos). In Utah, this company took up the name **Elk Mountain Cattle Company**, with the brand ELKM. They soon began herding their stock into White Canyon and other canyons close to the Colorado River. Since their supply lines were so long and competition so tough, they only lasted 4 or 5 years, then sold out to the Bluff Pool. Some local ranchers believe it was these Texans who may have built some of the first stock trails down into the canyons of the Colorado near Hite.

In 1891, enter 2 of the most important characters in the building up and development of livestock ranges in the western half of San Juan County, and in the canyons leading directly into what is now Lake Powell. They were the **Scorup brothers, Al & Jim**. For more than half a century these 2 men dominated the scene. According to family members, Al was the one who did all the buying, selling and big deal making, while Jim did most of the range development, steer wrestling and cow punchin' out on the range. It very likely could have been the Scorup Brothers who built and developed many of the stock trails on the east side of Lake Powell and on the north side of the San Juan Arm.

Most of the information about the Scorups, comes from a book written by **Stena Scorup**, sister of the 2 brothers, titled **J. A. Scorup: A Utah Cattleman**. As the story goes, 19-year-old Al made a deal with cattleman Claude Sanford, who had about 150 head of Texas Longhorns grazing somewhere in White Canyon. The deal agreed to was that Scorup was to get a third of the calves if he would just go down there, round them up, and bring them back to Salina (in central Utah), where the Scorup family lived.

So on March 20, 1891, Al left home alone with 2 horses, 2 quilts, some grub, and a $5 bill in his pocket. He rode to the Colorado River, and with his horses swam across, and began to look for Sanford's cattle. This was no easy task, as the Longhorns were wild as buckskins, and soon his grub stake was about gone. He sold one steer to some prospectors along the Colorado for $20, then bought a sack of flour from **Cass Hite** (read more about him later) for $11 (this was during the gold rush days along the Colorado River). The rest of the $20 went for salt pork and pinto beans.

This didn't last long either, so instead of heading home, he shoved the Longhorns into a side-canyon, and headed east, getting a job with the Elk Mountain Cattle Company driving 350 steers from Elk Ridge to Ridgeway, Colorado, a distance of 500 kms (320 miles). On that drive, which put $75 in his pocket, he made friends with several Bluff cowboys. He was then talked into going back to Bluff, where he stayed in the Bayles Hotel, and had a chance to meet the local girls. One of the daughters of the hotel owner, who was working as a cook, later became his wife. In later years Al recalled that *Bluff girls were cowboy shy [most cowboys were gentiles], and they along with their parents were dyed-in-the-wool Mormons.*

He didn't stay long in Bluff, but did get acquainted with the folks there, which helped him land a job a few years later. On his way back to White Canyon and Sanford's cattle, he met 5 armed Texans wranglers working for the Elk Mountain outfit. They were tough hombres and they told Al; *see here, youngster, we've scattered your cattle and we mean to use all this feed for our own stuff. You'd better go way back where you came from.*

So Al moved on quickly, but called in on prospector Charley Fry (of Fry Canyon), who he had made friends with while in White Canyon earlier that season. Fry said he'd look after the Longhorns while Scorup headed back to Salina for help. Upon arriving home, he talked his father, brother Jim, and the Hugentoblers, to go back with him. When they moved out, which was in November of 1891, they took with them 150 head of their own family cattle, apparently to leave on the east side of the river.

When they reached the **Dandy Crossing at Hite**, they had a hell of a time getting the cattle across. With the river high at that moment, they enlisted the help of several miners, and with the aid of Cass Hite's rowboat, finally got the herd across. When the Scorups arrived at the camp of the Texans, they were surprised to see Al return, but didn't give the Scorups any trouble. As it turned out, the Texans had rounded up Sanford's Longhorns and were on their way out of the country. When they finally did leave, that left White Canyon to the Scorup herd.

The Scorup brothers decided to stay the winter with big dreams of building up their own herd. During that winter, and for many years afterwards, they stayed in alcove caves in the canyons, one of which was near **Collins Spring** in the middle part of **Grand Gulch** (which drains into the upper end of the San Juan Arm of the lake). They lived on sourdough, beans, dried fruit, and venison.

After a couple of years of wrangling and competing for range with the Bluff Pool, which had moved into White Canyon when the Texans and the Elk Mountain Cattle Company moved out, they began to feel the effects of the drought for the first time. During the winter of 1893-94, the Scorups lost 60% of their small herd, and the Bluff Pool lost half of theirs. In the spring, The Pool rounded up 600 head and left White Canyon to the Scorups. That year was the beginning of a drought period, which lasted several years. This extended drought was one reason for the big cattle operators leaving San Juan County in the late 1890's.

Not long after these events, the Bluff Pool hired Al to be their foreman, paying him $37.50 a month. Brother Jim stayed with their own little herd. Later in the fall of 1894, Al moved part of the Bluff herd to Denver, where they were sold for $13 a head. Upon returning to Utah, he headed for Salt Lake City, where he and Emma Bayles were married in January, 1895.

Later, in the winter of 1895-96, Al made a contract with the Bluff Pool to gather wild cattle from the area west of Bluff and near the upper end of the San Juan Arm of Lake Powell. He was to get $5 a head. Al used some of the young buckaroos from town and gathered 2000 head. That translated into $10,000, which was enough to get the Scorup Brothers back in the cattle business.

Al worked for the Bluff Pool until 1898. That's when it collapsed, which was due in part to the drought. The Scorups then bought out most of the Co-op and had all of the area between the San Juan, the Colorado, and the Abajos Mountains as their range, with no competition. They summered their stock on Elk Ridge and the Abajos, and wintered them in White Canyon and other drainages to the south, such as **Red, Cedar, Knowles, Moqui, Lake, The Rincon, Cottonwood, Wilson Creek, San Juan, Navajo, Castle Creek** and **Mikes Canyons**.

During this period of time there were lots of wild horses out on the range, possibly left-overs from the Wilson herd which had been on Wilson and Gray Mesas. They were eating grass the cattle needed, so they were eliminated when ever possible. Al later stated that on one roundup, they shot 700 head of horses.

Throughout the years, the Scorups had some experiences worth telling. In the winter of 1900-1901, Jim Scorup and cowhand Henry Knowles ran into members of Butch Cassidy's Wild Bunch camping along the Colorado near Dandy Crossing. They surprised each other and everyone drew revolvers, but put them away moments later. Jim later stated that Butch Cassidy himself actually pointed his six-shooter at Henry, but neither side wanted any trouble (This same **Henry Knowles**, along with his brother, once ran cattle on Mancos Mesa east of Good Hope Bay, beginning some time around 1890. They were a small outfit and the first to be on the Mancos. They are also the ones credited with building the stock trail down into, and naming Knowles Canyon.)

Another time, the Scorups went to Ephraim (located in central Utah north of Richfield & I-15) and bought 30 pure-breed Hereford bulls to increase the quality of their herd. When they got those stubborn critters to Dandy Crossing, they had to use Cass Hite's rowboat again to take the bulls across, one at a time. That was in December, and not a pleasant undertaking.

In 1908, Jim finally got off the range long enough to get married. That was to Elmina Humphreys, a Salina school teacher. In the years after the turn of the century things went well for the Scorup Brothers outfit. Their herd increased, and prices remained good. They built up the herd to thousands of head. Their headquarters was at Bluff, but in 1917 the brothers began to seek an alternate life style. One reason for this was the death of Jim's wife Elmina. This forced Jim to want to live closer to his 4 children, one boy and 3 girls. So while Al moved his family to Provo (Al's original home is still standing and owned by family members at 237 East, Center Street) so their 6 girls could get a better education, Jim moved back to Salina, where they had other livestock interests at a place called Lost Creek. In March of 1918, all the Bluff holdings were sold for a total of $291,700. Everything seemed OK. But,...

Al Scorup had developed into a big time cattleman and dreamer, and wanted more challenges. Less than a month after selling the herd, he headed for Moab, where he met the Somerville brothers, Bill and

Big Time Cattle Companies & Their Ranges--1890

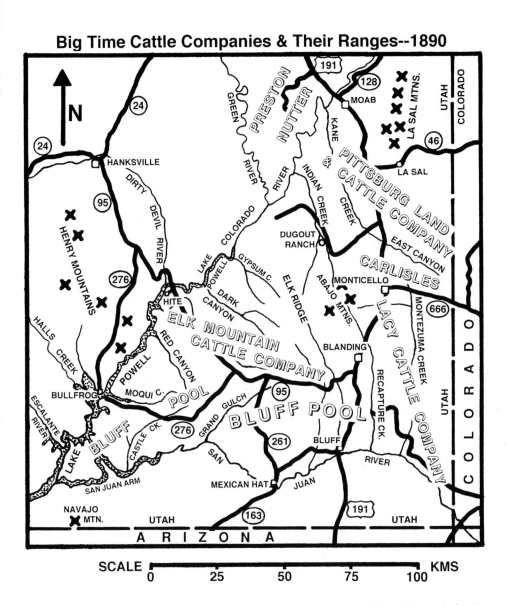

Andrew. They discussed the purchase of the **Indian Creek Cattle Company** owned by David Goude-lock and others. Goudelock had moved to Indian Creek in 1895, and had built it into a first class oper-ation. In the years since, this same ranch became known as The Dugout, or the Dugout Ranch. John Scorup, grandson of Jim Scorup, now living in Monticello and retired from the BLM, believes it was Goudelock who first built and used the old stock trails leading down into Gypsum and Dark Canyons.

As it turned out, Al Scorup (without telling his brother Jim), along with the Somervilles, and Joe Titus, paid a total of $426,000 for the **Dugout Ranch**. The new company was to be called the **Scorup-Somerville Corporation**. Al looked out for the Indian Creek holdings, while Jim stayed on in Salina to care for that end of the business. Their new range included the north slopes of the Abajos in summer, and the canyons leading into Cataract Canyon to the west and northwest as winter range.

After this purchase, the Scorup-Somerville outfit went through good years and bad. By far the worst disaster came in the winter of 1919-20. That's when Al really started feeling or getting old. To begin with, on Thanksgiving Day, 1919, it snowed heavily and they had nearly a meter of snow on the ground and the cows couldn't get at the grass. There was no hay to buy either. Everyone suffered. The company lost nearly 2000 head of cattle alone; 300 in the feed lot. Al paid a trapper $1.50 apiece to skin as many carcasses as possible, then sold the hides. And if this wasn't enough, in February, 1920, Al got a telegram from Salina, saying brother Jim was ill. By the time he got to Salina, Jim had died. Jim's four children ended up being raised by their grandmother Humphreys, and in the end got almost nothing of an inheritance.

Because of that winter, many stockmen folded, but Scorup got through. Then finally in the 1920's the

13

Big Time Cattle Companies & Their Ranges--1900

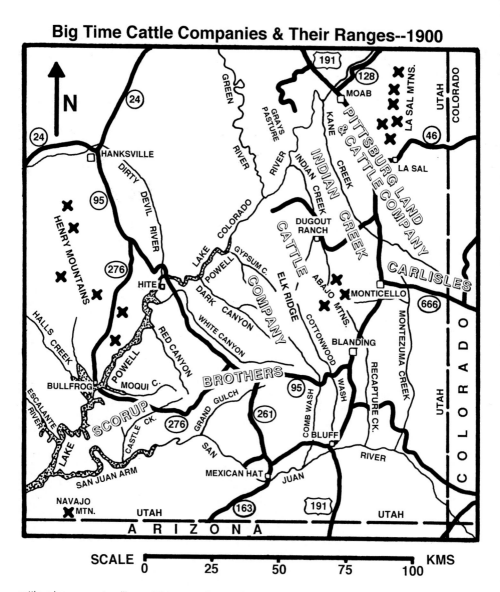

SCALE 0   25   50   75   100   **KMS**

cattle prices rose steadily, and things got better. In 1926, Scorup, the Somervilles, and Jacob Adams (the man Al sold most of their Bluff holdings to in 1918), combined their stock and ranges, to create the **Scorup & Somerville Cattle Company**. This new and bigger outfit held grazing rights from the canyon country near Moab, south to the San Juan River. It included all the canyons on the east side of present-day Lake Powell and Cataract Canyon. It covered nearly 800,000 square hectares, or about 2 million square acres, all west of the Abajo Mountains.

As the years passed, Al Scorup continued to ride with the cowboys, at least during roundup and branding times. He stayed in the saddle until he was nearly 80 years of age, and until he had a stroke. Not long after that, and while in a wheelchair, he passed the reins of the **S & S Cattle Company** to his son-in-law, **Harve Williams**. Al died soon after on October 5, 1959.

In 1965, the Scorup & Somerville Cattle Company came to an end. The entire outfit was sold to **Charley Redd** of La Sal. A few years later, Redd divided his holdings and sold part of it to Ken Schmidt of Colorado, while giving the other part to his son **Robert Redd**.

Sometime in the mid-1970's, Schmidt sold most of his stock & grazing rights to the late **Melvin Dalton** of Monticello. Another part of the original range in White Canyon and the Woodenshoes (north of Natural Bridges National Monument) country at the head of Dark Canyon, went to **Cloyd** and **Sandy Johnson**. Later, Sandy and his **Woodenshoe Cattle Company**, got all that range & cattle and in 2007, he still winters cattle between Dark Canyon and the big east-west ridge between White & Red Canyons. After Melvin's death in the late 1990's, his son **Val Dalton** took over and in 2007 still runs cows from Red Canyon south to the San Juan Arm of the lake and east to Grand Gulch. His outfit is called the **TY Cattle Company**. East of the northern parts of Grand Gulch (but not down in the canyon) is alloted to Ken

Black of Blanding; east of the southern end of Grand Gulch is alloted to Ron Ebberts of Egnar, Colorado.

In 1997, **The Nature Conservancy** bought the Dugout Ranch from **Robert Redd**, ex-wife **Heidi,** & their **2 sons, Matt & Adam**. As part of the deal, Heidi got a 10 year lease and still operates the Dugout Ranch using Forest Service and BLM grazing allotments on public lands from Dark Canyon north into Beef Basin and to the boundary of Canyonlands NP. Heidi has a lease on 25 acres of land, terminating on her death. Their outfit is still called the **Indian Creek Cattle Company.** As of 12/2007 & as this book goes to press, negotiations are underway about a new lease, perhaps just for the boys (?).

The Glen Canyon & San Juan River Gold Rushes

The gold rush in Glen Canyon of the Colorado and along the San Juan River started when wandering prospectors tried to figure out where the Navajos got all the silver for their jewelry. Two prospectors who may or may not have found that place were killed by Indians in Monument Valley in March, 1880. They was **James Merrick** and **Ernest Mitchell**. When their bodies were later examined, silver ore samples were found. This led to the belief that Merrick & Mitchell had found the Navajo silver mine. Rumors spread, and before long the place was crawling with prospectors all the way from Monument Valley to Navajo Mountain.

One of those out looking for El Dorado was **Cass Hite**, an old miner from Telluride, Colorado. According to David Lavender, he'd got into some sort of trouble that recommended speedy departure from the Colorado mountains. Monument Valley seemed a good place to lie low, and he might even utilize his time trying to find Pish-la-ki (the Merrick & Mitchell Mine). Somehow Hite made friends with the Navajo Chief Hoskaninni, even living with him in his hogan for one year. In the end the chief told him there was gold in Glen Canyon. Cass took off, crossed the San Juan and headed down White Canyon to the Colorado River at what later became **Hite**, or Hite Ferry. Hite himself called the place **Dandy Crossing**.

He arrived in September, 1883, and did indeed find gold, although it was a very fine dust and hard to separate from the sand. At first Hite prospected for gold, but it was slim pickin's. When the **Hole-in-the-Rock Mormons** found out this was a better route than their old Hole-in-the-Rock Trail between the settlements of western Utah and Bluff, they began to use it, along with **Halls Crossing**. That's when Hite built a small rock store & post office (in his name) to catch their business. According to Lavender, 2 miners even built a row boat and operated it on call. Mail and supplies came in from Hanksville once a week.

Slowly but surely, Hite collected a pouch of gold dust, by doing a little prospecting and with his small business. He showed it around now and then, and suddenly the rumor spread that he had a secret mine. He was followed, threatened, bribed and cajoled to reveal its location. Of course the mine didn't exist, but when he said so, it was believed he was being sly. To keep from being pestered to death, he finally touched off one of the weirdest gold rushes in American history.

Hite said the gold came from riffles farther down the canyon. The tale spread like wildfire. Hundreds of miners rushed into the grim gorge, and tore it's gravel bars to pieces. Eventually even staid Eastern capital fell prey to the excitement and organized the **Hoskaninni Mining Company** (Lavender). Hite then settled into the business of keeping his small store alive and extracted gold from the pockets of prospectors.

From Dandy Crossing, prospectors spread out all over Glen Canyon. Entry points other than at Hite were at Halls Crossing, Hole-in-the-Rock, Crossing of the Fathers (Ute Ford), and at Lee's Ferry. The San Juan River also had a gold rush, beginning is **1892-93**, but it offered the same kind of fine gold that was found in Glen Canyon.

In 1889, a group of men under the guidance of **Frank M. Brown** reached the mouth of North Wash, just west across the channel from present-day, rather the former, Hite Marina (in 2007, the marina part of the business was gone, and now it's just called Hite). He was the president of a company that hoped to build a railroad from Colorado to California via the canyon of the Colorado River. His chief engineer was **Robert Brewster Stanton**, a man who specialized in mountain railways. The purpose of the trip was to determine the feasibility of a railway through the canyon. That trip ended in disaster when Brown and 2 others were drowned just below Lee's Ferry in Marble Canyon. Stanton later finished the trip downriver and thought the plan was possible, but the railway was never started. However, Stanton remembered the placer mining activity in Glen Canyon.

Late in the century, after most miners had given up gold mining, Stanton returned to Glen Canyon as the chief engineer and founder of the **Hoskaninni Company**. With investors money, he re-claimed all of Glen Canyon, from North Wash down to Lee's Ferry, with 145 new mining claims. This was in 1898-99. After that they were required to make improvements on the claims to keep them valid. Crews were sent throughout the canyon to make roads and trails and make it appear like some thing was really happening.

In the meantime, a dredge was being built and later shipped from Chicago by rail. From Green River, Utah, it was loaded onto wagons and hauled to the river at **Stanton Canyon** (just east of Bullfrog Marina) and to nearby **Camp Stone**, named after the company president. The assembly began in July, 1900, and by January, 1901, the dredge was in operation. It worked only for a short time, then shut down, a total failure. It simply couldn't separate the fine gold dust from the sands. After that, things were pretty quiet along the river for a while, as one colorful chapter in the history of Glen Canyon ended.

But not long after one chapter ended, another was about to begin. The lead character in the new drama was **Charles H. Spencer**. His career began on the **San Juan River** in about 1900. Not much is known about his early days, but the first we hear of him was at **Williams Bar**, otherwise known as Williamsburg, just upstream or east of the mouth of Copper Canyon. Spencer apparently built a little red rock cabin, near where a boiler and other equipment was found years later. That was in 1908.

He later discovered the Wingate Sandstone held small quantities of gold and silver, so after he got investors interested, he moved operations downriver. There he set up Camp Ibex, otherwise known as **Spencer Camp**, under the Wingate Cliffs. They put their rock crusher to work in June, 1909, then again the following winter. But as it turned out, they had a hard time getting the gold out of the sandstone, so that ended in failure too.

Next stop for big-time dreamer Spencer was **Lee's Ferry**. He became head engineer for the **American Placer Corporation**, which re-filed on claims in the area, as well as around Pahreah, up the Paria River in Utah. Their plans were to use a boiler to create steam to run a sluicing operation and attempt to separate gold from the clay beds of the Chinle Formation. They thought if they could get coal from mines in upper Warm Creek Canyon down to Lee's Ferry, they could run the operation, and surely then

Big Time Cattle Companies & Their Ranges--1930

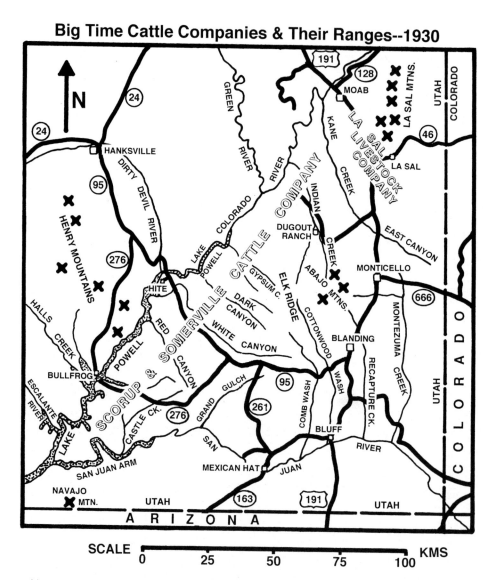

could get at the gold. But after several attempts to use 2 different steamboats and a barge on the river to get coal to the Ferry, it became apparent they still couldn't get the gold out of the Chinle clays. After the venture at Lee's Ferry, Spencer tried once again at **Pahreah, Utah**, but had the same results.

After the big-time promoters left the canyon, things became very quiet until the 1930's and the Great Depression. Then there was another flurry of activity in and around the canyon, but it didn't amount to much. There was another period of exploration as well after World War II and in the 1950's. Those were the **uranium boom days**. Anywhere on the Colorado Plateau where the Chinle Formation is exposed, men and bulldozers went looking for uranium deposits. The Chinle forms a talus slope, then usually a bench not far below the big Wingate Sandstone walls. There are several areas around the lake where you can still see uranium mining exploration tracks, including the areas southwest of Hite, around The Rincon, and in the upper San Juan River Arm.

Over the years, and at a very slow rate, interest gradually shifted from mining or prospecting, to recreation. The first boat load of people said to have gone down the river just for the fun of it was in 1909. That's when **Julius Stone**, the big loser in the Hoskaninni Company and Stanton Dredge scheme, with **Nathaniel Galloway** as guide, rafted through the canyons from Green River, Wyoming, to Needles, California. In 1911, **Ellsworth and Kolb**, fotographed the canyons using Dellenbaugh's book, *A Canyon Voyage*, as a guide.

After World War II, and with the coming of inflatable rafts, there was renewed interest in the canyons. **Bert Loper** and **Norman D. Nevills** were a couple of the more prominent river guides, and David E. Rust was the one who began commercial tours in Glen Canyon. Just about the time river runners were getting in the water, in came the dam builders, which changed the character of recreation in the Glen

Canyon area forever.

The Dam Builders

In 1921, the U.S. Geological Survey (USGS) and the Southern California Edison Company sponsored a joint effort to map the Colorado River from the confluence of the Green and the Colorado down to Lee's Ferry, including the San Juan River. The next year the first really good maps of the river were released. This coincided with a big conference between all the states bordering the Colorado River Basin. It had to do with water allocations and distribution, as well as flood control and hydroelectricity.

The result was the **Colorado River Pact**. It separated the river into the upper and lower basins. The **Upper Basin States** included **Utah, Colorado, New Mexico** and **Wyoming**. The **Lower Basin States** were **Nevada, Arizona** and **California**. The dividing line was at **Lee's Ferry**. The flow of the Colorado River would be divided there. A certain percentage of the annual flow was to pass Lee's Ferry in order for the upper basin states to fulfill their obligation to the lower basin states. But the only way that could be accomplished would be to erect a series of dams upstream so spring floods and heavy runoff during above average water years could be stored and released during drier periods. This was the real beginning of the Glen Canyon Dam project.

By 1952, the **Bureau of Reclamation** had completed a master plan for water development in the upper basin states. After much debate, this master plan was passed by Congress on April 11, 1956. The law authorized four large dams to be built above Lee's Ferry. The first one started was the **Glen Canyon Dam**, located just south of the Utah-Arizona state line, and about 24 kms upstream from the mouth of the Paria River.

The actual construction, or at least preliminary work, began on **October 1, 1956**. Tunnels were blasted and the river diverted into these diversions on February 11, 1959. The very first concrete for the dam was poured on **June 17, 1960**; the last bucket poured was on **September 13, 1963**.

The thickness of the dam at bedrock is 91 meters, while the thickness at the crest is about 8 meters. The height of the dam above bedrock is 216 meters, and 179 meters above the Colorado River.

When the reservoir is completely full, the elevation is to be set at 1128 meters or 3700 feet. When full, the lake is 298 kms long, with a shoreline of about 3136 kms. The water first started backing up in the new lake on **March 13, 1963**, and it took until **June 22, 1980**, to reach the high water mark (**HWM**) for the first time. However, on **July 14, 1983**, the lake reached its all time high point of **1130 meters**. This was due to rapid and heavy runoff after a winter of unusually deep snows all over the upper basin. That historic high level was only 2 meters below the crest of the dam.

The dam has 8 hydroelectric generators, the first of which began to operate on September 4, 1964. By February 28, 1966, all eight were in operation.

For those interested in touring the dam, go to the **Carl Hayden Visitor Center** just west of the Glen Canyon Bridge. There are guided tours going down into the dam, plus park rangers who interpret the scene and sell books and maps.

It was on October 27, 1972, that the region around Lake Powell was established as the **Glen Canyon National Recreation Area**. It is now administered by the National Park Service (NPS).

Over the years, and as Lake Powell has grown in size, it has also grown in popularity. It seems that through Lake Powell the nation has recently discovered the wonders of the Colorado Plateau. Below is a chart showing the visitations to the Glen Canyon National Recreation Area. Keep in mind that the GCNRA covers all the lake at the HWM and bordering areas, and downriver from the Glen Canyon Dam to as far as Lee's Ferry. On lands bordering the Navajo Nation, the GCNRA extends up to the 1134 meter mark (that's 6 meters, or 20 feet above the HWM). The visitation figures include Lee's Ferry, but not traffic going across the bridge near the dam on Highway 89A.

Total Visits to the Glen Canyon National Recreation Area

1962.............................9,282	1977....................2,127,419	1992..........................3,620,558
1963..............................44,285	1978....................2,211,818	1993..........................3,615,024
1964............................196,422	1979....................1,733,282	1994..........................2.844,999*
1965............................303,548	1980....................1,646,968	1995..........................2,538,684
1966............................359,659	1981....................1,820,163	1996..........................2,532,087
1967............................590,037	1982....................1,826,572	1997..........................2,455,736
1968............................654,505	1983....................1,975,273	1998..........................2,467,199
1969............................781,250	1984....................2,052,642	1999..........................2,667,249
1970............................788,482	1985....................2,160,524	2000..........................2,594,064
1971............................687,721	1986....................2,484,024	2001..........................2,363,807
1972............................970,922	1987....................2,883,412	2002..........................2,128,379
1973.........................1,209,116	1988....................3,564,944	2003..........................1,896,797
1974.........................1,159,383	1989....................3,483,904	2004..........................1,861,773
1975.........................1,139,275	1990....................3,103,431	2005..........................1,928,274
1976.........................1,061,716	1991....................3,210,890	2006..........................1,904,350

* A computer error was found in previous years that allowed duplicate counts in total number of visitors. This error was corrected in 1994 and as a result numbers show a decrease over the previous year. The NPS is confident in the numbers shown after 1994 as far as actual counts go.

Of all the entry points to Lake Powell, or rather the GCNRA, the Wahweap-Stateline complex is perhaps the busiest, followed by Bullfrog or Antelope Point, Lee's Ferry (which is the entry point for rafting down the Grand Canyon), Halls Crossing and Hite (as of 2007 it had only a gravel launching area, and no marina facilities).

The new Antelope Point Marina is located just northeast of Page and northwest of the Navajo Power Plant. In the future, the Antelope Point Marina may be the busiest on the lake because it's closer to Rainbow Bridge than Wahweap & Stateline.

After 1989, the San Juan Marina at Piute Farms in the San Juan River Arm was closed and will never be reopened. By 2007, the lake only extended about halfway up the San Juan Arm anyway.

Sedimentation and the Filling Up of Lake Powell

For those who have wondered how long it will take for Lake Powell to fill up with sediment, here is some of the latest information. The Bureau of Reclamation (BOR) has released one of its studies titled, *Lake Powell 1986 Sedimentation Study Report*. Here is a brief summary of that report and some conclusions drawn by one employee of the National Park Service.

It was found that in recent years, the amount of sediment being carried downstream and into the lake, is less than what was recorded in the Colorado River and other tributaries earlier in the 1900's. Several reasons were sited for this change. First, erosion has been reduced, in part at least, by reduced grazing of livestock on public lands, and by better range management. Second, new upstream reservoirs have begun to trap small amounts of sediment.

Because less sediment is entering the lake, new figures were calculated. The BOR now puts the annual amount of sediment entering the lake at 35,000 acre-feet/year. The original carrying capacity of Lake Powell was set at 27,000,000 acre-feet. By simple division, this means it will take 771 years for the lake to fill with sediments to capacity (to the HWM). In coming up with these figures, they may or may not be taking into account the fact that new sediment entering the lake will settle upon older layers, causing compression of the old. If all factors remain constant, the lake will fill up to the HWM in 771 years, if settling and compression are not taken into account.

As you ponder of these figures, here are a couple of things to keep in mind. As the lake gets close to being filled, muddy water will begin to pass through the penstocks, instead of dropping its sediment behind the dam. Also keep in mind, that the penstocks are 15 meters (50 feet) below the HWM, and 50% of the lakes water storage capacity is in the top 15 meters of the reservoir. When that point is reached, then the ability to generate electric power will diminish, but there will still be some ability to store heavy winter runoff. There should also be at least some water around for boating and other forms of recreation.

However, it's likely impossible for the lake to fill to capacity with sediments. It seems that at sometime in the future, the upper end of the lake will end up being one big mud flat, covered with tamarack, tumbleweeds and cheat grass, with the Colorado and San Juan Rivers meandering down the middle. But closer to the dam, there should always be some lake remaining. How much is still a guess. At that point in time, most of the functions for which the dam was originally built, will have run their course.

An aerial view of **Rainbow Bridge** looking north, northwest. To the right, and just out of sight, is an overhang or alcove cave where tourists used to camp before the coming of Lake Powell. Rainbow Bridge is in Bridge Canyon, and to the upper left, just out of sight, is Lake Powell and the floating docks.

The floating docks for **Rainbow Bridge**. This picture was taken on **7/24/2007-WL1099.78m /3608.18'**, and boaters had to walk 1 1/2 kms to reach the bottom of Rainbow Bridge. Also floating in the background left, are toilets.

The head of **Forbidding Canyon's Inlet** on **9/11/2007-WL1098.03m/3602.42'**. There's usually a mass of logs & other debris where the stream enters the lake, but it's not as hard to get through as it might first appear. Forbidding is one of the better canyon hikes in this book.

Part II--Introduction to Boating, Hiking and Camping

Marinas on Lake Powell

Wahweap and Stateline Marinas

Wahweap Marina, just south of the Utah-Arizona line, is still the busiest entry point on the lake. It's located just a few kms north of the dam, and 10 kms (6 miles) northwest of Page, Arizona. The main commercial enterprise at Wahweap is operated by **ARAMARK**, which runs most of the concessions on the lake. Their facilities include a lodge/hotel, with dining room, gift shop, lounge and swimming pool. The **Lake Powell Resort Lobby** is headquarters for scheduled and charter lake cruise boats. Most popular are tour boats heading for **Rainbow Bridge**. In the three months of summer, there are as many as 4 or 5 tour boats a day going to Rainbow Bridge at the cost of around US$132 per person. Sign up for a tour at the **tour boat desk** in the **Resort Lobby**, Tele. 928-645-1070. Call for updated information.

Near the lodge/hotel is a cement boat launching ramp, a fuel dock with regular gas and Diesel, a floating dock & store, another shore-side store, long and short term parking, and a gas station for automobiles. Also provided are **boat rentals** which are found only at the **Stateline Marina**, located just northwest of Wahweap, a sports store with fishing and boating supplies and private boat storage facilities. These are all operated by the ARAMARK, P.O. Box 1597, Page, Arizona, 86040, or call the Lake Powell Resort front desk at Tele. 928-645-2433. For boat rentals, reservations or other information for any of the marinas on the lake call toll free at **800-528-6154**. Or check their website **lakepowell.com**.

West of the lodge/hotel & gas station is a large campground and RV park, both of which are now operated by ARAMARK. Just northwest of the Wahweap operation and campground, and on the Utah side of the line, is the **Stateline Marina**. It's facilities include boat rentals (Tele. 928-645-1129/1128) and boat repairs, a small store, a large public boat-launching ramp & parking lot, a fuel dock, boat pump-out facilities, house boat storage, a fish cleaning station, swimming beach, day-use picnic sites and toilets.

In addition, there is a National Park Service ranger station but this is not a visitor center. The main place to get information & books, etc., is at the **Glen Canyon Dam** and the **Carl Hayden Visitor Center**, Tele. 928-608-6404. See the map on the next page.

Antelope Point Marina

This newest of Lake Powell's marinas is located northeast of Page and northwest of the Navajo Power Plant. To get there, drive southeast and downhill out of the center of Page, then at the signal light, turn east on **State Highway 98**. Drive to a point just beyond **Antelope Canyon** and just before the power plant, then at the sign turn north (directly north from the entry to Antelope Canyon) on a newly paved road and drive 8 kms (5 miles) to the new site. The nice thing about Antelope Point is, it's located

Looking northeast from just below the **Lake Powell Resort Lodge at Wahweap**. This is the Tour Boat Dock with **Castle Rock** in the background. The boat to the lower left-hand corner is one that takes tourists to Rainbow Bridge.

Area Map--Wahweap & Stateline Marinas and Glen Canyon Dam & Page, Arizona

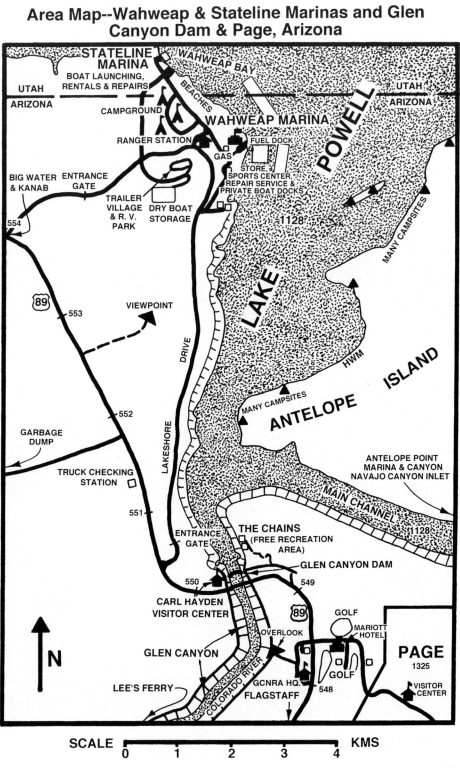

This aerial picture looking almost due west, shows most of the **Wahweap Marina** complex. In the foreground is the floating marina where private boats are stored; to the right is where houseboats are anchored; upper center is **Stateline Marina** where you can rent boats; center is **Lake Powell Resort Lodge**; in the far upper left is **Lone Rock Beach & Lone Rock**. This foto was taken on **10/7/2007-WL1097.8m/3601.66'** with rather low lake levels. This part of the lake is known as **Wahweap Bay**.

The **Antelope Point public launching ramp** looking southwest; to the right is the breakwater, upper left is parking (as well as along the ramp itself); and to the lower left, and just out of sight, is the floating Antelope Point Marina. This aerial foto was taken on Sunday, **10/7/2007-WL1097.8m/3601.66'**. In October, there are fewer boats & boaters than in the summer months.

Antelope Point Marina looking north. Left, and just out of sight, is the public launch ramp; center is parking; left, and in the channel is boat rentals; right is private houseboat storge; center is eating facilities; upper part of the narrow channel is a no-wake zone where boats pass going between Wahweap & Stateline Marinas, and upper Lake Powell. Foto taken on **10/7/2007-WL1097.8m/3601.66'**

in the main channel of the Colorado River 8M (13K) uplake from the Glen Canyon Dam. This means it's closer to the main body of the lake than is Wahweap/Stateline Marinas. This is especially nice when the lake level is below 1103 meters (3620') when the **Castle Rock Cut** is closed. When the CR Cut is closed, all boat traffic from Wahweap must go uplake via the old channel and right by Antelope Point. This means an extra 20 kms (12 miles) of boating from Wahweap. However, in early or mid-2008, earth moving equipment will be taken to Castle Rock by barge, and a deeper cut made. The plan is to dig down to 1097,3 meters (3600'), which is the long run will save fuel/pollution. The thinking by all concerned is, the lake may never again fill up, or go much lower than the new CR Cut will be.

July 6, 1999, marked the completion of the first stage of construction at the Antelope Point Marina. At that time a National Park Service public cement launch ramp and 2 toilets were completed. Construction was done by GMF-Antelope, LLC, out of Phoenix which got the low bid (the only bid!). As of the summer of 2007, everything was completed and up & running. This new marina is owned and operated as a **joint venture** by **Antelope Point Holdings, LLC**, which is a private non-Indian company and the Navajo Nation. It's an official concessioner of the National Park Service.

Here's what you'll find in addition to the public launch ramp. On land is a large concession parking lot, dry storage area for boats & repairs, and a paved & metal gangway leading down to everything else, which is a totally **floating marina**. On the water and at the east end, is a large docking area for **private yachts & houseboats**; in the middle is a fairly large **store** (open from 7am to 8pm--Arizona time), plus a **food & beverage hall** which includes a fast food section (ice cream & burgers), a cafeteria which serves pizzas and meals, and a bar. The eating hall is open from 6:30am to 10pm in summer--perhaps fewer hours in the off season (?).

On the west end of the floating marina is a **small store** selling ice, oil, maps, T shirts, boaters supplies, etc, plus a **fueling dock** which sells regular gas & Diesel. The fuel dock is up & running from 7am to 7pm; but if the pumps are working correctly, you can buy gas anytime with a credit card. Fill up water bottles/tanks there as well. Just to the west of that are the **boat rental docks**. You can rent houseboat and smaller speedboats & personnel watercraft. As of the summer of 2007, lots of boaters going to or from Wahweap/Stateline, were stopping at Antelope for refreshments.

For updates, see their website **antelopepointlakepowell.com**. For reservation & information call 928-645-5900, x5. For houseboat reservations call 800-255-5561, or for marina, slip and moorage information call 928-645-5900 x1. Their mailing address is Antelope Point Marina, PO Box 880, Page, Arizona, 86040.

Dangling Rope Marina

This is the only marina on the lake with **boater access only--no roads to this place**. It's located about 66 kms (41 miles) uplake from the dam, about halfway up Dangling Rope Inlet, and almost due south of the southern end of Fiftymile Mountain. It's also on the route to Rainbow Bridge.

Dangling Rope is a **floating marina** which has a small **store**, equipped with basic food and camping supplies (including lots of ice), a snack bar with ice cream, a covered picnic area with tables, garbage disposal bins, and a small NPS ranger station (which isn't open very often!). They have a telefon where calls can be made via a cellular hookup, but they seem to work only part of the time and are a bit expensive (in 2007, all calls were free because of an electrical glitch!). Calls can be made with a calling card only. There is also an information board with a button you push to get the latest weather forecast (but it wasn't working in 2007!) You can post letters from this marina, but they'll be post marked Page, Arizona.

At the eastern end of the floating marina is a **fuel dock** which sells regular gas, but apparently no Diesel fuel. There is no more premixed 50 to 1 gas sold at any of the marinas on the lake. To give some idea of the cost of gasoline, in late July, 2007, regular gas cost $4.41 a gallon. During the same week, the cheapest regular in Page sold for about $2.92.

They also have a **repair and maintenance shop**, boat pump out, drinking and flushing water facilities, and a cold water tap. Electricity at Dangling Rope is supplied by photovoltaic **solar panels** located on the hill behind the marina next to employee housing. The backup is a propane powered generator. For updated information call the Dangling Rope Marina store at 928-645-2969, or call the the NPS dispatch in Page at 928-608-6301 which can connect you to the ranger station or any other local number. Or try their website **lakepowell.com**.

One odd thing about this place is that although it's located in Utah they still use Arizona time. During the winter months, these 2 times are the same, but when daylight savings time rolls around, Arizona does not participate. The Navajo Nation uses daylight savings time, as does Utah and everywhere else in the west. In the summer season, the store and gas station are open from **7am until 7pm, Arizona time** (fewer hours during the fall, winter and spring). The ice cream window is open from 8am until 5:30pm, Arizona time. The busiest times for the marina are from about 10am to 5pm. The main reason they prefer to use Arizona time is that Page and Wahweap use it, so for them it's less confusing to stay on the same clock as the company headquarters, which is **ARAMARK (Lake Powell Resorts & Marinas)**. Also, most of the visitors to Dangling Rope begin at Wahweap, Stateline or Antelope Point Marinas, and are already on Arizona time.

Some food prices at Dangling Rope are nearly double what you'd pay in the cheapest supermarkets in Utah and Arizona. Dangling Rope gets all it's supplies from Wahweap and is regularly serviced by barge-carrying container units. The garbage is hauled out in containers on barges too, which are hooked onto big trucks at Wahweap and taken to a disposal site. Gasoline is brought in almost daily in summer in a large Chevron gas boat. This marina is closed in winter--from mid-November to early March.

Bullfrog Marina

Most boaters from Utah end up at Bullfrog located due south of Hanksville and the Henry Mountains, and in about the middle of this long reservoir. It's the 2nd or 3rd busiest port on the lake. At Bullfrog, you'll find the Defiance House Lodge with dining room, a gasoline station which performs minor repairs, and a curio shop. There is a dock-side store with all the basics, including fishing tackle, food, drinks, and other supplies. Nearby is a fuel dock, which sells regular gas and Diesel fuel--no one sells the premixed 50 to 1 gas on the lake anymore. You can rent houseboats or smaller speed boats, or join group tours of the lake. These facilities all belong to the main concessioner on the lake, **ARAMARK (Lake Powell Resorts & Marina)**. Their mailing address is Bullfrog Resort & Marina, Box 4055, Lake Powell, Utah, 84533. You can call ARAMARK's main switchboard at 435-684-3000 for local information or other numbers; or ARAMARK'S toll free reservations number at 800-528-6154; or **lakepowell.com**.

There is a public cement boat launch ramp (but no more drinking &/or flushing water there) and rest-

Looking southeast from a hill overlooking **Dangling Rope Marina**. At the far end is the fuel dock & small marina store; coming back this way is a repair shop; garbage disposal barges; parking docks for visitor's boats; NPS ranger station & pay telefone; and the main marina store & ice cream booth (ice cream is very popular in summer!). Left is the covered picnic tables & ice storage containers.

Bullfrog and Halls Crossing Marinas

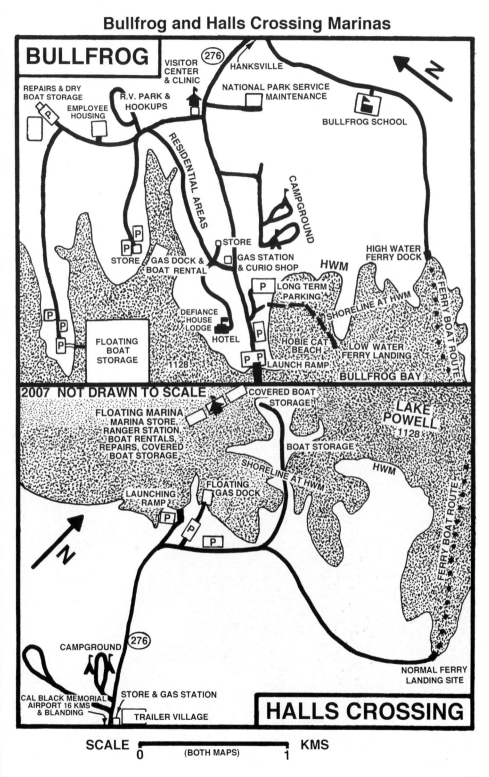

BULLFROG

REPAIRS & DRY BOAT STORAGE

EMPLOYEE HOUSING

R.V. PARK & HOOKUPS

VISITOR CENTER & CLINIC

276

HANKSVILLE

NATIONAL PARK SERVICE MAINTENANCE

BULLFROG SCHOOL

RESIDENTIAL AREAS

CAMPGROUND

STORE

GAS DOCK & BOAT RENTAL

STORE

GAS STATION & CURIO SHOP

HWM

HIGH WATER FERRY DOCK

LONG TERM PARKING

SHORELINE AT HWM

FERRY BOAT ROUTE

DEFIANCE HOUSE LODGE

HOTEL

1128

FLOATING BOAT STORAGE

HOBIE CAT BEACH

LOW WATER FERRY LANDING

LAUNCH RAMP

BULLFROG BAY

2007 NOT DRAWN TO SCALE

COVERED BOAT STORAGE

LAKE POWELL
1128

FLOATING MARINA
MARINA STORE, RANGER STATION, BOAT RENTALS, REPAIRS, COVERED BOAT STORAGE

BOAT STORAGE

SHORELINE AT HWM

HWM

LAUNCHING RAMP

FLOATING GAS DOCK

FERRY BOAT ROUTE

CAMPGROUND

276

NORMAL FERRY LANDING SITE

CAL BLACK MEMORIAL AIRPORT 16 KMS & BLANDING

STORE & GAS STATION

TRAILER VILLAGE

HALLS CROSSING

SCALE

0   (BOTH MAPS)   1   KMS

25

rooms and a fish cleaning station nearby. In the public housing section is an RV park, a small camp-ground and a day-use picnic site. The National Park Service has a new **visitor center** along the main highway leading into Bullfrog, Tele. 435-684-7423/7400/7424. In the same building is a **clinic** which is open for about 6 months of the year, Tele. 435-684-2288. Bullfrog has a small **school** with grades 1-12, which handles local children as well as those from Halls Crossing.

Located on the highway north of Bullfrog about 16 kms (10 miles), and outside the Glen Canyon National Recreation Area, is the the **Off Shore Marina**. It has two gas stations, store and boat storage & repairs all near **mile post 30**. They have a main office switchboard Tele. 435-788-2254. Just down the road south near **mile post 31** is a new gas station with an A & W outlet (Tele. 435-788-2220) and post office. North of this complex is **Ticaboo** between **mile posts 27 & 28**. It was originally built as a company town for the uranium mines in the southern Henry Mountains, but is now switching to tourism to stay alive. Located there is a motel (Tele. 435-788-2110), restaurant, gas station & C Store, mobile home park with RV hookups, a few new homes and boat storage. In July of 2007, the cheapest gas was at Ticaboo, then Off Shore Marina, and then the station at Bullfrog--but the price difference between all of them was only about 5 cents.

Bullfrog is also the terminal for the **ferry boat**, the **John Atlantic Burr (JAB)**. The regular launch site is south of the school (same paved road) on the east side of the Bullfrog area, but when the lake levels are low, they switch the landing site to **Hobie Cat Beach** which is about 800m east of the normal public launch ramp at Bullfrog. This site is unpaved, as is the road leading to it.

The JAB was originally 30m long and 13m wide. It has two 8V-71 Detroit Diesel engines and a 9450 liter fuel tank. It originally held 8 cars and two buses and could haul a maximum of 150 passengers, but during the winter of 1996, the boat was lengthened to handle more and bigger vehicles.

This ferry was designed by the Alexander Love and Co., from Victoria, British Columbia, but was constructed by Mark Steel Co., Salt Lake City, Utah. It was named after John Atlantic Burr, a pioneer Utah rancher born in 1846 aboard a ship somewhere in the Atlantic Ocean. Funding for this venture was the Utah Department of Transportation. They paid for the boat's design, construction and transportation to the lake. The ferry boat launch facilities were provided by the National Park Service (NPS), and it is operated by Lake Powell Resorts & Marinas--ARAMARK.

The John Atlantic Burr (JAB) runs year-round (except for February which is the month for maintenance) between Bullfrog and Halls Crossing, a distance of about 5 kms and takes about 25 minutes. Here's a price list as of 7/2007: for foot passengers, $5. For all vehicles (the price includes vehicle, driver and passengers) under 20' (about 6m), $20. All vehicles over 20' (6m), $1.25 per/foot. Motorcycles $10.

The JAB begins and ends at **Halls Crossing**. In the summer season, which is May 15 through October 15, departures in 2007 were at 8am, 10am, noon, 2pm, 4pm and 6pm. **Departures from Bullfrog** were at 9am, 11am, 1pm, 5pm and 7pm.

During the winter season departures from Halls Crossing should be at 8am, 10am, noon and 2pm. From Bullfrog departures should be at 9am, 11am, 1pm and 3pm. The last ferry of the day takes school children back to Halls Crossing for the night. For updated information & schedules call the main switchboard at Bullfrog (see above) or ARAMARK at Halls Crossing, Tele. 435-684-7000.

Bullfrog Marina on **9/25/2007-WL1097.86m/3601.85'**. Near the center are the covered docks for private boats, and the marina store & fueling docks nearby to the right. Since the higher lake levels of the late 1980's, everything has been pushed further out into **Bullfrog Bay**. Lower left is the end of the public launching ramp; to the left of that is Hobie Cat Beach & the low-water ferry dock.

Looking southeast at the public launch ramp & parking with low water levels at **Bullfrog** on **9/25/2007-WL1097.86m/3601.85'**. To the left is the gravel road leading to the low-water ferry boat dock above; just below that is **Hobie Cat Beach**.

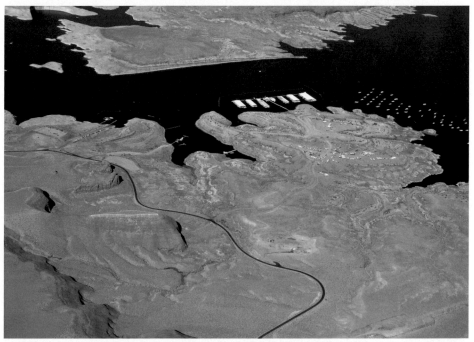

Looking southwest at **Halls Crossing Marina** on **9/25/2007-WL1097.86m/3601.85'**. On land near the middle are dry docks & repair facilities. In the water left is the public launch ramp; near the middle and in the small inlet with 2 forks is the fuel dock; above in the middle are the covered boat storage, marina store & snack bar and ranger station; to the right is the floating houseboat storage.

If ferry service should shut down for any reason you will see the closure notice stated clearly on some big signs as you turn off Highway 95 onto Highway 276, at both ends of this paved road. Or call the visitor center in advance for the latest information.

Halls Crossing Marina
This marina is just across the main channel from Bullfrog Bay and about 5 kms across the lake from Bullfrog Marina. It's at about the halfway point along Highway 276, the paved road that makes a loop to the south from Highway 95. One part of this road ends at Bullfrog, the other at Halls Crossing. The ferry boat completes the loop across the lake. See Bullfrog Marina for ferry boat information.

At Halls Crossing you'll find a campground, a pump-out station, trailer village, mobile home rentals with a small store, boat storage and a gas station & garage that can make minor repairs. The marina has a floating houseboat dock with repair facilities, and fishing & house boats for rent. It has a store with limited food items, souvenirs, fishing tackle and other boater's supplies. The fuel dock supplies regular gas only and it's located southeast of where the 2007 floating dock was situated and where the ferry used to land. These facilities are operated by ARAMARK, Box 5101, Lake Powell, Utah, 84533, Tele. 435-684-7000, or try their website **lakepowell.com**. The National Park Service maintains a small office and visitor center next to the little store at the dock but it's not open very often, Tele. 435-684-7460.

Hite (no more marina as of 2007)
Hite is located at the upper end of Lake Powell, about halfway between Blanding and Hanksville, and just south of Highway 95 (turn off between mile posts 48 & 49). This area used to have a marina complex which was about 8 kms or 5 miles north of where the old Hite town and ferry used to be located before Lake Powell days. At Hite today is a **small store** with most basic needs for fishermen and campers, but in 2007, it was only open 3 hours a day, from 11am to 2pm. With the store is a **gas station**, which carries regular gas & Diesel. You can buy fuel 24 hours a day with a credit card. ARAMARK still has accommodations in the employee housing area in the form of **5 mobil homes for rent**. Call ARAMARK at Tele. 800-528-6154 for information & reservations. Or try their website **lakepowell.com.** There's also a new NPS ranger station with fire engine, visitor center & self-registration fee station and public Tele. just west of the store--but it's seldom open, Tele. 435-648-2457.

ARAMARK's floating dock or marina is now (2007) gone because of low lake levels. In 2002, all **their facilities were towed to Halls Crossing**. Even if we again have a wet weather cycle, and the lake level rises substantially, don't expect anyone to reinstall a marina complex at Hite.

Near where the marina used to be is the same cement launching ramp, but in 2007, it was high & dry. However, the NPS did cobble together a **graveled launching site** and small dock below the cement portion. The problem with this is, it can be muddy, unless the NPS adds more gravel. In the meantime, if the water level is high enough, you launch at your own risk (a 4WD might be handy).

Above the old cement launching ramp is a **primitive campground** without water; however, between the launch ramp and campground are some **cement toilets with drinking water**. There's no charge for camping because there's no facilities to speak of. The concessioner is again ARAMARK with the mailing address Hite Marina, Box 501, Lake Powell, Utah, 84533. The Tele. number at the gas station

Hite and Vicinity (No More Marina)

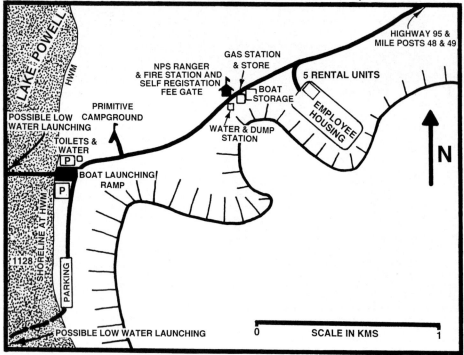

Looking east at the **former Hite Marina** on **9/25/2007-WL1097.86m/3601.85'**. To the upper left is the ranger station and Hite store & gas station. The white place upper left, is the cement launch ramp; to the right of that is where Hite Marina was located--low water was its demise! Lower left is the end of North Wash with clear water; in the middle is the Colorado--no boats launched that day!

On **7/8/2007-WL1100.55m/3610.85'**, this is what greeted anyone who wanted to launch from **Hite**. About 2 months after this foto was taken, water was too low for launching. Notice the cement ramp in the distance. Anytime water is less than 1100 meters (3608') altitude, you can't launch at Hite.

& store is 435-684-2278.

Navajo Nation Marinas

During the 1980's there was a marina at the upper end of the **San Juan River Arm** of Lake Powell run by a Navajo-operated company headquartered in Blanding, Utah. However, in the late summer of 1989, a huge flood came down **Piute Farms Wash** and apparently took out most of those facilities. It has not operated since.

At one time there was a plan to move the old San Juan Marina to the mouth of Copper Canyon; however, with the drought and lower water conditions of the 1990's & 2000's, that plan was scrapped. The reason was, in late August of 1991, lake waters barely reached the mouth of Copper Canyon. So building a marina there wouldn't have been much better than at Piute Farms. The **Antelope Point Marina** has replaced the San Juan Marina. In the future, Antelope may be the busiest & the best on the lake.

Other Possible Launch Sites

Just a little west of Wahweap & Stateline Marinas is **Lone Rock Beach** (see Map 42A). You can get there from Highway 89 and from a point between the state line and mile post 1 on the Utah side. It's about 3 kms (2 miles) to the beach, which has half a dozen stationary vault toilets at the HWM, 7 portable toilets, and cement & brick facility with drinking water, showers, toilets and pay telefon right at the end of the paved road. Lone Rock has a great sandy beach, where you can camp or park right at the shoreline. You can also launch a boat, but beware of deep sand in some places getting down to the beach. One disadvantage to camping at Lone Rock is this is the only place in the GCNRA where ORV's are allowed. At times they can make a lot of noise. **ATV's & motorcycles** are allowed only in a fenced area just south of the beach on the sandy hill side which is east of the fee station.

Near the south end of the lake, and entering the upper part of Warm Creek Bay, is **Crosby Canyon** (see **Map 40**). To get there by car, drive to **Big Water, Utah**, located on Highway 89 about 11 kms (7 miles) northwest of the Utah-Arizona line. Between mile posts 7 & 8 turn northward; after 500 meters (.3 mile) turn right or east, and follow the signs toward Escalante along the **Warm Creek Road**. After 8.3 km (5.1 miles) on a good partly-paved road, you'll pass the **Wiregrass Canyon Trailhead**, but continue on to where the road crosses Crosby Canyon (15.6 kms/9.7 miles from Highway 89). From there, it's about 5 kms (3 miles) down to the HWM. You can likely drive to the lake--but you better have a 4WD--and perhaps launch a small boat (?). You can camp for free, but there's nothing around in the way of improvements or facilities. The county sometimes grades the road down Crosby Canyon, but with low lake levels, don't bet on being able to launch anything from there.

Just north of Bullfrog as you're about to drop down over the hill to the marina, you'll see a dirt road turning off to the left or east. This road takes you down to what's left of **Stanton Canyon** (see **Map 13**). At the end of the road, you can wander about and pick the camping place of your choice. There are now 4 or 5 vault toilets scattered about. Sometimes it's possible to launch there, but that will depend on lake levels and the size of your craft. Camping fee is $6, but it's a little primitive and seems overpriced for what you get. There's no drinking water available, and no garbage pickup, so haul out everything you take in. Leave garbage at the dumpster next to the highway.

Another vehicle access point to the lake is in **Upper Bullfrog Bay** (see **Map 13** again). About 10 kms

The **ferry** at **Halls Crossing** on **10/11/2007-WL1097.66m/3601.52'** with pretty low water. This ferry departs from Bullfrog at odd hours; 9am, 11, 1pm, 3 & 5, while departing from Halls Crossing on the even hours of 8am, 10, 12noon, 2pm & 4. School children leave Halls at 8am, return after 3pm.

(6 miles) north of the boat ramp at Bullfrog on **Highway 276** is the beginning of the **Bullfrog-Notom-Burr Trail Road**. It runs northwest along the Waterpocket Fold to Highway 24 just east of the headquarters of Capitol Reef National Park. About halfway along this road, it is intersected by the Burr Trail, which connects to Boulder and Escalante (because of this connection, some refer to this entire road as the Burr Trail Road). From the beginning of the Bullfrog-Notom-Burr Trail Road on Highway 276, drive northwest between 5 and 10 kms, to find one of 2 places to turn left to reach the lake. These are designated **Bullfrog North** and **Bullfrog South**. With low lake levels in 2007, both sites were closed--until higher water returns. These sites have vault toilets but no one to collect garbage but you. Contact the Bullfrog Visitor Center to see if this area is open, Tele. 435-684-7423/7400/7424.

Just north of Hite on the west side of the lake and Dirty Devil River Bridge, is another primitive camping and possible boat launching area next to Highway 95 and near the mouth of the **Dirty Devil River**. Only one problem with camping here, during times of low lake levels, it's impossible to launch a boat. Since the NPS started collecting fees for camping and boating on and around the lake, there have been several toilets installed in this area but no drinking water. There's a self-serve fee collection box, but no one has stayed there for years, so surely no one was checking the box as of 2007 (?).

To reach 2 more camping areas on the lake with vehicle access, drive south from the turnoff to Hite (which is between mile posts 48 & 49) to **mile post 53** on Highway 95; then turn west and after about 3 kms (2 miles) on an improved gravel road, you'll arrive at the lake in **Farley Canyon** (see Map 5). This is another primitive-type camping area with toilets, but no water or garbage collection. You can camp there for a fee, and launch a boat (depending on lake levels).

Just around the corner from the Farley Canyon turnoff, is one of 2 improved but rough dirt roads heading south off the highway to campsites along the upper **White Canyon Inlet** (see Map 5). The first entry place is on the west side of canyon, and although you can camp there, you can't launch a boat even if the lake level is high. Or drive a bit further east and to between **mile posts 54 & 55**, and turn south at the sign pointing out White Canyon. From the highway, it's about 4 kms (2 1/2 miles) to the lake on a rough road, whereas it's about 3 kms (2 miles) to the high water mark (HWM) via the west side road. In the late 1980's when the lake level was very high, some people were launching boats from the east side of While Canyon, but normally there is no way to get a boat to the water. There is nothing in the way of camping facilities on either side of White Canyon Inlet and the last time the author saw the place it was a tamarack jungle. In 2007, no one was going there.

Important Tele. Numbers & Websites for GCNRA & Lake Powell

ARAMARK Concessions on Lake Powell ....lakepowell.com
Glen Canyon National Recreation Area..nps.gov/glca
Antelope Point Marina ....antelopepointlakepowell.com

Glen Canyon National Recreation Area Concession Services

ARAMARK Reservations	800-528-6154	Lake Powell Resort (Wahweap)	928-645-2433
Stateline Marina	928-645-1129	Dangling Rope Marina Store	928-645-2969
Bullfrog Resort & Marina	435-684-3000	Halls Crossing Marina	435-684-7000
Lake Powell Ferry	435-684-3000	Hite Store	435-684-2278
Antelope Point Marina	928-645-5900 x5		

National Park Service--Glen Canyon National Recreation Area

NPS Headquarters-Page	928-608-6200	Visitor Center-GC Dam	928-608-6404
Lee's Ferry Ranger Station	928-355-2234	Bullfrog Visitor Center	435-684-7400
Halls Crossing RS	435-684-7460	Hite RS & Visitor Center	435-684-2457
NPS Dispatch-Page, AZ	928-608-6301		

Weather and Climate of Lake Powell

One of the nicer things to say about Lake Powell is it almost always has good weather. This is especially true in summer and fall. As you can see in the climographs below, it does have some warm temperatures in summer, and occasionally cold days in winter, but because it's at the lowest elevation in the area, the winters are usually rather mild. It's a dry semi-arid region, so sun and good weather are the rule; rain and bad weather more the exception. The normal boating season is from about mid-March through late October. Each year is a little different. Below is a brief summery of the weather for each season of the year.

Winter The northern end of the lake, such as in Cataract and Narrow Canyons, will freeze over in some places, but it's never heavy ice. The reason it's colder and subject to some icing is that it's further north and the lake is confined to a deep, shaded, narrow canyon where temperature inversions are more common. The rest of the lake is more open and not subject to such temperature extremes.

Occasionally there are boaters out on the lake in winter, but usually on the southern end. In dry weather spells, the days are calm and rather pleasant, and hiking can be invigorating. The nights are normally crispy with cold weather bedding and clothing required! **If riding in an open boat, you'll need the same kind of clothes as snowmobilers use!** So don't forget your winter mukluks! In bad weather, it'll be a miserable trip, but good weather is more the norm in this semi-desert landscape. Generally speaking, the time period which is the coldest and most uncomfortable will be from about December 1, until mid or late February. This is a period of time when you'll have very short days and long nights, so take plenty of ways to light the night.

Spring Spring is a pleasant time to visit Lake Powell, especially for hiking and/or fishing. The water is far too cold to swim, but some people try water skiing with wetsuits. The days are usually nice and the nights aren't so cold, but spring time does bring more windy conditions than at any other season. Another nice thing about spring, the days are longer and nights shorter than in winter or in fall. For example, April 21, has the same amount of daylight as does August 21. Late in the fall, such as in October, the nights are becoming very long. In early spring, and if riding in an open boat, you'll still need winter-type clothes, so bundle up good. In March of 2001, the author used a heavy down-filled jacket with hood, winter mountaineering mittens, plus he wrapped himself in a blue plastic sheet--and he using a little 10hp outboard!

Summer Summers are very enjoyable. The mornings are usually calm, but there are often breezes in the afternoon. Evenings are again calm. By Memorial Day or early June the water temperatures are getting warm enough for swimming and water skiing. In the middle of summer there are some really hot days, but it seems cooler right on the water, and you can always jump in and cool off. In the afternoons, you can expect some clouds to build up, but if there are showers, they don't last long. Over the years, this writer has had many mid-night wakeup calls because of passing thunder storms in the night. Strong gusty winds always accompany thunder storms, so remain alert if you're in a small boat, and head for cover quick.

Fall In some ways, fall is similar to the spring season temperature wise, but the days are getting very short, the nights long. Camping and fishing are usually good. There are cold fronts going through the area in fall too, but usually not as often as in spring. When bad weather comes, it usually doesn't last long. In bays or canyons which have gamble oak or cottonwood trees, the fall colors make for great fotography. Mid to late October through the first week or so of November is the best time to get color fotos.

Climographs for Lake Powell Weather
Below are climographs from 3 different weather stations near the lake. They are Hite in the north, Bullfrog Marina in about the middle (both in Utah), and Page, Arizona at the southern end. Each is either on the lake, or very near the shoreline.

When converting Fahrenheit (F) to Centigrade (C), keep in mind that 0° C is equal to 32° F which is freezing; 10° C is equal to 50° F; 20° C is 68° F; 30° C is 86° F; and 38° C is 100° F. Also, 0° F is about -18° C. For every 10 degrees of change on the Centigrade scale, the Fahrenheit thermometer changes 18 degrees--or 5°C = 9°F. To convert, the author took the temperature in F, then -32, and multiplied that by .555. That equals C. To convert precipitation from inches to centimeters, multiply inches by 2.54, which gives centimeters (cms). This means one inch is roughly 2 1/2 cms.

Hite, Utah, 1158m elevation, from 1949-1986 (the earlier figures could only have come from Hite Ferry, formerly located on the Colorado River. Since about the mid-1960's, they would have come from the present-day marina site). The marina is now closed, but there is a gas station & store at Hite.

Month	Max(C°) Average	Max(C°) Record	Min(C°) Average	Min(C°) Record	Precip Av(Cms)
January	8.1(46F)	19.4(67F)	-3.1(26F)	-18.9(-2F)	1.47(.58in)
February	11.9(64F)	23.9(75F)	-0.8(31F)	-17.8(-1F)	.79(.31in)
March	16.7(62F)	28.3(83F)	2.9(37F)	-11.1(12F)	1.45(.57in)
April	22.3(73F)	35.5(96F)	7.4(45F)	-6.7(20F)	1.14(.45in)
May	27.9(82F)	39.4(103F)	12.9(56F)	-0.6(31F)	1.04(.41in)
June	34.1(94F)	44.4(112F)	18.2(65F)	1.7(34F)	.61(.24in)
July	37.2(99F)	43.3(110F)	22.4(72F)	7.2(45F)	1.45(.57in)
August	35.9(97F)	42.7(109F)	21.4(71F)	12.2(54F)	1.35(.53in)
September	31.5(89F)	41.1(106F)	16.2(61F)	3.3(38F)	1.68(.66in)
October	23.3(74F)	37.2(99F)	9.1(58F)	-2.2(28F)	2.62(1.03in)
November	14.8(59F)	25.5(78F)	2.5(36F)	-8.9(16F)	1.68(.66in)
December	8.8(49F)	20.6(69F)	-1.9(30F)	-14.4(6F)	1.14(.45in)
Annual	**23.0(73F)**	**44.4(112F)**	**9.1(58F)**	**-18.9(-2F)**	**16.41(6.46in)**

Bullfrog Marina, Utah, 1165m elevation, 1967-1986

Month	Max(C°) Average	Max(C°) Record	Min(C°) Average	Min(C°) Record	Precip Av(Cms)
January	7.2(45F)	19.4(68F)	-4.1(25F)	16.1(3)	1.37(.54in)
February	11.4(52F)	22.2(72F)	-1.0(30F)	-14.4(6F)	.91(.36in)
March	16.5(62F)	28.3(83F)	2.8(37F)	-9.4(15F)	1.83(.72in)
April	21.5(71F)	32.2(90F)	6.4(44F)	-6.1(21F)	.58(.23in)
May	27.8(82F)	37.2(98F)	11.8(53F)	-0.6(31F)	1.17(.46in)
June	34.1(94F)	43.3(110F)	17.1(63F)	5.6(42F)	.46(.18in)
July	37.3(99F)	43.3(110F)	21.2(70F)	12.2(54F)	1.14(.45in)
August	35.8(97F)	41.6(107F)	20.2(68F)	7.8(46F)	1.07(.42in)
September	30.7(87F)	38.3(100F)	15.0(59F)	6.7(44F)	1.50(.51in)
October	22.4(72F)	33.3(92F)	7.9(46F)	-3.9(25F)	2.64(1.04in)
November	14.3(58F)	25.5(78F)	2.0(36F)	-10.4(13F)	1.70(.67in)
December	8.3(46F)	20.5(68F)	-2.9(27F)	-15.0(5F)	1.35(.53in)
Annual	**22.4(73F)**	**43.3(110F)**	**8.2(47F)**	**-16.1(3F)**	**15.72(6.19in)**

Page, Arizona, Elevation 1335m. Based on a 25 year average?

Month	Max(C°) Average	Max(C°) Record	Min(C°) Average	Min(C°) Record	Precip Av(cms)
January	5.5(42F)	17.8(65F)	-4.4(24F)	-23.9(-12F)	1.19(.47in)
February	10.5(51F)	20.5(69F)	-1.0(30F)	-13.3(8F)	1.09(.43in)
March	14.4(58F)	27.8(83F)	2.2(36F)	-7.8(18F)	1.85(.73in)
April	20.0(68F)	32.2(90F)	6.1(43F)	-3.9(25F)	.86(.34in)
May	26.6(80F)	36.1(96F)	11.7(53F)	-.5(31F)	1.09(.43in)
June	32.7(91F)	46.1(115F)	16.7(62F)	5.5(42F)	.51(.20in)
July	36.1(97F)	42.2(108F)	20.5((69F)	13.3(56F)	1.19(.47in)
August	34.4(94F)	41.1(106F)	19.5(67F)	7.8(46F)	1.70(.67in)
September	29.4(85F)	37.7(100F)	14.4(58F)	4.4(26F)	1.37(.54in)
October	21.6(71F)	33.9(94F)	8.3(47F)	-4.4(24F)	1.92(.78in)
November	12.8(55F)	23.3(74F)	1.7(35F)	-8.9(16F)	1.50(.59in)
December	7.8(46F)	19.4(67F)	-2.8(27F)	-17.2(1F)	1.30(.51in)
Annual.	**21.0(70F)**	**46.1(115F)**	**7.7(46F)**	**-23.9(-12F)**	**15.60(6.14in)**

Surface Temperature of Lake Powell Water(Centigrade)

January ....7.8C(46F)	July ....25.5C(78F)
February ....7.8C(46F)	August................26.1C(79F)
March................?12.2C(54F)	September ....23.3C(74F)
April...................?12.2C(54F)	October................19.4C(67F)
May ....17.8C(64F)	November ....16.1C(61F)
June ....21.6C(71F)	December ....10.5C(51F)

Data taken at Wahweap Marina (?) by ARAMARK (?). Something is wrong with March & April figures.

Hiking Season Around Lake Powell

There are times during winter when you may find very nice weather, but nights are cold and very long. Special care and equipment are needed for the hardy souls who venture out in winter. Remember, if riding in an open boat, you'll need all the clothes you can wear! This goes for early spring, plus morning cruising during much of the year as well.

Generally speaking the best time to hike in this area temperature wise is from mid or late March until early or mid-May, and then in October (but the days are getting short then!). Again, if riding in an open boat, especially in the morning hours, you'll need winter clothes.

Sometimes the period from late May through mid-June can be pleasant too, but it starts to get hot in June. Generally speaking, hiking from Memorial Day (end of May) until Labor Day (first Monday in September) is a little unpleasant and on the hot side. But the author has hiked a lot in all the summer months and somehow survived. On one of those days, the temperature in Hanksville, was 43°C (110°F)! It was the hottest June and July in history, but he hiked in it and so can you; just plan to drink lots of water, and jump in the lake occasionally with your clothes on. September can be warm too, but it's usually a good month for hiking.

Hiking Equipment

There will be 2 kinds of hikers reading this book. First, the serious hiker, the one who goes to the lake with the intention of walking. Others will be fishermen, water skiers, or just boaters out camping and soaking up rays with family and friends. For those unfamiliar with what to take, here is a list of items or equipment the professional hiker takes on an average half day trek up one of the side-canyons from Lake Powell.

Most of the hikes in this book are into canyons where the walking generally isn't very difficult and the way isn't too rugged or difficult. For the most part, a pair of running shoes is the best footwear. They are light weight and comfortable, and you'll almost never get blisters. If you take an older pair, you won't feel bad if they get wet while wading in a stream. Many canyons have small streams and wading is required in some, if not most. Most athletic shoes today are made of synthetic materials and are ideal for making wading-type shoes.

On other hikes, you'll be climbing up to canyon rims; for example, to the top of Fiftymile Mountain. For this type of climbing, a pair of rugged leather boots might be best. Under each hike in this book, is a brief statement as to which type of boots or shoes would be best for that particular trek.

Because most people visiting the lake will do so in warmer weather, shorts or cutoffs are generally preferred, as opposed to long pants. A pair of loose fitting shorts with zippered or buttoned pockets are best. However, in the spring and fall months, you will surely want long pants for early mornings and evenings in camp.

In the summer months, the best shirt to have is a plain cotton T shirt, or one that's made from a 50/50 blend of cotton/polyester. In the spring or fall season, you'll want a long sleeved shirt too. Any kind will do, but one with pockets is best. The author usually has a flannel shirt, plus a sweat shirt with hood, if it's extra cool.

For those of us with light colored skin, some kind of hat is required to prevent sunburn and skin cancer. The big cowboy hats work fine, but they're not good in windy conditions. The author uses an adjustable baseball cap and sewn a kind of cancer curtain around the sides and back--similar to the French Foreign Legion caps seen in the movies. This keeps the sun off the vital parts of the face and neck. You should also take a sun screen lotion for the hands, arms & legs, especially if you don't have the time to get a tan the slow and safer way. It's the repeated sun burning of the skin which eventually causes skin cancer--not necessarily getting a slow tan.

The serious hiker will take and use a small day pack. These come in various sizes, but must be large enough for the following items: a 1 and/or 2 liter water bottle (on a hot summer day you'll need up to 4 liters!), a light lunch, and in the cooler seasons, a pair of long pants and long sleeved shirt or jacket. In a small pack pocket, the author always has a short nylon cord, bandaids, extra pens, small notebook, a compass, map, toilet paper and perhaps sun glasses.

In his pants pockets, he carries chapstick (lip balm) and pocket knife (wallet in a zippered pack pocket). A camera is a must for most people visiting Lake Powell, along with extra batteries for today's digital cameras. A camera stand of some kind or tripod is good in the deep, dark canyons, of which there are many in this country. A lightweight walking stick is sometimes good in places, especially if you're in a stream valley and wading over slick rocks or into deep pools.

Originally, the author thought there would also be some longer 2 or 3 day hikes in this book, but as it turned out, almost all are of the half day, or day variety. In a few canyons you could backpack in for a night or two in order to see it all, but overnight hiking is seldom done by Lake Powell boaters.

Fotography in Deep, Dark, Canyons (updated January, 2007)

Here are some tips on cameras, carrying cases, and how to come home with good pictures on your first trip down a deep, dark, slot-type canyon.

Film cameras are all but history now, so in this edition, it's **digital fotography only**. First thing to consider when buying a camera is the size. In today's world you can get really good pictures with a small camera--there's no need to buy something that weights a ton or is dreadfully bulky. If you're a hiker, you'll want a small camera--period! Start with one that fits in your shirt pocket.

Next thing to look for in a camera is one that fits into a small, plastic carrying case. This writer has **2 Canons, Power Shot A550 & A560**, both of which shoot at **7.1 mega pixels (mp)**; and almost all pictures in this book were taken with these. Both these cameras fit perfectly into a **Pelican #1010 plastic** case that can be carried on a second belt around the waist for easy and quick access; remember, a camera in the pack does not take pictures! This is the smallest case Pelican makes, and it, and both the A550 & A560 cameras are a perfect fit. **Otter** also makes small plastic cases for cameras & cell fones.

The reason for a plastic case or box is to protect a very sensitive piece of electronic equipment. **Dust** and **water** are the 2 biggest enemies of all cameras, and the #1010 box is the best thing this writer has ever seen. He can swim through potholes worry-free with it attached to his belt, and it doesn't scratch the LCD screen. Plus, damage from dust is almost a thing of the past. The only negative thing about this way of carrying a camera is, if you're not alert, you can drop it while taking it out of the case.

Another thing to look for in a camera is its ability to take good pictures in **low light situations**. For example, in darker slots, all cameras automatically go down to lower shutter speeds, but you want one that raises the ISO settings automatically to adjust to the low light.

Here's an example, when set on **automatic**, the Canon A550, goes down to 1/8 of a second in low light and with an ISO setting of perhaps 100 or 200. With a little less light, it automatically pushes the ISO up to as much as 400--but the shutter speed stays at 1/8. If you're careful, you can hold your hand & camera against a wall, and get good crisp pictures at 1/8--but not less than that. If the shutter speed goes down to 1/4 second or less, you'll need a tripod, or set it on a rock.

When the camera is set on **manual**, and in low light conditions, it always pushes the ISO up to 600 or 800. Along with the higher ISO setting, the shutter speed then goes up as well to maybe 1/15 or 1/30 of a second. This is good for hand-held shooting, but although it might look good on the LCD screen, the quality isn't as good as pictures shot at low ISO's--same as with the old fashioned film cameras. The higher the ISO, the more "noise" there is in digital images, which translates to the *equivalency* of *graininess in film*, and a lower quality picture. **The lower the ISO, the better the foto quality.**

Here's something few people think about when choosing a camera; the **battery**. The smallest & thinnest cameras come with a one-of-kind size battery that fits only one camera and can only be bought in specialty fotographic stores. They also cost a small fortune. You must always carry one or more backup batteries, so it's best to have a camera that uses **AA's**. These can be purchased in any store, gas station, kiosk or supermarket in the world!

When it comes to AA's batteries, best to spend a little extra in the beginning and get the **rechargables** which normally come with a recharging kit that works at home or in your car. That way, you'll always have fresh batteries. Or you can buy new alkaline batteries anywhere.

If you enjoy taking pictures with people in most scenes, then prior to your trip, inform everyone to wear **colorful clothing**. The author prefers red, something like the University of Utah's color. Others prefer bright yellow, orange or blue. This not only gives your fotos additional color, but it helps to separate the person from the background. If you're shooting B+W, sometimes you can't tell a person from a rock.

Squeeze the Trigger! When ever you're taking pictures, regardless of how bright or dark the scene is, press the **shutter release button slowly.** Otherwise your picture will be blurred. It's just like shooting a gun; if you jerk the trigger, you'll miss the target. Remember, your finger does not determine how fast the camera's lens opens & closes! This is the biggest difference between good & bad pictures, or between professionals & amateur fotographers. **Squeeze the Trigger Slowly!**

When in a place like **Labyrinth, Face or Antelope Canyons**, avoid taking a foto when there's some sunlight in your subject area. If you do, part of the picture will be washed out with too much light; the other part will be dark or totally black. Instead, take a picture where the sunlight is being bounced off an upper wall and diffused down into the dark corners. One exception to this rule would be if you're after special effects. In the case of **Antelope Canyon**, there is one place **(The Crack)** where a shaft of sunlight reaches the bottom at around high noon. Some fotographers set their camera on a tripod, then throw sand in the air which creates dust in the shaft of light. This technique exaggerates the small sunny part adding a pleasing effect to the picture.

Another way to get a good foto with bright sun covering half the scene is to wait for a cloud to cover the sky, then the light is diffused, eliminating the harsh difference between sun & shadow. The best time to take fotos in slot canyons is generally in late morning or early afternoon. This way you can easily find places where the sun isn't shining directly down into the narrows, but instead is shining on an upper wall, and the light is bounced or diffused down into the otherwise dark slot.

If you're in a slot at or near high noon, you can get really good light & colors, and no sun, if you back up or walk forward a little, or around a corner. If at all possible, move around just enough to keep that one little streak of sunlight out of you picture. Or, if you do get a small sunny steak, you can sometime clone-stamp-it-out at home on your computer using **Photoshop**.

If you should slip while wading, or somehow drop your camera in water, here are the steps to take. Immediately take out the batteries. Open the camera (if possible) and shake and blow out any water. Allow it to sit in the hot sun to dry, turning it occasionally to help evaporate any water inside. If you're near your car, start the engine, turn on the heater, and hang the camera in front of a vent. The warmer the camera gets, the quicker the water evaporates. The quicker the water evaporates, the less corrosion there will be on the electrical system and less rust on metal parts.

If your camera is under water for just a nano second or so, there may not be any water deep inside. In this case, by following the above steps, you may be back in business again in half an hour, especially if the water is clear, no sand has gotten inside, and if the sun is warm. The author had several of these little accidents with each of his older mechanical Pentax K-1000's film cameras. The last several times, no repair work was needed because he did the right things to get the camera dry fast. But he has lost about 4 digitals since 2003. Fortunately, each camera had an extended warranty (had he been using a small Pelican case, most of those cameras would have been saved!).

Regarding the author drowning several of the older Canon A60 digitals, the good thing was, he never lost any images because **memory cards** are well sealed. With his extended warranty, the cameras were replaced without charge.

However, ff you drop a digital into water, it likely can't be repaired, so they throw it away. When buying a new camera, pay a little more and get an **extended warranty**; that way if you drown a camera in the warranty period, they'll replace it free (read the small print!). Ritz or affiliated camera stores offer such extended warranties, but the cost of the warranty for digital cameras is almost double that of film cameras. At this stage in fotographic history, it seems fewer people know how to fix digital cameras.

Preserving Archaeology Sites

In the side-canyons leading to Lake Powell, there are many ancient cultural sites such as Anasazi or Fremont cliff dwellings or granaries, petroglyph and pictograph panels, and flint-chip sites. The author has marked some he found on the individual canyon maps.

34

However, if too many people visit these sites, damage will occur; not so much by vandals or pot hunters, but simply by careless visitors. It's highly unlikely you will ever discover any ruins which have not already been recorded and studied. And it's true the simple cliff dwellings or granaries you see will never contribute anything more to our present understanding of the Anasazi people. But regardless of how simple the sites may be, it's important to prevent any further damage to them and make as little impact as possible. Many more interested people will follow in your footsteps, so it's important to leave the sites in as good a condition as possible.

Here's a list of things you can do to help preserve these Anasazi ruins. First, don't allow children to climb all over the walls or any part of the structure. Some may seem solid, but in time all walls will tumble down. Please stand back and look, take pictures, and leave it as-is for the next visitor. Second, if the ruins are under an overhang approachable via a steep talus slope, try to get there from the side instead of scrambling straight up the talus. Undercutting ruins is a big problem for some lake-side sites and most damage occurs simply by thoughtless individuals.

Third, if mother nature calls and you have to use the toilet, please don't do it in or near any ruins. Defecate as far from these sites as possible, or use the toilet all campers must now have while on the lake. And fourth, keep in mind it is against Federal law to damage any ancient artifacts. Part of the Federal law states, *No person may excavate, remove, damage, or otherwise alter or deface any archaeological resource located on public lands or Indian lands unless such activity is pursuant to a permit issued.....* Simply picking up a potsherd or corn cob and taking it home is illegal. As is putting your initials on a wall next to petroglyphs. And one last reminder, the NPS archaeologists ask visitors to report any significant new finds to them at any ranger station or the park headquarters at Page, Arizona.

Insects and Pests

Here's some good news. There are very few insects of any kind to bother you while you're on the lake as a boater, fisherman, or hiker. On or near most lakes, one might expect to find mosquitos, but not so with Lake Powell. First, it's a dry semi-arid land, and there aren't many places for them to breed and reproduce. In other words, there are few if any swampy places. Also, much of the shoreline is smooth, solid rock, commonly known in these parts as **slickrock**. Mosquitos simply can't survive in such an environment.

In the canyons, it's much the same way, but there are small streams and lush vegetation in many. If you walk into these areas in the day time only, you won't see any, or at least very few **mosquitos**; but if you were to camp in the same areas, you might. The variety of mosquitos in this region only come out at night, so if you're camping on the lake, but away from streams or lush vegetation, you'll find few if any of these insects. The only mosquitos the author remembers on Lake Powell was while setting up his tent one evening right where **Lake Creek** entered the inlet. The next morning, there were none.

Other insects you may encounter are tiny **gnats**, or midges. These sometimes get in your hair and bite hard, although they are very small. On one occasion, the author was camping next to his car near the lake at the head of White Canyon Inlet and was nearly eaten alive. However, there was no wind that afternoon and he must have just been in the wrong spot, because he has seldom encountered these gnats at any other time. These pests seem to occupy a niche away from the lake, so in most cases they won't bother boaters. One NPS employee told the author they seem to disappear around the middle of July or when the monsoon season sets in.

The common **house fly** is something almost never seen. The only time you may see flies is if you arrive at a camping place which is often used, and if others before you have left food scraps around. Other places the author saw small flies, which resembled the Australian **bush fly**, was at the mouths of several canyons on the Navajo Nation lands. There you may see semi-wild or feral Navajo donkeys hanging around the shoreline. In these cases with all the dung piles around, expect to encounter more flies. Other than in those places, house or bush flies hardly seem to exist.

Another pest you may encounter is the big **gray horse fly**. It's likely you'll never see these unless you go hiking, then you may find them flying around and biting your bare legs; but a pair of long pants solves this minor problem. However, these flies seem to be found only in dry washes, which have an occasional seep or enough moisture to grow tamaracks. Up and away from the tamaracks, the horse fly doesn't seem to exist.

The author once docked at the HWM at the very end of the inlet to Bowns Canyon. He then hiked upcanyon for half a day. When he returned, he noticed several **ravens** (there are apparently no crows on Lake Powell according to someone at the NPS) flying around making lots of noise. He soon discovered they had raided his boat and gobbled up 3 loaves of bread and a small sack of raisins. On his 2007 trip to Bowns Canyon, the same ravens (or their offspring) rummaged through a large bucket looking for food--and found none. But they must have flipped out his 2-cycle oil measureing cup and dropped it in the water; it was never seen after that. The same thing happen while on a backpacking trip into West Canyon. In that case, his Lake Powell map came up missing! The lesson here is, don't leave anything small lying around in or on your boat when you're out hiking--especially food! Pay special attention to ravens if you're docking in popular camping areas.

One last pest. On several occasions the author found **mice** in his boat. This was always after it had been tied up against an embankment overnight, which either allowed them to hop right in, or they may have climbed in along the rope. They ate into bread sacks and other packages made of plastic or paper. After a few bad experiences, all food was put into containers such as plastic boxes with tight lids and that ended the problem. For most people, it's likely mice won't be able to get into their boat. However, at night they can get into food that's placed around your tent if it's not carefully packaged. Just place your food in waterproof plastic containers with lids and you'll have no problem.

Drinking Water

For the most part, drinking water isn't a problem on Lake Powell, because everyone takes enough in their boat to sustain them for the duration of their trip. However, there are times when you may have to replenish your supplies especially if you're out hiking, especially in hot summer weather. The best place to do this is right at a spring where it comes out of the ground.

There are small streams or springs in almost every canyon entering the lake, and some have reasonably safe water to drink. However, many streams have **beaver**, which seem to migrate from one canyon to another, looking for fresh food supplies. When you see fresh sign of beaver, then it's best not to drink from the stream. Instead, head upcanyon to the spring source if possible.

In the days before Lake Powell, there were **cattle** grazing in many of the side-canyons but today, there are only a handful of places where they can muddy up a stream or spring. When you see fresh sign of cattle, also beware of the water quality and pollution.

On every hike the author has made, he started out with a bottle of culinary water, but in most canyons he found some kind of spring or stream, and in almost every case, sampled that water. He has never gotten sick. In summer heat, you may have to take 2 or 3 or more liters of water on some hikes, or plan to drink from springs or streams. In the description of each canyon, is a short discussion on where you can find safe drinking water.

One problem many people have is, they have had very little experience when it comes to deciding what is good safe water, and what is bad. Without that experience it's difficult to make such a determination. This is the reason the US Public Health Service tells the National Park Service to insist that all campers treat, filter or boil all surface water. Another reason why the NPS tells everyone to drink only treated, filtered or boiled water is to save themselves from lawsuits.

Lake water is another possible source, and believe it or not, it's some of the safest around. In the early 1990's, an unnamed source told the author about lake water samples taken by the NPS. Samples taken near marinas, beaches, and other crowded campsites, nearly always showed some kind of pollution, and were considered unfit to drink. Samples taken near the shore line next to Navajo Nation lands and where livestock graze near the lake, also showed pollution, but **Giardia** apparently has never been found. Samples taken out in the main channel and away from congested areas, usually didn't pass rigid public health standards either, but neither has anything been found that would make a person sick. Keep in mind US drinking water standards are among the highest in the world.

On one fuel stop at Dangling Rope Marina, the author mistakenly filled his jugs with water coming from the tap marked **flushing water**. This water is pumped right out of the lake without treatment. He drank that water for 5 days, until he returned to the same dock to find the mistake. But there were no ill effects. Another boater told of running out of water and instead of boiling some to drink, they just took it from the main channel and used it as it was. No one suffered. If you do run out of water, and have to take some from the lake, be sure to take it from the main channel and away from livestock areas or popular campsites. It's best to do something with the water before drinking it, but the chances are good you'll go on living even if you don't.

Camping on Lake Powell

Campgrounds in the GCNRA

Most of the following are quotations from a National Park Service hand-out on camping. The NPS in the Glen Canyon National Recreation Area, formerly operated developed campgrounds at Wahweap, Bullfrog and Hall's Crossing. However, in the mid-1990's, they were turned over to ARAMARK, the concessioner on Lake Powell. Even though they are now operated by a private company, the general rules should remain the same. These 3 campgrounds are operated on a first-come, first-served basis and no advanced reservation can be made. However, reservations can be made at the RV parks shown below. There is an undeveloped, designated camping area at Hite, which does not require a fee, and the camp-

The ramp leading to the new **Antelope Point Marina**. It isn't that far from the parking lot, but the rides are apparently free (?). In the center background is the store, resturant & snack bar; to the left is the fuel dock (with a credit card, you can gas-up 24 hours a day); left of that and out of sight is boat rentals and a small store; to the far right and out of sight are the floating private houseboat docks.

ground at Lee's Ferry is still run by the NPS.

Camping in developed campgrounds in the GCNRA is limited to 8 people or 2 vehicles per site for up to 14 days per visit. Group sites are available for larger groups in some areas. For more information regarding the campgrounds, please refer to the chart below, or call **ARAMARK** toll free at 800-528-6154; or the **NPS** at 928-608-6200 or 6404. They can redirect your call.

The National Park Service requests that visitors be aware of and adhere to the regulations governing the use of the developed campgrounds.

Regulations:
1. Fires are permitted in fire grates only, not on the ground.
2. Quiet hours are between 10pm and 6am.
3. Pets must be leashed and under control at all times.
4. Use of fireworks and firearms is prohibited (the same throughout the lake and GCNRA).
5. Trash and waste refuse must be disposed of in the receptacle provided.

Facilities at Developed Campgrounds
These facilities can, and probably will change to some extent as time goes on. Expect some changes in the tables below. For updated information see **nps.gov/glca**, or **nps.gov/rabr**, or **lakepowell.com**.

	Number of Sites	Camping Fee	Camping Limit (Days)	Open all Year	Self-Registration	Reservations	Overflow Loop	Group Camping Area (Reservations only)	Dump Station	Restrooms	Running Water	Showers	Hookups	Picnic Tables	Grill/Fire Grate
Wahweap	189	yes	14	yes	yes	no	yes	yes	yes	yes	yes	**	no	yes	yes
Bullfrog	75	yes	14	yes	yes	no	yes	no	yes	yes	yes	yes	no	yes	no
H. Crossing	60	yes	14	no	yes	no	no	no	no	yes	yes	yes	no	yes	yes
Hite	12	no	14	yes	yes	no	no	no	*	*	*	no	no	yes	no
Lee's Ferry	54	yes	14	yes	yes	no	no	no	no	yes	yes	yes	no	no	yes	yes

* A dump station, restrooms, and running water are available at the Hite store & gas station, or next door at ranger station, but are not located in the designated camping area.
** Public shower facilities are available from the concessioner, but not the campground.

Camping at RV parks
At Wahweap, Bullfrog and Hall's Crossing Marinas, campsites with utility hookups suitable for RV's are available through the concessioner. Registration for these RV sites is through the concession operation at each marina.

During the busy summer months advanced reservations are recommended. For advanced reservations, call ARAMARK toll free at **800-528-6154**. Or for more information, call one of the numbers below.

	Number of Sites	Camping Fee	Reservations	Open Year-Round	Water Hookups	Electric Hookups	Sewage Hookups	Tent Sites	Showers	Laundry	For More Information
Wahweap	143	*	yes	yes	yes	yes	yes	yes	yes	yes	928-645-2433
Bullfrog	23	*	yes	yes	yes	yes	yes	yes	yes	**	435-684-3032
H. Crossing	32	*	yes	yes	yes	yes	yes	yes	yes	yes	435-684-7008
Hite			No RV camping facilities with hookups are available.								
Lee's Ferry			No RV camping facilities with hookups are available.								

* Fees vary depending on the season and hookup services required.
** Laundry facilities are provided at Bullfrog Marina and are located a short distance from the RV park.

Lakeshore and Boat Camping
Many visitors to Glen Canyon National Recreation Area & Lake Powell enjoy the peace and solitude of camping on the lake shore. Here are some common-sense rules to follow while camping, many of which are contained in National Park Service handouts on the subject.

Camping is permitted anywhere on the lake outside of a one mile (1 1/2 kms) zone around developed areas. Camping is prohibited in Rainbow Bridge National Monument. When camping on the lake, the NPS requests that all campfires be built below the high water mark (HWM) and in existing fire rings if possible. Respect the wishes of your camp neighbors by not having all-night parties and/or noise. **Fireworks** are not allowed anywhere in GCNRA. **Haul out all trash** and discard in receptacles provided at each marina. No trash may be left on the shore or thrown in the lake. Burying trash is not an acceptable method of disposal. Garbage bags may be given out free of charge at ranger stations and at marinas (These were nowhere to be found in 2007!, so to be properly prepared, take several leaf bags or other containers to carry out garbage).

Some lakeshore camping areas can be accessed by vehicle--depending on lake levels. These include: **Lone Rock Beach** near Wahweap; **Crosby Canyon** north of Wahweap at the upper end of Warm Creek Bay; **Stanton Creek** (Canyon) and **Upper Bullfrog Bay north and south** sites in the Bullfrog area (both closed in 2007); and **Farley Canyon, White Canyon** (not possible in 2007) and the **Dirty Devil River** (not possible in 2007) sites near Hite. There is a fee and registration required for camping in these areas--except Crosby Canyon (**Note**: with the lake as low as it's been in the late 1990's and 2000s, this policy will likely not be enforced as nobody normally wants to camp in those places anyway--especially if they can't launch a boat). Please take out all you take in. Vault toilets are located in some of these areas (not at White Canyon or Crosby Canyon sites). Like most other sources, Lake Powell's water should be boiled or treated with chemicals prior to drinking (NPS).

Tips on Camping and Boating, and Equipment Needed

For those who will be going out on the lake camping for the first time, here are some things you should take. First and perhaps most important, is a **shovel**. With it you can level a tent site. You'll sleep much better if you bed down on a flat spot, and make a shallow depression for your body.

In order to tie your boat down securely, take at least **two long ropes**, of about 20m (60'), but 30m (100') might be better. Long ones are important, because it's sometimes hard to find a place to tie down. In sandy beach-type areas, it is sometimes helpful to have a **metal stake** or pole you can pound into the ground to tie your boat to. In slickrock areas, it's sometimes best to have a couple of **anchors** which you can place into cracks in the rock to hold your boat away from the rocky shore line.

If your tent requires stakes, a **hammer** is sometimes a lot easier to use than a rock for driving the stakes in. In slickrock areas, many people are now using the new little pop or dome tents, which can be used without stakes. Many people also take plastic tarps. These can cover equipment or the boat, and with several poles and ropes, can make a nice shade canopy. In the heat of summer, this is nice to have during the middle of the day.

If you plan to go out on an extended trip where there will be no ice, remove the lid of your ice chest, put a small amount of water in the bottom, then cover everything with a wet towel. The water in the bottom will keep the towel wet, and the very low humidity at Lake Powell will evaporative rapidly, thus keeping everything reasonably cool. Keep the cooler in the shade and exposed to a breeze if possible.

If you're going out for an extended camping trip, be sure to have lots of **jugs**, or some kind of containers to carry lots of drinking water. That way you can get by without having to take the time to hunt for a safe place to stock up.

One last item that's very important is a **radio**. Having one will enable you to listen to the latest weather forecasts. If a big storm is coming, it's nice to be forewarned, especially if you're planning to hike into one of the really narrow slot-type drainages such as West Canyon. It's to your advantage to be warned about high winds, especially if you're in a small boat. One thing to remember about radios, make sure it's a good one, because there are few radio stations in the immediate area and normally you get good reception only after sunset and before sunrise. The exceptions are **2 stations out of Page, Arizona**. They're at **1340 AM and 93.3 FM** on the dial. If you're in the lower third of the lake and about as far away as Rainbow Bridge, you can usually pickup their signal if you're out on the lake or in an open area. These 2 stations can be heard during daytime hours, then they cut power at sunset, and may not be heard at night (?). Also, a radio with short wave bands will often get better reception for the BBC than from local stations. Satellite radio (XM/Sirius) is great, but you need a good power source & their special antenna, and you won't receive a signal if you're camped next to a big wall to the south.

Fees & Regulations, Portable Toilets & Waste Disposal Sites

Since 1997 everyone must pay a fee as they enter the GCNRA & Lake Powell area. Here is the Fee Schedule for Fiscal Year 2007.

Entrance Fees	1-7 Days	Annual Pass
1. Individual	$7	$30
2. Vehicle	$15	$30
3. Boats (First Vessel)	$16	$30
(Each Additional Vessel)	$8	$30
4. NPS Annual Pass		$80
5. NPS Senior/Lifetime		$10
6. Lee's Ferry (Camping per Night)	$12	
7. Stanton, Hite, Farley, Dirty Devil (Camping/Night)	$6	
8. Shoreline Camping/Backcountry	Free	

Also new since 1997, everybody camping on the lake shore must have with them some kind of **portable toilet**. The reason is, over the years the number of visitors to Lake Powell has increased greatly; therefore the number of "cat holes" being dug along the shoreline and below the HWM to bury human waste has increased dramatically. Some of these cat holes were dug when lake levels were low in the early 1990's, then when higher water levels returned in the mid-1990's, the NPS found higher bacteria count in the waters of some inlets near popular beaches and campsites.

Disposal of human waste is best accomplished through the use of a portable toilet system. Dump stations are located in all developed campgrounds and floating dump/pump stations for boats are located at all marinas.

So campers are more willing to cooperate with this new push to clean up beaches and camping areas, the NPS has installed **8 floating toilet & dump/pump stations** around the lake. These small platforms contain an always-clean **toilet** plus hand pumps and hoses to draw waste from your portable toilet into submerged tanks under the station.

These **toilets & dump/pump stations** are located at the mouth of **Warm Creek Bay** north of **Castle Rock**, mouth of **Face Canyon**, lower **Rock Creek Bay, Oak Creek Bay,** mouth of the **Escalante River Inlet**, northwest side of **The Rincon, Halls Creek Bay,** inside the mouth of **Forgotten Canyon** and in the west side of **Good Hope Bay**. None are in the San Juan River Arm of he lake.

Part III--Geology, Maps and Odds & Ends

Geology of Glen Canyon and the Lake Powell Country

Most of the exposed rock surrounding Lake Powell is sedimentary in nature. They were laid down millions of years ago during an age when shallow seas repeatedly invaded and retreated from the area, so the layers vary greatly in composition. Some of the deposits are actual sea sediments like limestone, some are wind-blown shore deposits, and some are silt from sluggish streams and delta areas. Others, such as the thick sandstone beds in the Cedar Mesa, Entrada, Navajo, and Wingate Sandstone formations were originally sandy deserts like some parts of the Sahara. Whatever the source, these deposits compacted by the weight of new deposits laid on top, hardened into the rocks we see & know today. The different layers, varying in degree of hardness, erode at different rates. This differential erosion has created the spectacular scenery we have today in the Glen Canyon and Lake Powell areas as well as in the nearby Grand Canyon and Monument Valley.

Here's a quick rundown on how each type of sedimentary rock was formed. The rock type which dominates all others around Lake Powell is **sandstone**. This rock began as a sea of sand, like much of the Sahara Desert today. Then the land likely sank and was covered by shallow seas which deposited other sediments on top. The sand froze in place, and with time the grains were cemented together to form sandstone. Later the land rose, and erosion began to take place, leaving the spires, buttes and mesas we see today on the Colorado Plateau.

Another important sedimentary rock commonly found in the cliffs and mesas of Lake Powell country is **mudstone**. The history of mudstone began around the shorelines of fresh water lakes or shallow seas, and at or near the mouths of rivers which were heavily loaded with mud or slit. The present-day delta of the Mississippi River will probably end up as a type of mudstone--perhaps 100-200 million years from now (?). You will recognize mudstone by its brown color and fine texture. Another rock that's very similar to mudstone, is **siltstone**. This is also a very fine textured stone, but it can come in different colors.

Another common sedimentary rock found in Lake Powell country is shale. Shale is seen as thin layers of rock which often appear as shingle-like plates. In various places in the world it's used as roofing for homes. It is often gray in color, but thin beds of red shale are common, especially in the Moenkopi. Shale is formed from fine sediments settling to the bottoms of fresh water lakes. Each layer of shale would likely indicate one year's muddy sedimentation of the heavy spring runoff. Shale, when put under heat and pressure, can evolve into slate.

Another important rock type is **limestone**. All limestone was formed at the bottom of deep ocean. After a period of sedimentation, the sea floor was raised along with other layers which formed over the limestone. Still later, the land rose higher, then began the process of erosion. This is the stage we see today around Lake Powell. Limestone has a gray color and is composed of the remains of marine shell fish which sank to the sea floor and decayed. It normally has some marine fossils, and because of its high content of lime, this is the rock from which cement is derived. Limestone is seen only in the northern end of the lake in Cataract Canyon--plus a thin lens in the middle of the Navajo Sandstone.

Not all of the rock in the area is sedimentary. **Igneous rock** exists in this region in the form of **laccoliths**, such as the **Henry Mountains** and **Navajo Mountain**. These laccoliths formed when molten rock inside the earth called magma, tried to push up through the sedimentary layers, bulging the overlying rock into a dome-shaped mountain but not breaking through to form a volcano. These rocks eventually cooled in place forming crystals and were later exposed by erosion.

Usually smooth and rounded, laccolithic mountains become more ragged looking as erosion wears away the sedimentary layers, exposing jagged fins of **granitic-type rock**. Occasionally, the entire intrusive neck comes into view. In the Henry Mountains, the intrusive rock is exposed in many places, while on Navajo Mountain, the underlying intrusive rock has yet to be exposed.

Geologic formations are not stagnant; their forms are constantly changing as erosion continuously wears away at the stone. Even large plateaus slowly turn into mesas, mesas evolve into buttes, buttes become spires, and spires crumble. The eventual fate of all formations, regardless of shape or size, is collapse and/or erosion.

Geologic Formations and Where They're Exposed

Below is a list of all the formations found within just a few short kms of the shore of Lake Powell. The youngest rocks are the **Straight Cliffs Formation**, found at the top of Fiftymile Mountain/Kaiparowits Plateau just north of the Dangling Rope Marina. The oldest rocks, the **Paradox Formation**, are found in the far upper or northern end of the lake in Cataract Canyon.

Straight Cliffs Formation Type Locality: The long straight cliffs on the northeast side of the Kaiparowits Plateau, usually known as Fiftymile Mountain, Kane County, Utah. This formation is a cliff-maker and is seen as the upper-most layer of rocks on top of the Kaiparowits. This is a light colored brown or yellow sandstone, sometimes mixed with shale and mudstone. In the southern parts where this formation is exposed, it's divided into four members: Drip Tank, John Henry, Smoky Hollow and Tibbet Canyon. About 333 meters thick.

Tropic Shale Type Locality: In Bryce Valley just east of Bryce Canyon National Park around the small town of Tropic, Garfield County, Utah. This is a dark gray marine shale, with thin layers of sandstone near the top, and thin fossiliferous limestone in the lower part. This formation makes a bench and is the first layer below the Straight Cliffs Formation on the **Kaiparowits Plateau** above the Fiftymile or Navajo Bench. However, it is buried by talus and landslide debris, and seldom exposed at that location. It's also seen above the lake in **Wahweap** and **Warm Creek Canyons**. 185 to 195 meters thick.

Dakota Sandstone Type Locality: Near Dakota City, Dakota County, Nebraska. This is generally a pale brown, course-grained sandstone, with some beds of mudstone and some coal seams. It's sometimes seen on the outskirts of the first broad bench below the top-most cliffs of the **Kaiparowits Plateau**, and to the west and southwest just above the flat-topped benches which were created by the Morrison Formation below. It's the bed where the **Spencer Coal Mines** are found in **Crosby Canyon**, a tributary to **Warm Creek**. It's a cliff-making formation, but it hardly forms a cliff in this region because it's so thin, 10 to 30 meters thick.

Morrison Formation Type Locality: Near Morrison, Jefferson County, Colorado. Made up mostly of continental beds of sandstone, but with conglomeritic sandstone and mudstones. This formation is def-

Geology Cross-Section--Lake Powell & Kaiparowits Plateau to Cataract Canyon

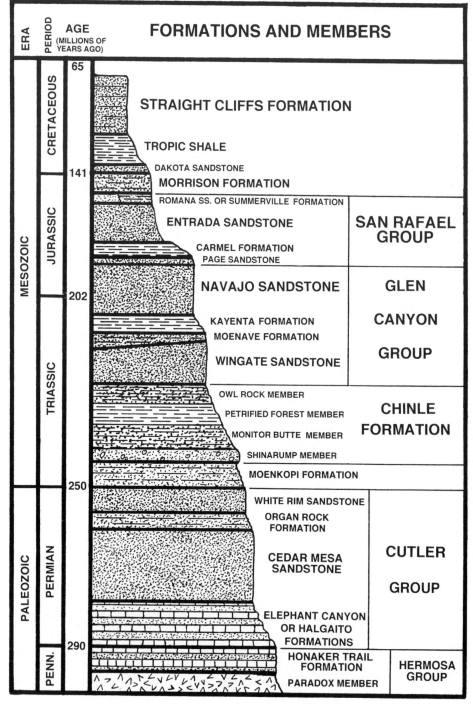

ERA	PERIOD	AGE (MILLIONS OF YEARS AGO)	FORMATIONS AND MEMBERS	
MESOZOIC	CRETACEOUS	65	STRAIGHT CLIFFS FORMATION	
			TROPIC SHALE	
		141	DAKOTA SANDSTONE	
			MORRISON FORMATION	
	JURASSIC		ROMANA SS. OR SUMMERVILLE FORMATION	SAN RAFAEL GROUP
			ENTRADA SANDSTONE	
			CARMEL FORMATION	
			PAGE SANDSTONE	
		202	NAVAJO SANDSTONE	GLEN
	TRIASSIC		KAYENTA FORMATION	CANYON
			MOENAVE FORMATION	
			WINGATE SANDSTONE	GROUP
			OWL ROCK MEMBER	CHINLE FORMATION
			PETRIFIED FOREST MEMBER	
			MONITOR BUTTE MEMBER	
			SHINARUMP MEMBER	
			MOENKOPI FORMATION	
PALEOZOIC	PERMIAN	250	WHITE RIM SANDSTONE	CUTLER GROUP
			ORGAN ROCK FORMATION	
			CEDAR MESA SANDSTONE	
			ELEPHANT CANYON OR HALGAITO FORMATIONS	
	PENN.	290	HONAKER TRAIL FORMATION	HERMOSA GROUP
			PARADOX MEMBER	

40

initely a cliff-former, and seen just uplake, or east of Wahweap, and in the cliffs on both sides of the lake. It forms the upper half of the cliffs in **Warm Creek, Padre, Last Chance, Rock Creek, and Dangling Rope Bays**, and others to the east and south of the lake. It's the top layer on **Cummings Mesa**, and on **Padres, Dominguez, Boundary and Tower Buttes**. 0 to 155 meters thick.

Summerville Formation/Romana Sandstone Type Locality: Summerville Point, north end of the San Rafael Swell, Emery County, Utah: and Romana Mesa between Warm Creek & Padre Bays, Lake Powell, Kane County, Utah. The **Summerville** is found east of the Waterpocket Fold; whereas the Romana, which occupies the same niche or position, is found west of the Waterpocket Fold. Both are reddish to pale brown sandstone, mixed with shaley siltstone. **The Romana** is the narrow band found in the middle of the big cliffs formed by the Morrison and the Entrada Formations above **Warm Creek, Padre, Last Chance, Rock Creek** and **Dangling Rope Bays**; and in the cliffs above **Wetherill, West, Face and Labyrinth Canyons**. 5 to 25 meters thick.

Entrada Sandstone Type Locality: Entrada Point, north end of the San Rafael Swell, Emery County, Utah. In the Lake Powell area, it is mostly the reddish brown massive, or solid sandstone you see in the walls of the big cliffs between **Wahweap** and **Dangling Rope Marina**, and on both the north and south sides of the lake. Generally, this forms the lower half of the cliffs, with the Morrison and Summerville/Romana Formation making up the top half. 185 to 230 meters thick.

Carmel Formation Type Locality: Mount Carmel, Kane County, Utah. These are thin beds of dusky red limy siltstone, and reddish brown sandstone, with occasional pink limestone beds. It is seen to form the benches where camping is so good in Gunsight Canyon, Warm Creek, Labyrinth and Face Canyon Bays, and at the upper end of the three bays forming Rock Creek. It's also the bench where employee housing sits at the Dangling Rope Marina. It's always a bench-former and always on top of the ever-present Page/Navajo Sandstone. 60 to 120 meters thick.

NOTE: Carmel Formation, Page Sandstone and Navajo Sandstone Updates In recent years more detailed studies have been made of the Carmel and Navajo formations. It's been found in the Lake Powell Country, and the middle part of the Paria River in Utah, there are divisions in the lower Carmel and upper Navajo and geologists have come up with a new cross section. On top is the Carmel Formation, which in some areas to the west has about 3 members. Next, and what used to be the top of the Navajo, but now is called the **Page Sandstone** (type locality: Manson Mesa, Page, Arizona), which includes the **Thousand Pockets Tongue**. From all the author can gather, both of these members are one in the same formation (?). Under the Page Sandstone in some sites is the **Judd Hollow Tongue of the Carmel Formation**. Then immediately under this thin layer is the main body of the Navajo Sandstone. Presently, only a few of the very latest geologic maps have any mention of this new classification which dates from the early to mid-1980's, or later. All other geology maps retain the older and still-used names of just the Carmel and Navajo Formations. Read the new book, **Geology of Utah's Parks and Monuments** for more information; see it under Further Reading.

Navajo Sandstone Type Locality: Navajo Canyon, Coconino County, Arizona. This thick layer of solid or massive sandstone is usually pale brown or buff colored. It's a cliff-maker, and the one which makes up many of the very narrow slot canyons on the Colorado Plateau. It's seen in **Navajo Canyon**, all the canyons of the **Escalante River Arm**, in the area of the **Great Bend** of the San Juan River Arm, the **Tapestry Wall area**, and on top of the big walls forming the bluffs to the west of Hite. Also, a limestone lens within the Navajo makes **Piñon Falls in Chaol Canyon**. **Rainbow Bridge** is perhaps the best example of the Navajo Sandstone. It's also the most prominent formation making the walls of **Zion National Park** and in the **Paria River Canyon**, both west of Lake Powell. 290 to 425 meters thick.

Kayenta Formation Type Locality: Just north of the town of Kayenta, Navajo County, Arizona. This is the reddish brown fluvial-made (under water) sandstone, siltstone and shale layer which is always sandwiched in between the Navajo above, and the Wingate (or Moenave) below. This one is a bench-former and often has several minor terraces itself. It can be seen in the **upper Escalante River Canyon**, in the area of the **mouth of Bowns** and **Long Canyons**, and between **Good Hope Bay** and **Hite**. 75 to 120 meters thick.

Moenave Formation Type Locality: Near Moenave and Tuba City, Coconino County, Arizona. Mostly a reddish brown sandstone with thin layers of siltstone and mudstone. This formation is exposed in the big cliffs you see to the **south of the San Juan Arm** of the lake. It's near the top of the massive Wingate Sandstone walls on Piute Mesa. It thins out completely by The Rincon, and is non-existent in areas to the north. It replaces the Wingate Sandstone to the west around Zion Park, and south into Arizona. The cliffs east of **Lee's Ferry**, are mostly Moenave, with just a little Wingate. 0 to 125 meters thick.

Wingate Sandstone Type Locality: Cliffs north of Fort Wingate, McKinley County, New Mexico. Reddish brown to light brown, fine grained, and massive cross-bedded sandstone. This one makes the big cliffs or walls surrounding **The Rincon**, in the **lower part** of the wall in the area of the mouth of **Bowns and Long Canyons**, surrounding **Good Hope Bay**, and in **Twomile & Fourmile Canyons**. It's seen in the lower San Juan Arm and it makes most of the big wall you see on the north and east side of Piute Mesa where the **Williams Trail** zig zags up the steepest part. 70 to 105 meters thick.

Chinle Formation Type Locality: Chinle Valley, Apache County, Arizona. There is great variation between the four main members of the Chinle, but mostly it's famous for many clay beds. The upper-most layer is the **Owl Rock Member** which is a reddish brown silty mudstone. Below that, the **Petrified Forest Member** has lots of petrified wood. It was in these clay beds that Charles H. Spencer tried to dig out gold at Lee's Ferry and later at Pahreah, Utah. A reddish brown mudstone is the third layer from the top, and is called the **Monitor Butte Member**. The lowest member is the **Shinarump Conglomerate**. It's a light colored, course sandstone and conglomerate, again with lots of petrified wood. In some localities, it's known as the **Black Ledge**, because it's often covered with black desert varnish. It's famous also as one of the primary formations on the Colorado Plateau which contains **uranium**. It's an area-wide formation and uranium was mined in it from the San Rafael Swell in the north, and south to Arizona. Many of the old mine exploration tracks you see in the San Juan Arm, and in the area of **Hite** and **The Rincon**, led miners to explore this member of the Chinle. 15 to 380 meters thick.

Moenkopi Formation Type Locality: Moenkopi Wash, Coconino County, Arizona. In some places there are some thin beds of limestone in this formation, but mostly it's a dark reddish chocolate brown, ripplemarked sandstone, with thin lenses of shale and mudstone. The Moenkopi is seen in the ledges across the channel from Hite, and in the area of **Piute Canyon, Zahn Bay** and **Nokai Dome** in the San Juan Arm. Most of the dark reddish-brown soil you see as you drive along White Canyon east of Hite is derived from the Moenkopi. 90 to 120 meters thick.

41

White Rim Sandstone Type Locality: White Rim escarpment between the Green and Colorado Rivers, San Juan County, Utah. A white to yellow, thin, fine grained, cross-bedded, massive sandstone in the **White Canyon** and **Dirty Devil River Canyon** areas. Around Lake Powell it's seen in the lower part of the Dirty Devil River, around White Canyon, and also surrounding Zahn Bay and on the slopes of Nokai Dome in the San Juan Arm. 0 to 120 meters thick.

Organ Rock Shale Type Locality: Organ Rock, Monument Valley, San Juan County, Utah. This is a reddish brown siltstone with sandy shales. It forms a slope and ledge on the **cliffs across** the **channel** from **Hite**, and on both sides of **Zahn Bay** in the San Juan Arm of the lake. Some of these rocks appear similar to the rocks seen in Goblin Valley next to Utah's San Rafael Swell. 90 to 150 meters thick.

Cedar Mesa Sandstone Type Locality: Cedar Mesa, west and northwest of Mexican Hat, San Juan County, Utah. This covers the top of the massive mesa south and southwest of the Abajo Mountains. It's a mostly white to pale yellow, cross-bedded, massive sandstone. It's always a big cliff-maker which forms some of the finest slot canyons around, especially in lower White Canyon. This is the same formation where all or most of the Anasazi ruins are found in the areas south of the Abajos, especially in **Grand Gulch** and nearby canyons. You can see this one as the massive sandstone walls in **Narrow Canyon**, and as you get further up and into **Cataract Canyon** this is the top-most layer on those high walls. It's also the top layer as you hike into all the tributary canyons of Cataract. 365 to 400 meters thick.

Elephant Canyon Formation (Fades to **Rico Formation** in Colorado, and **Halgaito Shale** along the San Juan River near Monument Valley) Type Locality: In Elephant Canyon, Canyonlands National Park, near Moab, Utah (Near **Rico**, Dolores County, Colorado; and **Halgaito** Springs, southwest of Mexican Hat, San Juan County, Utah). The **Elephant Canyon (Rico) Formation** is made of cherty limestones, some dolomites, and interbedded with pale reddish sandstones. This one forms a cliff, but with some slopes and terraces. You can see this one only in the far upper end of the lake in **Cataract Canyon**. These are the oldest rocks exposed in Canyonlands NP and best seen near the mouth of **Gypsum Canyon** (the **Halgaito** has more shale and occupies the same stratigraphic position, but with some differences in composition. It's found in the upper end of the San Juan Arm of Lake Powell at or just above the HWM). 125 to 450 meters thick.

Honaker Trail Formation Type Locality: Upstream from the end of the San Juan Arm Inlet of Lake Powell at **Goosenecks State Park** and the nearby Honaker Trail, Utah. It also covers large areas along the Colorado River in **Canyonlands National Park**, Utah. This formation is composed of dark colored thick limestone, interbedded with gray cherty limestone, and red & gray shales and sandstones. These rocks form ledges, terraces and slopes. You can see this one only in upper **Cataract Canyon** down as far as Dark Canyon, and maybe Mille Crag Bend, and in the eastern end of the San Juan Arm of the lake. Some geologists have called this strata simply the Upper Member of the Hermosa Group. 300 to 500 meters thick.

Paradox Formation Type Locality: Paradox Valley, Montrose County, Colorado. You may not be able to see this one, as it's difficult to differentiate with the member above, and much of it is covered with talus. This is a slope & cliff-maker and you may see it only in the upper end of Cataract Canyon near the mouths of **Palmer and Gypsum Canyons**. It's basically black shales and limestone, interbedded with salt anhydrite and gypsum. The author believes this is the blackish rock you see at **Gypsum Falls** in Gypsum Canyon. The Paradox Formation is a result of a large anticline in western Colorado and eastern Utah. In the middle parts of the anticline, the beds are composed of salts, a result of evaporation of a large shallow inland sea (perhaps similar to the Caspian Sea). But along the outer fringes, one sees mostly limestone beds. This would be the result of marine shell fish sedimentation during younger stages of the same salty sea. Since we see mostly limestone beds in Cataract Canyon, it's assumed this region was along the outer-most edges of that ancient sea. 150 to 1500 meters thick.

Pinkerton Trail Formation Type Locality: Pinkerton Trail, along the San Juan River Gorge west of Mexican Hat, San Juan County, Utah. This formation is a pinkish gray series of limestones beds with intertongues of siltstone. It also contains gypsum beds. This one is seen only in the lowest end of the San Juan River Canyon **above Clay Hills Crossing** and the HWM of Lake Powell. 45 to 60 meters thick.

Maps of Lake Powell Country

One thing to keep in mind when using this book as your guide to Lake Powell: you must also have one of the following maps which shows the entire lake. There are several full sized maps of the lake available, one of which must be used along with this book. The most popular one is **Stan Jones' Boating and Exploring Map of Lake Powell**. It's double sided with lots of information about boating rules and regulations, wildlife, fishing regulations, etc. By itself, it maybe the best map of the lake, and one this author recommends. It's also the best selling lake map available. Stan Jones, who lives in Page, Arizona, apparently updates the information almost every year, but the map seems to stay the same.

Another good one is called **Lake Powell Map Guide**. It too is double sided, with lots of tidbits of information, including weather and water temperatures, fishing and boating tips, and a little about the marinas. This one is published by the American Adventures Association.

Still another commercial map of the lake is titled **Lake Powell, Finding Your Way.** This one is published by someone in Chico, California, and uses the 1:62,500 scale USGS maps of the region as its base. It shows the lake in 4 sections and it may be the most accurate of all the lake maps available when it comes to showing the inlets and bays. Perhaps the best thing about this one is that it specializes in showing all the buoys on the lake. Beyond that, it has little information. One last map which might interest some is by **Trails Illustrated/National Geographic** titled, **Glen Canyon & Capitol Reef Area.** It's based on the USGS 1:250,000 scale maps and is made out of plastic, therefore waterproof. This map will outlast all other maps about 10 fold! All or most of these maps can be purchased in the marina stores and visitor centers around the lake and in other nearby private businesses.

In addition to these, there are some free maps put out by the National Park Service (NPS). One is called **Glen Canyon: Official Map and Guide**. It's a good one and has a little information about all aspects of the lake, plus the locations of the new toilets & dump/pump stations. Another one put out by the NPS is titled **Glen Canyon Dam and National Recreation Area.** It's very similar to the one above, but appears to be an older version. It's an adequate map as well. Both of these maps can be found at National Park Service Visitor Centers around the lake, and in some cases at visitor centers at the other national parks in the region. Sometimes BLM offices will carry them as well.

There are 2 more maps showing all of Lake Powell. The **Utah Travel Council** has a series of maps covering the state, and in the old series **Map #1, Southeastern Utah**, covers the lake very well, especially the access roads leading to the GCNRA. This a good map, but it shows nothing of the lake on the Arizona side of the line. In the new map series, look for the one titled, **Southeastern Utah**. Both the old and the new cover about the same area.

One more map put out by the USGS, the Bureau of Reclamation and the NPS, is called **Glen Canyon National Recreation Area**. It's based on the 1:250,000 scale USGS maps of the region and is the very best one to show the northern end of the lake in Cataract Canyon (up to the confluence of the Green and Colorado Rivers).

Shown on the index map, next page, are the **USGS 1:100,000 scale metric topographic maps** of southeastern Utah. It takes five of these to cover the lake, and are undoubtedly the best all around maps available. The ones you'll need are: **Hanksville, Hite Crossing, Navajo Mountain, Smoky Mountain and Glen Canyon Dam**. In addition to these USGS maps, the Bureau of Land Management (BLM) also puts out maps which are identical except theirs come in different colors which depict land ownership. For example, public lands are shown in yellow, private lands are in white, Forest Service lands are in green, etc. If you buy any of the BLM maps, be sure to order those in the series called Surface Management Status. These are easier to read than maps having to do with mineral leases.

Some of the good things about these USGS (or BLM) metric maps dating from the 1980's are that all show the lake at the HWM, they show most of the newer roads leading to the lake and the marinas, and they show lots more detail than any of the maps above, which show the entire lake. This makes them good for both boating and hiking.

In addition to these newer metric maps, there are much older USGS maps of the area at **1:62,500 scale** (**15' quads**). These maps are actually **out of print**, but some may still be available while supplies last. These are good maps but they're old, most dating from the 1950's. They were made when Lake Powell was just a dream, so they don't have the newer access roads, marinas, or the lake's shore line. These 15 minute maps can be good for hiking, but unfortunately when stocks are sold out, **they won't be reprinted**.

You'll have to swim through parts of **For-bidding Canyon/Aztec Creek**, at least after big floods have scoured out deep pools.

The replacement for the 1:62,500 scale maps will be those at **1:24,000 scale or 7 1/2' quads**. The entire state and nation are now covered with this scale of maps. These maps are very detailed, but sometimes you need 2 or 3 maps for just one hike. The **small squares** on these maps represent **1 kilometer (km)** and are geared to **GPS navigation systems** (the larger squares with thin red lines are **square miles or sections** and are only shown on maps which contain private or state trust land). These quads are all quite new and show the lake at the HWM and new access roads. The best map for hiking is listed under each of the hiking areas in this book. That short list includes the 1:100,000, 1:24,000 and 1:62,500 scale maps, if available.

General Information: Odds and Ends

One of the first things you'll have to do before getting on the lake, and before you even begin to plan a trip, is to get a **large map covering the entire lake**. You can't use this book effectively unless you have one. See Maps of Lake Powell Country, on the previous page for a list of the maps available.

The map you buy should show all or many of the **buoys** one sees while boating on the lake. The buoys in the middle of the channel, which tell boaters where deeper water and where the old Colorado River channel is, also have numbers and sometimes letters on them. Those with letters don't seem to mean a lot, but those with numbers, indicate the number of miles uplake from the Glen Canyon Dam. The **dam** is at **mile 0**.

There are no buoys in the San Juan Arm of the lake to indicate mileage & kilomage. Neither are there buoys at the mouths of any of the side-canyons. The numbers the author uses in that part, are the old river runner's distances before Lake Powell came to be. In the north end of the lake in Cataract Canyon, there are no buoys either. On the individual canyon maps, the author has extended the **mileage & kilomage** from the dam, to show relative distances.

In this book, and on the various maps of the canyons, there will be numbers and letters such as M24 (K38). This means there is a buoy in that area that is marked with a number indicating the miles from the dam. The second letter & number are not on the buoys, but it is the conversion from miles to **kilometers (kms)**. In this case 24 miles equals 38 kms, the distance uplake from Glen Canyon Dam. Another example, the Ten Cent Campsite in Cataract Canyon at the upper end of Lake Powell is measured at **M171 (K274)** from or above the Glen Canyon Dam.

The reason each of the buoys marked in this book are labeled with miles & kms is because most of the rest of this book is in **metrics**. It's not meant to confuse people, but for some it will. The reason it's used here is that when the day comes for the USA to change over to metrics, the author won't have to change his books. The author feels that day is fast approaching.

In 1975, the US Congress passed a resolution to begin the process of changing over to the metric system. They did this because the USA is the only country on earth still officially using the antiquated British System of measurement. This progressive move ended with the Reagan Administration in 1981.

Use the **Metric Conversion Table** for help in the conversion process. It's easy to learn and use once you get started. Just keep a few things in mind: 1 mile is just over 1.5 kms, 2 miles is about 3 kms, and 6 miles is about 10 kms. Also, 100 meters is a little more than 100 yards, 2000 meters is about 6600 feet, and 3000 meters is about 10,000 feet. A liter and a quart are roughly the same, and one US gallon jug holds about 3 3/4 liters.

When it comes to the subject of **boating regulations**, this is something you'll have to get more of in another place. The regulations for Lake Powell appear to be virtually the same as for other waters in the states of Utah and Arizona. There's no difference when you cross the state line. Briefly, **all boats** with **motors** must be **licensed** with the numbers showing on the boat. Boats must have a **fire extinguisher, a life jacket for each passenger, a set of oars or paddles, and a whistle or horn** of some kind. Other highly recommended items would be: an anchor or anchor line, a shovel, simple tool kit and at least one, but better still, 2 long ropes. Also, plenty of gasoline (more than you think you'll need), food, water, and the camping gear of your choice. Always have the **boat registration** in your possession.

Before going to Lake Powell for the first time, it's best to check your own state's requirements for equipment and other safety devices. Also, have a map of the lake which gives more information than this book. **Stan Jones' Map of Lake Powell Country** is perhaps the best all-around. His map and other sources should be consulted concerning the markings on other buoys, travel at night, boater's right-of-ways, fishing, etc,.

For the most part, there is little or no danger of hitting a piece of **driftwood** on Lake Powell, but there are a couple of areas where you'll have to be observant. The worst place the author encountered was in the upper end of Navajo Canyon Inlet. Driftwood is very thick near the south end, but some floaters make it to the halfway mark. The other place is Cataract Canyon in the northern end of the lake, where the Colorado River enters. The water is always a little muddy in that region, but there isn't as much floating wood as you might expect; sand or silt bars can be bigger problems than driftwood.

If you're hiking into any of the narrow **slot canyons** around the lake, remember to stay out if **bad weather** is threatening. **Flash floods** of the magnitude which can wash people out of narrow canyons don't come very often, but when they do, you'd better not be in their way. Most of the big gully-washer-type floods come in the late summer and early fall. They come about during cloudburst-type storms with high winds, thunder and lightning. The all-day type rainstorms which pass over the area in winter, usually put some running water in these narrow canyons, but low flow ankle-deep water is not a problem. On August 12, 1997, 11 people drowned in **Antelope Canyon** just east of Page, Arizona.

Here's the situation on the **boundaries of the GCNRA** as it relates to the lands of the **Navajo Nation**. If you're boating and camping in areas on the south side of the lake between Wahweap and the mouth of the San Juan River Arm, and on the south side of the San Juan Arm itself, you'll be on the Navajo Nation side of the lake. However, the line between the recreation area and the Navajo land is set at 1134 meters or 3720 feet. This means the boundary is 6 meters above the **High Water Mark (HWM) of 1128 meters or 3700 feet**. So, when you camp anywhere near the lake, you're within the boundaries of the GCNRA.

Index to 1:100,000 Scale Topographic Maps of Lake Powell

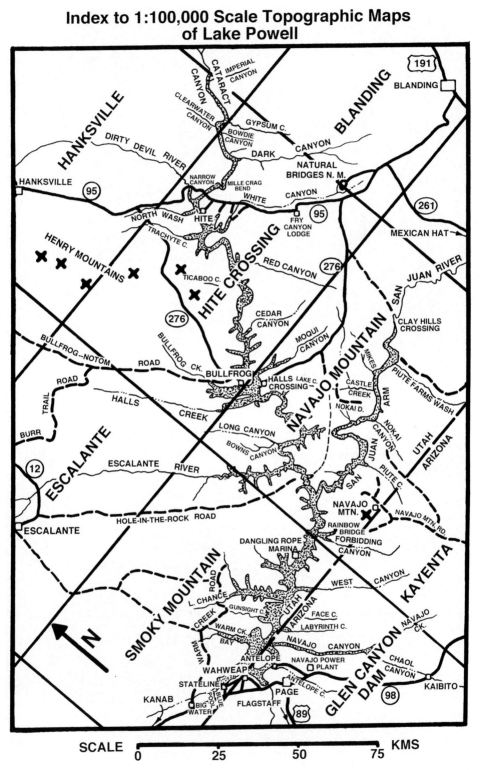

A big alcove cave in the **South Fork of Iceberg Canyon**. This is one of the most colorful scenes on Lake Powell. Be there when the sun is shining into the front of the cave, or on the opposite wall.

Looking southwest from the launching ramp at **Halls Crossing Marina**. You can launch a boat, stock up on water, or flush your tanks with flushing water at this ramp & dock.

Reference Map of Canyons and Hikes

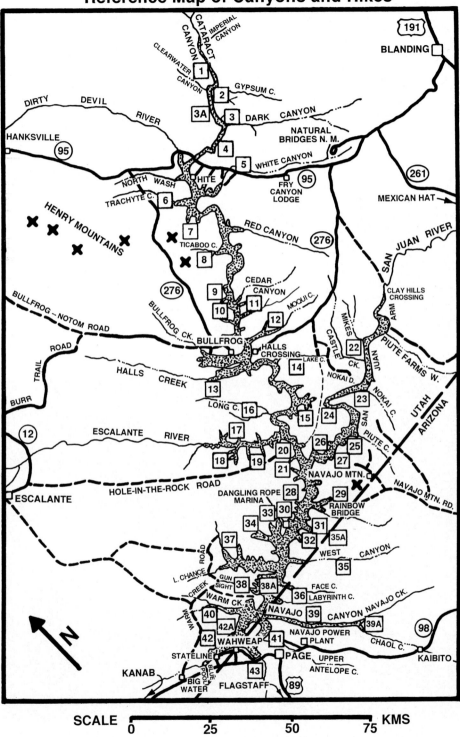

SCALE 0 25 50 75 KMS

Cataract, Imperial and Calf Canyons

Location & Campsites The 3 canyons featured on this map are located right at the uppermost end of Lake Powell. When the lake is at maximum capacity, the elevation is said to be **1128 meters (3700 feet)** and reaches into Cataract Canyon to about M172 (K276) from Glen Canyon Dam. This upper end also reaches as far as what rafters call the **Ten Cent Campsite** just north of the mouth of Imperial Canyon. On some maps, the Calf Canyon shown here is called Waterhole Canyon; but boaters maps seem to use the name Calf most often.

Also shown on the map is the lower part of Cataract Canyon unaffected by Lake Powell. **Cataract Canyon** begins at, or just below, the confluence of the Green and Colorado Rivers. The canyon is famous for its many rapids, the first of which begins just below Spanish Bottom in the heart of Canyonlands National Park. Cataract Canyon officially ends at **Mille Crag Bend**, which is the beginning of **Narrow Canyon**. Narrow Canyon ends at about the highway bridge north of Hite. Before the lake came to be, there were about 62 rapids in Cataract Canyon (according to Dellenbaugh's diary), but today there are only 25 above the HWM. As of 7/2007, and because of the drought which started in about the year 2000, there were half a dozen small rapids between the HWM and the Gypsum Canyon Horse Trail.

As you boat up Cataract Canyon you'll notice a slight current. Its speed will vary with the amount of water entering the lake, how close you are to the upper end at any given moment, and the water level in the lake at any given moment. On the author's first visit when the lake level was about 2 meters below the HWM, he could detect a slight current as far downcanyon as Mille Crag Bend. As you'd expect, the lower the lake level, the more pronounced the current is throughout Cataract and Narrow Canyons. In 2005, with the water level the lowest in 25-30 years, there was no lake in front of the old Hite Marina--only the Colorado River.

Needless to say, the upper end of the lake always has water that is less than crystal clear. During the spring runoff, cloudy or muddy water is seen downlake past Hite. On one late September visit the cloudy water only extended downcanyon to the beginning of Mille Crag Bend. That was when the lake was full.

As you boat uplake, there used to be a floating sign around Mille Crag Bend stating: *Swift currents, shallow sand bars, and driftwood beyond this point. Campsites above here are needed by River Rafters. Please limit upstream camping.* Partly because of this sign (it was nowhere to be found in 2007), but mostly because of the slightly muddy water, the author has never seen other Lake Powell boaters in Cataract Canyon; only the rafters drifting downlake and the occasional canoeist or kayaker. Actually, there are more campsites than this sign might indicate, but everyone wants the nice sandy beach-type sites, which are definitely limited. However, when the water levels are 4 or 5 meters or more below the HWM, there are many silt bars exposed. Not all of these make the greatest campsites, but you can pitch a tent or dock a boat up against some of them.

Rafters actually **reserve campsites** they want between **Spanish Bottom and Hite** by signing a register located at **the Confluence** of the **Green & Colorado Rivers**. The major campsites below the HWM are at the mouths of: **Gypsum, Clearwater and Dark Canyons**. Not all of these are occupied each night, and there are many other smaller sites to choose from, especially above Dark Canyon.

In this mapped area, the very best sandy camping place is right at the HWM at the very upper end

From **Ocean Point** looking almost straight down at the mouth of **Gypsum Canyon**. Notice the tamaracks (tamarisks) which follow the HWM into the former Gypsum Bay and along the shoreline.

Map 1, Cataract, Imperial and Calf Canyons

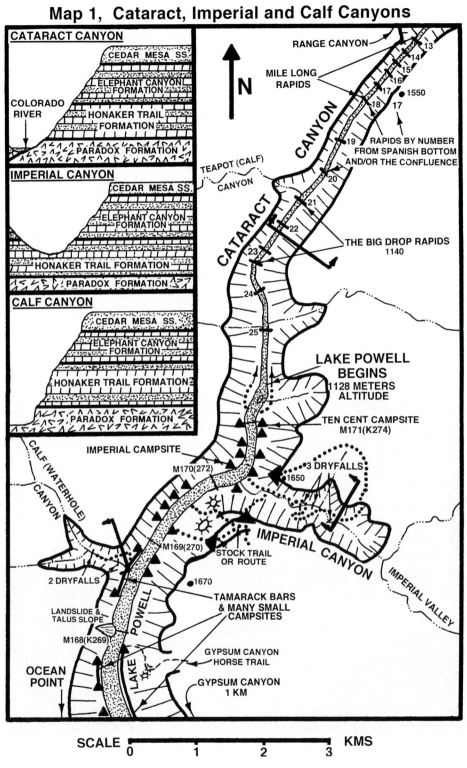

CATARACT CANYON

CEDAR MESA SS.

ELEPHANT CANYON FORMATION

COLORADO RIVER

HONAKER TRAIL FORMATION

PARADOX FORMATION

IMPERIAL CANYON

CEDAR MESA SS.

ELEPHANT CANYON FORMATION

HONAKER TRAIL FORMATION

PARADOX FORMATION

CALF CANYON

CEDAR MESA SS.

ELEPHANT CANYON FORMATION

HONAKER TRAIL FORMATION

PARADOX FORMATION

N

RANGE CANYON

MILE LONG RAPIDS

1550

RAPIDS BY NUMBER FROM SPANISH BOTTOM AND/OR THE CONFLUENCE

TEAPOT (CALF) CANYON

CATARACT CANYON

THE BIG DROP RAPIDS
1140

LAKE POWELL BEGINS
1128 METERS ALTITUDE

TEN CENT CAMPSITE
M171(K274)

3 DRYFALLS

IMPERIAL CAMPSITE

M170(272)

1650

IMPERIAL CANYON

CALF (WATERHOLE) CANYON

M169(270)

STOCK TRAIL OR ROUTE

IMPERIAL VALLEY

2 DRYFALLS

1670

TAMARACK BARS & MANY SMALL CAMPSITES

LANDSLIDE & TALUS SLOPE

M168(K269)

LAKE POWELL

OCEAN POINT

GYPSUM CANYON HORSE TRAIL

GYPSUM CANYON
1 KM

SCALE
0   1   2   3   KMS

49

of the lake. It's called **Ten Cent Campsite** by the rafting crowd. It's a large beach on the east side of the river/lake at M171 (K274). There's another smaller sandy site just across the channel to the west. Just down around the bend, and across from the mouth of Imperial Canyon, is the **Imperial Campsite**. Both of these sites are regularly used by river runners during the 6 month rafting season. If the lake is high, and you decide to camp at either of these sites, do so at one end or the other, so when the rafters come in during the afternoons, you'll all have plenty of room.

Downcanyon a bit further, there are numerous campsites with tamaracks, all of which are of questionable quality. There used to be one very good little sandy site just north of the mouth of Calf Canyon, but it, as well as all other silt bar campsites are ever changing. In Cataract Canyon, possible campsite locations will always change depending on water levels and whether the lake is rising or falling. The sites exposed when the lake is low will be mostly silt bars, and not as desirable as the sandy beaches.

One of the worst things about camping in the far upper end of the lake is when you want to bathe, you'll often be standing in mud ankle deep, sometimes deeper. Therefore the best place to wash is from the top of an exposed rock or boulder near the water's edge. The current always keeps such places free of mud or silt.

Hiking Routes or Trails The first hike here is up the lower end of the present-day river part of **Cataract Canyon**. Hopefully you can tie down somewhere between Ten Cent and Imperial Campsites. There are no trails from these campsites up along the river, but the walking is fairly easy and you can walk on either side. Staying close to the river is usually the best place to walk. There are however, some places with lots of driftwood and others with large boulders. Some parts are even sandy. Even though the hike is almost a flat track, you'll feel it in your legs if you're not in good shape, because of all the rock-hopping involved. If you have the inclination, you could walk all the way through the remaining part of Cataract Canyon to the Confluence of the Green and Colorado Rivers.

One destination on this hike would be **Teapot Canyon**, about 3 kms above the HWM. You could also go to as far as the mouth of Range Canyon on a day-hike, but perhaps the best plan would be to go to the first really big rapids along the river. There are 3 rapids (the author counted 4) in a short stretch of river called the **Big Drop Rapids**. On river runners maps, they are numbered 21, 22, and 23. Most of the time, the rafters stop just before going through each so they can safely plot their course. If you arrive around midday, you may meet some of these people taking the plunge through white water.

Begin the walk up **Imperial Canyon** from anywhere along the wide-open mouth. After about 1 km, the canyon constricts, and you'll reach some narrows and a big dryfall. A good climber with equipment could scale this one, but not the ordinary hiker. At the dryfall, regress about 100 meters and climb due north, first on a talus slope, then up through 2 cliff bands. This part is almost vertical and for the experienced hiker-climber only. Take a short rope to help those not accustomed to rock climbing. This is the most difficult part of the hike, with the descent being much more risky than the ascent. The author had no trouble doing this pitch alone in 1988, but in 2001 and with 2 camera bags, he decided it was too risky. Part of that wall seems to have collapsed as well (?).

Once through these ledges, you'll be on a bench or terrace. Walk east into the narrows again where you'll be above one dryfall, but below still another. Instead of trying to climb up the second, head west on the same level but on the south side of the canyon to a point directly across from where you scaled the first cliffs. From there, route-find upslope to the south through about 3 easy-to-climb ledges. Once

The head of Lake Powell in **Cataract Canyon** as seen from the air and looking west. To the right is the upcanyon side. In the middle is the mouth of **Imperial Canyon** & **Rapids**. Look closely and you can see the HWM which is a thin line of tamaracks near the center of the picture.

on the next terrace, bench-walk east again and into the upper canyon basin.

About 300 meters above the second dryfall, route-find left and onto still another easy-to-reach terrace to avoid a third dryfall (follow map carefully). After you pass this last dropoff, gradually veer to the left or north, and walk up the steep but easy-to-climb talus slope to the canyon rim. To reach the overlook of Cataract Canyon at 1650 meters altitude, first walk due north before turning west, to avoid a minor drainage. You'll come out at a point where you can look straight down on the Imperial and Ten Cent Campsites. About midday or just after noon would be the best time to take fotos.

About halfway between the mouths of Imperial and Calf Canyons on the east side of the river/lake, are 2 easy and interesting ways to the rim of Cataract Canyon. These routes (in places it might be an old stock trail?) go up to the rim of the canyon overlooking the mouth of Imperial Canyon.

To get onto either of these routes, boat north from the mouth of Calf Canyon about 1 or 1 1/2 kms. As you do, observe a couple of big slide areas coming down from the rim to your right or east. Probably the easiest route to climb is the second, or the one furtherest north. Dock at the bottom and walk up a steep but easy-to-climb talus slope. As you do, you'll first be walking east, then will gradually veer northeast. At the top of this first slope will be a small butte on your left, and a low ridge to your right or southeast. Walk to the southeast and over an easy-to-climb little ridge. At the top, look east to find still another rim about 300 meters away. Walk toward it but veer left just a bit. On the lower part of this slope you'll find some stone cairns and what looks like a very old & faded trail. Near the top, veer to the left and skirt to the north of this rim. Once on the north side, this faded trail zig zags up to the south. Once on top of this slope or rim, again walk south and look for an easy way up one last minor bench or terrace. Observe the map, and use your head to route-find up this route.

As you near the top, you'll have some fine views to the north into both Imperial and Cataract Canyons. Due north and alongside the river, will be the Imperial Campsite. If you want, you can return via another steep gully about 300-400 meters to the south of the route just described.

A 3rd route to this same overlook, and one that's a bit less complicated, is to walk to a point just inside the mouth of Imperial Canyon and look for an easy-to-climb slope heading south, southwest as shown on the map.

The last hike in this area is a short climb into the middle basin of **Calf Canyon**. About 200 meters from the lake is a big dryfall perhaps 70 meters high. You can't climb into the canyon from there, so look to the north side of the now tamarack-filled bay, and you'll see a slide area. Bushwhack through the tamaracks and walk up this steep, but easy-to-climb talus slope. At a convenient location, and at about the same elevation as the top of the first dryfall, veer to the left or west, and bench-walk to a point just above the dropoff. From there you'll climb over a little rise and down into the middle basin.

After another 400 meters or so, you'll come to yet another big dryfall, perhaps 80-90 meters in height. This one is in an alcove that's rather dark in the afternoons. There will likely be several large potholes in the middle basin, especially at the bottom of the upper dryfall. From this middle part it appears there is no way to the upper basin of Calf Canyon. The **Gypsum Canyon Horse Trail** will be discussed in the next section.

Hike Length & Time Needed In **Cataract Canyon**, from the Ten Cent Campsite to the mouth of Teapot is about 3 1/2 kms. Since it's slow walking for part of the way, plan to take 1 1/2 hours each way, or about 3 hours round-trip. If you hike to Range Canyon, it will likely be an all-day trip.

From near the top of the **Gypsum Canyon Horse Trail** looking southwest. Far left is Palmer Canyon; above right is **Ocean Point**; closer, and to lower right is the little butte you pass on this trail.

To make the climb up **Imperial Canyon** to the rim and back, will take most people 5-6 hours. The author did it in 4 hours on his first try. The distance is only 3 to 4 kms one way, but it can't be done quickly. The Calf Canyon hike is only about 1 km in length, and can be completed in a couple of hours. Going up to the east rim between Calf and Imperial Canyons will take a couple of hours, one way. On his 2 climbs in the rim near Calf Canyon, the author did it in about 2 hours round-trip each time, which was about the same time as it took to reach the same overlook from the mouth of Imperial Canyon in 2001. In 2007, and because of low water levels and all the rapids (see foto below), he didn't even get up to the mouth of Imperial Canyon or the HWM.

Boots or Shoes For all hikes a pair of rugged boots are best, but running shoes would work fine for the walk up Cataract Canyon.

Water There are no springs in this area, so take your own water on each hike.

Main Attractions A hike up one of the most spectacular canyons in the world and a chance to see rafters run some of the best rapids anywhere. Also, some interesting climbing to the rim of the plateau for some excellent views of Cataract Canyon.

Hiking Maps USGS or BLM map Hanksville (1:100,000); Teapot Rock (1:24,000--7 1/2' quad); Orange Cliffs (1:62,500) if available; or Canyonlands National Park (1:62,500).

From **Ocean Point** looking north down at the upper end of Lake Powell in **Cataract Canyon**. This foto was taken on **7/5/2007-WL1100.68m/3611.11'**. The water seen here is really the Colorado River (not the lake), complete with rapids. The **Gypsum Canyon Horse Trail** begins in the lower right-hand side just below or downstream from the big landslide & talus slope on the left.

One of many small sandy campsites in upper **Cataract Canyon**. Looking downstream south & a little east, at the mouth of **Gypsum Canyon**. Picture was taken on **7/3/2007-WL1100.73m/3611.27'**. On that day, the first rapids in Cataract were about 500 meters upstream (behind) from this campsite.

Looking northeast at a typical wall of **Upper Cataract Canyon**. This picture was taken at the mouth of **Gypsum Canyon** on **7/3/2007-WL1100.73m/3611.27'**. The boulders in the foreground were brought down by floods from Gypsum Canyon.

Gypsum, Palmer, Easter Pasture, Clearwater & Bowdie Canyons and the Ocean Point Hike

Location & Campsites There are 5 canyons on this map; **Gypsum, Palmer, Easter Pasture, Clearwater and Bowdie**. Combined with Easter Pasture Canyon is a hike to the rim of Cataract Canyon at a place called **Ocean Point**. Also featured is the old **Gypsum Canyon Horse Trail** up to the east rim of Cataract just north of the mouth of Gypsum, and another route out of Gypsum to the east rim. These hikes are found not far below the upper end of the lake and the HWM in Cataract Canyon. The mouth of Gypsum Canyon is near M166 (K266), while Bowdie Canyon empties into the lake at about M161 (K258). These distances are miles (kilometers) uplake from Glen Canyon Dam.

There are many campsite symbols on this map, almost all of which are silt bars with lots of tamaracks. It's in this section the lake, the water is starting to move more slowly, therefore silt is deposited, especially next to shore and at the mouths of the many tiny coves or inlets. When the lake is high and near the HWM, you will see many little ponds of water behind the silt bars. During times of low water, there's one straight main channel with dike-like silt bars on either side. In many places now, the highest parts of some of these silt bars are so thick with tamaracks, that it's impossible to find an open place for a tent. Therefore you'll just have to boat along until you find a bar 1-2 meters above the water level and large enough for a tent. Above the mouth of Dark Canyon, there are many small sites.

With so much silt being deposited along the shoreline, it's sometimes a little unpleasant for camping. Just under water will be thick mud; and just above, the tamaracks. When everything is covered with mud, it's difficult to enjoy a bath or swimming. Look for large boulders to stand on at water level.

When the lake level is low, with much larger silt bars exposed, it sometimes means more campsites. But you'll have to look for places where the water is deep right next to the silt bar, otherwise it's hard to get out of your boat--without stepping into a quagmire. Other than this minor problem, Cataract Canyon is a nice quiet area to visit. Your only company will be the occasional rafting party heading downlake.

About the only camping place regularly used by rafters on this map is in the area of **Clearwater Canyon** (there's good drinking water just up the canyon a ways). One site may be inside the shallow bay or right at the mouth; the other just across from the bay on the east side. Both of these sites change depending on water levels and whether the lake is rising or falling. During times of low water levels, you won't be able to boat into Clearwater Inlet as it's filled in with sand & silt and covered with tamaracks. There are other generally good sites at the mouth of **Gypsum, Easter Pasture** and **Bowdie Canyons**, depending on lake levels.

The author spent time in this region within a day or two of **7/21/2007-WL1099.93m/3608.67'**, and found the lake extended up to just above the bottom of the Gypsum Canyon Horse Trail. That's where the first rapids were encountered. If the lake drops much more than on 7/21/2007, it'll be hard to get to the mouth of Gypsum Canyon. Let's hope the drought breaks soon.

It's in this region that the oldest rocks seen along the shores of Lake Powell are exposed. These belong to the **Paradox Member** of the **Hermosa Formation**. They are exposed in just a few places between Spanish Bottom (upper end or the beginning of Cataract Canyon) and Palmer Canyon. It's difficult to see differences in the rocks of the Paradox (some are gypsum) from those above in the Honaker

From **Ocean Point** looking southeast into the mouth of **Gypsum Canyon**. This foto was taken on **7/5/2007-WL1100.68m/3611.11'**, and on that date the first rapids were about 1 km up **Cataract Canyon** (which is to the lower left in this picture) from the mouth of Gypsum.

54

Map 2, Gypsum, Palmer, Easter Pasture, Clearwater & Bowdie Canyons and the Ocean Point Hike

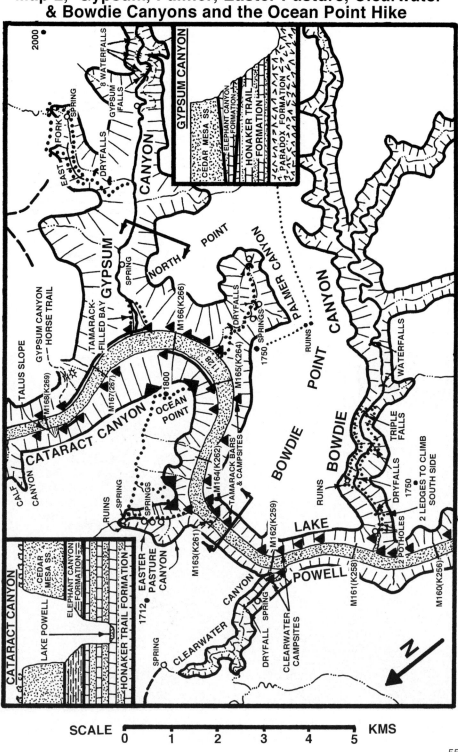

SCALE

0   1   2   3   4   5   KMS

Trail Formation.
Hiking Routes or Trails After the author was in this area twice, he had a chance to discuss an old trail down into Gypsum Canyon with John Scorup, formerly of the BLM in Monticello. John is a grandson of Jim Scorup, of the old **Scorup Brothers cattle outfit**. He stated the **Gypsum Canyon Horse Trail**, which had been built long ago, came down from the rim about 1 1/2 kms up Cataract Canyon from the mouth of Gypsum on the east side. This he guesses, was built by David Goudelock of the **Dugout Ranch** sometime around 1900 or soon after. John Scorup was probably the last cowboy to take horses down this trail to winter in the lower end of Gypsum Canyon.
   Here's how to get up this old historic trail. From the mouth of Gypsum, boat upcanyon about 1 1/2 kms and stop at a point about where the tamaracks end on the east bank. It's about 600 meters below the **Big Talus Slope** on the west side of the river/lake. Tie-down, then walk up to just above the HWM and tamaracks and look for 4 stone cairns marking the lower end of the trail. See the map. The cairns and the trail zig zag straight up the slope. After a short distance, the trail itself will become more visible as it ascends a minor ridge while heading due east. About halfway up to the rim, the trail then turns and runs southeast along a contour line. After crossing a talus slope, and going in and out of **2 steep drainages**, you'll arrive at a kind of divide or pass with a narrow buttress on your right or south. At that point the trail levels out for 150 meters, then turns left with cairns marking the way as the trail zig zags northeast until you're basically out of the canyon. Follow the cairns closely all the way--the author erected many on his 2 trips there. From the higher levels, it heads east and soon disappears in the rough country just south of Imperial Canyon. About 3 kms east of where it leaves Cataract Canyon it apparently meets an old road in a large depression.
   From the lake, walk right up the **Gypsum Canyon dry creek bed** as it cuts through the middle of the former inlet which is now filled in with sands, rocks and tamaracks. After a ways, you may see running water part way upcanyon, but in a long dry spell, it dries up completely. The dry creek bed is rather wide in most places and walking is easy. There are no trees, willows or tamaracks to slow you down after you leave the bay/inlet area.
   The canyon is very broad in the lower end, then gradually constricts. After about 8 kms, you'll come to a couple of tight gooseneck bends, then **Gypsum Falls**. The author estimates it to be about 40-45 meters high and is completely enclosed, making a rather dark secluded scene. This is surely the most spectacular waterfall leading to Lake Powell. The water appears to cascade over the Paradox Member, which in this case seems to be a dark limestone. Note: on 7/4/2007, the falls were bone dry, with only 3 pools of stagnant water in the first km below the falls.
   If you want to see upper Gypsum Canyon here's what you do. Backtrack from the waterfall less than a km, then scramble upon a steep talused ridge coming down from the west. Once on this ridge, you'll find a big horn sheep trail. Continue upridge until you're on an obvious terrace, then bench-walk into the canyon on a big game trail. Along the way you'll have some great views down on Gypsum Falls.
   Just beyond Gypsum Falls you'll drop down to the creek to find 2 smaller falls just above the main waterfall. Continue upcanyon on the right side passing 3 waterfalls in limestone. After you reach a side-canyon coming in from the right, you'll pass 2 more waterfalls, number 7 & 8. When you reach the 9th

From the air looking northwest up **Cataract Canyon**. Below and to the right is **Gypsum Canyon** coming in from the southeast; **Ocean Point** is to the upper left; and Calf Canyon is in the upper middle part of this picture.

waterfall, backup about 100 meters and route-find upslope west to a cliff band which thins to 5-6 meters high. There is no trail up a 75-meter-long talus slope, so you'll have to use your eyes & head to locate the only reasonable route up through the cliff band.

This cliff is quite an easy climb (always more difficult coming down!) but you'll need a short rope to raise or lower large packs. Once on the terrace above, bench-walk upcanyon around waterfall 9, then skirt around waterfall 10 which is just above the 9th. From these 2 waterfalls you'll need more than one day to continue up Gypsum Canyon and into Beef Basin or lower Fable Valley (which is not far beyond waterfalls 9 & 10). For this trip and a possible loop-hike involving Bowdie Canyon, see this writers other book, *Non-Technical Canyon Hiking Guide to the Colorado Plateau, 5th Edition (or later)*.

In 1995, Bob Bruington of North Ogden, Utah, along with some friends, hiked down through Fable Valley and Gypsum Canyon, floated in cheap plastic rafts down to the mouth of Bowdie Canyon, then hiked up Bowdie and back to their vehicles at the head of Fable Valley. Five days round-trip.

John W. Powell hiked up Gypsum Canyon to Gypsum Falls in 1869, during the first of his 2 epic river journeys, then later found a way out of the canyon in an eastern side-canyon. The author finally found the route Powell must have taken to reach the canyon rim. As you walk up from the bottom of Gypsum, you will pass 2 side-canyons on the left or east before reaching the waterfall. It's the **second one** you'll be interested in, the one called **East Fork** on this map.

Right where the dry creek bed of East Fork meets Gypsum Creek, turn left or east, and walk up on a low bench on the north side. From there you'll see a big dryfall at the mouth of East Fork. Your goal then is to walk up a steep talus slope on the left side to the top of a high bench or terrace northwest of the dropoff. This allows you to enter the upper basin above a couple of blocking dryfalls. Once inside the upper basin, you'll have a choice of 2 routes out to the rim. To explain the way, the author's circular route will be described.

As you enter the upper basin, continue on the same horizontal bench until you're in the bottom of the dry creek bed about halfway into the upper basin. At that point you'll see several cottonwood trees and willows indicating a seasonal seep. Continue upcanyon southeast along the easiest route. Higher up, you'll come to another green spot with cottonwoods where a year-round spring is located. There are no cattle or beaver in this area, so this water should be good to drink as is.

From this spring, head up along the south side of the little drainage coming down into the canyon from the east. Then walk east to within about 50 meters of the highest dryfall, which forms the upper-most

rim. There on the south side, you'll come to a 10-meter-high crack in the yellow sandstone. This crack is steep, but it has lots of good hand and foot holds, and is easy to climb. You can return this same way, but there's another way in or out about 600 meters to the northwest.

From the rim above the spring and first exit, walk northwest to find a shallow drainage dropping off the top. Right where that dry creek falls over the rim, look for an easy way down with 2 minor dropoffs. From there, walk down to the west a ways, then when you reach the first terrace, veer right or northwest, and bench-walk another 700-800 meters. When you reach a landslide area, walk down to the terrace you were on when you entered the upper basin at the beginning of the hike. It was in this area the author ran into a desert big horn ram.

Gypsum Falls on 7/4/2007. This is normally a real waterfall with a small stream, but in the summer of 2007, and after about 7 years of almost continuous drought, it was bone dry.

J.W. Powell's Report In Powell's book on his explorations of the Colorado, he describes his party's exploration of Gypsum Canyon. On July 26, 1869, he wrote: *About ten o'clock, Powell, Bradley, Howland, Hall, and I start up a side canyon to the east. We soon come to pools of water; then to a brook, which is lost in the sands below; and passing up the brook, we see that the canyon narrows, the walls close in and are often overhanging, and at last we find ourselves in a vast amphitheater, with a pool of deep, clear, cold water on the bottom.* This was what is now known as **Gypsum Falls**. They tried to get out of the canyon there, but failed. The party then retreated and each member set out to find a route to the rim by himself.

Powell went up a side-canyon on the northeast, and after some work, found a route up. Near the top he states: *I came to a place where the wall is again broken down, so I can climb up still farther; and in an hour I reach the summit. I hang up my barometer to give it a few minutes time to settle, and occupy myself in collecting resin from the pinyon pines, which are found in great abundance.* One of the principal objects in making this climb was to get this resin for the purpose of smearing our boats. At the end of that day's entry he states: *Great quantities of gypsum are found at the bottom of the gorge; so we name it Gypsum Canyon.*

In reading Powell's account of his river expeditions, keep in mind he had but one arm; he lost the other in the Civil War. In Dellenbaugh's Diary, **Canyon Voyage**, he makes a statement concerning Powell's handicap. The scene was somewhere in middle Cataract Canyon and on September 20, 1871 (Powell's second trip) he states: *The Major having no right arm, he sometimes got in a difficult situation when climbing, if his right side came against a smooth surface where there was nothing opposite. We had learned to go down by the same route followed up, because otherwise one is never sure of arriving at the bottom, as a ledge half-way down might compel a return to the summit. We remembered that at one point there was no way for him to hold on, the cliff being smooth on the right, while on the left was empty air, with a sheer drop of several hundred feet. The footing too was narrow. I climbed down first, and, bracing myself below with my back to the abyss, I was able to plant my right foot securely in such a manner that my right knee formed a solid step for him at the critical moment. On this improvised step he placed his left foot, and in a twinkling had made the passage in safety.*

The first canyon downstream from Gypsum is **Palmer Canyon**. If you stay in the creek bed, you can only walk into it about 1 km, then you come to some high dryfalls. But there's a way around these and into the upper basin. Tie-down your boat just west of the mouth of Palmer and walk up an obvious ridge until you're on a terrace at the same elevation as the top of the first dryfall. Then bench-walk at the same level around the falls and into the upper basin. Or you can begin at the bottom of the canyon about 300 meters below the falls. At that point, look up to the southwest and locate an easy route up the steep talus slope to the same level or terrace as the top of the dryfall. Walk up the slope to that bench and bench-walk south into the canyon.

As you walk into the upper basin, you'll first be in a dry creek bed, but after a ways, you'll come to the first spring and maybe some running water. Not far beyond that, you'll come to the place where a short side-canyon comes in from the west. It may have some running water, and you'll have to skirt around a dropoff and pourover pool to the left. Above this, there are several minor dryfalls you'll have to get around. Finally, you'll reach a point at about the bottom of the Cedar Mesa Sandstone, where there may be a trickle of running water and an unclimbable wall. It appears this is the end of the line

Boating northeast up **Cataract Canyon** between Clearwater and Easter Pasture Canyons.
Ahead and to the left next to the shadows is the mouth of **Easter Pasture**.

for hikers and no way out of Palmer Canyon to the rim.

In the 1940's, a team of archaeologists from the **Carnegie Museum** of Pittsburgh, explored the upper parts of this canyon (what they called John Palmer Canyon) from the rim, and found 3 different Anasazi ruins. One site was said to be in a crack in the Navajo Sandstone (it could only be the Cedar Mesa Sandstone!). The other 2 sites were only 150 meters above the elevation of the river, and about 1 1/2 kms from the Colorado. These were surely incorrect, as the author later found. There seems to be no ruins inside Palmer Canyon, but in the cliffs just above the rim to the southwest and in what might be called the **upper Palmer drainage**, there are some ruins.

These 3 sites were called the Andrew Delaney, Henrys, and Sandy Camp sites. There were Mesa Verde style potsherds found at all three ruins, one of which was dated between 1026 AD to 1127 AD; another dated from between 1070 AD to 1164 AD. You can get to these only from the rim, and the upper part of Bowdie Canyon's north fork.

There's no trail up **Easter Pasture Canyon**, but you can easily climb through it up to the rim. For some reason, the big cliffs or ledges which block passage in other nearby canyons, have been filled in with avalanche debris in this one. This makes it one of the few side-canyons in Cataract which you can exit. Just walk up this steep and mostly-dry creek bed. After wading through tamaracks next to the lake and after another 600-700 meters, you'll come to one big hackberry (?) tree. Below its branches is a small seep. Not far above that are 3 cottonwoods and another trickle of water. On the author's September, 2001 (and July, 2007) trips to this canyon, these **2 springs** were nearly dry.

Further up, you'll come to 3 cliff bands, which you pass on the left, or north side. After these cliffs, walk to the right or south 75 meters, across a very small stream, then climb up a talus slope to avoid one little waterfall. Above this is a dry section of the canyon, but just ahead is a big dryfall and right beneath it are several places where the water seeps out from under the lowest part of the Cedar Mesa Sandstone. About 30 meters left (west) of the main spring are **4 small Fremont Indian structures**; one was a living quarters, the other 3 were for food storage. They're all in bad condition today, mainly because they were not well-built in the first place.

From the upper spring, veer east and route-find up through the minor ledges. To reach the top of the plateau, which is the top of the Cedar Mesa Sandstone, you'll have to zig zag up through half a dozen ledges. There are easy ways up through each, but you have to look for them. The easy routes are on the south side of a minor drainage.

Once on top, route-find southwest to where you can look down into lower Easter Pasture and Cataract Canyons. Nice views. But to reach the best canyon overlook on Lake Powell, which is **Ocean Point**, go due east from the spring and ruins, but stay away from the canyon rim to avoid the head of a minor drainage. When you reach the rim of Cataract, veer south to the Ocean Point itself. From various locations in that area, you can see up and down Cataract, and into Gypsum and Palmer Canyons. The altitude of the lake at the HWM is 1128 meters; while Ocean Point is about 1800. This is nearly 700 vertical meters (2300 ft) above the water, and one of the best hikes around.

In **Clearwater Canyon**, you simply walk up along the little stream with a small waterfall or two. However, you can't go far, as you'll come to a big dryfall less than 2 kms up from the mouth of the canyon. Along the way you'll see some cottonwood trees, a result of the small, clear, year-round flowing stream in the canyon. The author once saw a rattlesnake there, only one of 3 he's seen while doing the foot-

From the mouth of **Easter Pasture Canyon** (to the left out of sight) looking southeast uplake. Notice the mud bars or caked mud at the shoreline--but there's usually sandy places around to camp on.

work for 5 editions of this book.

J. W. Powell's Report From Powell's diary, which centered mostly on his 1869 trip down the Colorado, he mentions the area around Clearwater Canyon. On July 27 he states: *We have more rapids and falls until noon; then we come to a narrow place in the canyon, with vertical walls for several hundred feet, above which are steep steps and sloping rocks back to the summits. The river is very narrow, and we make our way with great care and much anxiety, hugging the wall on the left and carefully examining the way before us. Late in the afternoon we.... discover a flock of mountain sheep on the rocks more than a hundred feet [30 meters] above us. We land quickly in a cove out of sight, and away go all the hunters with their guns, for the sheep have not discovered us. Soon we hear firing, and those of us who have remained in the boats climb up to see what success the hunters have had.*

They ended up with 2 young desert big horns, which they apparently needed very badly as he later writes: *We lash our prizes to the deck of one of the boats and go on for a short distance; but fresh meat is too tempting for us, and we stop early to have a feast......We care not for bread or beans or dried apples to-night; coffee and mutton are all we ask.* Apparently they made no stops at either Easter Pasture, Clearwater or Bowdie Canyons, all of which are in this very deep and narrow section.

Bowdie Canyon makes one of the better hikes in this book. In times of low water levels, you'll have to tie-up your boat right at the mouth of the small inlet because it's now full of sand & silt and tamaracks. However, you can always walk up the dry creek bed which gets cleared out with each flash flood.

From just above the former inlet and the HWM, you will enter a narrow limestone section where you may find a trickle of water and a couple of minor water/dryfalls. After walking a short distance, you'll come to a **large pothole** which is full of water year-round. You can pass this on the right side without swimming. Or as one kayaker later told the author, you can backtrack a ways, climb up a steep talus slope, then contour or bench-walk into the canyon. But the author still hasn't tried it.

Just above the first large pothole is a 2nd one which is sometimes dry, but a chest-deep wade right after floods. About 250 meters past that you'll come to a blocking dryfall. From there backtrack 100 meters or so, and walk straight up the talus slope on the south side, then climb (a little difficult for some) up through 2 ledges, one above the other. Look for 2 stone cairns marking the way. If you're taking big packs, or have inexperienced hikers, take a short rope for these **2 ledges**. After that, bench-walk east and back into the bottom of the canyon.

After you're back in the canyon bottom, walk another 400 meters, then climb up on the right or south side to skirt the 2nd dryfall/waterfall. After another km, you'll have to leave the dry creek bed and head up a talus slope to the south again. After passing 3-4 cliff bands, contour east on a big horn & hikers trail. If you don't do this, you'll run into another blocking dryfall. After you reach the point above the **Triple Falls**, then you can reenter the creek bed, which may have a little running water. If it's not flowing, there will always be some springs or potholes around (by going all the way up Bowdie, you can exit Cataract Canyon and make it to the top of the Dark Canyon Plateau). So as not to backtrack, you can also come down on the north side of the Triple Falls as shown on the map. For more information on the upper end of Bowdie, see the author's book, *Non-Technical Canyon Hiking Guide to the Colorado Plateau.*

About 2 kms into Bowdie and high on the north side of the canyon, is lots of green vegetation and springs. Just to the left or north side of the highest spring, are **5 Anasazi structures**. To get there, climb up over 2 minor ledges to the left just before the 2nd dryfall/waterfall, then route-find up. These ruins have a roof-less kiva with corncobs, several granaries, and a very well-preserved family dwelling. Just inside the dwelling's doorway is a wind deflection wall, the first this writer has seen. These ruins seem untouched and unexplored by white men.

Hike Length & Time Needed It's about 8-9 kms from the lake to the big waterfall in **Gypsum Canyon**. The author did the round-trip hike in about 4 1/2 hours. On his 4th hike in the area when he walked up to the 9th waterfall, he did it round-trip in just over 8 hours. Some hikers may want 5-6 hours or more for the hike to Gypsum Falls and back; or maybe 8-12 hours to reach the 9th waterfall and return. Or backpack in, camp, and explore the upper end of the canyon and Fable Valley. See the book above for more details on how to hike down from the top.

It's about 2 1/2 kms from the lake to the ruins and spring in **Easter Pasture Canyon**, and about 7 kms from the lake to **Ocean Point**. The author hiked for about 7 hours (5 hours on a 3rd trip), but he did some back tracking and re-fotographing because of a brief rainstorm earlier that morning. Most people will want all or most of a day to do the Ocean Point hike, so take plenty of water and a lunch.

You can go up **Clearwater Canyon** only about 2 kms or less, so it will take just about an hour for this hike. In **Bowdie Canyon**, you can hike for an hour or two, or all day. The author hiked up to the ruins and back in less than 4 hours (another time he did the same hike, but included a loop around **Triple Falls** and back in 5 1/2 hours), but you may want 5-7 hours, round-trip.

Boots or Shoes Use rugged hiking boots in Gypsum, Palmer and Easter Pasture Canyons, but any shoe will be OK in Clearwater. In Bowdie, take wading-type shoes just in case.

Water There may be some running water in lower **Gypsum Canyon** below the falls, but it can dry up almost completely. This water comes from springs below Beef Basin, so it can't be too bad if you have to drink it as is. About one bend below Gypsum Falls, several seeps come out on the left at creek level. Another one comes out on the right 250 meters below the waterfall.

There may be several little springs & some running water in the upper basin of **Palmer Canyon**, which should always be safe to drink. In **Easter Pasture Canyon**, there's water at several locations, but the best is at the spring source near the Fremont Indian ruins. In **Clearwater Canyon**, there is a spring about 300 meters above the HWM. It should be good water anywhere along this stream's short course. There are a number of springs and running water in **Bowdie Canyon**, beginning at the HWM and beyond.

Main Attractions One of the best waterfalls (and series of waterfalls) near Lake Powell, 2 hikes to Fremont or Anasazi ruins, and to the best overlook in Cataract Canyon. You'll see the deepest and steepest part of Cataract which is between Easter Pasture and Bowdie Canyons, and a chance to see big horn sheep on the cliffs and crags of Bowdie Point. With all the water/dryfalls, Gypsum & Bowdie Canyons are 2 of the best hikes around.

Hiking Maps USGS or BLM maps Hanksville & Hite Crossing (1:100,000); Teapot Rock, Clearwater Canyon, Bowdie Canyon East & Bowdie Canyon West (1:24,000--7 1/2' quads) for hiking; Orange Cliffs and Mouth of Dark Canyon (1:62,500) if available; or Canyonlands National Park (1:62,500).

Above A private party of 2 rafting down **Cataract Canyon** just south or below the mouth of Clearwater Canyon.

Left About 500 meters into the lower end of **Clearwater Canyon** you'll find reflective pools and running water. If you need more drinking water, this is the place to stock up.

Above This is one of 5 Anasazi structures located in the lower part of **Bowdie Canyon**. These are just a few meters above the highest springs on the slopes shown on the map.

Right Looking down **Bowie Canyon** from just below the ruins shown above. To reach the ruins, leave the canyon bottom next to the trees & pool shown below, and climb up toward the lower right-hand side of this picture.

Above In **Bowdie Canyon**, this is the waterfall & spring located directly below the ruins shown on the opposite page.

Left This is what the author calls **Triple Falls** on the **Bowdie Canyon** map. You can't climb these dry-falls, but you can reach the top by walking up one of 2 talus slopes on either side of the canyon wall further downstream; once on a high bench, then contour into the canyon to the top of Triple Falls.

Cove, Rockfall and Dark Canyons

Location & Campsites Cove, Rockfall and Dark Canyons are all located in the upper end of Lake Powell, and in the lower end of **Cataract Canyon**. The mouth of Cove is very near M156 (K249), Rockfall is at about M154 (K246), and the mouth of Dark Canyon is M153 (K245) uplake from Glen Canyon Dam. Rockfall Canyon gets its name from a big **rockfall** or land slide about 400 meters upcanyon from the HWM. You can see where it has fallen off the high wall as you boat downcanyon from the north.

Dark Canyon has its beginnings on the western slopes of the Abajo Mountains and in the area north and east of Natural Bridges National Monument. Most of this canyon has been set aside as an official wilderness area and is a popular hiking region.

Most people who hike into Dark enter at Peavine or Woodenshoe Canyons on the southwest slopes of the Abajos, or via the **Sundance Trail**. The Sundance is reached by Road #2081, which begins about half a km above the **Hite turnoff** on **Highway 95** (near mile post 49). Or **best** to start near mile post 53, and drive northeast on Road #2731 for 8.1 kms (5 miles), and turn right on Road #2081. At Km 13.4 (Mile 8.3) turn left onto Road #256 and proceed to Km 18.6 (Mile 11.5) which is just past **Squaw & Papoose Rocks**. At that point turn left and drive 200 meters to the Sundance Trailhead. The trail on the mesa top is marked with cairns and is well-used. The last part of the Sundance Trail is down the steep side of lower Dark Canyon. Only the lower quarter or so of the drainage is shown on this map, as that's normally the only area of interest to Lake Powell boaters.

At or near the mouth of **Cove Canyon**, there are few if any campsites whether the lake is high or low. The former good sandy campsite at the head of **Rockfall Canyon Bay** used to be a regular stop for river runners, but it's now filled in with rocks & sand. However, the huge floods of 10/2006, washed a nice corridor through the silt bar at the entry to the bay, and you can now reach the upper canyon easily, plus there's a nice sandy campsite (**7/3/2007-WL1100.73m/3611.19'**) at the mouth of Rockfall Canyon Bay--all dependent on lake levels of course.

River runners often make **Dark Canyon** one of their campsites. If the lake level ever returns to or near the HWM, you might boat into the inlet a ways and find some sandy beaches to camp on. However, the inlet is now mostly filled in and since the 1990's, rafters have camped at the very mouth of the bay where there's at least one really good campsite on the sandy silt bars. On **7/5/2007-WL1100.68m /3611.11'**, it was a nice place. Expect changes in this campsite depending on water levels and whether the lake is rising or falling.

Hiking Routes or Trails The first drainage covered here is **Cove Canyon**. When you first look at the bottom of this canyon from the lake, it appears to be un-hikable, but there is a way into a middle basin. From the mouth of the little bay, boat uplake to the northeast about 2 kms, and tie-down on the left or west side where you see a landslide debris slope coming down from above. Walk straight up this steep slope (in 7/2007, and with low water, this did not look easy!) until you're at or just above the Elephant Canyon bench which is about halfway up to the rim (at that point it appears you can continue to climb north and reach the canyon rim, as shown by the words, *possible exit*, on the map). Once on this in-

Map 3A, Cove Canyon

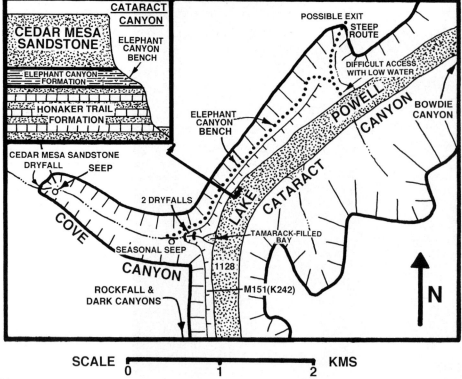

SCALE 0   1   2   KMS

Map 3, Rockfall and Dark Canyons

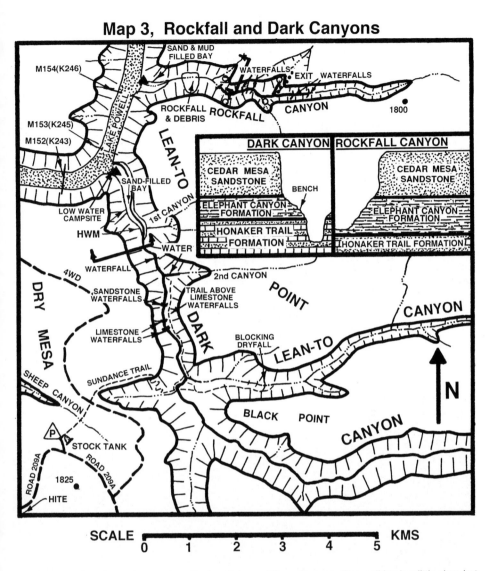

SCALE ‖▬▬▬▬▬▬▬▬▬▬▬‖ KMS
0   1   2   3   4   5

termediate level, walk southwest along the bench toward Cove Canyon. The walking is a little slow, but not difficult.

Once you reach Cove Canyon, you'll have to drop down a ways to reach the dry creek bed. At that point, you'll be above 2 big dryfalls, which appear to be in the Honaker Trail Formation. Just above the second dryfall, you may see a minor seep, a pool or two, and some cottonwood trees.

From that point, you can walk upcanyon about 1 km before coming to a blocking dryfall in the Cedar Mesa Sandstone. Along most of the way there will be cottonwood trees, but likely no running water, unless you arrive at the end of a wet spell. The walking is easy and fast. At the upper end you'll find some big boulders just below another dropoff and a minor seep at the bottom. It's likely some water will be there at all times.

The bottom end of **Rockfall Canyon** and its little bay are now (7/2007) filled in with sand & boulders from big floods and it's easy walking right from your boat. A little ways upcanyon, a large slab of Cedar Mesa Sandstone once broke off near the top of the wall on the south side and created a rock dam. After the crash, water backed up behind this dam during times of flash flooding, and filled in with sand. There's a flat sandy area behind the rocks, which looks like an **old lake bed**. Finally water burst through its dam and you now climb up through one of two "V" cuts.

Above the dam, it's easy boulder hopping for a ways, then the canyon narrows and you come to several limestone ledges which can be passed easily. From this area on up, you may see at times a small trickle of water most of the way upcanyon. It's in this part where you'll find a number of small fotogenic cascades and several waterfalls. Not far above what used to be a potty-like bridge & waterfall (taken out by the floods of 10/2006), you'll have to climb up to the right or south side, to avoid 3 waterfalls. Not far beyond, is a side-canyon entering from the north. On this side-canyon's east side, you can climb out onto the plateau, the only such exit in the canyon. It would take some time, but you could walk across the plateau west to a point overlooking Cataract Canyon.

If you continue up Rockfall Canyon, you'll have to pass another water/dryfall on the south, or right side, then after a walk through a small forest of cottonwood trees, you'll come to a blocking dryfall, which appears to be the bottom part of the Cedar Mesa Sandstone. All the way up to that point you'll see numerous springs on the south side canyon wall.

Dark Canyon In the bottom end, there are some hiker-made trails. but often times you'll just be walking along one side of the stream or the other. Dark Canyon Creek is one of the largest to enter Lake Powell and it flows year-round. However, in 7/2007, the last 2 kms was bone dry, and there were just a few pool up to within 1 km of the Sundance Trail. Beyond that there was running water.

Just after you pass the **2nd little canyon** on the left (see map), you'll come to a narrow section. First, you pass through some deep pools, before coming to a sandstone waterfall, then you may be stopped by several limestone ledges or chokestones in some short narrows. At that point you'll likely have to regress to the 2nd canyon, and follow a good cairned trail up to a major bench just above the narrows. This will put you on top of the limestone beds which created some of the waterfalls in that lower section. On that terrace you'll find a much-used hiker's trail which bypasses the waterfalls.

Beyond the limestone waterfalls, you'll drop back down into the creek bed and not far beyond, the canyon begins to open up. To the left is **Lean-to Canyon**; to the right the lower end of the **Sundance Trail**, the popular entry/exit route into the lower end of the canyon. You can walk into Lean-to Canyon on its east side, as there's a hiker-made trail going that way from near the bottom of the Sundance. With some route finding skills, you can bypass one big dryfall, then climb out the upper end (see the author's other book, *Non-Technical Canyon Guide to the Colorado Plateau, 5th Ed.* for a better description. If you stay in the bottom of Lean-to, you'll eventually come to the same type of formations as you find in Rockfall Canyon, and will be blocked by dryfalls. Above Lean-to, Dark Canyon is interesting, but not many Lake Powellers get that far.

Hike Length & Time Needed To hike to the end of **Cove Canyon** will take about half a day. The author hurried up and back just before dark, and did it round-trip in less than 3 hours. You can only walk 4-5 kms up **Rockfall Canyon**, but it's slow going, so you'll need at least half a day just to reach the blocking dryfall in the upper end and return. Much more time would be needed to exit the canyon, reach the rim of Cataract and return.

It's only 4-5 kms from the HWM in **Dark Canyon** to the bottom end of the **Sundance Trail**. You'll likely need at least 5-6 hours for a round-trip hike to the Sundance and back The author got to very near that trail, and returned in less than 3 hours once. In 7/2007, he did the same thing in 3 1/4 hours. On another hike he walked up Lean-to Canyon to the dryfall in 4 hours, round-trip.

Boots or Shoes Hiking boots are best in Cove and Rockfall Canyons, but it might pay to have waders in Dark Canyon. However, the author used leather hiking boots going up Dark and into Lean-to on one trip, and never did get them wet.

Water You will likely find some water in upper Cove Canyon, but it's best to take your own. There are several springs with good water in Rockfall Canyon, originating at the contact point between the Cedar Mesa Sandstone above, and the Elephant Canyon Formation below. The creek in Dark Canyon begins to flow about halfway down its long course, so the water couldn't be too bad as there are no cattle in the lower end of this drainage.

Main Attractions A chance to exit Cataract near Cove Canyon. Rockfall Canyon; good water, waterfalls, and a chance to exit to the rim. Dark Canyon; a very deep and rugged gorge, perhaps the most

This camp on **7/3/2007-WL1100.73m/3611.19'** was on a sandbar at the mouth of **Rockfall Canyon**.

spectacular to enter the upper end of Lake Powell. The best part of Dark Canyon is below Lean-to with all the waterfalls.

Hiking Maps USGS or BLM map Hite Crossing (1:100,000); Bowdie Canyon West & Indian Head Pass (1:24,000--7 1/2' quads) for hiking; Mouth of Dark Canyon (1:62,500) if available; or Canyonlands National Park (1:62,500).

J.W. Powell's Report On July 28, 1869, Powell must have been very near Rockfall and Dark Canyons when he wrote: *During the afternoon we run a chute more than half a mile [800 meters] in length, narrow and rapid. This chute has a floor of marble; the rocks dip in the direction in which we are going, and the fall of the stream conforms to the inclination of the beds; so we float on water that is gliding down an inclined plane.... After this the walls suddenly close in, so that the canyon is narrower than we have ever known it. The water fills it from wall to wall, giving us no landing place at the foot of the cliff; the river is very swift and the canyon very torturous, so that we can see but a few hundred yards ahead; the walls tower over us, often overhanging so as almost to shut out the light. I stand on deck, watching with intense anxiety, lest this may lead us into some danger; but we glide along, with no obstruction, no falls, no rocks, and in a mile and a half [2 1/2 kms] emerge from the narrow gorge into a more open and broken portion of the canyon. Now that it is past, it seems a very simple thing indeed to run through such a place, but the fear of what might be ahead made a deep impression on us.*

From the air looking northwest. Upper left to lower right: Cove Canyon, then **Cataract Canyon**, Rockfall Canyon (right), and **Dark Canyon** below the airplane. Also, on the right are the 2 side-drainages entering Dark Canyon from the east.

67

Above About 2 kms up **Rockfall Canyon** is what was used to be a natural bridge just to the right of the author; however, it was washed away, probably in the big floods of 10/2006.

Right This is part of the upper limestone narrows in **Dark Canyon**. There is now a good hiker's trail on the rim just above the creek on the left. This picture was taken on 7/5/2007, and although there were pools in some places, there was no running water in the lower end of Dark Canyon at that time.

Lower **Dark Canyon** and 2 small waterfalls in the sandstone part of the narrows. This picture was taken on 7/5/2007, and although there were pools around, there was no running water at that time.

Rafters breaking camp at the mouth of **Clearwater Canyon**. This picture was taken on **7/5/2007-WL1100.68m/3611.11'**, with low lake levels and lots of mud bars in **Cataract Canyon**.

Freddies Cistern and Sheep, Narrow & Rock Canyons

Location & Campsites The mouth of **Sheep Canyon** is located at the point separating lower **Cataract Canyon** and the upper part of **Narrow Canyon**. It's also M147 (K235) from Glen Canyon Dam. Sheep Canyon drains into the Colorado River Canyon at a place known as **Mille Crag Bend**, which is a very distinguishable feature on the map.

There may be several campsites in the area. The best used to be what rafters called **Sheep Canyon Campsite**, but it's only useable when the lake levels are high; when the lake is low, you can't get to it or any of the other high water sites. In times of low water, as it was on **7/8/2007-WL1100.55m/3610.70'**, you'll have silt bars which are covered with tamaracks, or you'll just get out of your boat in mud! As of 7/2007, there were no good campsites in the Mille Crag Bend area.

Hiking Routes or Trails About the only place you can hike in this area is into **Sheep Canyon**. There are no trails up this drainage, you just route-find up along the dry creek bed. However, in 7/2007, you couldn't even get past the tamarack-covered silt bars! If you do get beyond the bushwhack, it's slow-and-go all the way because you weave in and out of large boulders. After about 3 kms, you'll be able to climb up the slope to the left, or north, and get out onto the canyon rim easily. There's one good viewpoint there, or you could rim-walk west for a better view of the lake and Mille Crag Bend.

Hike Length & Time Needed In Sheep Canyon, the first place you come to where you can exit is about 3 kms from the lake. In less than half a day, you can hike the canyon and get up on the rim for some fine views. The author spent 2 2/3 hour on his round-trip hike. You may want up to 4 hours, round-trip.

Boots or Shoes Hiking boots are best, but running-type shoes will do.

Water There are no springs or streams in the area. Take your own water.

Main Attractions From above, good views of Mille Crag Bend and the canyon.

Hiking Maps USGS or BLM map Hite Crossing (1:100,000); Sewing Machine & Copper Point (1:24,000--7 1/2' quads) for hiking; or Browns Rim (1:62,500) if available.

J.W. Powell's Report On July 28, 1869, the Powell Party passed this way, and here is an excerpt from Powell's diary: *At three o'clock we arrive at the foot of Cataract Canyon. Here a long canyon valley comes down from the east, and the river turns sharply to the west in a continuation of the line of the lateral valley [Sheep Canyon]. In the bend on the right vast numbers of crags and pinnacles and tower-shaped rocks are seen. We call it Mille Crag Bend.*

And now we wheel into another canyon on swift water unobstructed by rocks. This new canyon is very narrow and very straight, with walls vertical below and terraced above. Where we enter it the brink of the cliff is 1,300 feet [400 meters] above the water, but the rocks dip to the west, and as the course of the canyon is in that direction the walls are seen slowly to decrease in altitude. Floating down this narrow channel and looking out through the canyon crevice away in the distance, the river is seen to turn again to the left, and beyond this point, away many miles, a great mountain is seen. Still floating down, we see other mountains, now on the right, now on the left, until a great mountain range is unfolded to view [Henry Mountains]. We name this Narrow Canyon, and it terminates at the bend of the river below.

As we go down to this point we discover the mouth of a stream which enters from the right. Into this our little boat is turned. The water is exceedingly muddy and has an unpleasant odor. One of the men in the boat following, seeing what we have done, shouts to Dunn and asks whether it is a trout stream. Dunn replies, much disgusted, that it is a "dirty devil," and by this name the river is to be known hereafter.

Aerial view of **Mille Crag Bend** looking north, northeast. To the lower right is the mouth of **Sheep Canyon**, and all the green you see are tamaracks (tamarisk).

Map 4, Freddies Cistern and Sheep, Narrow & Rock Canyons

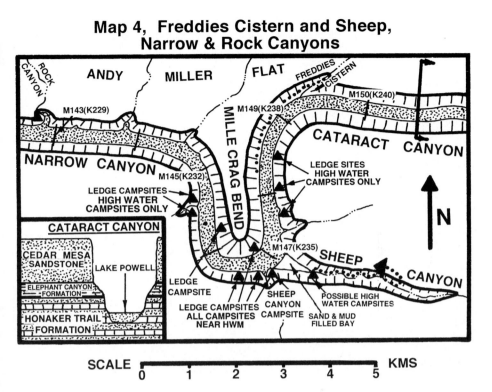

SCALE
0   1   2   3   4   5   KMS

In this area of lower Cataract, Mille Crag Bend, and Narrow Canyon, **Dellenbaugh's Diary** states on September 29, 1871: *Morning brought a continuation of the rain, which fell in a deluge, driving us to the shelter of a projecting ledge, from which comparatively dry retreat we watched the rain cascades that soon began their display. Everywhere they came plunging over the walls, all sizes, and varying their volume with every variation in the downpour. Some dropped a thousand feet [300 meters] to vanish in spray; others were broken into many falls. By half-past eight we were able to proceed, running the rapid without any trouble, but a wave drenched me so that all my efforts to keep out of the rain went for nothing. By ten o'clock we had run four more rapids, and arrived at the place the Major had named Mille-crag Bend, from the multitude of rugged pinnacles into which the cliffs broke. On the left we camped to permit the Major and Prof. to make their prospective climb to the top. A large canyon entered from the left [Sheep Canyon], terminating Cataract Canyon, which we credited with forty-one miles [66 kms], and in which I counted sixty-two rapids and cataracts,..... The Major and Prof. reached the summit at an altitude of fifteen hundred feet [450 meters]. They had a wide view over the unknown country, and saw mountains to the west with snow on their summits [Henry Mountains].*

Near our camp some caves were discovered, twenty feet deep [6 meters] and nearly six feet [2 meters] in height, which had once been occupied by natives. Walls had been laid across the entrances, and inside were corncobs and other evidences usual in this region, now so well known. Pottery fragments were also abundant. These caves are now surely filled with silt somewhere under the mouth of Sheep Canyon.

Other Canyons On this map is another short canyon which may not be hikable. This is **Freddies Cistern**. It's a long drainage, but you see only the last part as it falls over the Cedar Mesa Sandstone walls. The author went only part way up this from the lake on a late evening hike, and it appeared you couldn't get into the upper part of the drainage. At a later date, he viewed the top end of Freddies from above and from the Hite Road running along the west side of Cataract Canyon. From that vantage point it appeared a person could get up. However, there is still one problem down below. There are some ledges just above the lake which will block entry to the drainage. When the lake levels are low, as it was in the early 2000's, you'd have to tie your boat up way downcanyon somewhere along Mill Crag Bend in order to get upon one of those intermittent ledges, then walk 2-3 kms to the actual beginning of Freddies Cistern Canyon.

Still another canyon, part of which is on this map, is **Narrow Canyon**. This short section of the former Colorado River lies between Mille Crag Bend (the end of Cataract Canyon), and the mouth of the Dirty Devil River, which is the beginning of Glen Canyon. There was never any mining, nor any other activities in this section of the Colorado.

Another interesting drainage, but with no hiking possibilities, is **lower Rock Canyon**. It's located west of Mille Crag Bend in about the middle part of Narrow Canyon. It's a long drainage, but you can see the very bottom end below a high dryfall. Sometimes you may find a campsite in the back end of the tiny inlet, but in 7/2007, it was completely fill in with tamaracks. On ledges just above the HWM, are several flat spots which could be used by someone with a tent that don't use stakes (it's mostly on slickrock). There are even places which are sandy, but they're right where water comes down during flash floods. When the lake level is low, you may not get close to this one because of the brush.

Silt bars in **Cataract Canyon**. These are just across the channel from the mouth of **Rockfall Canyon**.

From the air and almost directly above Hite, looking north at the Highway 95 bridge over the **Colorado River/Upper Lake Powell**. This bridge marks the end of Narrow Canyon.

Above This picture was taken on **7/8/2007- WL1100.55m/3610.70'**. It shows one of 2 more-or-less homemade launching ramps at **Hite**. This is the one below the end of the cement ramp that most people have known for years. The other possible launch site is just to the south and below where the old floating Hite Marina used to be. By 9/2007, the water level was so low, it was impossible to launch a boat from either of these sites.

Left From the air looking south from above the lower end of the **Dirty Devil River**. Lower left, the bridge over the Dirty Devil; to the right is the Dirty Devil high-water camping & launching area; and in the upper part of the picture is the Colorado River/Upper Lake Powell. Just beyond the top of this foto is the Hite area.

Dirty Devil River, North Wash, and Farley & White Canyons

Location & Campsites Of all the drainages discussed in this section, **White Canyon** is the only one with hiking possibilities. White Canyon Inlet is located 7-8 kms south of Hite. Out in the main channel you will likely find a buoy marked M135 (K216) or M135 A. From the main channel you can boat into the common mouth of both Farley or White Canyons. Also, as shown on the map, you can drive from Highway 95 down into **White or Farley Canyons**. Of the two, Farley is the only one with any camping facilities or where you can launch a boat. Even when lake levels are low as was the case on **7/8/2007-WL1100.55m/3610.70'**, you could still launch from Farley, but the ramp and facilities were not good. As you boat into upper White Canyon Inlet, you'll find several good sites for putting up a tent from a boat. However, when the lake levels are low you can't boat very far into this inlet. After the 1990's, no one was driving to, and/or camping in this bay, nor were there any boaters going that way from the lake.

Hiking Routes or Trails The lower end of **White Canyon** is one of the most exciting non-technical slot canyon hikes on the entire Colorado Plateau. Non-boaters normally visit the most interesting part of the canyon, called the **Black Hole**. They enter the canyon near **mile post 57** on **Highway 95**, and leave at one of 2 exits leading toward **mile post 55**, as shown on the map. Boaters can walk up the canyon from the lake, but if the lake level is low as it was in 7/2007, you'll have to walk a couple of kms just to reach the end of the canyon. Best to do the Black Hole from your car and the highway.

Walking up lower White Canyon from the lake, the drainage at first is shallow, but gets deeper with every bend. If there has been a recent rainstorm, expect to wade through some pools beginning below the highway bridge. It's moderately narrow and deep until after about 10-11 kms, then it really tightens up, and you'll have to start wading, then you'll have to swim to get through the narrowest parts.

There is one section of the Black Hole where you have to walk under a large pile of tree trunks and other debris. This pile of debris is about 10 meters above and forms a tunnel 15 meters in length. Just above this tunnel is the main part where you'll have to swim a total of 4 long frigid pools (one is down-canyon from the tunnel) for a total of about 150 meters. However, it could be difficult to get through going upcanyon if the potholes are low on water. Because of this, it's best to hike downcanyon rather than up.

Something else that's very important, don't hike into this canyon during periods of bad weather. Also, be aware this is a long drainage, and floods beginning upcanyon near Natural Bridges National Monument will take 18-24 hours to reach this lower section. Always check on weather and other conditions with the rangers or someone at the store at Hite before entering this canyon.

If you do go through the Black Hole, here are some tips. First, put everything that can get damaged by water in a boater's waterproof **dry bag**, then put that inside a small day-pack. This will include a lunch, wallet, car keys, perhaps dry clothes, etc. So you get lots of good pictures, use a small plastic waterproof case for your camera and wear it on a belt around your waist. Pelican and Otter make good cases. Also include a **short rope about 10 meters long** to help less-experienced hikers. Take water, and an **empty plastic water bottle** in your pack. This will add to flotation because you will swim through the long pools with the pack on your back. Another thing, if you have a **wetsuit**, take it. The climate is dry and the water evaporates quickly, leaving behind refrigerator-cold water that never sees the sun. **Hypothermia** is a real danger. Do this hike only in warm or hot weather--from about **June 1 to mid-September**. Start hiking after 10am and arrive at the Black Hole swimming part about 2pm for more light

This picture of the **Black Hole** in **White Canyon** was taken on 6/21/2004. The flood that brought in all these logs occured in 9/2003; then the 10/2006 floods scoured them out (Steve Tyler foto).

Map 5, Farley and Lower White Canyons

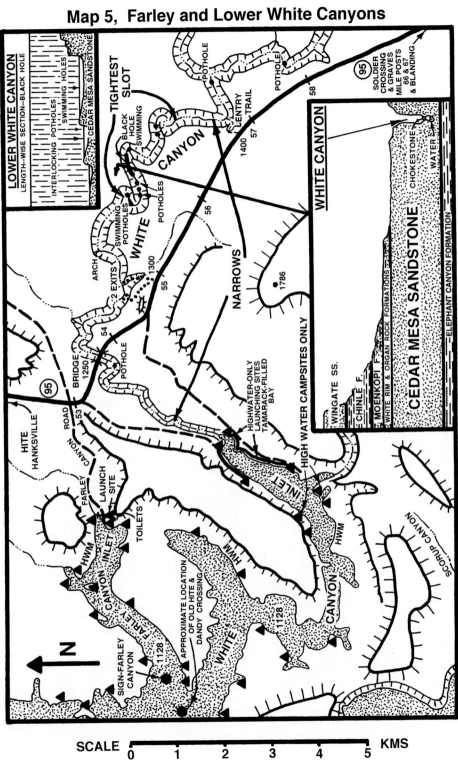

SCALE

0   1   2   3   4   5   KMS

and warmer temps. During spring or fall, using a wetsuit is mandatory. Also, the first of 2 exits leading south toward mile post 55 can be difficult for some; this means the **2nd exit is a little easier**. Look for cairns on the left or south side of the canyon wall. Also, if you're taking younger people through, you might equip them with life preservers.

The entry at mile post 57 is easy. Walk due north on a hiker's trail from a big sign at the entry park-ing lot. You'll then enter White Canyon via a small side-canyon or cleft, then just head downcanyon. Each group should have at least one experienced slot canyon hiker. Go prepared, and this can be one of the best hikes on or near Lake Powell.

Hike Length & Time Needed You might consider seeing the lower end of White Canyon from your boat (only if the lake level is high), and the Black Hole part from your car. If you do the mile post 57 to mile post 55 loop, it will still take about 5-7 hours.

Boots or Shoes Wading-type shoes.

Water There will always be pothole water in White Canyon, but take your own drinking water.

Main Attractions One of the most exciting and challenging slot canyon hikes found anywhere.

Hiking Maps USGS or BLM map Hite Crossing (1:100,000); Copper Point (1:24,000--7 1/2' quad) for hiking; or Browns Rim (1:62,500) if available.

Other Canyons and J.W. Powell's & Dellenbaugh's Diaries Just north of the former Hite Marina (in 2007, the marina was gone due to low water, but a small store & gas station, and motel were still there) and the mouth of North Wash is where the Dirty Devil River enters the lake. This was a stopping place for both of Powell's River Expeditions. On the first trip the Dirty Devil was given its name. During the second expedition, here are some of the things written in Dellenbaugh's Diary for September 30, 1871: *Having now accomplished a distance down this turbulent river of nearly six hundred miles [1000 kms], with a descent toward sea-level of 2607 feet [800 meters], without a serious accident, we were all in a happy frame of mind, notwithstanding the exceedingly diminutive food supply that remained. We felt that we could overcome almost anything in the line of rapids the world might afford, and Steward declared our party was so efficient he would be willing to "run the Gates of Hell".....*

Apparently they were considering still another trip down the river in the future, for they decided to leave one of their 3 boats at the mouth of the Dirty Devil. Their supplies were low anyway and they had no need for 3 boats. Dellenbaugh went on to say: *The Cañonita was chosen and the day after our ar-rival, Sunday, October 1st, we ran her down a short distance on the right, and there carried her back about two hundred feet [60 meters] to a low cliff and up thirty or forty feet [10 to 12 meters] above the prevailing stage of water, where we hid her under an enormous mass of rock which had so fallen from the top......*

The **Dirty Devil River** is a long drainage with a sinuous lower canyon, but in the summer of 1988 with the lake level 2 meters below the HWM, boaters could only go up a short distance. As the name im-plies, this is a very muddy stream much of the time, and the upper inlet is filling up with sediment rap-idly. Because of the north-south situation of the canyon and the prevailing south winds, the driftwood is constantly pushed into the northern part of the inlet. This, along with the sand or silt bars, makes it impossible to get to the end of the lake waters.

By the early 2000's, there was no inlet whatsoever; just the Dirty Devil draining directly into the Col-orado River. For about 3 years, the lake didn't even make it up that far; and the nearby Dirty Devil

On June 21, 2004, the **Black Hole** in **White Canyon** had lots of swimming through "log soup" like this. However, by 10/2006, big floods took out all or most of the logs.

campsite next to Highway 95, was high & dry and unused. You can still use that campsite, but you have to pay a fee (?), and you can't even begin to launch a boat from there.

Back to history. According to C. Gregory Crampton, one of the men who researched the historic sites in Glen Canyon before Lake Powell times: *during the gold mining period in Glen Canyon, the Dirty Devil marked the practical upper limits of prospecting. It does not appear from any records or from physical evidence that any extensive placering took place above it. Robert B. Stanton in 1897, in anticipation of mining operations for the Hoskaninni Company, actually surveyed two dam sites in the narrow lower canyon of the Dirty Devil. He planned to use the dammed waters of the river downstream along the Colorado for mining purposes, and for the generation of electric power.*

North Wash Going back in time to the second Powell Expedition of 1871. From the Dirty Devil River and their camp, part of the men went downstream a ways to the mouth of North Wash where they found an Indian trail. This is where: *Prof. and Cap. climbed out, after following the trail up the gulch six miles [10 kms], and they saw that it went toward the Unknown Mountains [Henry Mountains], which now lay very near us on the west. Steward.... with his glass was able to study their formation and determined that lava from below had spread out between the sedimentary strata, forming what he called "blisters." He could see where one side of a blister had been eroded, showing the surrounding stratification.* These blisters were later called **laccoliths** by G.K. Gilbert in his study of the Henry Mountains in the mid-1870's.

As the 1871 party left the mouth of North Wash, they were traveling in 2 boats, the Dean and the Nell. Dellenbaugh went on to say: *Each man had charge of a cabin and this was Cap's special pride. He daily packed it so methodically that it became a standing joke with us, and we often asked him whether he always placed the thermometer back of the fifth rib or in front of the third, or some such nonsensical question, which of course Cap took in good part and only arranged his cabin still more carefully.*

Just across the lake from present-day Hite and the little launching areas, is the mouth of **North Wash**. If you're driving south from Hanksville heading for Hite, this is the canyon the present-day highway runs through. In the years just before Lake Powell, the road across southeastern Utah went down North Wash, then south or down along the Colorado River to Hite and Dandy Crossing where the ferry was located; then up White Canyon. But originally, and in the days of Cass Hite and the Glen Canyon Gold Rush (about 1884 to 1900), the main trail into this region was down **Trachyte Creek**, across the river at Hite ferry and up White Canyon to Bluff.

In 1889, **Robert B. Stanton**, who was originally a railroad engineer, brought boats down to the Colorado via North Wash and went down the river. He worked for a group of investors who were considering running a railroad down the Colorado River to California. Read more on his story under **Map 12, Stanton Canyon**, and in this book's **Introduction**.

The original name for North Wash was Crescent Creek, but sometime during the later gold rush days its name was changed. The upper part of this drainage on the east side of Mt. Ellen, is still called Crescent Creek. There was much placer mining activity along the mouth of North Wash prior to about 1900, then during the 1950's uranium boom, there was still more activity in the lower end of the canyon where the Chinle clay beds are exposed.

Farley Canyon This drainage shares the same common mouth with White Canyon. Farley is one of the places you can drive to from Highway 95 (about 3 kms/2 miles) and launch a boat. There are many good campsites (with a couple of toilets) at the end of the improved graveled road, as well as

More swimming in "log soup" in the **Black Hole**. By 10/2006, these logs and other debris were gone.

other sites (boater access only) along the inlet leading to the main channel of the lake. If you're driving to this launch site, turn west off Highway 95 near mile post 53, about 7 kms (4 miles) south of the turnoff to Hite.

The first Powell Expedition stopped at the very mouth of White & Farley Canyon on July 29, 1869. In his diary for that day Powell states: *We enter a canyon to-day, with low, red walls. A short distance below it's head we discover the ruins of an old building on the left wall. There is a narrow plain between the river and the wall just here, and on the brink of a rock 200 feet [60 meters] high stands this old house. Its walls are of stone, laid in mortar with much regularity. It was probably built three stories high; the lower story is yet almost intact; the second is much broken down, and scarcely anything is left of the third. Great quantities of flint chips are found on the rocks near by, and many arrowheads, some perfect, others broken; and fragments of pottery are strewn about in great profusion. On the face of the cliff, under the building and along down the river for 200 or 300 yards [180 to 270 meters], there are many etchings [petroglyphs].*

In the days of the gold rush when the tiny town of Hite was in its hey day, this structure was given the name **Fort Moqui.** It seems that everyone who passed that way stopped and had a look around. Crampton, who studied the site just before Lake Powell covered this site, made a list of the names which were inscribed on the walls of Fort Moqui. The oldest readable date was from 1884. Read more on Hite and the ferry under *Map 6, Trachyte and Swett Canyons.*

It was on October 2, 1871 and during the second Powell Expedition, that Dellenbaugh describes the state of the river below the mouth of White Canyon and Hite: *The river, some three hundred and fifty feet [110 meters] wide, was low, causing many shoals, which formed the small rapids. We often had to walk alongside the boats, but otherwise these places were easy. A trifle more water would have done away with them, or at least would have enabled us to ignore them completely.*

An interesting event happened in the middle part of White Canyon in 1884. The story actually began on July 7, near the Utah-Colorado state line in a tributary canyon in the lower end of Montezuma Creek. There was an argument between a group of Piutes and several cowboys over the rightful ownership of a horse. The whites were quick to claim the horse, and ended up shooting and wounding one Indian by the name of Brooks. Then there was a big shootout with 2 cowboys being wounded as they tried to leave the scene.

The cowboys escaped and headed for Colorado where they rounded up a group of whites including soldiers, and began hot pursuit. The Piutes, which included a whole band of men, women and children, went north and northwest around the southern part of the Abajo Mountains. All the while, they stayed just out of rifle range, and just ahead of their pursuers. From the area of the **Woodenshoe Buttes,** just north of Natural Bridges National Monument, they headed southwest into White Canyon.

In the middle part White Canyon, the Indians headed south over what has been known ever since as **Piute Pass.** To reach the top of Piute Pass, it was necessary to go up a narrow trail under some cliffs. The Indians waited on top, while 2 white men advanced into a trap. There was another gun battle and the 2 whites were shot and left to lie in the hot sun. That day was **July 14, 1884.** The Piutes pinned down the rest of the soldiers, not allowing them to come to aid their wounded companions. In the night the Piutes took all the valuables from the 2 men, who were by then dead. One of the men was a soldier named Worthington, the other a cowboy named Wilson.

From Piute Pass, the Indians headed south into Red Canyon and to the Colorado River. From there a trail went south along the river to what is now **Good Hope Bay.** They got to the canyon rim along an **old trail** on the southwest side of the bay (this was later developed into a stock trail which you can see and use today). From the rim (according to the late Melvin Dalton of Monticello) they must have dropped down into a north fork of **Cedar Canyon,** then moved up the main fork, over a divide, and down into the upper end of **Moqui Canyon** (cowboys always knew this as **North Gulch**). They left upper Moqui by way of a big sand slide north of **Burnt Spring,** and finally headed southwest to **Lake Pagahrit.**

The **Hite Ferry** which was in operation until July, 1963 (Crampton foto).

The Piutes camped at Lake Pagahrit for one week. They vented some of their frustration toward the whites by shooting all the cattle they saw. They feasted on some of the beef while other cows were shot with arrows and left to run around looking like pin cushions. When they left Lake Pagahrit, it's believed they headed southwest over **Wilson** and **Gray Mesas**, then down **Wilson Canyon** to the **San Juan**. The soldiers and cowboys in pursuit, lost the trail not far from Pagahrit, and never knew for sure which way they went.

Perhaps the first man to write about this story was Albert R. Lyman. In his book, ***The Outlaw of Navajo Mountain,*** he called much of this route, at least that part from White Canyon to the San Juan, **The Old Trail**. It was quite obviously a trail well-known by the various Indian groups, but not the whites. It appears Lyman had gotten at least part of his information from some of the Piute Indians who were in that group.

The place where the 2 white men were buried is located between **mile posts 66 & 67** on Highway 95 southeast of Hite (see foto on page 97). Look for the sign stating **Soldier's Grave**. It's just off the paved highway north and at the beginning of a road which crosses White Canyon and heads east towards Cheesebox Canyon. The graves are in a small fenced enclosure.

Sometime in 2007, someone erected a new chain link fence around the graves, plus a large metal sign telling the story.

This was the 2nd of 2 big log jams in the **Black Hole** of **White Canyon** in the summer of 2004. They were deposited by big floods in 9/2003, and all were taken out by even bigger floods of 10/2006.

Trachyte and Swett Creek Canyons

Location & Campsites The bay to **Trachyte Creek Canyon** is located about 8 kms southwest of present-day Hite. The buoy in the channel reads M134 (K214). The bay is about 5 kms long at full pool and seems to be a fairly popular place to fish and camp, although there aren't many good campsites. There will always be some kind of camping place at the very mouth of both Trachyte or Swett Creeks (only during times of high water), and several more in the inlet leading out in the lake, but they are on the less-desirable clay beds of the Chinle Formation.

Hiking Routes or Trails Trachyte Creek is a wide canyon with a year-round flowing stream. Parts of this drainage are used during the winter months for cattle grazing, so you'll find some trails, but normally you just walk in or beside the small creek. This canyon has no obstructions and it was the original route from Hanksville to Hite and/or Dandy Crossing before the road was built down North Wash--which was the better route for wagons. Three kms up Trachyte Creek from the HWM is a side-drainage coming in from the left or west. This is **Woodruff Canyon**. You can walk up Woodruff quite easily; first past one large chokestone which has made a pool of water on the lee-side (maybe some wading), then up and over one waterfall on the right, and finally up along a small stream to Highway 276 near mile post 12.

About 5 kms past Woodruff Canyon is **Trail Canyon**. This drainage is featureless, but it's an easy and quick way to enter or exit the Trachyte Valley from the highway. Another canyon and small stream enters Trachyte Creek from the west about 1 km above or north of Trail Canyon. This is **Maidenwater Creek**, and it's the most interesting side-drainage to Trachyte Creek. It has a live beaver population and small year-round stream. You may encounter several large chokestones and pools, but these change with every flood. There are also some pretty good fotogenic narrows. However, for Maidenwater, it's easier & faster to hike down from the highway, then return via Trail Canyon.

Now for **Swett Creek** which is the first canyon you'll come to on the left as you walk up Trachyte Creek from the lake. You'll first come to water pouring over a limestone ledge (sometimes it's a dryfall as in 7/2007), then the canyon narrows and deepens. About 4 kms from the lake you'll come to the Wingate Narrows. In April, 2001, there was a big chokestone & pool at the beginning of this semi slot. Further along, the canyon turns to a slot where it winds through the Navajo Sandstone. You can walk all the way to Highway 276, to between mile posts 13 & 14. In the **South Fork of Swett Creek**, you will find a moderately narrow canyon, with several minor seeps and places where large boulders have cluttered the creek bed. The author has been in this canyon twice.

Hike Length & Time Needed All the hikes to the various side-canyons discussed here are day hikes, with none being too long. However, the walk to the upper parts of Maidenwater (about 10 kms) is an all-day affair, as is the hike to the highway through Swett Creek. To go halfway up the South Fork of Swett Creek and back, is half a day or less. If the lake levels are real low as on **7/8/2007-WL1100.55m /3610.70'**, it's best to hike from the highway.

Boots or Shoes Wading shoes for Trachyte drainage and dry weather boots or shoes into Swett Creek.

Water Don't drink the water in the Trachyte Canyons; cattle graze somewhere in that drainage much of the year. However, there is at least one spring near the creek just above the confluence with Woodruff

This 3-meter-high water/dryfall is located about 1 km up **Swett Creek** from its confluence with **Trachyte Creek**. This picture was taken on 7/8/2007 during a long drought. On all his previous trips, the author found this to be a waterfall; but on this day it was bone dry.

Map 6, Trachyte and Swett Creek Canyons

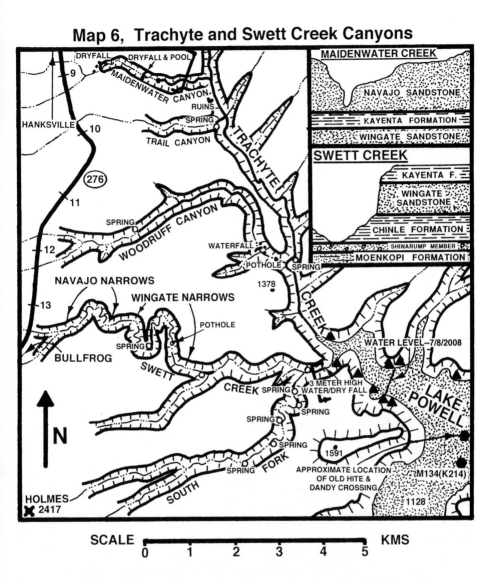

SCALE 0 1 2 3 4 5 **KMS**

Canyon. There's also a good spring in lower Trail Canyon which should be drinkable as is.

The author recalls at least three minor seeps along Swett Creek. Take water where it comes out of the ground and it should be good as it seems there are no cattle in Swett Creek. South Fork seeps have good water but there's not much to see.

Main Attractions Good narrows, wading in some deep pools, a live beaver population, and a small Anasazi shelter along Trachyte Creek between Trail and Maidenwater Canyons. Also a nice 3-meter-high waterfall/dryfall in Swett Canyon.

Hiking Maps USGS or BLM map Hite Crossing (1:100,000); Mount Holmes & Hite South (1:24,000--7 1/2' quads) for hiking; or Browns Rim & Mt. Hillers (1:62,500) if available.

History of Hite and Dandy Crossing Much of the following information comes from the work of C. Gregory Crampton who studied Glen Canyon in the late 1950's and early 1960's. His research has been written up in the *Anthropological Papers* published by the University of Utah.

According to Crampton who interviewed Art Chaffin in 1960, the first white occupant in the Hite area was **Joshua Swett**, a squaw man, who allegedly stole horses on one side of the river and sold them on the other. He arrived in 1872 and built a cabin at the mouth of Swett Creek, about 6-7 kms from the Colorado. When Hite arrived in 1883, Swett left. Then Hite moved the Swett Cabin down to the river where it stayed until Lake Powell covered it in 1964.

The town of **Hite** was founded upon the arrival of **Cass Hite** to Glen Canyon on September 19, 1883. He had fled Arizona under threats of being scalped by Navajos, and had entered the area via White Canyon to the east. Chief Hoskaninni of the Navajos had told him of gold in the canyon. The location where Cass Hite first settled, and what was later known as Hite City, is about 8 kms south or downstream from the present-day Hite, and near the mouths of White and Trachyte Canyons.

When Hite first reached the Colorado from the east through White Canyon, he found a good place to cross, which he called **Dandy Crossing**. As it turned out, it was the best place to cross the Colorado in all of Glen Canyon. The normal way through southeastern Utah in the days after Hite's arrival, was to pass through Hanksville, south and down Trachyte Creek (later, the normal route went down North Wash), cross at Dandy Crossing, then up White Canyon and on to Blanding or Bluff.

Soon after Hite arrived, he discovered gold in the sand bars of the Colorado. This led to 2 minor gold rushes; one lasting from about 1884 until around 1890; the other from about 1893 until 1900. Crampton believes there were probably no more than a 1000 men in the canyon at any one time, so the Glen Canyon Gold Rush wasn't of the same magnitude as the California or Yukon Gold Rushes.

As it turned out, the gold was very hard to get out of the sand. It was in the form of fine dust, which tended to float away in the panning process. Another problem miners encountered was the lack of water. It proved difficult to get river water up to the higher bars, where most of the gold was located. There were a few side-canyon streams, but they flooded periodically washing everything away. Water wheels were used in a place or two, but with little success, and pumping the muddy water out of the river quickly wore out the pump's gears. The best way to get the gold was simply with a shovel, some form of sluice, and a pan.

After Hite moved the Swett Cabin down to the river, he was followed by his 2 brothers. The family ran the post office (which opened in 1889), and a store for many years. The Hite brothers stayed in the canyon until Cass Hite died at his ranch on **Ticaboo Creek** in 1914 (see **Map 8, Ticaboo Creek**).

Cass Hite may have put his name on the town and ferry crossing, but he never did build or operate a real ferry himself. For years those who wanted to cross just swam their animals over, or floated their wagons across on driftwood logs found along the river. There was never really a ferry, and it was never a ford, because animals always had to swim. Actually, Hite did have a small row boat, which some people either borrowed or rented. The Scorups used it several times in the 1890's to help get some of their stubborn cows across the river.

In 1907 or 1908, a man named **Harshberger** built and operated the first real ferry in the area, but it was about 5 kms upstream or north of Hite, where the later Hite Ferry was located. The boat itself measured about 4 x 9 meters. At the time, the price of copper was high, and Harshberger had found some deposits in upper White Canyon and established a mine. With the use of the ferry, he was able to take the copper to the railway at Green River via North Wash and Hanksville. Apparently Harshberger's ferry service stopped, when the price of copper dropped after only a year or two.

There is no record of regular ferry service at Hite again until 1946. **Arthur L. Chaffin** moved to Hite in 1932, and ran a farm. It was he and other local people who, over the years, opened a real road from Hanksville to Hite. Finally the state got involved, and built a road from Hanksville to Blanding. It was Art Chaffin who supplied the last link. He opened the first auto ferry service at Hite on September 17, 1946. This ferry, along with a small store, ran continuously until June 5, 1964, when the rising waters of Lake Powell forced the closure.

Because of the opening of the road and ferry, more mineral exploration began in the area. Uranium was found in upper White Canyon, and in 1949, the Vanadium Corporation of America and the Atomic Energy Commission opened an experimental mill just across the river from Hite at the mouth of White

Right at the junction of **Swett Creek** and its **South Fork**, is this unusual & fotogenic rock. The South Fork heads off to the left.

Canyon. Shortly thereafter, a one-room school opened with 30 pupils. One of the teachers at White Canyon was the late great **Pearl Biddlecome Baker**, the same cowgirl who grew up on the Robbers Roost Ranch and who later wrote the books, *The Wild Bunch at Robbers Roost* and *Robbers Roost Recollections* and several others. A post office opened as well. The school closed about the time the mill shut down in 1954, but the post office stayed open until 1964.

About 2 kms up the **South Fork** of **Swett Creek** is this colorful undercut made from Wingate Sandstone with an added touch of desert varnish.

Twomile, Fourmile, Scorup, Blue Notch and Red Canyons

Location & Campsites The 2 hikable canyons on this map, **Twomile & Fourmile**, are only 2-3 kms apart, and together they are 12-14 kms southwest or downlake from Hite. The buoy nearest Twomile Canyon Bay is marked M132 (K211); while near Fourmile Canyon Inlet one is labeled M130B (K208).

This is an area with limited campsites; the shoreline is either rough & rocky, which makes less than desirable campsites, or in some cases the Chinle clay beds extend down to the shore. In other places the Shinarump Member of the Chinle is exposed at the high water shoreline, and it creates a flat-top bench and a low cliff. As of **7/7/2007-WL1100.58m/3610.70'**, the shoreline was covered with cheat grass, tumbleweed & tamaracks. Not many places to pitch a tent! In Twomile, there is normally one sandy place right where the creek bed enters the lake, regardless of lake levels. In Fourmile, there are some small sites available, at least when the lake is high.

Hiking Routes or Trails In **Twomile Canyon**, you'll begin at about where the Shinarump Member of the Chinle Formation is exposed. First you'll pass a dryfall, then a series of potholes as the usually-dry stream bed drops down through a sandstone layer (Shinarump). About 1 km above the potholes is a steep place in the canyon where boulders have come down near a spring. In hot weather, you'll enjoy drinking this spring water; it seems very cold on a hot day and tastes good too. Drink it where it flows from beneath a large boulder right in the creek bed.

On the author's visit he went around the south side of these big boulders located at what he is calling **Coldwater Spring**. However, in talking about the canyon with the late Riter Ekker, an old-time cattleman from Hanksville, he was told of a trail of some kind around the north side of these boulders and on the slope with all the cottonwood trees and other greenery. According to Ekker, years ago a man named Tom Humphrey ran cattle in Twomile Canyon and he built a trail around the boulders which allowed his stock to graze both the upper and lower ends of the drainage. On a second trip up, the author found no trace of a trail, but the slope is gradually slipping away, so over the years the trail seems to have disappeared.

Above Coldwater Spring, it's fairly easy walking, with about 3 more minor seeps (maybe dry?) with good water. In the upper end, you can route-find up to the right or north, and exit the canyon. It's possible to climb Mt. Holmes from the lake via this canyon, but low water levels will make it a long hike.

Fourmile Canyon is similar to Twomile with the same geologic formations. Right at the HWM is a good little seep and running water, which the author drank on 3 different trips. There are several seeps and flowing water for short distances in the lower end of the canyon. About 1 1/2 kms up the drainage from the HWM is the scene of a **big wall collapse** dating from the mid-1990's. During flashfloods, this blocks the normally-dry Fourmile Canyon Creek to create 2 small ponds of up to 5 meters deep just above the blockage. Pass this on the **left** going upcanyon. A couple of the boulders are the size of small apartment houses! Halfway up the canyon, you'll come to some deep narrows and potholes. This is where the stream bed cuts deep into the Wingate Sandstone. Further up is **Fourmile Spring**, once used by stockmen.

From near Fourmile Spring, you could walk north and climb the rugged Mt. Holmes. Or you could continue straight up the canyon to the west, go over a pass, and end up on **Highway 276** at **mile post 20**. From near that pass, you could climb south and reach the summit of Mt. Ellsworth, but it's a lot eas-

Aerial view looking west at **Fourmile Canyon** left, and **Twomile** on the right. In the background is **Mt. Ellsworth** left, **Mt. Holmes** right. Of the 2 canyons, Fourmile is the more interesting.

Map 7, Twomile and Fourmile Canyons

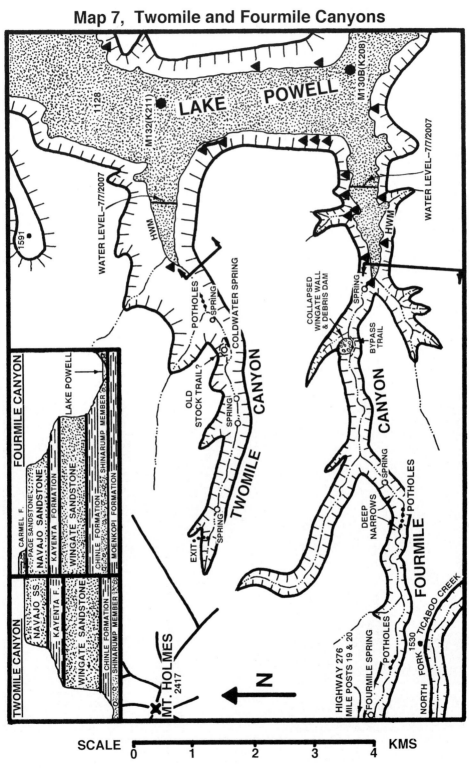

SCALE

0   1   2   3   4   KMS

ier to climb from the highway and mile post 20.

You could also walk south from the upper end of Fourmile, and drop down into the upper end of the North Fork of Ticaboo Creek, which is described in detail under the next map.

Hike Length & Time Needed It's about 6 kms from the HWM to the exit in upper Twomile Canyon. The author's trip lasted 3 1/2 hours, so you'll need at least half a day round-trip, maybe more. The author once walked from Highway 276 to the lake in Fourmile Canyon in 8 1/2 hours, round-trip. A long hike. He's also been up from the lake several times on half-day hikes.

Boots or Shoes Any kind of light weight hiking boots or shoes will be fine.

Water There are several seeps and springs in both canyons which the author drank from. Hopefully, most of these seeps will be flowing on a year-round basis. Take water from the spring source and it should be drinkable as is.

Main Attractions Solitude in seldom visited canyons, and for hardy climbers, a chance to climb either of the 2 peaks making up the Little Rockies part of the Henry Mountains. The Little Rockies are Mts. Ellsworth at 2510 meters, and Holmes at 2417 meters.

Hiking Maps USGS or BLM map Hite Crossing (1:100,000); Mount Holmes & Hite South (1:24,000--7 1/2' quads) for hiking; or Browns Rim (1:62,500) if available.

Other Canyons and History Just a few kms south or downlake from Two & Fourmile Canyons, and on the east side of the lake, are 3 more drainages, 2 of which share a common mouth. These are **Scorup, Red and Blue Notch Canyons**. Look at one of the maps showing all of Lake Powell as these drainages are not shown on the map in this book. Nor do they have interesting hiking possibilities.

About 5-6 kms downlake from Fourmile (near buoy M169 (K206), around the big horseshoe-shaped bend called **The Horn**, and on the east side of the lake, is a small drainage called **Scorup Canyon**. If you were to walk up this short drainage, you'd end up in the lower end of White Canyon, just over a low divide. It got its name from the Scorup Brothers cattle outfit who ran livestock in this area from 1891 until 1965. Read about the Scorups in the **Introduction** to this book under *History of the Cattle Industry*.

Just inside the broad mouth of Red Canyon, which is located at about M125 (K198) and buoy O & N, and just after you pass around **Castle Butte** on your left, you can enter the short inlet of **Blue Notch Canyon**. This is a short tributary of the much larger Red Canyon. At the end of the inlet, you will see a road. This 4WD track leaves Highway 95 between mile posts 59 & 60, and runs southwest over Blue Notch Pass and down to the lake. Before Lake Powell, this road was used for access to copper and uranium mines in the area. There may be a number of good campsites in this inlet, but are likely to be covered with tamaracks, cheat grass & tumbleweeds; even if the water gets up that far again (?).

If you continue southeast from the mouth of Blue Notch, you'll be in the larger **Red Canyon Bay**. This is another bay with shallow water along the shoreline. Some of the shoreline rocks are part of the Moenkopi Formation, while just above these reddish siltstones are the clay beds of the Chinle Formation. There are many uranium mines, prospects and old mining exploration roads in this canyon above the lake. Uranium mining was most active in Red Canyon in the 1950's.

The roads you see heading southeast from the head of the inlet eventually reach pavement on Highway 276, which links Highway 95 and Halls Crossing Marina. The canyon has running water in some places and at certain times, but since it comes out of clay beds, it won't taste good.

This picture was taken on **7/8/2007-WL1100.55m/3610.70'** at **Hite**. The NPS had extended the launching ramp using gravel to cover mud well beyond the end of the cement ramp shown here. By **9/8/2007**, the water level had fallen to **1098.14m/3602.85'** and no boats could be launched.

In the pre-Lake Powell days, there was an interesting old miner's log cabin located at the mouth of Red Canyon. It measured 3 x 5 meters, was built with squared logs, and had a stone fireplace. No one seems to know for sure who built it or when it was built, but it surely must have been built during the gold rush days, sometime between 1884 & 1900. In 1909, a miner named **Albert "Bert" Loper** moved in and lived there for 5 years. Loper called it his **Hermitage**. He apparently left in 1914, the same year Cass Hite died at his ranch on Ticaboo Creek (see next map).

It's been said that Loper dammed Red Creek in order to have water to run his placer mining operation on a nearby river bar and to irrigate a small farm of about one hectare (2 acres). Loper brought several pieces of farm equipment to the canyon. In later years (1952) it was reported by a river runner that a family was living in the cabin and doing a little farming themselves.

In his later years, Bert Loper became a river guide and took many people down the Colorado. He did this until he was 80 years of age. In July of 1949, he was drowned in the Colorado River somewhere in the Grand Canyon. Read about the life of Bert Loper in the book, *Trail on the Water*, by the late great Pearl Bittlecome Baker, the gal who grew up on the Robbers Roost Ranch east of Hanksville.

This is part of the deep narrows in the upper end of **Fourmile Canyon**.

Ticaboo Creek and South Fork Canyons

Location & Campsites The mouth of **Ticaboo Creek** is about 27 kms (17 miles) southwest of Hite and near to what should be M122 (K195) from the Glen Canyon Dam. Near this bay is a buoy marked "I".
There are not many campsites in this region, either in Ticaboo Bay or the main channel. However, there will always be one or 2 good sandy campsites at the head of the inlet regardless of the lake level. Not far away, there are some really great sandy beaches south of Ticaboo and on the southeastern shore of **Good Hope Bay** (see next map).

Hiking Routes or Trails Right at the HWM at the upper end of the Ticaboo Bay, you'll find running water and a nice spring coming out of a crack in the wall on the left. The author calls this **Wall Spring**. This will be one of the best places around to stock up on water. About 150 meters above this spring is the beginning of running water which used to flow past the now-submerged **Ticaboo Ranch** belonging to **Cass Hite**, and on to the Colorado River (read more on Cass Hite below).

Just upcanyon a short distance from the beginning of the running water, is a fork in the drainage. The one on the right or north, is the main fork of Ticaboo Creek. The one on the left or south, is the **South Fork of Ticaboo**. South Fork is the most interesting canyon in the immediate area. After 4-5 kms, you'll see a short side-drainage to the left, or south. Up this a ways, and on the east side, is a large cave once used by Indians, probably what we call today the Fremonts. After another 3-4 kms, and just before the canyon begins to really narrow, look to your left on the south side wall to locate an **old stock trail**.

One resident of Hanksville told the author this trail had been built during the Great Depression of the 1930's by CCC crews. However, the late Riter Ekker of Hanksville, told the author that Keith Taylor of Teasdale, Utah (located just west of Capitol Reef National Park), who used to have a permit to run cattle in the canyon, did most of the work on this trail during the 1940's & '50's. The author guesses the trail has been there a long time, going back to Anasazi or Fremont Indian times, but that Taylor was probably the last to use and maintain the **South Fork Trail**.

At the top of this trail is a metal water storage tank called the **Ticaboo Stock Tank**. It holds water from a small spring located about 300 meters above to the south. Beside the storage tank is a watering trough, both of which should have water year-round. This was installed by the BLM in recent years to provide water and water storage for the cattle belonging to the grazing permit holders.

Continuing up the South Fork. The canyon gradually narrows to almost nothing, then it's blocked by a big dropoff in the Navajo Sandstone. There are several little side-cracks in the upper end which are worth looking at.

Now back to the main **Ticaboo Canyon**. Less than 1 km above where the South Fork enters, and on the left wall, is what the author calls the **Ledge Spring**. Water flows from the bottom of the Navajo Sandstone above and over several ledges. The flowing water ends 40 meters downcanyon. As you walk upcanyon the walls gradually fade away and it becomes more shallow. Four or 5 kms above the Ledge Spring, you'll come to cottonwood trees and willows, and a stream flowing for about 200 meters (after a long dry spell, this could dry up?). In March of 2001, the author met a group of college students from Minnesota camped there.

Not far above this wooded area is a place where 3 canyons come together. They are called the **Mid-**

Ticaboo Stock Tank, located on the rim of the upper part of **Ticaboo Creek's South Fork**. You can hike or drive to this place; and there's always water inside the tank, and in a watering trough nearby. In the background is the southeastern face of Mt. Ellsworth.

Map 8, Ticaboo Creek and South Fork Canyons

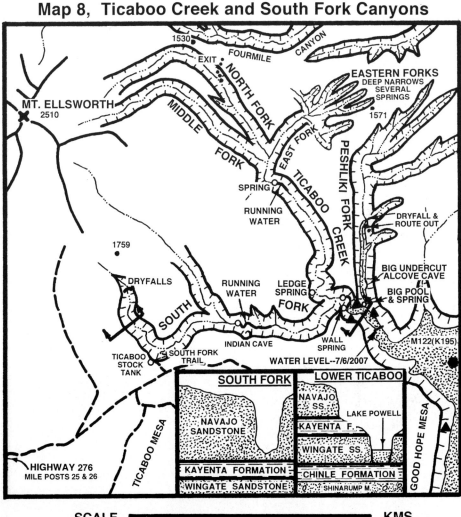

dle, North and East Forks. The **Middle Fork** hasn't got too much to look at and it gradually widens and becomes more open & shallow the higher you go. In the **North Fork**, you'll pass through some moderately narrow sections of the upper Navajo Sandstone, then after about 3 kms, you'll come to the emerging Kayenta Formation which makes some shallow narrows. At that point you can walk up the slope to the right or east, and exit the canyon. From there you'll have a fine view of the **Little Rockies, Mts. Ellsworth & Holmes**, or drop down into Fourmile Canyon.

In this area, the most interesting canyon is **East Fork(s) of Ticaboo**. About 1 1/2 kms above where the North Fork enters, East Fork separates into several canyons with high walls made of Navajo Sandstone. There you'll find seeps & water and lots of bushwhacking if you attempt to reach the upper end of either fork.

Back to the lake and **Peshliki Fork**. You'll be able to get into this canyon by walking up an old trail on the west side of a big dryfall near the mouth of the canyon. At the bottom of that dryfall is a nice spring & deep pool. Upcanyon is a **big undercut or alcove cave**, then it narrows near the upper end of the main canyon with another big dryfall. Just before that is a **steep gully** to the south where you can exit the gorge. From there you can wander at will into several upper forks.

Hike Length & Time Needed It's about 11 kms from the HWM to the exit in North Fork. The author did this one in less than 4 1/2 hours, round-trip. You'll need about half a day for this which is pretty easy walking all the way. On another trip, the author drove from Highway 276 to the Ticaboo Stock Tank, then walked down the trail and through the canyon to the lake and back in about half a day. In late March of 2001, he camped at the lake and with an early morning start hiked up Middle Fork a ways, then into one of the canyons of the East Fork, and finally returning to South Fork and Ticaboo Tank. From there back to his boat took a total of 10 hours. Long hike! In July, 2007, he walked into Peshliki Fork, past the big alcove, exited the lower canyon, and went most of the way up the upper east fork, and back, all in 4 1/3 hours.

Boots or Shoes Any boots or shoes will be OK.

Water There doesn't seem to be any cattle in any of these canyons today, so all water should be good for drinking, especially at the source of each spring or seep. Also at Ticaboo Stock Tank.

Main Attractions An Indian cave, the narrows and the old stock trail in upper **South Fork**, great views of the mountains, and several narrow side-canyons. In **Peshliki Fork**, an interesting alcove.

Hiking Maps USGS or BLM map Hite Crossing (1:100,000); Ticaboo Mesa & perhaps Mount Holmes (1:24,000--7 1/2' quads) for hiking; or Browns Rim & Mt. Ellsworth (1:62.500) if available.

Cass Hite's Ticaboo Ranch Quoting from Crampton's University of Utah *Anthropological Paper #72*: *At the point where Ticaboo Creek emerges from a narrow canyon about a mile [1 1/2 kms] from the Colorado River, Cass Hite established a home--usually called Ticaboo Ranch--where he lived much of the time he was in Glen Canyon after 1883. There in an open area of about 3 acres [about 1.2 hectares] alongside Ticaboo Creek is where he built a cabin, the chimney of which is still standing [1959, and before Lake Powell covered the area]. The foundations of the cabin on the outside measured about 18 by 30 feet [6 by 10 meters] and may have consisted of more than one room.* Crampton goes on to say there were many objects of various kinds lying about.

The cabin was near the canyon wall just to the west, and the area was fenced. There was a corral in one place, and nearby a fenced-off vineyard. Crampton continues: *A few of the vines, though they had not been irrigated in years, still clung to life. When Julius Stone visited Cass Hite at Ticaboo Ranch October 23, 1909, his host treated him to grapes and melons fresh off the vine, and was given a sackful of raisins to take along.*

Crampton also noted, right next to the corral and vineyard was a large boulder which had rolled down the slope. It was covered with petroglyphs.

Hite always had good water at the cabin, but just downstream, Ticaboo Creek sank into the sands of a gravel bar. Upstream about half a mile (800 meters) was a fine stream where it flowed over bedrock and a low waterfall: *In 1914 Cass Hite died at his ranch at Ticaboo and is buried there. The grave is marked by a rectangular enclosure composed of boards nailed to four posts. Another grave along side that of Hite, and with a similar enclosure, is reported to be the resting place of one Frank Dehlin.* The water of Lake Powell covered these ruins and historic site sometime in 1964.

J.W. Powell's Report Powell mentions finding ruins near what later would be Hite, then in the afternoon of July 29, 1869, he says: *then we run down fifteen miles [24 kms] farther, and discover another group [of ruins]. The principal building was situated on a summit of the hill. A part of the walls are standing, to the height of eight or ten feet [2 1/2 to 3 meters], and the mortar yet remains in some places. The house was in the shape of an L, with five rooms on the ground floor,--one in the angle and two in each extension. In the space in the angle there is a deep excavation. From what we know of the people in the Province of Tusayan [Hopi Land], who are, doubtless, of the same race as the former inhabitants of these ruins, we conclude that this was a kiva, or underground chamber in which their religious ceremonies were performed.* These ruins must have been not far upriver from the mouth of Ticaboo Creek (?).

In the lower end of **Ticaboo Creek**, and just above the HWM, is what the author calls **Wall Spring**. This foto was taken on 7/6/2007, but one year earlier, there were many small trees--literally a forest of cottonwoods--growing here. They were taken out by the big floods of 10/2006.

In the lower 1 km of **Peshliki Fork**, is this Big Undercut Alcove Cave, as shown of the map. It's been carved out of the Wingate Sandstone Formation, which makes a colorful fotogenic scene.

The remains of **Cass Hite's cabin** at his ranch on lower **Ticaboo Creek**. This picture was taken in the late 1950's, and at that time, grapes were still growing near the cabin even though they hadn't been watered in years (Crampton foto).

Good Hope Bay, The Old Trail and Sevenmile & Cedar Canyons

Location & Campsites The 2 drainages featured here are **Sevenmile & Cedar Canyons**. The buoy nearest the mouth of Sevenmile is M113 (K181); while near the mouth of Cedar Canyon Inlet is buoy M110 (K176). The name Sevenmile came about because the mouth of this canyon was 7 miles (11 kms) down Glen Canyon from Cass Hite's Ticaboo Ranch on **Ticaboo Creek**. Before Lake Powell came to be, there was a wagon road and/or trail running along the west side of the river all the way from Hite & Dandy Crossing to Sevenmile Canyon.

There should be several campsites in each canyon inlet, some better than others. At the upper end of each inlet, you'll find at least one small campsite which will likely be sandy. If you like lots of sand for camping, then consider heading for **Good Hope Bay**. On the southeast and eastern sides of this bay are many sandy beaches, as well as some springs. The best spring puts out a lot of water that's good tasting and cold--at least in hot weather. The author counted 8-9 springs on the hillsides below the Wingate Sandstone walls. In the western part of the bay is a **toilet & dump/pump station**.

Also shown is **Warm Creek Bay**. In times of high water, all walls rise vertically from the water, but when the lake level is low, as it was on **7/6/2007-WL1100.63m/3610.95'**, then there will be 3 good places for houseboats to tie-down (but no sandy beaches) as shown on the map. One of those places will be in a big alcove directly below where flood waters fall during rainy periods. See foto on front cover.

Hiking Routes or Trails The main **Sevenmile Canyon** is as deep and narrow as any canyon on Lake Powell. From the HWM in the upper end of the inlet, you'll first encounter a small stream lined with cottonwood trees and other water loving plants. There are enough people hiking up this canyon to have created some hiker-made trails. These trails extend all the way upcanyon to the big boulders & narrows, which is the end of hiking for all except a few adventurous individuals. If you can get above these boulders, you'll see a short slot, at least 3 upclimbs, then you can exit the canyon completely on the left or west side in the upper end of the drainage.

Paralleling the main fork to the east is what the author calls the **East Fork** (this has an **East & West Branch** higher up). It has a short inlet with probably a couple of campsites, depending on lake levels.

After walking about 200-300 meters above the HWM, you'll come to a dryfall, below which is a minor spring (which may dry up during long dry spells). You can skirt this minor obstacle on the left or west. Then you walk right up the dry creek bed and into some pretty good narrows with very high Navajo walls. About 1 km above the dryfall you'll come to a place with large boulders jammed into the gorge. For people coming downcanyon, this is the last rappel. For information on the 2 upper branches, which has rappels & great slots, see the author's other book, *Technical Slot Canyon*

Lower Sevenmile Canyon. This picture was taken on **7/6/2007-WL1100.63m/ 3610.95'**. With lake levels that low, you'll find this fotogenic groove not too far from your boat; it's shown on the map as, *Low Water Groove*.

Map 9, Good Hope Bay, The Old Trail, and Sevenmile & Cedar Canyons

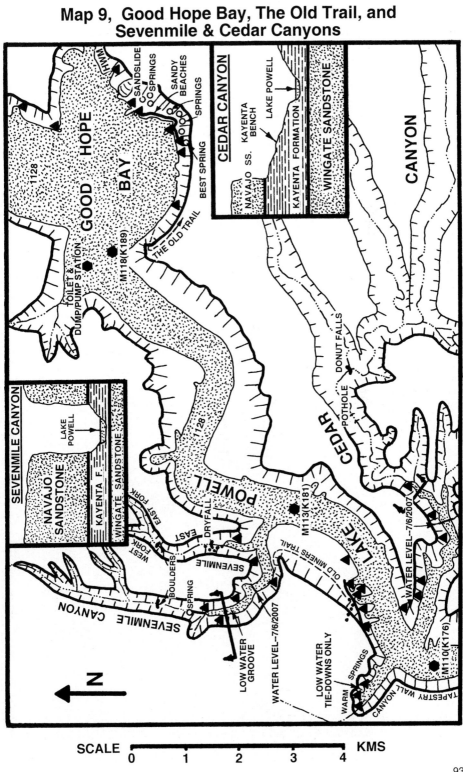

SCALE

0   1   2   3   4   KMS

Guide to the Colorado Plateau, 2nd Edition.
    Across the inlet south of the mouth of East Fork you may be able to find an **old miners trail** heading up to the east and southeast to the top of the Kayenta bench. This trail, according to Crampton, was apparently used by miners during the Glen Canyon Gold Rush days from about 1884 until 1900. It started at Hite and went south along the west bank of the river. It was a wagon road at first, then gradually narrowed to a horse trail. It's shown on old river maps running south to Sevenmile, then up over the rim and southwest to the head of Hansen Creek, where a wagon road ran down to the river in the dry creek bed. Going north along Hansen Creek was the standard route to Hanksville from these parts.
    This is what the author found. He boated into the main inlet about a km past the mouth of East Fork, and tied-down where the Kayenta bench is seen coming out of the water. At that point there's a faint trail, which follows the rising bench as it curves around to the southeast and south and below the big Navajo walls above to the west.
    On top of the Kayenta bench, there are about half a dozen stone cairns marking a route around to the southwest and nearly to the mouth of Warm Springs Canyon. When the cairns end, someone on foot can easily walk up one of several routes to the top of the Navajo rim. While this is an easy walk for the infantry, the cavalry could never make it. The author never saw any cairns on the slickrock, nor any steps cut. It seems if this was indeed a real trail, it was not used by horses, but by foot traffic only (however, the author may have missed a place where steps could be cut in the slickrock?). You could also get to this old miners trail by docking along the main channel about 2 kms northeast of the mouth of Warm Springs Canyon.
    Cedar Canyon is not as impressive as Sevenmile. Its walls aren't very high, and they're set back away from the dry creek bed. As you head up Cedar Canyon above the HWM, you'll be walking along Kayenta benches or ledges all or most of the way. You can go up for half a day, or more, but maps seem to indicate it doesn't get any more interesting, scenery wise.
    As you go upcanyon, you'll have to pass by several small dryfalls, before reaching what the author calls **Donut Falls**. There, flood waters have created a small donut or potty-shaped bridge across the top of an unusual dryfall. There are also several places with potholes and interesting erosional features in the various layers of the Kayenta Formation.
    There are 2 short hikes leading off from **Good Hope Bay**, which are discussed below.
Hike Length & Time Needed Most people can only walk about 1 km up **Sevenmile** beyond the HWM, something the author did twice in 7/2007 was into the narrows; it took 2 hours round-trip. In **East Fork**, the time and distance are about the same as in the main fork. It's about 5 kms from the HWM to Donut Falls in **Cedar Canyon**. This might take only 3 hours or so round-trip. The author did this one in an even 2 hours. Walking along the **old miners trail** to the final rim will take only an hour or so.
Boots or Shoes Any kind of boots or shoes will be OK in either canyon.
Water There likely will be a small year-round stream in the lower part of Sevenmile Canyon (above the HWM). There are no cattle or deer there, so it should be good drinking--unless you see fresh sign of beaver--then don't drink it! East Fork is dry except for a minor seep under the dryfall. The author found a number of potholes in Cedar Canyon, but otherwise it's dry with no springs (up to Donut Falls).
Main Attractions Sevenmile Canyon is very deep, narrow and fotogenic, and Cedar Canyon has some

This is part of the **South Fork Trail** in the **South Fork of Ticaboo Canyon**. You can drive to the beginning of this trail and park at the Ticaboo Tank, as shown on **Map 8**.

interesting erosional potholes and other features in the Kayenta Formation. From the rim above the old miners trail, you will have some good views of the lake & region in all directions.

Hiking Maps USGS or BLM map Hite Crossing (1:100,000); Ticaboo Mesa & Knowles Canyon (1:24,000--7 1/2' quads) for hiking; or Mt. Ellsworth & Mancos Mesa (1:62,500) if available.

History and Good Hope Bay In the upper right hand corner of this map is **Good Hope Bay**. It has some of the best campsites around, plus there's a couple of interesting short hikes. On the southwest side of the bay is an **old stock trail** used during the time before Lake Powell, to take cattle and other livestock to or from the river. The Piutes and Navajos knew this as **The Old Trail**.

To find this trail, first locate the second-most-westerly talus slope which can be climbed to the rim in the southwest corner of the bay. The author once placed a large cairn near the bottom just above the HWM, however, since that time a big rock slide has fallen onto the lower 1/3 of the trail. When you get there, tie your boat up on the **west side** of the big rock slide and scramble straight up the slope until you find the trail which is just under the big vertical wall. There are a few other people doing this hike now, so when you reach the trail you'll know it; then it's very easy to follow. Altogether it runs diagonally about 400 meters up to the rim (from the HWM), it then disappears on the flats.

At the rim, where you'll have fine views to the west & north and the Henry Mountains, is a rock wall which kept the livestock either in, or out of the canyon. This stock trail appears to be part of The Old Trail, discussed by Albert R. Lyman in his book, **_The Outlaw of Navajo Mountain_**. This was an old Indian trail or route which began somewhere near the Woodenshoe Buttes, then ran down White Canyon and south along the Colorado River, and finally over the mesa tops to the San Juan River. In 1884, a band of Piutes had an altercation with some cowboys and there was a shoot-out near the Utah-Colorado state line. Later, when cowboys and soldiers followed the Piutes, there was still another gun battle on the rim of White Canyon. Two white men were killed in an ambush, and the Piutes escaped to Navajo Mountain along this trail. Read all the details under **Map 5 and White Canyon**.

A second short hike is up the big prominent **sandslide** on the east side of Good Hope Bay. The author had thought there might be a trail up this slope, but if there ever was one, it's now lost in time. Cattle could likely be taken up the sandslide, but then they'd have to bench-walk to the south for several kms before they could find flat ground. One nice thing about taking the time for this hike is, from the top you'll have perhaps the best view anywhere of the Henry Mountains to the northwest.

Under the lake waters and on the west side of the bay, is what used to be called **Good Hope Bar**. This was one of the better placer gold mining gravel bars in Glen Canyon during the gold rush which lasted from about 1884 until 1900. Gold was discovered in February of 1887, and a company founded by Cass Hite and J. S. Burgess. At some point in time, and before 1897, Burgess and Hite built a 12-meter-high water wheel on the river's edge. When Stanton visited the place in 1897, he called this the **Egyptian Wheel**, which must have reminded him of water wheels on the Nile River.

This wheel was connected to a 225-meter-long, 12-meter-high flume, which took water to a reservoir a distance

The upper end of **Sevenmile Canyon** just below where _boulders_ are shown on the map. These Navajo Sandstone walls are about as high as any around.

away, where it was used in the placer mining operation. In later years, when uranium prospecting was in full swing, there was a landing strip built along the bar on the west side of the river. When Crampton's group visited the bar in 1964, they found such things as shovels, a post-hole digger, drills, cogwheels, scrapers and screens. Now that era has vanished under the lake waters.

The **Ryan Cabin** was located along the Colorado oppossite the **mouth of Sevenmile Canyon**. In 1897, Robert B. Stanton called it O'Keefe's Lone Star Rock House. It was built during the Glen Canyon Gold Rush by miners Mike Ryan or Timothy O'Keefe sometime before 1897 (Crampton foto).

From the air looking southwest at **Good Hope Bay** on **9/25/2007-WL1087.96m/3601.85'**. To the left are lots of beaches and good sandy campsites; to the upper right, and near the point, is where **The Old Trail** is located. Just visible in the far distance to the upper right is **Sevenmile Canyon Inlet**.

From the top of **The Old Trail** looking east at the east side of **Good Hope Bay**. In the upper left can be seen a big sand slide; walk up that and get on a bench, then bench-walk south to The Old Trail.

This is the place known as **Soldiers Graves** as of 10/2007--with new sign & fence. It's located along Highway 95 between mile posts 66 & 67 not far west of the now-closed (2007) Fry Canyon Lodge.

Tapestry Wall Hike, and Smith Fork & Warm Springs Canyon

Location & Campsites The mouth of **Smith Fork Canyon** is about 20 kms northeast or uplake from the mouth of Bullfrog Bay. The closest buoy is marked M106 (K170); the one in front of **Tapestry Wall** is M110 (K176)--that's 110 miles or 176 kms uplake from Glen Canyon Dam.

There aren't many campsites in this immediate area. The reason is, the Navajo Sandstone walls come right down to the water's edge. There are a couple of sites at or near the beginning of the **Tapestry Wall Hike**, and there should be one or 2 good sandy sites at or near the head of Smith Fork Canyon Inlet right where the creek flows into the lake. There could also be a couple of possible sites along Smith Fork Inlet. **Warm Springs Canyon** has sheer walls above the HWM, but in times of low water levels, as it was on **7/6/2007-WL1100.63m/3610.95'**, there will be 3 good places for houseboats to tie-down (but no sandy beaches). These are exceptionally fotogenic campsites.

Hiking Routes or Trails **Smith Fork** is one of the premier narrow or slot canyon hikes in this book. As you walk upcanyon, you'll find some cottonwood trees growing along side the small stream which begins to flow maybe 200 meters above the HWM. In this same area there is a short side-canyon coming in from the right or northeast. It's narrow and dark for a ways and ends in a cool grotto with a pool. Above that is one of the best technical slot canyons around (see the author's book, *Technical Slot Canyon Guide to the Colorado Plateau, 2nd Ed.* for more details). About 750 meters back down the inlet from the HWM is still another side-canyon with similar pool and dryfall.

The narrows begin about 500 meters above the HWM. For a short distance, this slot is impressive. Above the best narrows, the canyon isn't so deep, but still narrow. You'll find several little side-canyons, which could prove interesting and there are a couple of chokestones you'll have to climb over. In the upper end you'll come to a large rockfall, which will stop most hikers, but the canyon opens up above that point anyway. All along the canyon bottom you'll see dark colored granitic-type boulders. These came all the way down from Mt. Ellsworth to the north.

Now for the **Tapestry Wall Hike**. Tie-down and/or camp just across the channel from the mouth of Knowles Canyon. There are several campsites in the back of a small inlet. From this tiny cove just south of a free-standing flat & gravel-topped butte, head up a shallow drainage in the slickrock to the west. In places it can be steep, but there are several different ways to choose from. After the first steep part, it's easy hiking for the whole family.

As you walk up to the west, you'll also be looking down on another shallow drainage to the north. This one has many potholes, which are often filled with water. After a ways, begin to veer right or north, then just below the rim of the Carmel Formation, cross the upper part of this little drainage to the east side. Finally, you'll climb onto the **Carmel rim** where a cattle trail was built, then it's an easy stroll to the top of the wall, where a little pyramid of limestone, a part of the Carmel Formation, is found. This little pyramid is the highest point around. On top is a USGS bench mark reading *Mancus, 1952*. From there you'll have excellent views of the Henry Mountains to the northwest, and of the lake 226 meters (or more) below.

Hike Length & Time Needed In **Smith Fork**, you can walk upcanyon about 3-4 kms. The author made this hike up to the rockfall and back in about 2 hours, but you may want a little more. On a second trip, he explored above the rockfall and returned in 2 1/2 hours. In 2001, he refotographed several scenes

Warm Springs Canyon Bay on **7/6/2007-WL1100.63m/3610.95'**. With low lake levels, this is a great tie-down camp for houseboats. Notice the HWM on the cliff to the right; and look at the top where flood waters pour into the bay. With high lake levels there are no places to even tie-down.

Map 10, Tapestry Wall Hike, and Smith Fork & Warm Springs Canyon

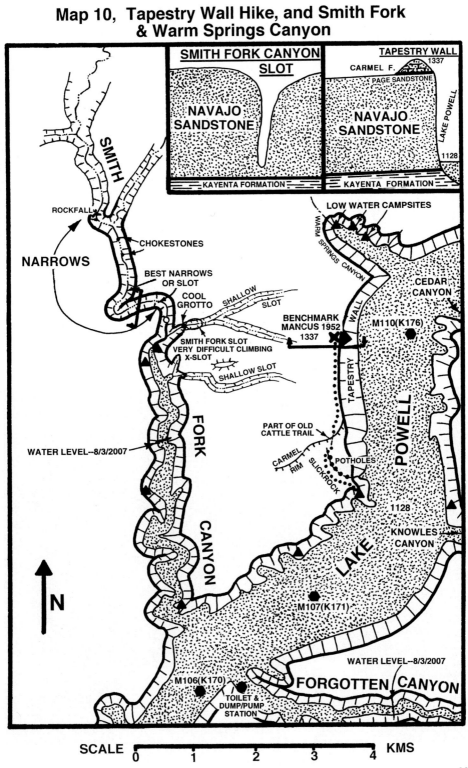

SMITH FORK CANYON SLOT

NAVAJO SANDSTONE

KAYENTA FORMATION

TAPESTRY WALL

CARMEL F.

1337

PAGE SANDSTONE

NAVAJO SANDSTONE

LAKE POWELL

1128

KAYENTA FORMATION

SMITH

ROCKFALL

NARROWS

CHOKESTONES

BEST NARROWS OR SLOT

COOL GROTTO

SHALLOW SLOT

SMITH FORK SLOT VERY DIFFICULT CLIMBING X-SLOT

SHALLOW SLOT

BENCHMARK MANCUS 1952
1337

LOW WATER CAMPSITES

WARM SPRINGS CANYON

CEDAR CANYON

M110(K176)

TAPESTRY WALL

FORK

CANYON

WATER LEVEL--8/3/2007

PART OF OLD CATTLE TRAIL

CARMEL RIM

SLICKROCK

POTHOLES

POWELL

1128

KNOWLES CANYON

LAKE

M107(K171)

N

WATER LEVEL--8/3/2007

M106(K170)

TOILET & DUMP/PUMP STATION

FORGOTTEN CANYON

SCALE

0   1   2   3   4   KMS

in the best places. Stay out of this drainage in times of bad weather. From the lake to the top of **Tapestry Wall** is about 3-3 1/2 kms, and will take most people 2-3 hours round-trip. The author did the round-trip in 1 1/4 & 2 hours on 3 occasions.

Boots or Shoes Any dry weather boots or shoes will do on Tapestry Wall, as most of the hike is on slickrock. After rains, take wading shoes into Smith Fork; otherwise it's a dry hike.

Water After rains you'll find lots of pothole water on the Tapestry Wall Hike. Also, a small year-round seep exists in the lower end of Smith Fork. There are no cattle or beaver there, so it should be good drinking as is--if you take it from the spring source! And if you don't see any fresh signs of beaver.

Main Attractions Some of the best narrows anywhere, and great views from the top of Tapestry Wall.

Hiking Maps USGS or BLM map Hite Crossing (1:100,000); Knowles Canyon & Bullfrog (1:24,000--7 1/2' quads) for hiking; or Mt. Ellsworth (1:62,500) if available.

J.W. Powell's Report and History On July 29, 1869, the Powell Party began at what would later be known as Hite, and ended up in the area of Tapestry Wall. Here's part of what he wrote that day: *And now I climb the wall and go out into the back country for a walk. The sandstone through which the canyon is cut is red and homogeneous, being the same as that through which Labyrinth Canyon runs* [Wingate Sandstone now below the lake]. *The smooth, naked rock [Navajo Sandstone] stretches out on either side of the river for many miles, but curiously carved mounds and cones are scattered everywhere and deep holes are worn out. Many of these pockets are filled with water. In one of these holes or wells, 20 feet [6 meters] deep, I find a tree growing. The excavation is so narrow that I can step from it's brink to a limb on the tree and descend to the bottom of the well down a growing ladder. Many of these pockets are potholes, being found in the courses of little rills or brooks that run during the rains which occasionally fall in the region.*

Just north of **Tapestry Wall**, just across the main channel from the mouth of Cedar Canyon, and near buoy marked M110 (K176), is a short narrow bay with high vertical Navajo Sandstone walls throughout its entire length. This is **Warm Springs Canyon Inlet**. At the very end of the inlet is a high dryfall. The name Warm Springs was given to it by early-day prospectors, although there were never any warm springs in the canyon. There was however, a small year-round stream flowing out the bottom end before the coming of Lake Powell and was a regular waterhole stop for river runners.

Just across the river from the mouth of Warm Springs Creek, and down the Colorado River about 2 kms, was another historic site called **Olympia Bar**. It was an important placer mining site dating back to as early as the 1890's. When Crampton was there in the early 1960's studying the historic sites of Glen Canyon, he noticed extensive placer mining operations had occurred. At several locations there was a terrace about 60 meters above the level of the river, where gravel beds had been dug out and taken down to river levels by means of chutes.

At one point, a water wheel had been placed in the river to lift water to a flume, which carried it to a nearby gravel bar. Geologist Charles B. Hunt was there in 1953, and reported this wheel was the one originally located at Good Hope Bar, further upstream. It was moved to Olympia Bar in 1910, and was called the **Bennett Wheel**, according to Frank Bennett (this Frank Bennett is the same fellow who in 1920-21, drilled for oil at Oil Seep Bar, downriver and across from The Rincon. See **Map 15**). At various places on the bar were found ore cars, old wooden tracks, scrapers, screens, wooden wheel barrows, and remains of the old camp.

The **Smith Fork** narrows. In this part are both granitic & sandstone cobblestones. The granite boulders have been washed down all the way from Mt. Ellsworth to the north.

An aerial view of **Tapestry Wall**; to the right of the 'Wall is **Warm Springs Canyon Bay**; to the lower left is the end of **Cedar Canyon**. This picture was taken on **9/25/2007-WL1097.86m/3601.85'**.

Looking north from very near the summit of **Tapestry Wall**. In the upper left are the summit and Mts. Ellsworth & Holmes. This foto was taken on **7/7/2007-WL1100.58m/3610.80'**.

Above Looking south-east from the top of **Tapestry Wall**. To the left is the main channel and the mouth of Knowles Canyon. In the lower right is the benchmark reading *Mancus, 1952*. The wood you see apparently dates from the time the survey was taken and the bench mark installed.

Right This is the very end of **Smith Fork Slot** which begins at the top of Tapestry Wall. This is a very difficult slot involving high stemming up to 15 meters above the bottom. On the map this is called the **Cool Grotto**.

Above A nice campsite in **Cedar Canyon Inlet.** This is one canyon that may have more campsites in times of low lake levels than when the water is high. This picture was taken on **7/7/2007-WL1100.58m/3610.80'.**

Left The narrows of **Smith Fork**. This section is about 1 km above the HWM.

Knowles, Forgotten, Hansen & Crystal Springs Canyons

Location & Campsites The mouths of **Forgotten** and **Knowles Canyons** are located about 20 kms northeast, or uplake, from the mouth of **Bullfrog Bay**. Near the mouth of **Forgotten Inlet** is a buoy marked M106 (K170), while near Knowles is a buoy reading M107A (K171). There is a **toilet & dump/pump station** just inside the mouth of **Forgotten Canyon Inlet**.

Knowles and Forgotten Inlets are long and narrow, with a few small tent sites in the upper ends of each; plus lots of tie-down places for houseboats. Knowles Inlet has the Kayenta Formation exposed forming ledges just below the Navajo Sandstone walls. Right where the small streams of each canyon enters the lake, should be at least one sandy campsite. **Hansen Creek Inlet** has many good sandy campsites, especially in the upper end, and regardless of water levels. **Crystal Springs Canyon Inlet** has one excellent sandy campsite at the upper end of the inlet under an overhang, and several smaller & sandy places, plus other nearby rocky tie-down places (as seen on **8/3/2007-WL1099.42m/3606.98'**).

Hiking Routes or Trails There are hiker-made trails running up **Forgotten Canyon**, but halfway up these tend to disappear and the upper part is more pristine. It has a year-round stream, which is lined with willows, cottonwoods and gamble oak. At the end of the canyon you'll find a high dryfall blocking the way. Under it is a spring and sometimes a pool of water. The benches you'll be walking on are made of the Kayenta Formation, while the walls above are all Navajo Sandstone.

The **North Fork of Forgotten** is similar to the main canyon, with a small stream from end to end, and a big dryfall at the head of the canyon. The author found lots of fresh sign of beaver, including beaver dams. Take wading shoes if going there--it's filled with brush as well with maybe some bushwhacking.

In the upper end of **Lone Pine Fork** is a big dropoff or dryfall of nearly 100 meters; this is one of the grandest scenes on the lake. Below the dryfall is a pool and 300 meters of big cottonwood trees along with some running water. Nice hike. All forks of Forgotten are box canyons with no exits.

About 1 km up Forgotten Canyon Inlet above the mouth of North Fork, look to the left or north side and into south-facing alcoves. Located there are **2 Anasazi ruins**. The first site is called **Crumbling Kiva**; the second is known as **Defiance House**. This one gets it's name from a pictograph on the wall, which shows 3 warriors with shields & clubs. The Defiance House Ruins have been restored by the NPS and there are several good sandy beaches just across the inlet (On **8/3/2007-WL1099.42m/3606.98'**, boats could only get up to Crumbling Kiva Ruins). Both sites are discussed below.

Knowles Canyon is very similar to Forgotten, but has a wider inlet. The canyon has running water throughout most of its lower course, and water in a few places higher up; therefore it has trees and some brush. The hike can be a bushwhack until you get up past the HWM, then you stay mostly in the dry creek bed, or on some hiker-made trails. Higher up you may find cattle trails, which makes life easier. This canyon has at least one entry trail in the end, so there are cattle around from October to June each year, and deer year-round. As you near the upper end of the canyon, you'll have a couple of dryfalls and pourover pools to pass. Look to the right, or south side of each, for cattle trails by-passing the obstructions. These 2 pourovers are less than a km apart.

As you pass the upper falls on the south side, continue veering to the right until you're heading back in a southwest direction. Look for stone cairns and obvious routes up through the last series of ledges. As you near the top, evidence of a **constructed cattle trail** will be seen in places. This trail was surely

When you boat up **Forgotten Canyon's Inlet**, the first Anasazi structures you come to are these, **Crumbling Kiva Ruins**. These are pretty much intact, but haven't been rebuilt or stabilized.

Map 11, Knowles, Forgotten & Crystal Springs Canyons

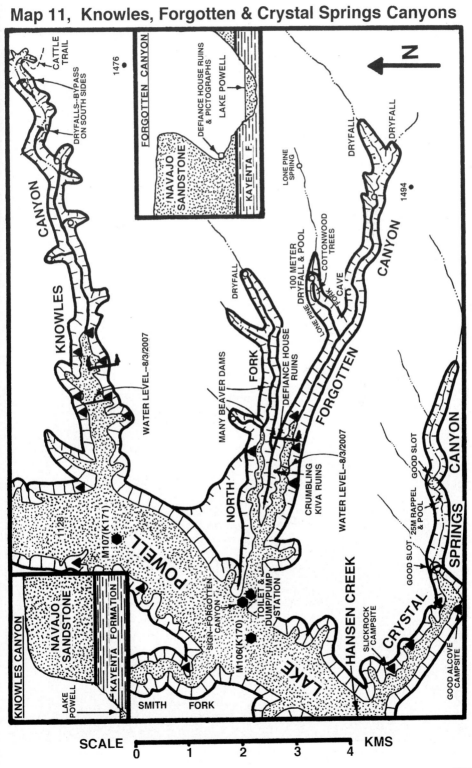

SCALE

0   1   2   3   4   KMS

built by 2 brothers named **Knowles**. It's not certain when they were in this part of the country, but according to John Redd of Monticello, it was in the 1880's or 1890's.

Hike Length & Time Needed From the HWM to the head of the **main fork of Forgotten Canyon** is 7-8 kms, and will take at least half a day for a round-trip hike--more when the lake is low. The **North Fork of Forgotten** is shorter, around 5 kms to the headwall. The author did this in 2 2/3 hours, while his hike in the main fork lasted about 3 hours, round-trip. It's about 7 kms from the HWM to the **cattle trail** in **Knowles Canyon**. This took the author just over 3 hours to complete; but he started very near the HWM. Most people will want 4-5 hours for this hike, or longer when the lake is really low.

Boots or Shoes There is running water in all canyons, so it's best to use a wading-type shoe.

Water The small streams in all forks of **Forgotten Canyon** are clear, but there's likely to be beaver in parts of each. Don't drink the water if you see fresh signs of beaver--drink only at the spring source to be safe. In **Knowles**, what water you may find is suspect because of the cattle. Normally, cattle are permitted in these canyons from October 1 until mid-June, then they're removed for the summer.

Main Attractions Moderately narrow canyons, high dryfalls, one historic cattle trail, many springs and small streams with good tasting water, and Anasazi ruins in Forgotten Canyon.

Hiking Maps USGS or BLM map Hite Crossing (1:100,000); Knowles Canyon & Mancos Mesa (1:24,000--7 1/2' quads) for hiking; or Mt. Ellsworth (1:62,500) if available.

Anasazi Ruins and History Studies made in Glen Canyon in the late 1950's and early 1960's by researchers from the **University of Utah and University of Northern Arizona Archaeology Departments**, included the ruins in **Forgotten Canyon**. Their studies indicate both of these habitation sites were occupied for short periods of time. They surmise this because the trash heaps were very small. This would indicate they were camps associated with seasonal agriculture, or were possible short-lived attempts to settle and establish year-round homes. The length of habitation at **Crumbling Kiva** site was estimated to be from about 1225 to 1250 AD; while the **Defiance House** structures were occupied from 1250 to 1285 AD, or thereabouts.

Pottery remains from Crumbling Kiva site, which was closer to the Colorado River, indicated it was used mostly by people who came up the river and are considered to be part of the **Kayenta Anasazi** group. The Defiance House homes, it is theorized, were built by a group of people believed to have come from the east, and from over the high mesa country around the Abajo Mountains. These people have been classed as the **Mesa Verde Anasazi**. But keep in mind, this is a box canyon and all who entered came via the river. This could only mean there were 2 groups, separated by long time periods.

Crumbling Kiva has not been restored and is in poor condition--so please don't help the aging process. The Defiance House site has been stabilized and there's a short trail from the water to the occupied ledge. This may be the most visited archaeology site on the lake. It's been restored to what the NPS believes is close to the original condition.

Just off the map to the west, and across the channel from the mouth of Crystal Springs Canyon is **Hansen Creek Inlet**. Near each of these 2 canyons is a buoy marked M104 (K166). Hansen Creek today is an inlet with low canyon walls or no walls at all. For the most part the rocks exposed at the shoreline are from the Carmel Formation; that's the reason for the low bench around the HWM, or in some cases no bench at all. On the northeast shoreline, the Carmel Formation is often exposed, while

On **8/3/2007-WL1099.42m/3606.98'**, this was as far as anyone was boating up **Forgotten Canyon**. This picture was taken from the Crumbling Kiva Ruins.

some of the bluffs on the southwest shore are made of the Entrada Sandstone. Because of all the sand in the area, there are numerous beaches and good campsites, many of which offer good views of the Henry Mountains to the north. There are no real hiking places here, at least down near the lake.

Hansen Creek was an important canyon to the miners during the **Glen Canyon Gold Rush**, which lasted from about 1884 until 1900. This canyon offered an easy route from the Henry Mountains to the Colorado and a wagon road was opened as early as 1888. Hansen Creek was the only easy and usable route into Glen Canyon between Hite and Halls Crossing on the west side of the river. It served 3 important mining locations along the river; **California, Smith and Moqui Bars**.

Across the river and upstream about 2 kms from the mouth of Hansen Creek, and just below the mouth of Forgotten Canyon, was the **California Bar**. It was first mined in 1888 by miners Hawthorn, Brown, Keeler and Haskell. Sometime later, Bert Loper and Louis Chaffin worked it over. Supplies for the mining operation were brought down Hansen Creek, then usually ferried across the river. Chaffin, who was interviewed by Crampton, stated that on one occasion when the river was low, he was able to drive a team of horses and a wagon across. Robert B. Stanton, who was staking out claims there in 1899, stated that $30,000 worth of gold had been taken from the bar up to that point. This bar saw intermittent activity until the mid-1940's.

Most of the gold bearing gravels at California Bar were on a low terrace. The gravel was loaded into ore cars, taken to the edge of the terrace and dumped down a chute. Here's what was found in the area in the early 1960's. About 300 meters upstream from this area was a large steam boiler and a second placer mining site. There were scattered remains including ore cars, tracks, a chute, an old cook stove, and the walls of a 2 room rock house. Also on the bar, a grave was found marked: ***A. B. Tuner [Turner], died April 23, 1923, age 69***.

Just above, and just below the mouth of Hansen Creek, was a large sandy embankment. In the days before Lake Powell, it was known as **Smith Bar**. It's believed it was first prospected by a pair of **Smith brothers**, but the first dated claim was located by **N. and Theodore Hansen** and others in 1888. In 1961, researchers reported all that was left of the mining era were the remains of a small water reservoir, the ruins of 3 stone cabins, plus other miscellaneous camp litter. Right at the end of the road coming down Hansen Creek, was an abandoned steam boiler.

Across the channel from Hansen Creek is **Crystal Springs Canyon Inlet**. Today this is a moderately short inlet, with vertical Navajo Sandstone walls rising from the water's edge. It has several alcoves, one of which has a small but very nice sandy campsite (during times of low water, more sites are exposed below). Off to one end used to be toilet paper alley. Hopefully with the new rule that everyone camping on the lake must have some kind of portable toilet, this smelly situation will end.

The end of the inlet is nearby, and if the water level is just right, you can swim up a very narrow crack and with some climbing skills, get into the canyon's upper basin--maybe. There's a good slot canyon above, if you can get to it (We got into the upper canyon from the south where we tied-up our boat and walked overland. We rappelled in, then walked upcanyon into a good slot).

Just downstream from the mouths of Crystal Springs Canyon and Hansen Creek, and on the west side of the Colorado, was another mining site called **Moqui Bar**. Access to this gravel & sand bar was via both Hansen Creek Canyon, and an old trail which came off the low benches to the west.

Defiance House Ruins. Archeologist believe about 15-20 people lived here off & on from about 1250 to 1285 AD. Notice the pictographs just above the structure on the right.

The pictographs for which **Defiance House Ruins** are named.

One of several nice campsites in the upper end of **Forgotten Canyon Inlet**. This was the morning after a midnight wakeup call from a passing thunder storm. Beware of night-time storms during the monsoon season on Lake Powell and secure everything before going to bed.

Just inside the mouth of **Forgotten Canyon Inlet**, is this toilet & dump/pump station.

Right at the head of **Crystal Springs Canyon Inlet** is this huge alcove with campsite underneath.
This picture was taken on **8/3/2007-WL1099.42m/3606.98'**.

Moqui, North Gulch & Stanton Canyons

Location & Campsites The opening of the inlet to **Moqui Canyon** and its north fork called **North Gulch**, is just around the corner from **Bullfrog Bay** and **Halls Crossing Marina**. Buoy number M99 (K158) sits near the mouth of the bay.

Moqui Canyon Inlet is long, narrow and rather entrenched. It's one of the more popular canyons around; partly because it's close to 2 marinas, and because of its scenery, its Anasazi ruins, and its normally-good sandy campsites in the upper end of the inlet. As the lake levels rise and fall, there should always be one good big campsite at the head of navigation--if it isn't overgrown with tamaracks! There can be small campsites in **North Gulch** as well, but on **8/3/2007-WL1099.42m/3606.98'**, the lake ended just below the mouth of this main tributary.

Hiking Routes or Trails In August, 2007, all boats had to be tied down just below where the North Gulch entered **Moqui Canyon**. One short fun hike is to walk up Moqui about 1 km above North Gulch, then to the right or south climb up to the top of the **1st sandslide**. At the top of the slide, use a hiker-made **ledge trail** to reach the canyon rim. It's an easy hike with good views from the top. This trail is now hiker-made, but could have had its beginnings with Indians or the early-day cattlemen who roamed the area before 1900.

To hike Moqui, either climb up to the north side of the stream to the Kayenta ledges and locate a hiker's trail heading east upcanyon; or walk right up the sandy stream bottom. The lower part of the canyon is well-traveled, as there are some **good ruins** about 1 km east of the 1st sandslide on the north side of the creek. In 2007, it was difficult to get out of the channel and upon one of the benches.

Moqui has a year-round stream throughout the canyon, so it has some trees and willows. In some places you'll route-find through vegetation; but it's usually easier to wade in the middle of the shallow sandy stream, which is normally less than 5 cms deep. Big floods generally keep the main channel cleared of brush so there's very little if any bushwhacking.

About 3 kms above the **best ruins**, you'll be in an area with several springs issuing from the south side of the canyon wall and one small Anasazi site on a ledge just above the stream on the north side. The author saw no more ruins above that. Another 3 kms above the **3rd ruins**, a **2nd sandslide** appears on the south wall (it's the weathering of the Navajo Sandstone and the prevailing south winds which have created at least 4 sandslides which make entry/exit points to the canyon). You can easily walk up this slide to the rim. The author did just that, then made his way to **Camp Canyon** to the east, where he descended a **3rd sandslide**, and found running water and 2 easily-passable waterfalls in the Wingate Sandstone. Moqui Canyon goes on for many kms, but scenery seems less interesting to the east. In the early days of San Juan County, this main canyon was known to cowboys as North Gulch.

North Gulch is another seemingly endless canyon with a year-round flowing stream in normal years. The author didn't hike far up this creek, but he did find fresh sign of beaver, a beaver pond, some bushwhacking, and several good springs; this changes with every big flood. Big game guide Carl Mahon of Monticello, Utah, stated that you can walk out of the upper end of North Gulch, which used to be a regular cattle route in the early days of the cattle industry of San Juan County.

Hike Length & Time Needed When the lake level is at or near the HWM you can visit the **best ruins** in a few minutes; but an hour or more on **8/3/2007-WL1099.42m/3606.98'**. You can also climb the 1st sandslide and reach the canyon rim in less than half an hour. To hike up to Camp Canyon and back,

This picture (from an old slide) was taken in the fall of 1988 from the top of the 1st Sandslide & Ledge Trail looking north at the Henry Mountains. This was when water levels in **Moqui Canyon** were 2-3 meters below the HWM. However, on **8/3/2007-WL1099.42m/3606.98'**, it was a 10 minute walk getting to the base of this sandslide. In 2007, there was a waterfall just to the right of this foto.

Map 12, Moqui Canyon and North Gulch

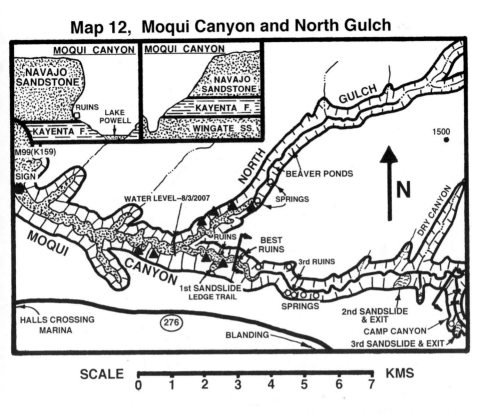

SCALE |———————————————————| KMS
0   1   2   3   4   5   6   7

One of several small granaries in **Moqui Canyon**.

similar to what the author did, will take all day, so it's best to take a lunch. The author did it in a little more than 5 hours round-trip. You can walk for many kms up North Gulch, so this leaves room for exploration.

Boots or Shoes Both canyons have streams so use wading-type shoes.

Water There are cattle and signs of beaver in both Moqui Canyon and North Gulch, so don't touch the stream water. Drinking water coming directly from unpolluted springs should be safe in either canyon.

Main Attractions A deep & narrow inlet, a well-watered and green desert valley, several good sandy campsites, and Anasazi ruins.

Hiking Maps USGS or BLM map Navajo Mountain (1:100,000); Halls Crossing NE, Mancos Mesa & Burnt Spring (1:24,000--7 1/2' quads) for hiking; or Lake Canyon & Mt. Ellsworth (1:62,500) if available.

Anasazi Ruins and History of Bullfrog Bay and Stanton Canyon During the pre-Lake Powell archaeological studies in Moqui Canyon, 100 sites were found. Many are now under water, and those upcanyon are less visible than the commonly seen cliff dwellings.

About 700-800 years ago, there were many inhabitants in Moqui Canyon. That's because of a sizable and year-round flowing stream, a broad alluvial-filled canyon bottom, many overhanging alcoves, and a number of natural entry/exits to the canyon (3 sandslides in this local area, and a 4th higher upcanyon). This place must have looked pretty good to an agricultural people.

Studies on cliff dwellings, and potsherds, now under water, indicated Moqui Canyon was inhabited from about 1125 to 1275 AD. In examining the potsherds in those sites, it was found that about half of the cultural affiliation came from the **Kayenta Anasazi**; about half from the **Mesa Verde group**. See the map on **page 9** which shows the location of various Indian groups. Those sites in the upper canyon indicated a strong tendency to have been influenced by the Mesa Verde people to the east and the Abajo Mountains, as opposed to Kayenta people who likely migrated up the Colorado River Gorge.

As you hike upcanyon, notice the soil or alluvial benches just back from the stream, but below the Navajo walls or the Kayenta benches. This erosion or down-cutting of the soil deposits, has taken place all over the Colorado Plateau, and the primary reason for it is believed to be overgrazing by white men's cattle herds. Lake Canyon is another good example of this recent downcutting, and the reason for it is obviously overgrazing. The author believes a similar pattern of downcutting may have occurred with a dense population of Anasazi, thus the eventual evacuation. If indeed that occurred, then these canyons refilled themselves with sand and soil up to the time of the cattle boom just before and after 1900. Since then there's been another cycle of down-cutting, but it seems to be abating now, perhaps even beginning to restore itself.

Not far west of the mouth of Moqui Canyon is **Bullfrog Bay**, which is the location of **Bullfrog Marina**, the number one launching site for northern Utah boaters. Bullfrog Bay is normally one of the largest open bodies of water on Lake Powell. The southern part of the bay is merely a transit corridor for boats going up or downlake, and to **Halls Crossing Marina** just south of Bullfrog on the southeast side of the lake.

The northern or upper part of the bay is very popular for water skiing and other water sports. It also has many sandy beaches and excellent campsites with both boater and automobile access (but not with low water like it was on **8/3/2007-WL1099.42m/3606.98'**. See **Map 13**, of Halls Creek and the Wa-

This waterfall is just upcanyon or east of the **1st Sandslide**. See map. This picture was taken on **8/3/2007-WL1099.42m/3606.98'**, and the morning after a heavy thunderstorm & flood. With low lake levels in the early 2000's, sand is still being washed downcanyon to the lake by floods.

terpocket Fold Canyons, for a better look at campsites in Bullfrog Bay.

Before Lake Powell, there was some minor rapids at the mouth of Bullfrog Creek, one of the few in the entire length of Glen Canyon. The river dropped only about a meter in 1 km, so it was mostly just a ripple. The Bullfrog drainage begins on the south slope of Mt. Hillers, and was originally called Pine Alcove Creek by the 1873 Wheeler Survey. The name Bullfrog probably came about during the gold rush days just before 1900.

As far as history of Glen Canyon goes, there were several sand bars in the vicinity of the mouth of Bullfrog Creek which were fairly important in the gold rush days. One was the **Wilson Bar**, right at the mouth of **Stanton Canyon**. It served as a camp for the **Hoskaninni Company**, when they were operating a dredge (see below).

Another of the more important sites in the area was **New Years Bar**. It was found directly across the river from the mouth of Stanton Canyon, and extending upstream. Records show it was placer mined from 1888, and mining equipment littered the area in 1959. At the upper end of the bar was one of the few sites where agriculture was undertaken in Glen Canyon. Crampton reported that a Dan E. Miller had planted melons, peanuts, and other crops sometime before August, 1958. By the next year, it had been abandoned. Left there was a trailer house, a one-room log cabin, a chicken coop, and corrals.

Perhaps the most important site in Glen Canyon, as far as mining history is concerned, was the **Hoskaninni Company** operations at **Camp Stone** and **Stanton Canyon**. This area was upstream a couple of kms from the mouth of Bullfrog Creek and had to do with the **Stanton Dredge**.

Robert Brewster Stanton was an engineer, educated at the University of Miami, in Ohio. One of his first jobs was in Colorado working on a railway line to Leadville. Surveying potential railroad grades became his specialty. He once met Frank M. Brown, who in 1889, founded the Colorado Canyon and Pacific Railroad Company for the purpose of constructing a watergrade railroad from Grand Junction, Colorado, to the seaboard, through the canyons of the Colorado River connecting the coal fields of the Rocky Mountains with southern California.

Brown hired Stanton to help assess the potential route. In 1889-90, they went down Glen Canyon surveying a route for the railway. However, while boating the Colorado just below Lee's Ferry, Brown and 2 others were drowned in the upper part of Marble Canyon. That pretty well ended the big plans for a railway through the Grand Canyon. But Stanton remembered the gold mining in Glen Canyon.

After a few years, Stanton and several interested business men, went back to Hite and made some tests of the gold diggings. They thought they had something, so on March 28, 1898, the Hoskaninni Company was founded, with **Julius F. Stone** as president, and Mills, Brooks, Morton and Ramsey as co-owners and investors. Robert B. Stanton was brought into the firm as a vice president, engineer and as superintendent.

In 1898, a crew made the trip from North Wash to Lee's Ferry and restaked all old claims. In all, the company had 145 claims from about 3 kms above Hite, down to Lee's Ferry, a distance of 265 kms.

Early in 1900, a contract was let out to the Bucyrus-Erie Company of Milwaukee, to build a gold dredge. Later in the spring it was shipped by rail to Green River, Utah. Moving the dredge the 160 kms to the river required the building of a road from the areas between the Granite and Trachyte Ranches, just east of the Henry Mountains, up Benson Creek to South or Stanton Pass between Mt. Hillers and Pennell, and down Hansen Creek, passing Stanton's Coal Mine on the way. From the lower part of Hansen Creek, the route went south over the low divide and down Stanton Canyon to the river. It took about 25 men and several wagons, with 4 to 8 horses each, and 75 to 100 horses total, to haul the dredge from Green River. It took 8 days.

Stanton ordered the dredge to be assembled not at the mouth of Stanton Canyon, where a dugway was built out of solid rock, but at a site about 1 1/2 kms upriver. This site was called **Camp Stone**, and was a couple of kms downstream from the mouth of Moqui Canyon. The dredge was built on a barge

Wagons taking parts & material for the Stanton Dredge down **Stanton Canyon** to the Colorado River. It was assembled in 1900 at Camp Stone. See more pictures on the next page (Stanton foto).

measuring about 12 x 25 meters. The construction started in June of 1900, and took about 7 months to complete (January, 1901). The dredge worked for about 6 months and quit; a total failure. It failed because the equipment was unable to separate the fine gold dust from the sand & gravel. Estimates on the total cost to the company ranged between $100,000 and $350,000.

Sometime later, the dredge was moved downstream to the mouth of Stanton Canyon, where it gradually sank in the river. For many years it was a regular stopping place for river runners on the Colorado. It now sits below about 100 meters of water.

Crampton reports in his ***Anthropological Paper #61***, that in 1902 or 1903, A. L. Chaffin operated a trading post at the site of the gold dredge, and directly across from New Years Bar. At that time it was a frequent stop for Navajos.

Camp Stone during the summer or fall of 1900. The Stanton Dredge was built nearby.

The **Stanton Dredge**. Work on it began in June, 1900, and it took about 7 months to complete. After January, 1901, it worked for about 6 months and quit; a total failure.

From the hilltop above **Halls Crossing Marina**, looking north across the eastern part of Bullfrog Bay toward the **Henry Mountains** to the north. These houseboats are anchored just north of the marina.

Aerial view of **Crystal Springs Canyon** looking westward. Can you see 2 boats? The main channel and the lower part of **Hansen Creek Inlet** are seen in the background at the top of the picture.

Halls Creek & Waterpocket Fold Hikes, and Halls Creek & Bullfrog Bays, and Lost Eden Canyon

Location & Campsites Halls Creek is the very long intermittent stream running down the middle of, the Waterpocket Fold. It begins in the north in **Capitol Reef National Park** and flows south to **Halls Creek Bay**. This large body of water is immediately next to and southwest of Bullfrog Bay. It's a quick ride to the mouth of Halls Creek, or along the face of the **Waterpocket Fold**, from the marinas at Bullfrog or Halls Crossing.

Halls Creek Bay is one of the best places on the lake for camping and water skiing. There are many sandy beaches, some of which are on small islands made of the Entrada Sandstone. Most campsites are on the south or southwest side of the bay, where it makes contact with the Waterpocket Fold. **Bullfrog Bay** is also popular for camping and water skiing, but is not a hiking area. If you long for peace and quiet, best to avoid these 2 bays, especially on weekends.

Hiking Routes or Trails The walk up **Halls Creek** to the narrows and **Hall Divide** is one of the longer day-hikes in this book. But it's also one of the best, because it has one of the most spectacular and deepest narrow gorges on the Colorado Plateau.

To begin, walk northward from your boat to and past the old **Baker Ranch** (just below the HWM) as shown on the map. It probably isn't visible, but there is an old road running north along the western side of the dry creek bed. This is the original road built and used by **Charles T. Hall** during his years at the ferry crossing on the Colorado River. More on Hall below.

This old road is all but invisible until you get further upstream near Hall Divide, then it's easy to find and follow. The road follows the dry creek until the stream channel takes a strange twisting course to the west. The road itself crosses over a natural divide, avoiding about 4 kms of canyon narrows. Perhaps a million years ago, the stream was already entrenched when the final uplift started to this part of the **Waterpocket Fold**. That's the reason the stream runs off to the west as it does, rather than cutting across the natural low point of the divide.

Once you reach this area, it's best to walk along the road to the north side of the narrows first, then walk downstream through the slot. This will also give you a chance to walk to the rim of the narrows and look down into this impressive gorge. The road you see there now was probably last used about the time the lake began to fill in the early 1960's.

Going through the narrows, you'll find a small stream, and at one point a big overhang about 100 meters high coming off the wall to the right or west--one of the highest around. There's also one place where the water was waist deep for the author, but the depth of that hole will vary with the season, and the length of time since the last flood. There are also several springs in this part, which seep out at the contact point between the Navajo Sandstone above, and the Kayenta Formation below.

As you walk along Halls Creek, the **Waterpocket Fold** is best seen to the west, but you're actually in the center of the fold (see the geology cross section on the map). To the west are many short and narrow drainages coming off this monocline. The top-most rock exposed is the Navajo Sandstone, and when it's subjected to erosion, it creates many potholes or waterpockets; thus the name of the fold.

This picture of the **Bullfrog-Halls Crossing Ferry** was taken on **8/3/2007-WL1099.42m/3606.98'**. With lake levels that low, they moved the ferry from it's normal docking site near the Bullfrog school, to **Hobie Cat Beach**, which is near the main public launching ramp ar Bullfrog.

Map 13, Halls Creek & Waterpocket Fold Hikes, and Halls Creek & Bullfrog Bays, and Lost Eden Canyon

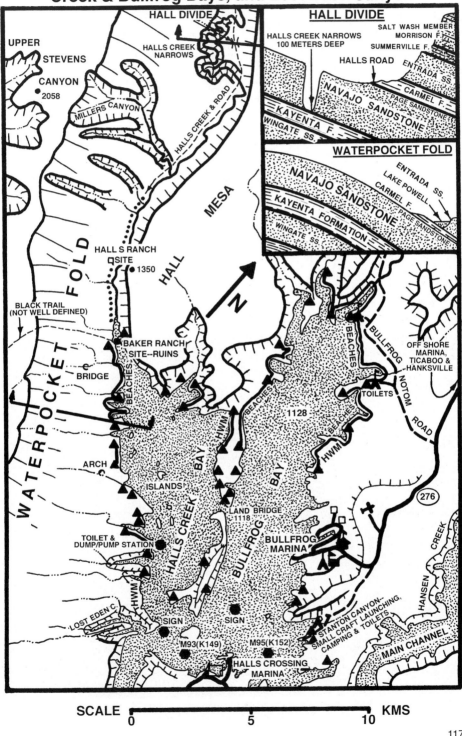

HALL DIVIDE

HALLS CREEK NARROWS

UPPER
STEVENS
CANYON
2058

MILLERS CANYON

HALLS CREEK & ROAD

MESA

HALL

FOLD

HALL S RANCH
SITE
1350

BLACK TRAIL
(NOT WELL DEFINED)

BAKER RANCH
SITE--RUINS

BRIDGE

BEACHES

ARCH

ISLANDS

TOILET &
DUMP/PUMP STATION

WATERPOCKET

HWM

HALLS CREEK BAY

LOST EDEN C

SIGN

SIGN

M93(K149)

M95(K152)

HALLS CROSSING
MARINA

HALL DIVIDE

HALLS CREEK NARROWS
100 METERS DEEP

SALT WASH MEMBER
MORRISON F.
SUMMERVILLE F.
HALLS ROAD
ENTRADA SS.
NAVAJO SANDSTONE
CARMEL F.
PAGE SANDSTONE
KAYENTA F.
WINGATE SS.

WATERPOCKET FOLD

NAVAJO SANDSTONE
ENTRADA SS.
LAKE POWELL
CARMEL F.
PAGE SANDSTONE
KAYENTA FORMATION
WINGATE SS.

N

BEACHES

BEACHES

1128

HWM

BEACHES

BULLFROG

NOTOM ROAD

OFF SHORE
MARINA,
TICABOO &
HANKSVILLE

TOILETS

276

BULLFROG BAY

LAND BRIDGE
1118

BULLFROG
MARINA

STANTON CANYON--
SMALL CRAFT LAUNCHING,
CAMPING & TOILETS

HANSEN CREEK

MAIN CHANNEL

SCALE
0   5   10   KMS

117

The largest side-canyon is **Miller's Creek**. It's deep and narrow at the mouth, and has a year-round flowing stream, complete with small fish or minnows. High to the west, it opens up and Kayenta and Wingate rocks are exposed below the Navajo.

Now back at the head of the inlet. Just southwest of where the old Baker Ranch was situated, and at the head of the bay during times of high lake levels, is a canyon with an interesting bridge. To get up this one, it's best to get out of the canyon itself, and walk up the slickrock slope. This would be true for hiking any of the little short slot canyons on the face of the Fold. The reason is, each slot canyon is very steep and narrow with one big pothole, pourover pool, or dryfall after another. It's easier to walk up the slickrock face in most places. Just pick a spot anywhere along the face of the Fold and start hiking. From on top, you'll have some fine views of the lake and the Henry Mountains to the north.

Another thing to look for is the beginning, or end, of the **Black Trail**, sometimes referred to as the **Baker Trail**. This old stock trail heads up the slickrock face of the Waterpocket Fold, then runs southeast along the top of this monocline. After a ways, it veers to the south and runs west of Long Canyon (**see Map 16, page 139**). When it reaches the **East Fork of Bowns Canyon**, it drops down in and runs nearly to the mouth of Bowns, then heads over a low divide on the Kayenta Bench, and follows this same bench southeast in Glen Canyon, then west and north into the mouth of the Escalante River Arm.

The last part is presently submerged. It then ran west out of the Escalante Canyon just north of the mouth of Clear Creek, connected to the Hole-in-the-Rock Road, then headed northwest to the town of Escalante.

The reason it got the name Black Trail, is that in a small alcove near the mouth of the Escalante is the signature written in charcoal, *J W Black, Feb. 2, 1896*. It probably was put there by a John Black, an early pioneer from the town of Boulder. Along the way, other trails headed off to the east, such as the **Schock Trail**, and the one running to **Oil Seep Bar**, just north of The Rincon. If there is any sign of the Black Trail near Baker Ranch, it will simply be some stone cairns up along the slickrock.

Hike Length & Time Needed From the HWM to the top of Hall Divide is about 14-15 kms. This means a round-trip hike will be over 30 kms; a long all-day walk, but the going is easy and fast. The author did this hike from the HWM, which included a side-trip up Miller's Creek, in 9 1/4 hours. Some people may need 12 hours or more round-trip. You can also hike to Halls Creek Narrows from the Bullfrog-Notom Road. For information on this alternate northern route, see this writers other book, *Non-Technical Canyon Guide to the Colorado Plateau, 5th Ed.* A hike to the top of the Waterpocket Fold directly from the lake will take a couple of hours round-trip. Any length of hike can be taken on the Fold.

Boots or Shoes For the Halls Creek hike, take wading shoes as you'll likely be wading often in the 4 kms of the narrows. Walking up the slickrock of the Fold can be done with any kind of boots or shoes, but a good pair of running shoes is ideal.

Water The narrows part of Halls Creek has running water much of the time, but it can dry up in June, the driest month of the year in Utah. The running water is in the narrows and sometimes just above. It'll probably be good to drink if you take it at or near a spring source, but there will be some cattle in the area north of the narrows during some of the winter months. Also, after rains there will be hundreds of potholes full of good water on the Waterpocket Fold. At the same time, there will be little seeps and some

In the middle part of **Halls Creek Narrows**, you'll find hanging gardens like this, a number of seeps or springs, and running water in the lower end.

sweet running water coming out the bottom of each slot canyon for a few days, or a week or two, after a good rainstorm.

Main Attractions Great slickrock hiking, and one of the deepest, narrowest and most impressive gorges on the Colorado Plateau. Also, interesting geology in the Waterpocket Fold.

Hiking Maps USGS or BLM map Hite Crossing (1:100,000); Hall Mesa, Stevens Canyon North & The Rincon (1:24,000--7 1/2' quads) for hiking; or Hall Mesa (1:62,500) if available.

Halls Crossing, Baker Ranch and other History The history of Halls Crossing begins further downstream at Hole-in-the-Rock. A man by the name of Charles T. Hall was a carpenter living in Escalante, Utah, when the San Juan Party made its epic journey from southwestern Utah, through the Hole-in-the-Rock in 1879-80. They made their way to, and settled Bluff, Utah, located on the San Juan River. Read more about that expedition's history under **Map 20**.

Hall was called upon by Mormon Church authorities to assist the party by building a boat to ferry wagons across the Colorado. He then stayed on the Colorado operating the ferry through 1880, but the route to the river was so incredibly difficult, almost no one gave him business. Later, Hall got word of a better route further upstream. He scouted the region, and moved the ferry upriver to what would later be known as **Halls Crossing** and **Halls Ferry**.

The approaches to Halls Crossing were much easier than to the Hole-in-the-Rock. From Escalante, the route went down Harris Wash to the Escalante River, up Silver Falls Creek to the Circle Cliffs, then descended Muley Twist Canyon to Halls Creek, thence to the river. On the east side, the route ascended the sand flats and slickrock slopes in the area between Moqui and Lake Canyons, then joined the Hole-in-the-Rock Trail to the east, which led to Bluff.

The ferry boat itself is said to have been built with materials from Escalante, some 80 kms away. It consisted of 2 pine logs with planks spanning the logs. It measured about 3 x 10 meters. Hall operated the ferry from 1881 to 1884. The reason he closed it was the completion of the railroad through eastern Utah in 1883, which eased transportation problems on both sides of the Colorado.

The best sources of information for the historic **Baker Ranch**, now sometimes lying below the waters of Lake Powell, comes from a number of papers and studies done by many people and various universities. Some of the research of the recent human history part of Glen Canyon was done by C. Gregory Crampton and is documented in the ***Anthropological Papers of the University of Utah***. These studies were done because of the construction of Glen Canyon Dam and the creation of Lake Powell. They of course concentrated their efforts on that part of the land which is below the HWM of Lake Powell at 1128 meters (3700 feet) elevation. Much of what is known of the Baker Ranch comes from Crampton's ***Anthropological Paper #61***. Here's part of what was stated in that report:

Within the Lake Powell Reservoir area there were a few areas put under cultivation in historic times. Baker Ranch on the right side of Halls Creek, 6 miles [10 kms] from Halls Crossing of the Colorado, was one of the largest of these. At one time approximately 100 acres [40 hectares] of pasture, alfalfa and corn were irrigated from waters diverted from the creek--this was before 1936 when Eugene Baker, after whom the place is named, patented 800 acres [about 320 hectares] of land in the vicinity.

The first (white) settler on lower Halls Creek, is believed to have been Charles Hall who maintained

The upper part of **Halls Creek Narrows** has cottonwood trees and some flowing water.

a small farm 2 miles [3 kms] above [north] Baker Ranch while operating the ferry at Halls Crossing, 1881-1884. Thomas William Smith (living in Green River, Utah, in 1962 and son of Thomas Smith who made the original location at Baker Ranch), stated that he remembers the old Hall place, which consisted of a log cabin 15 x 15 feet [5 by 5 meters]. He said that Charles Hall would climb over the slickrock slopes of the Waterpocket Fold to a point about 500 feet [150 meters] above the creek bed where he could see the ferry crossing 8 miles [13 kms] away. Smith thought there may have been some way for parties on the opposite side who wished to cross the river, to signal the ferryman. The site of Halls Ranch, which was referred to by name as late as 1922 (by other writers), has not been located by this author.

The second settler in lower Halls Creek, is believed to have been Thomas Smith who located the Baker Ranch site around 1900. According to Barbara Ekker of Hanksville, it was in 1907, the Thomas Smith family moved there. Smith was a polygamist, with two wives, Eliza and Sarah. In August 1907, all three filed claims on 800 acres [320 hectares] of land on lower Halls Creek, under the Desert Land Act of 1877. This must have been just the place Smith and his wives were looking for; a quiet and iso-lated place to live, and away from the law which frowned on a man having two wives.

In the course of time, Smith and family constructed several buildings including two log cabins and one stone structure. After several years of hardship, this property was transferred to Eugene Baker in about 1917. A public land survey of the vicinity was made in 1923. The survey notes reflect the improve-ments on the ranch, which then consisted of about 3 miles [5 kms] of fencing, one three-room frame house, a one-room log cabin, a one-room rock store-house and a large corral and stockyard. Twenty acres [8 hectares] of land, including fruit trees and alfalfa, were under cultivation at the time.

Crampton visited with a number of people and got first hand accounts from several individuals. One was: Carlyle Baker, son of Eugene Baker, living at Teasdale, Utah, in 1960, who stated that he spent a number of his younger years at the ranch. During the spring of the year, when storms broke over the Waterpocket Fold, enough water came down Halls Creek before June to irrigate up to 100 acres [40 hectares] of land on both sides of the stream. However, farming was only an adjunct to grazing and the uncertainties of the water supply, the hot climate of the summer months, and the sandy soil led to its abandonment by about 1940. The Bakers later sold the property to other interests who still use the ranch as a grazing headquarters (1962).

The Baker Ranch is just below the HWM of Lake Powell, but most of the time it's exposed, or at least what's left of it. When the lake is lower than about 5 meters below the HWM, then you can still see the ruins of the stone building seen in the fotograph below. Until it's completely covered with silt, you'll see other debris too, including an old cistern and stove.

Near the mouth of Halls Creek and the former ferry crossing were several sand bars which were im-portant locations during the Glen Canyon Gold Rush days. On the west side of the Colorado were **Halls Bar** just upstream, and **Burro Bar** just downstream, from the mouth of Halls Creek. Across the river downstream and around the corner was **Boston Bar**.

Boston Bar was the more important of the three. Operations at this site began in 1889, but it wasn't until 1899-1900 that significant work was done. During this time period, the Boston Placer Mining Com-pany, a corporation under the organization of Maine residents A.J. Strouse and Charles Sherwin, in-vested fairly heavy sums of money into the operation. But of course the venture failed in the end just like the Stanton Dredge. In place along the river in 1958-59, were pumps and gasoline motors, and older equipment such as a flume, sluice boxes, lumber, iron rails and other odds & ends.

Not far from where you leave Halls Crossing Marina, and just around the corner from the mouth of

An old picture of the **Baker Ranch** at the head of **Halls Creek Bay**. This foto was taken not long before the site was covered by the rising waters of Lake Powell (Hamilton Parker foto).

Halls Creek Bay, is the narrow and almost hidden inlet to **Lost Eden Canyon**. This inlet has three very narrow branches, the longest of which is about 1 1/2 kms. When the lake is at or near the HWM, there will be no campsites. However, you can get out of your boat in several places and walk along the Navajo slickrock. You could gain access to the southern end of the Waterpocket Fold from inside this inlet but there are not that many places to tie down your boat. When the lake is really low, there are a couple of nice slots with big potholes. The north fork and the middle fork both have some swimming and rappels.

Near the middle of Halls Creek Bay is a **toilet & dump/pump station** for longer-term campers who need to empty their waste tanks or port-a-potties.

Part of the deep slot in the lower end of the **Halls Creek Narrows**.

Lake & Annies Canyons, the Schock & Gretchen Bar Trails, and Lake Pagahrit

Location & Campsites **Lake Canyon** is the first major tributary on the east side of Lake Powell as you head south from Bullfrog or Halls Crossing Marinas. Buoy number M89 (K142) is near, and a buoy marked Lake Canyon, sits at the mouth of the inlet. **Lake Canyon Inlet** is rather long and narrow and its walls, made of Navajo Sandstone, rise vertically out of the water.

Near the middle of the inlet there can be several campsites, mainly on the north side, and all dependent on lake levels. At the head of the inlet where Lake Creek enters, there should always be a sandy (maybe muddy) campsite, regardless of how high or low the lake is.

The **Schock Trail** begins not far downlake from the mouth of Lake Canyon and on the north, or other, side of the channel. The buoy nearest the mouth of **Annies Canyon** is marked M84 (K134). Campsites in these parts are limited, because for the most part, the walls of the main channel and side-canyons come right down to the water. The walls are made of Navajo Sandstone. Just east of the beginning of the Schock Trail there are several tiny inlets in the gradual sloping Navajo. Depending on lake levels, these can make fine campsites (some with small patches of sand) or tie-down places.

In the upper end of the **north fork of Annies**, there's a **huge dryfall and alcove**, which makes another fine campsite which is completely overhung. The author was stuck there once for nearly 24 hours because of howling spring-time wind storm. On the hot afternoon of 8/4/2007, he observed 8-10 boats anchored there in the shade with kids swimming underneath this huge alcove. In the **middle fork of Annies**, there's also a possible campsite about where you begin hiking.

Hiking Routes or Trails If you like visiting Anasazi ruins, you'll enjoy the hike up **Lake Canyon**. You'll boat past one set of ruins about 1 km below the HWM; but this one's hard to find. Also, to the left under a south facing wall right at the HWM (and high on an alluvial bench), is another set of ruins--but this isn't much to look at. You'll have to climb up to this one from the west end of the bench.

As you walk upcanyon below the HWM, wade right in the creek; floods keep the stream channel open and free from tamaracks. Above the HWM, it's a more natural creek bed. There are livestock in the upper drainage from October to June, so in places there are cattle trails in and along the stream as well. In 2001, there were several deep beaver ponds just below the HWM which made progress up-canyon difficult. But, on **8/4/2007-WL1099.42m/3606.97'**, they were gone, washed away by the big floods of 10/2006. On a regular basis, plants grow in the stream channel for a while and clog things up, then every 3-4 years a big flood roars down and takes them out and cleans out the canyon bottom.

About 2 kms above the HWM, and just above where the creek bed makes a couple of gooseneck turns with a **waterfall**, you'll see high on the western wall, well-preserved **Anasazi ruins**. It's very difficult to reach these now, as the alluvial base has been washed away. If you wish to exit the canyon, you can do so by climbing up the slickrock slope immediately across the canyon east of these ruins. There's also an entry/exit about 200 meters downcanyon from the ruins and immediately east of the waterfall. About 1 km above these **wall ruins** is another easy way out of the canyon to the east using cow trails. Near that exit, and on the south side of a shallow meadow-type drainage, are 2 Anasazi struc-

About halfway up **Lake Canyon** (just past the waterfall), and on the right or west, is what this writer calls the **Wall Ruins**. Its base has been eroded away by big floods, and you can no longer climb up to the site.

Map 14, Lake & Annies Canyons, the Schock & Gretchen Bar Trails, and Lake Pagahrit

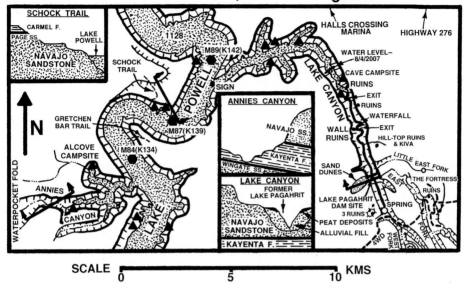

SCALE 0 ___ 5 ___ 10 KMS

tures on a **hill top**; one being a **kiva**, the other a dwelling.

From the area of these **hill-top ruins**, you can either walk upstream along the creek bed; or stay on the canyon rim. If you stay on the rim, you can reach a high point after walking less than 1 km. From this vantage point you can see ahead to where an old lake once was. This was called **Lake Pagahrit** (sometimes called **Hermit Lake**). The remains of this lake bed and natural dam is perhaps the most interesting feature in the canyon. More on this below.

To see other interesting places, walk up the **East Fork of Lake Canyon** about 2 kms. There you'll come to a sandy road in the wash bottom. Immediately east of that, is a small granary under a ledge. Also, up that road to the southeast about 200 meters, and on the left or east side, is where the road comes down from the canyon rim. About 100 meters southeast from the top of that dugway, is a big open Anasazi ruin called **The Fortress**. It's made of pieces of limestone from a lens in the Navajo Sandstone. It's a long hike from the lake to this site, so if you're in the area and have a car with higher clearance, you can leave Highway 276 immediate west of the **Cal Black Airport** (between mile posts 53 & 54) and head south for 7.1 kms (4.4 miles), then turn southwest onto **BLM Road #2541** and continue for another 3.7 kms (2.3 miles). That will put you right on the canyon rim near The Fortress.

If you get out of Lake Canyon on the west side of the former Lake Pagahrit, you'll find 3 more small crude **dwellings** on a flat **limestone hill-top**, plus another pile of rocks (a former Anasazi shelter) just north of those. About 650 meters southeast of these hill-top ruins, is the sandy 4WD road mentioned earlier in the East Fork. This track climbs out of the canyon and heads southwest over Grey & Wilson Mesas and to the **Hole-in-the-Rock Trail** & Cottonwood Canyon.

The **Schock Trail** is said to be an old cattle trail which began at the Baker Ranch (the **Baker Trail** at that point, see **Map 13**), then headed upon the slickrock of the Waterpocket Fold, and finally descended 300 meters to the Colorado River just below the mouth of Lake Canyon. However, because of it's steepness over slickrock it was likely used almost exclusively by prospectors rather than livestock. According to Crampton's studies on Glen Canyon prior to Lake Powell, the name of the trail is from one **W.H. Schock**, an old prospector who worked the river bars for 20 years after about 1898.

You'll have to look for the beginning of this trail. If the lake is high, it's about 200 meters west of the largest of the tiny inlets which can be used for camping, and 800 meters west of buoy M87 (K139). Tie-up your boat and get out and walk. Look for some steps cut and blasted out in steeper places and some stone cairns. It first zig zags up in a northerly direction, then once on an intermediate Navajo (perhaps Page?) Sandstone bench, it veers northwest. It tops out on the Carmel rim above, then disappears.

In **Annies Canyon**, the only place you can hike is from the end of the **middle fork inlet**. At that point the canyon is becoming wider because of the emergence of the Kayenta Formation. On 8/4/2007, **WL1099.42m/3606.97'**, you had to walk along a good hiker's trail to the left of a dryfall, then head up-canyon. As you climb, the canyon broadens and after about 4 kms you'll reach the top of the **Waterpocket Fold**. Get to a high point for good views in all directions. The view down on the Navajo Sandstone bluffs and domes is worth the easy walk.

Few people know of the **Gretchen Bar Trail**. It was built for one purpose according to Crampton's research, and that was to allow a 1930's model Caterpillar tractor down to the river. The Cat was used for mining at the Gretchen Bar (read more below).

This trail is located about 1 km southeast from the sharp corner of the old river bend, or about 2 kms north of the mouth of Annies Canyon and on the east side of the lake. Look for a large stone cairn just above the HWM on a little slickrock ridge jutting out into the lake a few meters. On the south side of this very minor ridge is an area which has been blasted out to form a narrow roadway. Walk up this and follow the half dozen or so cairns to the east. A bit further up, there's another minor ridge where some

123

blasting was done. At the very top of a prominent bluff, which can be seen faintly from the lake, is one last cairn. This one has an old piece of metal sticking up in the middle--some kind of a machine part. At that point the route/trail vanishes.

Hike Length & Time Needed It's about 6 kms from the HWM to the former dam of **Lake Pagahrit**. It isn't far and the traveling is mostly easy, but there are many things to see. That's why you'll need all or most of a day for this hike. The author spent over 4 hours walking to the dam and back on his first trip; most of a day on the second hike when he went all the way to the 4WD Road mentioned above.

The walk from the lake to the Carmel rim where the **Schock Trail** disappears is less than 2 kms. Once you locate the trail, you can do the whole thing in about an hour. It's about 4 kms to the top of **Annies Canyon**, and this hike can be done in maybe 3 hours round-trip, depending on how much you explore. The walk to the top of the **Gretchen Bar Trail** will take 15 minutes round-trip.

Boots or Shoes For Lake Canyon use wading shoes, but for all the other hikes any boots or shoes.

Water There's a year-round flow in Lake Creek, but there are cattle in the area most of the year, so don't drink water from the creek. Above the old dam site are several springs. They should have good drinking water--at the spring source only! There are no springs or streams on any of the other hikes, so take your own water from a culinary source.

Main Attractions Anasazi ruins and old lake deposits in Lake Canyon. Also, 2 old and historic miner's trails cut into slickrock, and an easy hike to the top of the Waterpocket Fold for some fine views.

Hiking Maps USGS or BLM map Navajo Mountain (1:100,000); The Rincon NE & Halls Crossing (1:24,000--7 1/2' quads) for hiking; or Lake Canyon & The Rincon (1:62,500) if available.

Anasazi Ruins, Lake Pagahrit, and Other History The University of Utah archaeological report on **Lake Canyon** conducted in 1959, states there were 77 sites observed in or near this canyon. Not all of these were the magnificent cliff dwellings so common in southern Utah canyons; some were hill-top dwellings while others were flint chip sites. There were also an unusually large number of food storage sites (granaries) observed. Still other sites were from the Navajos or early-day cattlemen. Some of the more interesting sites are now under water (the HWM).

Fowler's survey in 1959, indicated that Lake Canyon was outside the usual settlement pattern as found in other drainages flowing into Glen Canyon. In other canyons, potsherds indicate either Mesa Verde or Kayenta Anasazi cultures existed. But in Lake Canyon, there appeared to have been an odd mixture of both of these cultures into one, leading researchers to believe this was one of the first canyons settled in the region. Anasazi settlements in Lake Canyon spanned about 200 years, from about 1100 to 1300 AD.

In the late 1800's and early 1900's, there were Navajos in the region, as indicated by some circular pole structures, as well as parts of a buggy, a dutch oven, wire grills and water pipe. These artifacts were found in the area of **Lake Pagahrit**. Apparently the first time white men knew of the lake was in February of 1880, when the **Hole-in-the-Rock Party** passed that way on their journey to Bluff on the San Juan River. It was such an inviting place, they camped there for several days to make repairs to their wagons and rest their horses & livestock.

Ever since the Mormons passed through the Pagahrit country they had cattle grazing there year-round. From about 1880 until 1898, the cattle belonged to the **Bluff Pool**. Then the Mormons sold out to the **Scorup Brothers**, Al and Jim. Their Scorups ran cattle in the region until about 1965. Al Scorup

This is the **Hill-Top Ruins & Kiva** on the map. It's on a low hill on the east side of Lake Canyon not far above the Wall Ruins. This is a kiva, but there's another hole in the ground just to the left which was used as living quarters. The ground around is littered with potsherds & flint chips.

believed overgrazing in the drought years of the mid-1890's began to damage the range, then more grazing continued into the early 1900's. This led to the beginning of an erosional cycle and the eventual breaching of the lake's dam. It was **Jim S. Scorup** who witnessed the event. After 3 days of heavy rains, and on **November 3, 1915**, the water first started making a cut in the natural dam of the lake and it drained rapidly. Before that day the lake was reported to be about 12 meters deep and nearly 1 km long. Read more on the cattle industry in **Part 1--Introduction & History**, starting on **page 10**.

This was the beginning of this latest stage of downcutting of the alluvial benches you see so prominently exposed in the canyon today. All the ruins in the canyon were built while the stream was at that higher level. On top of these benches you'll find dead trees, which last grew when the water table was higher. They would have died sometime after 1915.

Here's what you'll find at Lake Pagahrit today. The dam of the lake was actually created by a slow moving sand dune pushed north, northeast by the prevailing southwesterly winds. This gradually filled in the canyon and the lake slowly developed behind it. It likely wasn't very deep; instead rather shallow and swampy. You can see deep beds of organic matter on the high benches where the lake once was even today. This looks like dead peat, something like you find in Ireland or in the northern tundra regions. The canyon is now "V" shaped and the stream runs at bedrock. With time, and if the area is not overused or abused any more, the place should again develop into a swamp or lake.

Here's something else to look for. As you walk upcanyon along the creek from the HWM, or on the rim, pay attention to the alluvial benches. There are a number of places along the way which have the same look as the old bed of Lake Pagahrit. One is immediately east or downcanyon from the waterfall. This seems to point to a former sand-filled canyon with one continuous swamp from top to bottom. In our time, it was cattle overgrazing the canyon which caused the recent downcutting.

It's this author's view that similar abuse or overuse by the Anasazi may have caused a similar event in their time resulting in downcutting and the lowering of the water table. This would have led to the loss of farmland and may have been a major cause for their departure from this canyon and others between about 1275 AD and 1300 AD.

Just below the mouth of Lake Canyon is what river runners used to call **Lake Canyon Rapids**. Actually, it wasn't really rapids, mostly just a fast ride over some ripples. This ripple was created by debris washed out of Lake Canyon during flash floods. When Stanton passed through the area in January, 1898, the river was jammed up with ice and they were lucky to have gotten their boats through without damage being done. The cause of the ice jam was the shallow quiet waters just above the ripples.

Just downstream from the bottom of the **Schock Trail**, was a place called **Anderson Bar**. Records show it was placer mined as early as 1889. In 1961, near the lower end of this gravel & sand embankment and about 50 meters from the river, was a dugout cabin consisting mainly of a fireplace chimney built of sandstone slabs and standing about 3 meters high. According to A. L. Chaffin and Crampton, that cabin was built by W. H. Schock, who lived in the area in 1898 and again in 1908-09.

Before Lake Powell came to be, one of the more important placer gold mining areas in this region was located just across the river from the mouth of Annies Canyon. It had many names over the years, such as Schock Bar and Anderson Camp, but the best known name was **Gretchen Bar**. It saw considerable placer mining dating from 1889, when 3 men--Harris, Davis and Vance, located the Hope Placer Mine.

It must have been a pleasant camp. There was a cool spring with some of the water being piped to

Looking west at a 3-meter-high waterfall about 250 meters below the **Wall Ruins**.

a nearby stone cabin. The cabin was built by W. H. Schock, perhaps in the 1890's. Spring water also watered fig, apricot and pomegranate trees, as well as grapes. Crampton reported that when his party inspected the place in 1961 these plants and trees were still alive and that they picked and ate delicious fruit from a fig tree.

There was all kinds of old mining equipment lying around atop this bar, which included sorting screens, a large boiler--dating from about 1900, sluicing tables, several gasoline motors and pumps, and a 1930's model "Thirty", 8 cylinder Caterpillar tractor, still attached to a Fresno scraper. It had been driven from Blanding, Utah, about 160 kms away, via the **old Mormon Hole-in-the-Rock Trail**. It was brought into the area west of Lake Canyon, then carefully taken down the slickrock just north of the bar. Several places had to be prepared by blasting the slickrock with dynamite. This is now known as the **Gretchen Bar Trail** (see more on the trail above).

The normal way the miners got to this site was via Escalante or the Loa areas, down Halls Creek to the Baker Ranch, then to the west on top of the Waterpocket Fold along the Baker or Black Trail. Finally, the Schock Trail veered to the east and dropped into Glen Canyon not far below the mouth of Lake Canyon. From there the route went down the west bank of the Colorado, and during times of low water, pack horses could make a ford of the river in front of Gretchen Bar.

This picture from an old slide dated 1989, shows part of the **Gretchen Bar Trail** with the lake level very near the HWM. It's easy to find even when the water is low as it was in 2007.

This picture was taken on the east side of the former **Lake Pagahrit** looking southwest. Both sides of this little valley show signs of the former lake bed. The top black layer resembles peat.

Looking southeast from a hill on the east side near what used to be the dam for **Lake Pagahrit**. Compare this with the B+W fotos on page 129. It was this migrating sand dune, created by prevailing south winds, that created the lake. After 3 days of heavy rain, the dam burst on November 3, 1915.

From the west side of the former **Lake Pagahrit** looking north toward the Henry Mountains. The white deposits on both sides are lake bed sediments. The former dam is to the left and out of sight.

About 2-3 kms up the **East Fork** of **Lake Canyon** from the former Lake Pagahrit, is this large Anasazi structure called **The Fortress** (looking west). It sits on a limestone lens within the Navajo Sandstone, and is made of limestone rocks. With a high-clearance vehicle, you can drive to this point.

The big **Alcove Campsite** at the head of the north fork of **Annies Canyon**. This picture was taken on **8/4/2007-WL1099.42m/3606.97'**. On that Sunday, 8-10 boats, with sunbathers & swimmers, were anchored underneath it.

Lake Pagahrit: Upper This foto was taken from the lake's dam, or just west of it, and looking southeast. In the middle & dead ahead in the far distance, is where a sandy 4WD road crosses what was then the upper end of the lake. Today, that same place is the head of an erosional gully. One more good flood and that 4WD road will be wiped out and will prevent vehicles from reaching the Hole-in-the-Rock Trail to the west. **Lower** This picture was taken from the upper end of the valley looking across the lake to the northeast. Not far to the right is where today's 4WD road leaves the canyon bottom heading for the Hole-in-the-Rock Trail (Albert R. Lyman fotos).

Left This foto shows ice jammed up behind the **Lake Canyon ripples** in the Colorado River. Robert B. Stanton took this picture in January of 1898.

129

Slickrock & Iceberg Canyons, and The Rincon & Rincon Overlook Hikes

Location & Campsites **Slickrock & Iceberg Canyons** and **The Rincon** are located about halfway between Hall's Crossing Marina and the mouth of the Escalante River. At the mouth of Slickrock Canyon is a buoy marked M81A (K130), and buoy M78 (K125) is at the mouth of Iceberg. The Rincon area is between buoys M77 (K123) and M78 (K125). These are distances in miles (kilometers) uplake from the Glen Canyon Dam.

Slickrock Canyon has several good sandy campsites, and many tie-down places, regardless of lake levels. These sites are found on the emerging Kayenta benches. **Iceberg Canyon** also has a number of campsites, but given its length, they are rather sparse. At high lake levels, Iceberg's campsites tend to be rather small and surrounded by water and vertical cliffs because the Navajo Sandstone walls came right down to the water's edge in most places. But on **8/4/2007-WL1099.42m/3606.97'** (low water levels), there were more possible tent sites, and even more tie-down places for houseboats. One of the best sites in the area, at least when the lake is high, sits at the mouth of Iceberg Canyon. It's a big sandy beach, but open to lake-size waves when the wind blows in from the north. Iceberg Canyon Inlet is one of the longest and deepest on the lake. Perhaps no other canyon on the lake has Navajo walls as high, as vertical and as spectacular as these.

An interesting feature in Iceberg is the large **rockfall** and resultant **dam** across the lower part of the **South Fork**. At one time, part of the eastern wall peeled off and created a dam. If the water level is at or very near the HWM, you can get your boat into the upper end of this inlet; otherwise boats are locked out. Both Slickrock and Iceberg have **Anasazi ruins**.

On the northern parts of **The Rincon** you'll find many good campsites. These beaches are made of sand from the Navajo and Wingate Sandstone, and the clay beds of the Chinle Formation. There are even more sandy beach-type sites on the western arm of The Rincon along what used to be called Butler Creek. Located in the lake northwest of The Rincon is a floating **toilet & dump/pump station**.

The name **rincon** is sometimes used in place of an **abandoned meander** or **abandoned stream channel**. These all mean the same thing. Rincon is used here to describe a giant abandoned meander of the Colorado River. It once flowed through this circular channel perhaps a million years ago. It may have been forced into that direction or position by the uplift called the **Waterpocket Fold**. This fold, sometimes called a monocline, begins far to the north around Thousand Lake Mountain and the north end of Capitol Reef National Park, and ends somewhere in Arizona. As time went on, parts of a gooseneck bend of the river closed in on each other, and finally a narrow wall was broken down and the river rushed through abandoning the old circular channel to the south. This left The Rincon Valley high & dry as we see today. Rincons or abandoned meanders are common features on the Colorado Plateau, but this is the largest of any in Lake Powell country. See foto below.

Hiking Routes or Trails Going up **Slickrock Canyon,** you may find hiker-made trails, mostly on the north side of the intermittent stream. Most of the time the creek will have a small flow of water. The canyon is lined with willows, cottonwoods and gamble oak. There is evidence of an older beaver pop-

Aerial view of the **Rincon** looking southwest on **9/25/2007-WL1097.86m/3601.85'**. Notice the sandslides on the right or western side. Cows used to be driven up the sand, then bench-walked around to the east side and out the top. The white spot in the water is the **toilet & dump/pump station**.

Map 15, Slickrock & Iceberg Canyons, and The Rincon & Rincon Overlook Hikes

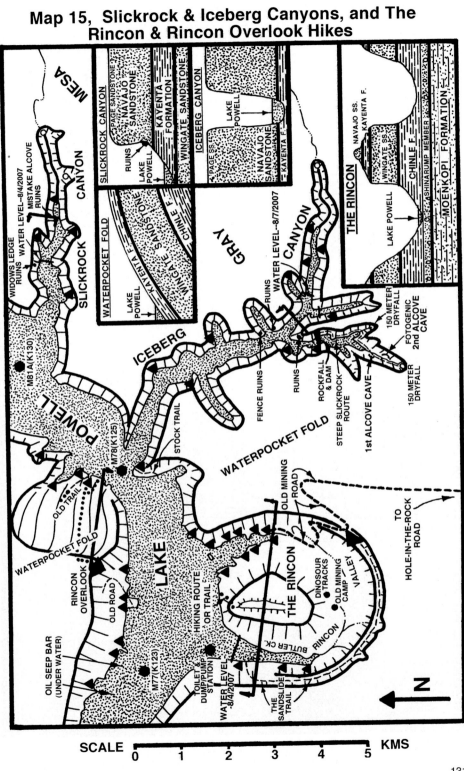

SCALE 0 1 2 3 4 5 KMS

ulation, but when the author visited the place, there were no new signs. There are small alcoves on both sides of the canyon, many of which have springs issuing from the bottom of the Navajo Sandstone and/or top of the Kayenta. At the end is a high dryfall with a seep at the bottom. This canyon shows no sign of being gutted by recent erosion as one sees in Lake, Moqui, or other area canyons.

There are 2 major Anasazi archaeology sites in **Slickrock Canyon**. The 1st is called **Widows Ledge Ruins**; the 2nd, **Mistake Alcove Ruins**. Over the years, these sites have been very popular with the public, and as a result of too much wear & tear, and maybe kids climbing on the walls, the NPS has erected chainlink fences around both sites and are now closed to closeup visitations.

In **Iceberg Canyon**, you have one rather short hike in the upper end of the main fork. This canyon bottom is littered with downed cottonwood trees the result of past beaver populations. On the author's 1st visit, there were no fresh sign, as beaver move from one canyon to another as food supplies dwindle. There's a hiker-made trail heading up this fork mostly on the north side of the year-round flowing stream. It ends at one of the highest dryfalls around.

In the **South Fork of Iceberg**, leave your boat close to the dam then walk across the rubble to the east side. From there, walk south on the east side of the upper inlet where you'll find a pretty good hiker's trail. After about 650 meters, you'll end up on top of a big slickrock **hogsback ridge**. From there, walk down to the west, then route-find south around the hogsback to the left and down to the lake. There are 2 steep sections on this downhill side, so it's best to wear a good pair of running shoes. A rope may help less-experienced hikers down the 2nd steep part which is near the water. When climbing back up, you'll have to use all-4's.

Once south of the hogsback ridge, walk along deer trails into the upper end of a **southeast fork** to find an alcove and dryfall approaching 150 meters in height! Or route-find your way, again on deer trails (occasionally used by hikers), up along the west side of the **main branch of South Fork**. After a ways, you'll come to the **1st Alcove Cave** measuring roughly 35 x 25 x 1 1/2 meters. There's evidence that Anasazi Indians camped there.

Beyond the 1st Cave, and after another 350 meters, head down, cross the small creek and enter the **2nd Alcove Cave**. This is one of the biggest alcove caves the author has seen. It measures approximately 90 x 60 x 20 meters. It's also the most fotogenic as you can see in the pictures on the cover and here. In a way it's very similar to The Wave in the Coyote Buttes (see the author's book on the **Paria River**), but here it's the rounded ceiling that has the fantastic color and stripping. Fotographers should be there between about 11am and 4pm or 5pm (best) on a sunny day for maximum light & color.

At the head of this same fork is another huge alcove & dryfall with a height approaching 150 vertical meters. To get into the west branch of South Fork, you'll need a raft of some kind, or maybe even swim in a place or two.

Now for **The Rincon** area. Perhaps the most popular hike would be the walk around the central butte of The Rincon and into the **Rincon Valley**. You can start on either side, but for this description, let's begin on the east side. Right in the bottom of the dry creek bed you'll see an old abandoned mining road. You can walk on this for a ways, but when it turns east, you continue southwest on some cow trails. Cows can graze this area from October to June every other year. Further on, and as you're heading west, take note of some of the large Wingate Sandstone boulders to your right. If the sun is right, you can see on the south side of one boulder, some kind of animal tracks, likely those of a small dinosaur. After another 200-300 meters, you'll come to some old barrels, buckets, etc. This is an old 1950's miner's campsite. The miners came to look for uranium in the Chinle clay beds.

Rockfall Dam in the **South Fork** of **Iceberg Canyon**. This foto is from a slide taken in 1988. With a small boat, you could, at that time, float into the the upper end of the South Fork. This Rockfall Dam is now covered with tamaracks & trees, as you can see in the foto on **page 137** from 8/4/2007.

On the west side of The Rincon is the canyon or drainage once called **Butler Creek**. In this area is an **old stock trail** which went from the rim to the river. Local cowboys called this the **Sandslide Trail**. This trail used to start or end just downstream from the mouth of Butler Creek on the Colorado. Then it must have gone up Butler Creek Canyon a ways before angling west up a sandslide to the top of the first major terrace, a **Kayenta Formation bench**. From the top of the Kayenta, the trail headed south at the same elevation until it either breached the Navajo Sandstone at a point about 2 kms to the south; or cattle could have been driven on around the same bench to where the old mining road now comes out of the Rincon Valley.

This stock trail was long used by cattlemen of San Juan County as a route by which livestock were driven to winter range in The Rincon Valley and adjacent areas, including Iceberg Canyon. After the road was built down the east side of The Rincon, this trail was abandoned. Today you can't see any trace of the trail but the route is still there. If you hike up the sandslide to the Kayenta bench you'll have some fine views of the Rincon Valley, a cross-section view of the Waterpocket Fold, and the lake.

One of the cowboys who worked in this area was Clarence Rogers of Blanding. He remembered an incident back in about 1920. A man named **Jacob Adams** had just bought the grazing rights for this region from big-time cattlemen **Jim & Al Scorup**. He took 100 head of cows to the Rincon Valley and left them there for the winter. The grass looked good enough for lots of livestock. But when Adams returned late in the spring, his cows had eaten everything down to the ground, and were in very poor condition. When he tried to push them back up the Sandslide, neither the cows or their new-born calves could make it. As a result he had to take them down to the river and move them north to the Gretchen Bar. From there, he got them out of Glen Canyon using the Gretchen Bar Trail.

Another hike is to the rim of The Rincon on the east side. Above the HWM at the south end of the inlet on the eastern side is the **old mining road** mentioned above. Follow it south, then east, as it zig zags up through the broken-down Wingate cliffs until you're on top of the Kayenta ledges. From there, you'll have fine views of the Rincon and lake. If you continue on this road, which is still used up to the point of this overlook, it first heads northeast, then turns south to meet the remains of the still older **Hole-in-the-Rock Trail**, dating from 1880. This is the easiest way to reach the rim and is a popular and easy hike for the whole family.

Another short hike with a good view is to the top of the **central butte** in the middle of The Rincon. Boat to the north side of the butte, and tie-up just northeast of the northern ridge. Walk southwest up a boulder & sagebrush covered slope which gets steeper the higher you climb. Higher up, and not far from the big Wingate cliffs, you'll begin to see signs of a hiker-made trail-of-sorts. When you reach the first cliffs, veer left or southeast and get on a little ridge, then go up again. Look for cracks in the upper-most cliffs. There are several cracks you can get into, then wander a bit, before exiting to the top. At that point, you'll be on a Kayenta bench, with good views of the lake. You may or may not be able to reach the very top which is capped with Navajo Sandstone.

Another interesting hike is one to the top of the **Waterpocket Fold** just across the lake north of The Rincon. From what the author is calling **The Rincon Overlook**, you will enjoy a good view looking south, and the interesting geology of the area. To do this hike, tie-up directly across the channel from the mouth of Iceberg Canyon in one of several tiny coves, then simply walk up the inclined slope to the west, but veer to the north a little to avoid some rougher & broken terrain. You'll be walking on top of

Mistake Alcove Ruins in **Slickrock Canyon**. This and the Widows Ledge Ruins, have been fenced off so you can't get up close (2007). Apparently the NPS thought they were being abused by thought-less individuals (?). Hopefully in the future they can be stabilized so everyone can see them upclose.

Kayenta slickrock all the way. Once you reach a high point of the Fold, turn left or south, and walk to the rim of the canyon. Below, and on the Chinle slopes, you'll see an old mining exploration track, and of course, have fine views of The Rincon and the southern extension of the Waterpocket Fold.

When the author first made this hike to the top of the Fold, he was unaware of an **old stock trail** up to the top in about the same area as his own route. This is how Crampton describes it: *This trail begins on the west side of the river, opposite the mouth of Iceberg Canyon, and ascends the steep eastern slope of the Waterpocket Fold. This trail, reportedly used by prospectors and by Indians before them, probably joins with the Black Trail [Baker Ranch--Escalante River Trail] at some point on the crest of the Waterpocket Fold.*

On another trip the author again went part way up the slope to check out this trail. He did find a couple of cairns but no other sign. Since it's not too steep, horses could have used any one of many routes. However, way up on top there are Navajo bluffs, which would channel all traffic into one of several narrow corridors. In one of these locations, it's possible you might find evidence of a real trail. This leaves room for someone to explore.

Hike Length & Time Needed You can only walk up **Slickrock** about 2 1/2 kms. It took the author only 1 1/2 hours for the round-trip hike. In **Iceberg**, you can walk less than 2 kms to the end of the main canyon. The author hurried on this one and did it in just over an hour. You should plan on 1-2 hours for each of these hikes. In the **South Fork of Iceberg**, it should take most people half a day to walk to the 2nd Alcove Cave and back--maybe 3-5 hours round-trip.

To hike around **The Rincon** is to walk about 5 kms--depending on lake levels. This round-trip hike can be done in a couple of hours. It's about 3 kms to the top of the mesa on the southeast side of The Rincon via the old road, and this too will take about 2 hours round-trip.

In 15 minutes you can walk from the lake up the **Sandslide Trail** to the Kayenta bench on the west side of The Rincon. In about half a day, one could walk up this old stock trail, and come down the road on the east side, then return to the boat.

To the top of the butte in the **middle of The Rincon** will take about an hour for most people. The hike up to **The Rincon Overlook** is about 2 kms, and will take perhaps 2-3 hours, round-trip.

Boots or Shoes There are small streams in the 2 canyons, but you can usually avoid getting wet feet, so any kind of boots or shoes are OK. All hikes around The Rincon are dry.

Water If you see fresh sign of beaver in either of the canyons better not drink the water unless it's taken directly from a spring (or filter it). If there is no new evidence of beaver, then it will likely be drinkable in the upper parts of both Iceberg and Slickrock Canyons. There are no springs in The Rincon area, so carry your own water.

Main Attractions Very high Navajo Sandstone walls, especially in Iceberg, several Anasazi ruins in each canyon, a huge rockfall & dam and fotogenic cave in Iceberg, some fine views of unusual geologic features in The Rincon area, and a number of good short hikes for the whole family.

Hiking Maps USGS or BLM map Navajo Mountain (1:100,000); The Rincon & Alcove Canyon (1:24,000--7 1/2' quads) for hiking; or Lake Canyon & The Rincon (1:62,500) if available.

Anasazi Ruins and Historic Sites There are at least 2 well-preserved ruins in **Slickrock Canyon**. Both sites were excavated before Lake Powell times and researchers found pottery which showed the inhabitants to be about half from the Mesa Verde group, half from the Kayenta clan. Quoting from the

Looking southwest at the **toilet & dump/pump station** located at the **Rincon**. Below the water is the now-drowned Butler Creek Canyon; in the background is the sandslide where cows used to be driven up to a bench where a trail took them around the Rincon and out to the east.

University of Utah Anthropological Paper #39: *Within the Glen Canyon Kayenta-Mesa Verde Group boundaries, Slick Rock [Canyon] occupies a unique position. Of canyons tributary to the Colorado River, it is the farthest downstream in which there is a significant evidence of Mesa Verde contact. As in Lake and Moqui Canyons, peoples of the two groups seem to have met and mingled peaceably, if pottery may be legitimately used as a criterion.* These sites were occupied sometime during the 1200's and abandoned before 1300 AD. The sites in Slickrock are called **Widow's Ledge & Mistake Alcove**.

In **Iceberg Canyon**, there are parts of 3 ruins visible; all storage structures or granaries, and frankly not very interesting to look at. The one called **Fence Ruins** is small and perhaps a granary. Fence was extensively studied because it was a major site with the main part of that group of shelters now under water. The Fence Ruins was occupied from about 1250 until 1280 AD.

A site named **Mat House** is somewhere in the dammed-off **South Fork inlet** but the author didn't see it. It may still be there and possible to see if you do some exploring beyond the rockfall dam and the inlet behind. Mat House is believed to have been used from about 1230 until 1250 AD. Near the mouth of the dammed-off inlet, there's a small storage structure tucked up underneath an overhang which appears to be authentic (?).

The old mining road into The Rincon has an interesting history according to Crampton's research. Sometime after World War II, the Hole-in-the-Rock Trail through Clay Hills Pass was replaced by a new road built by an oil company, which extended it to the top of **Nokai Dome**. This was very close to an overlook of the San Juan River. A few years later, beginning on July 4, 1957, a uranium company with Texas interests (a man named Howell), began repairing the Nokai Dome Road then extended it to the west along the old Hole-in-the-Rock Trail. From on top of Gray Mesa, the road went north to the east side of The Rincon, then dropped down to the river. It reached the river northeast of the central butte of The Rincon. If you see ATV's in this part, report this illegal activity to GCNRA rangers.

Before the lake covered the area, one of the most unusual sites in Glen Canyon was **Oil Seep Bar**. This area was just northwest of The Rincon and on the north side of the river. Just a few meters above the river were several natural oil seeps. Some travelers called them oil springs. Because of the remote location, no commercial drilling took place there until after World War I. In 1920-21, there were a number of places in southeastern Utah under investigation for possible oil drilling and The Rincon was one area of interest.

Under the supervision of **Frank Bennett**, who had been involved in various gold mining ventures in Glen Canyon since 1897, the **Henry Mountains Oil Company** drilled 4 wells at this site, which was sometimes called **Bennett's Oil Field**. Two of the wells, about 10 meters apart, were drilled in the seep area and a third, about 100 meters to the east. The fourth was drilled about 1 1/2 kms east of the seeps and just below the present-day HWM of the lake.

Operations began in July, 1920. Five tons of oil drilling equipment consisting of an Armstrong rig, a wooden frame, a large wooden bullwheel, a gasoline engine, and drill stems and bits, were brought by team & wagon from Richfield, Utah, to Halls Crossing. At that point, rafts were built and the equipment and supplies were floated downriver 32 kms to the drilling site. In November of the same year, part of the Stanton Dredge, marooned near Stanton Canyon, was dismantled and rafted down to Oil Seep Bar and used to build living quarters for workers.

Later, supplies were brought in by boat from Halls Crossing or by pack horses over the **Black Trail** from **Baker Ranch** (the Black Trail went south along the top of the Waterpocket Fold, then dropped down into Bowns Canyon, contoured along the Kayenta bench within Glen Canyon, and south to the

The site of 2 oil wells drilled by the Henry Mountains Oil Company. The location is just above where **Oil Well Bar** was located before the coming of Lake Powell (Crampton foto).

mouth of the Escalante River). From near the mouth of Bowns Canyon, they blasted out a trail down from the Kayenta bench and into the lower end of Bowns, then out Long Canyon and finally along the north side of the Colorado River to Oil Seep Bar (see **Map 16** on **Long & Bowns Canyons** for a look at **Bennett's Oil Field Trail**).

The oil wells proved unprofitable as the flow was sluggish and the operation shut down in 1921. When Crampton visited the site in 1961, a number of artifacts were found, including bits, drill stems, scrapers, 3 small cabins and a wagon. The drilling rig was later moved to Gretchen Bar and used for other things, and in the end parts of it ended up at Hite.

The **1st Alcove Cave** you come to when hiking up the **South Fork** of **Iceberg Canyon**. With the sun shining outside, and reflecting the light inside, these colors are natural--at least as seen through the lens of a Canon Sure Shot A550, 7.1mp. It was actually shot at 5mp.

From a high point on the trail into the **South Fork** of **Iceberg Canyon**, looking south into the back end of the fork with the 2 colorful alcove caves. During the late 1980's, all parts of this green valley was covered with water--now it's choked with brush--mostly tamaracks (tamarisk).

This is the **2nd Alcove Cave** in the upper end of **South Fork** of **Iceberg Canyon**. This is the real color and has not been enhanced by Photoshop.

From a high point on the trail into the **South Fork** of **Iceberg Canyon** looking northwest at the **Rock-fall Dam**. Today it's covered with tamaracks and small trees. On 8/4/2007, the small lake behind the dam was higher than the level of Lake Powel itself.

Long & Bowns Canyons and the Black Trail

Location & Campsites **Long and Bowns Canyons** share a common mouth, inlet or opening onto Lake Powell. Just after entering the lower end of Long Canyon, veer left and cruise up Bowns Inlet. Near the mouth of the Long/Bowns Canyon Inlet, and in the main channel, should be a buoy marked M74 (K118). These canyons form the first drainage north or uplake from the **Escalante River Arm**.

You'll find very few campsites in this part of Lake Powell. The reason is, the Wingate or Navajo Sandstone walls rise vertically right from the water. However, just to the west of the mouth of Long/Bowns Canyon Inlet are a couple of tie-down possibilities on the Kayenta Sandstone bench. These sites exist as the lake channel runs south, and the Wingate Sandstone dips under the water leaving the Kayenta benches exposed.

At the very end of Long Canyon Inlet, you should find at least one sandy campsite. There are no camping places in Bowns Inlet, but there are several tie-down places for houseboats. The author once camped in upper Bowns Inlet (in the late 1980's when the lake was near the HWM) on a sandy ledge just above the present-day dropoff, but a sad story came from that experience. While hiking up Bowns in 1988, **ravens gobbled up 3 loaves of bread** from his boat! A similar thing happened in 2001 in Long Canyon Inlet--so beware and **cover things up well**. This same event is happening all around Lake Powell at popular campsites.

One unique thing about these canyons is, there were, until September of 1988, wild horses and cattle in both. Actually, the best term to use instead of wild or semi-wild, would be **feral cattle or horses**. This means they were domestic at one time, then ran lose and became wild. These animals used to enter or exit this drainage complex in only one place, the **Black Trail** in the **East Fork of Bowns Canyon**. From there, they moved into Long Canyon via the Kayenta bench, which is above the lake and Wingate dryfalls. Read more on the removal of wild horses below.

Hiking Routes or Trails In **Bowns Canyon**, you'll have trouble getting directly into the drainage if the lake levels are below about 1120 meters (HWM is 1128m) because there will be a Wingate water/dry-fall to climb. In times of high water you simply boat in above the dropoff. In times of low water, as it was on **8/5/2007-WL1099.38m/3606.85'**, then a strong person might climb up a crack on the right with steep slickrock and continue upcanyon from there.

However, if you have trouble getting into the canyon at the very end of Bowns Inlet, head back out about 400 meters and on the left or northwest side, look for the remains of the **Bennett's Oil Field Trail**. It makes about 2 zigs and a zag up the rocky talus slope, then heads up to the right against the upper Wingate wall and into a short drainage. At the point where the trail crosses a minor dry creek bed, it's been blasted out with dynamite. Above that it disappears in the creek bed. About 100 meters beyond the blasted site, walk along the Kayenta bench into lower Bowns or Long Canyon.

Normally you'll tie-up your boat at the Bennett's Oil Field Trail, then bench-walk into lower Bowns. Not far in, you can get down into the lower section. About 200 meters above the HWM, you'll find a nice little 2 part, 4-meter-high waterfall & pool. Beyond that, in the first km or so above the HWM, you'll have a number of large boulders to get around but you'll find a hiker's trail which helps. Above that first section the canyon opens up and walking becomes easy. There will be a small stream in most places in this canyon all the way through the main fork. However, in some dry years, you may see just a few pools.

From the top of the constructed part of the **Bennetts Oil Field Trail** looking down onto the tiny **Bowns Canyon Inlet**. There's never any beaches here, just a place for houseboats to tie-down.

Map 16, Long & Bowns Canyons and the Black Trail

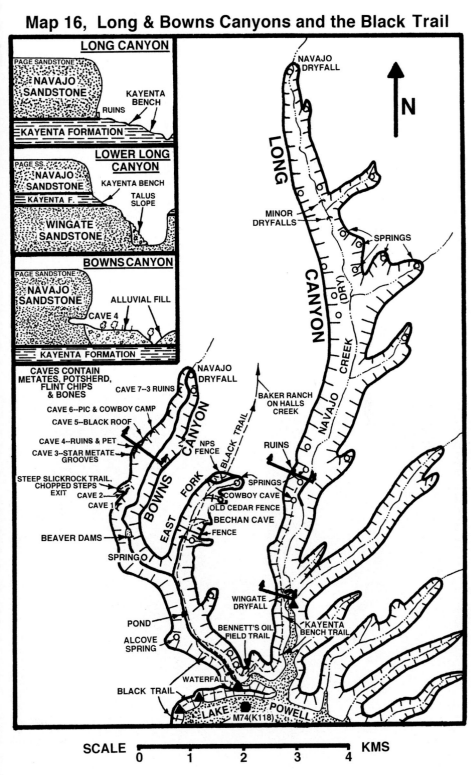

LONG CANYON

PAGE SANDSTONE
NAVAJO SANDSTONE
KAYENTA BENCH
RUINS
KAYENTA FORMATION

LOWER LONG CANYON

PAGE SS.
NAVAJO SANDSTONE
KAYENTA BENCH
KAYENTA F.
TALUS SLOPE
WINGATE SANDSTONE

BOWNS CANYON

PAGE SANDSTONE
NAVAJO SANDSTONE
ALLUVIAL FILL
CAVE 4
KAYENTA FORMATION

CAVES CONTAIN METATES, POTSHERD, FLINT CHIPS & BONES
CAVE 7--3 RUINS
CAVE 6--PIC & COWBOY CAMP
CAVE 5--BLACK ROOF
CAVE 4--RUINS & PET
CAVE 3--STAR METATE GROOVES
STEEP SLICKROCK TRAIL, CHOPPED STEPS EXIT
CAVE 2
CAVE 1
BEAVER DAMS
SPRING
POND
ALCOVE SPRING
BLACK TRAIL

NAVAJO DRYFALL

MINOR DRYFALLS
SPRINGS

BAKER RANCH ON HALLS CREEK
NAVAJO DRYFALL
BLACK TRAIL
NPS FENCE
RUINS
SPRINGS
COWBOY CAVE
OLD CEDAR FENCE
BECHAN CAVE
FENCE

LONG CANYON
NAVAJO CREEK (DRY)

BOWNS CANYON
EAST FORK

WINGATE DRYFALL
BENNETT'S OIL FIELD TRAIL
KAYENTA BENCH TRAIL

WATERFALL

LAKE POWELL
M74(K118)

N

SCALE
0   1   2   3   4
KMS

When you get out of lower Bowns with large boulders, you'll be on the **Kayenta bench**. At that point you can get onto this bench on the **west side** and walk along part of the old **Black Trail**, which heads out to the main channel towards the Escalante River. This trail is discussed more below. You can also turn to other way just up from the lake, and bench-walk into lower **Long Canyon**.

About 3 kms above the HWM in lower Bowns, the **East Fork** enters on the right. As you walk up the bottom of the East Fork drainage, you'll have a tiny running stream for about 1 km. At about the point where there's a dryfall, which will usually be the beginning of the running water, you can get out easily onto a low bench on either side (there's now a good hiker's trail on the east side as shown). No matter which side you walk up you may see parts of an **old fence** made of cedar trees, which must date back close to the year 1900. It may have been built by Will Bowns, who was known to have run cattle in the canyon between 1909 and 1913. It runs from one side of the canyon to the other about halfway up.

If you stay on the right or east side of East Fork, you'll notice a large cave not far beyond the old cedar fence. This is **Bechan Cave**, where researchers have found what they believe is mammoth dung about 12,000 years old. Read more on this cave below.

Just upcanyon another 300 meters and again on the right or east side is another large cave. This one is labeled **cowboy cave** on the map and it's nearly as big as Bechan Cave. There's a small spring below the entrance and the little alcove where it's located has been fenced off to form a corral or holding pen for livestock. This fence likely dates back to the early 1900's.

As you near the upper end of the East Fork, the main part of the drainage veers right or northeast and ends in a large alcove with a minor spring below. In this area, if you look due north or to the left a little, you can see on the lower part of the Navajo slickrock, a pile of old cedar posts or trees. This is at the bottom of the most gentle slope in the canyon, and is the lower end of a stock trail which was built by Will Bowns. This is part of the **Black (and Bowns)Trail** (discussed below) and is the only way livestock can enter either Bowns or Long Canyons. In several places along this part of the Black/Bowns Trail steps have been cut or blasted out of the rock. Higher up, the NPS has constructed a wire fence to keep cattle or horses from entering the canyon.

Now back to the **main fork of Bowns Canyon**. Start walking upon a bench on the right or east side to avoid the brushy bottom. After about 1 km, you'll have to cross to the west side just below a large beaver dam & pond. Even though the upper canyon is cut off from the lake (**8/5/2007-WL1099.38m /3606.85'**) there is still an active beaver population there.

Continue upcanyon on the west side. About 500m above the beaver pond, and on the left, will be the **1st of 7 big alcove-type caves** which used to be temporary home to Fremont Indians. This 1st one has metate grooves in large rocks, and scattered flint chips (the author found 3 broken arrowheads in one place). Just north of the 1st cave, is the **2nd alcove** with more m-grooves and broken bones from deer or big horn sheep. The Indians broke the bones to eat the marrow. Just above this 2nd cave is a **trail** out of the canyon. It has steps cut in steep slickrock in the lower part which goes right over the 2nd alcove. Higher up, more steps are cut up one steep place. Certainly cowboys, and perhaps horses, could use this, but not livestock.

The author calls the **3rd alcove**, **Star Cave**, because if has m-grooves on one boulder in the form of a star. See foto on page 142. The **4th alcove** has rock art, m-grooves on boulders, plus a simple

The top of the **Bennetts Oil Field Trail** just above **Bowns Canyon Bay**. The constructed part of this trail went down to about where the water line is shown to the upper left-hand corner of this picture.

shelter. The **5th cave**, has 6 more m-grooves on one big rock and black soot on the ceiling, indicating it was used a lot with campfires. The **6th alcove** was used as a **cowboy camp**, plus it has potsherds, pictographs and more m-grooves. The **7th alcove** has 3 rough shelters and a crude granary put together with mortar.

As you go up Bowns, you can walk along side the stream, but to see the caves, best to get up onto the alluvial bench. This bench, seen in many canyons entering Lake Powell, once was the floor of the canyon where the Fremont Indians must have had gardens and where until recently, many trees grew. The downcutting you see began in the early 1900's, sometime after the introduction of livestock. Because of this downcutting the water table dropped, thus a forest of dead trees is seen high and dry in places on this bench. Overgrazing is the reason for the recent and rapid erosion.

Now for **Long Canyon**. Just above the HWM in Long Canyon Inlet, you'll find a big Wingate dryfall and maybe a small stream flowing from beneath. You can't climb this dryfall, but about 100 meters below and on the left or west side, is a talus slope. Walk up this steep slope on an emerging trail to the terrace above, then bench-walk north and into the upper canyon. This bench is part of the Kayenta Formation.

Inside Long Canyon you don't find the same alluvial benches as found in Bowns. Instead, the Kayenta benches are exposed giving the canyon a slightly different look. It's easy walking right along the mostly dry creek bed, or on either side-bench and along the old wild horse trails. There is some running water in the lower end in what is called **Navajo Creek**, but not nearly as much as in Bowns. You will however find a number of small springs in the many alcoves which line each side of the drainage. The water seeps out at the Navajo-Kayenta contact.

Until 1988 there were wild horses in Long Canyon, along with at least one Anasazi ruin, as shown on the map. This one is under an overhang and has been trampled by cattle and horses. The author has walked all the way upcanyon on the west side, then returned via the dry creek bed. If you explore the short side-canyons on the east side, you could find something interesting. There are many green places at the upper ends of each alcove indicating the possibility of spring water and perhaps ruins.

Another way into Long Canyon is via the Kayenta bench which connects it with lower Bowns. The author once tied-down his boat at the bottom of Bennett's Oil Field Trail, climbed up on the Kayenta, then bench-walked around the corner into Long via what was obvious in places, a man-made trail. The author surmises, this **Bench Trail** was also built by Will Bowns in the same time frame as the other man-made trails in Bowns Canyon. From this bench you'll have a fine view down on the Wingate dryfall at the head of Long Canyon Inlet.

Hike Length & Time Needed Bowns Canyon; it should take all day to see both forks and do some exploring. **Long Canyon** is longer; about 12 kms from the Wingate dryfall to the upper end and the Navajo Sandstone headwall. If you enjoy exploring while hiking, and there are lots of places to explore, then plan on a full day's hike in Long Canyon.

Boots or Shoes In Bowns Canyon, you may have to do some wading, so wading shoes might be best. In Long Canyon, you'll be walking on a lot of Kayenta slickrock, so any kind of shoes will be OK.

Water The National Park Service (NPS) wild horse & cattle roundup in 1988 (read more below) has proved successful so the water quality in both canyons should be much better than before, but it's best

Bechan Cave in the **East Fork** of **Bowns Canyon**. About 1 meter under the surface of this dirt, mammoth dung has been found going back about 13,000 years.

141

not to drink direct from the streams in either canyon. However, there are many springs in both drainages. Drinking directly from a spring should be safe, but expect to find beaver in Bowns, so be careful.
Main Attractions Two green desert canyons (especially Bowns), interesting caves, waterfalls, and Fremont Indian ruins, metate grooves and rock art.
Hiking Maps USGS or BLM map Navajo Mountain (1:100,000); Davis Gulch, Stevens Canyon South, The Rincon & The Rincon NE (1:24,000--7 1/2' quads) for hiking; or The Rincon (1:62,500) if available.
The Black Trail and Will Bowns, Wild Horses and Bechan Cave Of all the trails in the Glen Canyon region, the **Black Trail** might have the most interesting history. It began along the Hole-in-the-Rock Road near the head of Clear Creek. It then veered east just north of Clear Creek Canyon and ran to the rim of the Escalante River. There it zig zagged down the a Navajo slickrock ledge to the river bottom just north of the mouth of Clear Creek. After running down the Escalante for 3 kms, it veered left or east and went up to and along the Kayenta bench which is just below the Navajo Sandstone walls. This bench is now under water in the lower end of the Escalante.

From the mouth of the Escalante, it continued to contour along the Kayenta bench to the east, then north for about 11 kms, to just below the mouth of Long Canyon. It then went around the corner and into lower Bowns Canyon, still on the same bench. A third of the way up Bowns, it headed north into the East Fork, and out on top of the Waterpocket Fold along the west side of upper Long Canyon. It continued north along the crest of the Waterpocket Fold, until somewhere above the Baker Ranch, then dropped off to the east and down to Hall's Creek and the Baker Ranch.

The reason it got the name Black Trail is because just east of the mouth of the Escalante River is a small alcove with the inscription, *J W Black, Feb. 2, 1896*, written in charcoal. It's not a certainty, but this was likely put there by a John Black, longtime resident of Escalante and Boulder who was born in 1871. Others have referred to the same route as the **Baker Ranch-Escalante Trail**.

According to Crampton's research on Glen Canyon, the creek in Long Canyon was at one time called Navajo Creek. Bowns Canyon gets it's name from an old cattleman who had a ranch on Sandy Creek just west of Mt. Ellen in the Henry Mountains. **William (Will) Bowns** used to winter cattle in these 2 canyons during the years between 1909 to 1913, but maybe earlier.

Bowns originally brought cattle into the area via the Escalante River Canyon, but sometime later he built the trail down into the East Fork of Bowns. At the same time he must have built the **cedar fences** and the **Bench Trail** connecting Bowns and Long Canyons. After that time, he brought cattle in via the Black or Bowns Trail described above. This new route allowed him to take cattle in or out of these canyons via the top of the Waterpocket Fold to the Baker Ranch, then along the eastern base of the Fold, which was an easier drive from his Sandy Ranch.

In the beginning, Bowns called this drainage **Meadow Canyon**. That must have been before all the erosion took place which has left Bowns Canyon half gutted today.

During the summer of 1988, the NPS made the decision to remove the **wild or feral horses and cattle** in Bowns and Long Canyons. These animals had multiplied to the point they were threatening the ecology in the area. They had eaten down the vegetation and made hundreds of trails creating the possibility of even more soil erosion.

So in the last days of September, 1988, a crew from the NPS and the Kane County Sheriffs office was sent in for a roundup. This land is administered by the NPS, but it was the duty of the Kane County

Inside **Cave 3** in the main fork of **Bowns Canyon**, is this unusual star-shaped set of metate grooves. Almost all caves in this canyon have metate grooves, flint chips, rock art and/or bone fragments.

Sheriff, Max Jackson, to remove the animals.

Several days before the roundup, a crew of 4 men were in lower Bowns preparing the place for entrapment. First, a trail was made down through the boulders to the head of the inlet where the animals were to be finally caught. This was when the lake level was at or near the HWM. The crew also fixed bright colored ribbons in places where the animals might get out of the trap.

On Saturday, October 1, the roundup began. One helicopter was used to locate and drive the horses and cattle out of upper Bowns, and off the mesa top, and down to the lower end of the Bowns Canyon. In the lower end, and on either side-bench, were 4 wranglers on horseback. In the end, 7 head of cattle and 5 horses were trapped and removed to Bullfrog Marina in a World War II landing craft. During the chase, one of the riders had an accident and his horse broke a leg. It was later destroyed. Two horses, a mare (female) and her foal (colt), managed to escape into Long Canyon. By 2001, there was no sign of any horses in Bowns and lower Long Canyons, so these 2 horses either left the canyon or have since died.

One of the alcoves in Bowns Canyon is called **Bechan Cave**. This cave is just another alcove like thousands of others on the Colorado Plateau, but researchers found **mammoth dung** inside.

It all started in November of 1982 when a team of NPS personnel entered Bowns Canyon to do a grazing survey. They found the cave and noticed someone had dug holes in the floor; this was obviously done by a pot hunter looking for Anasazi or Fremont artifacts. In the bottom of these small pits they noticed a blanket of dung which later proved interesting. Incidentally, few if any human artifacts have been found there although some parts of the cave were used as an Indian or cowboy campsite.

In February of 1983, a crew of NPS researchers and others from the University of Utah and Utah State University went to the site and did some legal digging of their own. They found the cave to be about 52 meters deep, 31 meters wide at the mouth, and about 9 meters in height. The cave is well lit during the afternoons, because it faces the southwest. Because of the steep slope right in front of the entrance there was no cattle or horse manure found inside.

In the test pits dug, they found a dung blanket about 1/3 of a meter deep, with some manure piles or boluses, in their original shape. Some of these **boluses** measured 23 x 17 x 9 cms (9 x 7 x 2.5 inches). Two of the boluses closely resembled those of African elephant dung. These later proved to be (with carbon 14 dating) 11,670 years old plus or minus 300 years, and 12,900 years old plus or minus 160 years. In the same dig, they found other dung which closely resembled that of elk and perhaps mountain goat or sheep.

In March and May of 1983, part of the same crew returned to do more digging. Their findings were later published by the *Carnegie Museum of Natural History, Special Publication No. 8, Pittsburgh, 1984.* It is titled *The Pleistocene Dung Blanket of Bechan Cave, Utah.*

In their digging they failed to find any bones of significance, although they did find bones of small mammals. Packrats had used the cave as well for at least 12,000 years. In the same level, dung from **ground sloth** was also found in abundance, as well as hair that closely resembled mammoth. In more recent layers above the dung, some charcoal was found but it was dated quite recently.

Examination of pollen showed a different type of vegetation and climate during that period of time. Found was pollen from water birch, blue spruce, elderberry, snowberry, currant, sledges and cattail. These are not found in the immediate area today, although they are found not far to the north in the Henry

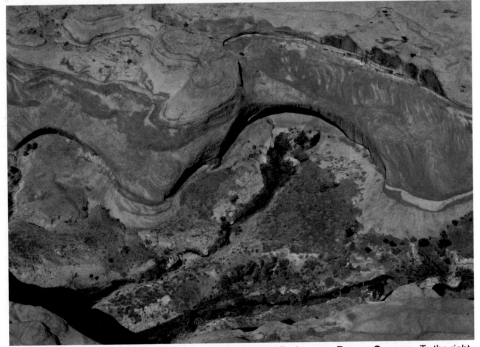

From the air looking down on **Cave 1** left, and **Cave 2** middle, in upper **Bowns Canyon**. To the right, and angling up to the top in the middle, is the slope with the steep slickrork trail. Steps are cut in the lower part, plus more steps are cut in the upper middle part where the trail meets the canyon rim.

Mountains.

The dating of material found in the cave closely approximates that of other finds in North America. Both the Columbian mammoth and the Shasta ground sloths disappeared from the continent about 11,000 years ago.

One thing that has puzzled the author, as well as the researchers is, how did these large mammals actually get into the canyon and cave? The front is presently very steep, which prevented livestock from entering. Apparently there was a larger sand dune in front of the cave during mammoth times. It's also interesting to speculate on how they could have gotten into the canyon itself. It's possible they could have come up from lower Bowns and the Colorado River, but it would be impossible today because of the Wingate dryfall blocking the way. Perhaps in those days the dryfall in the Wingate Sandstone may have been covered with windblown sand or soil making that route different than what we see today. They also may have come down the slickrock in the same area where Will Bowns later made his entry trail. However, some parts of that route are a little steep, perhaps too steep for cattle or horses, without some modification of the grade.

The lower end of the steep **slickrock trail** leading out of the main fork of **Bowns Canyon**. This is far too steep for cattle, but horses may have used it. Just above this section, the trail flattens out, then there's another steep part with steps cut & blasted out just as it goes over the rim.

One of the more interesting sets of metate grooves in **Bowns Canyon** is in **Cave 5**. If memory is correct, this is the cave with lots of black soot on the ceiling, indicating extended periods of fire building and camping/living inside.

This little waterfall (on this day it was a dryfall) is in the lower end of **Bowns Canyon**. However, on 8/5/2007, there was no running water at all at this point. Stream flows into Lake Powell have been down since about the year 2000 because of an extended drought.

Explorer, Fence and Cow Canyons, Escalante River Inlet

Location & Campsites Included here are 3 tributaries of the **Escalante River**. All enter from the east and all are in the upper or northern end of the **Escalante River Arm** or **Inlet** of the lake. It's in this upper end of the Escalante Inlet that geologic formations are seen rising out of the water. Because the benches of the Kayenta Formation are emerging there are more campsites available than downcanyon. You'll find a number of small and often sandy sites along the upper Escalante, and if the water levels rise above the 2007 levels **(8/7/2007-WL1099.34m/3606.71')**, you may find sites in the upper end of each inlet shown on this map (in 8/2007, you couldn't boat to Cow or Fence Canyons).

The uppermost end of the Escalante River Inlet, that part north of **Cow** and **Fence Canyons**, is normally full of muddy water & driftwood; or bone dry except for the river as it was in 2007. Therefore this place isn't considered a great hiking area, at least in times with boater access. When the lake levels are at or near the HWM, the inlet extends north to the mouth of Coyote Gulch. But very slowly, the mud and sand brought down by the Escalante River are filling in what used to be a lake. Even in the best of times with high lake levels, there are almost never any boaters going beyond the mouth of Cow and Fence Canyon. In the years to come, and depending on lake levels, feel lucky if you can boat into Explorer Canyon Inlet.

If you're interested in exploring the canyons above the HWM, consult this author's other book, **Non-Technical Canyon Hiking Guide to the Colorado Plateau, 5th Edition.**

Hiking Routes or Trails Like all side-drainages of the Escalante, **Explorer Canyon Inlet** is rather long and narrow, at least in times of high water. This canyon is one of the more interesting to visit in the Escalante. Boat as far upcanyon as possible, which wasn't very far in 8/2007. When the water is low, begin walking on the right or southwest side of the inlet. There's a good trail running along one of the benches. Stay on the right to about the HWM, then look up to see a **big, smooth, colorful Navajo Sandstone wall** that's free of desert varnish. At the bottom of it, are signs of Fremont Indian camps, plus the wall has some great striping & color for fotographers.

From this big Navajo wall, walk back down to the creek and cross over to the left or northwest side and look for another trail. Of the 2 trails on that side, the best one is the highest. It winds its way up and down and through, or just above the oak brush, and for the most part, on top of a slickrock bench just above the canyon bottom. About 100 meters above the HWM and a little ways above the main trail is the **first of 3 petroglyph panels**; this one is the best. About 2/3's the way up, and again on your left, and you'll see the **Zane Grey Arch** in the upper part of the Kayenta Formation. If you route-find above this arch, you'll find a **small granary** in a corner of an alcove about 30 meters away. Just around the corner from the arch you can climb up to a higher bench which allows good views down into the canyon. However, this route is a little steep and for experienced hikers only.

From where you can see the arch, the main trail winds around a buttress, and after about 75-100 meters, you'll see a good panel of petroglyphs on your left. The lower part has figures of humans with big horn sheep heads and horns. Higher on the wall are big horn sheep. This is one of the more unusual panels of rock art the author has seen. From this site walk upcanyon along the trail another 50 meters or less and you'll see another single petroglyph on the left. Between these 2 panels appears to be some kind of Fremont structure. Beyond this, the trail runs up to the springs at the bottom of the big dryfall which blocks the way to the mesa above.

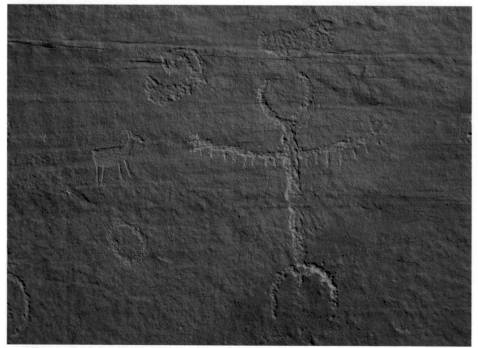

Hiking up **Explorer Canyon**, this is part of the first panel of rock art you'll come to. See map.

Map 17, Explorer, Fence and Cow Canyons

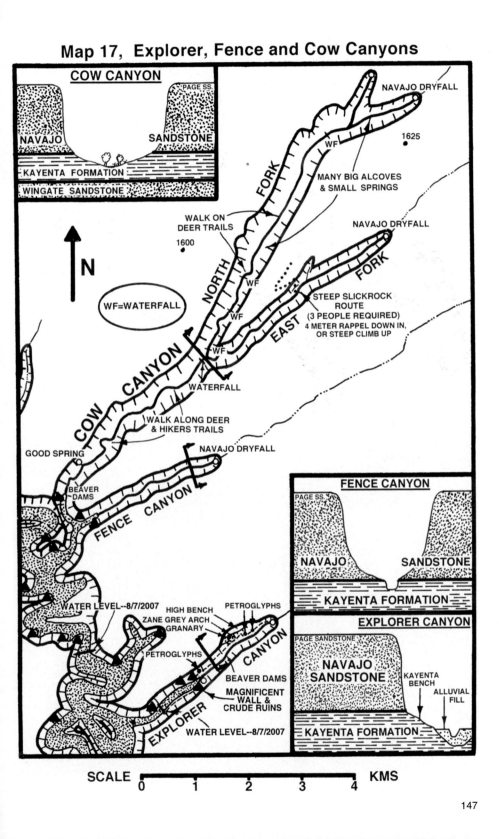

COW CANYON

PAGE SS.

NAVAJO SANDSTONE

KAYENTA FORMATION

WINGATE SANDSTONE

NAVAJO DRYFALL

1625

N

WF

MANY BIG ALCOVES & SMALL SPRINGS

WF=WATERFALL

FORK

NORTH

WALK ON DEER TRAILS

1600

NAVAJO DRYFALL

FORK

WF

EAST

STEEP SLICKROCK ROUTE (3 PEOPLE REQUIRED) 4 METER RAPPEL DOWN IN, OR STEEP CLIMB UP

WF

COW CANYON

WF

WATERFALL

WALK ALONG DEER & HIKERS TRAILS

GOOD SPRING

NAVAJO DRYFALL

BEAVER DAMS

FENCE CANYON

FENCE CANYON

PAGE SS.

NAVAJO SANDSTONE

KAYENTA FORMATION

WATER LEVEL--8/7/2007

HIGH BENCH

ZANE GREY ARCH GRANARY

PETROGLYPHS

PETROGLYPHS

CANYON

BEAVER DAMS

MAGNIFICENT WALL & CRUDE RUINS

EXPLORER

WATER LEVEL--8/7/2007

EXPLORER CANYON

PAGE SANDSTONE

NAVAJO SANDSTONE

KAYENTA BENCH

ALLUVIAL FILL

KAYENTA FORMATION

SCALE

0   1   2   3   4   KMS

Fence and Cow Canyons both share a common mouth, which is deep and narrow. The Navajo Sandstone walls rise to great heights at this point of the Escalante Canyon. **Fence** is the shorter canyon of the two and as you hike upstream, you'll be walking along Kayenta benches. The author used a series of deer trails on the left or north side of the year-round flowing stream but he could see trails on the other side as well. You'll have to use these trails, as the stream bottom is choked with tall grass, willows, trees, and in some places, beaver ponds. At the upper end of Fence, you will see a deep little groove in the top of the Kayenta Formation. Not far above this is the usual dryfall with good spring water seeping out at the bottom.

Fence and Cow Canyons share what the author once thought was a captive deer herd--at least that seemed to be the case in 1988. However, by 1991, the water was so low in the lake they could walk completely out of these canyons. It's also likely, they like beaver, swim from one canyon to another when they get boxed in by rising lake waters and/or run out of feed.

Of the 3 canyons discussed here, **Cow Canyon** is by far the longest. It has the same look as Fence; with the Kayenta benches along the lower end, big alcove caves and a year-round flowing stream choked with brush and water loving plants. There aren't too many hikers going up this one and the deer trails aren't as evident as in Fence Canyon, none-the-less you can walk upcanyon rather easily for the most part.

In some places you can walk right up the open creek bed; in other places you may have to bushwhack a little. One thing to remember, stay on a main deer trail. These trails are always crossing from one side of the creek to the other so if you stay on one there's very little bushwhacking and you likely won't get your feet wet. On his 2001 hike, the author had dry feet all the way.

Just below the confluence of the **North and East Forks** is an interesting waterfall pouring over a Kayenta ledge. This is just one of several waterfalls in the canyon. Above the confluence and in the North Fork, you'll find huge alcoves so prominent in all canyons made up of Navajo Sandstone. At the head of the North Fork is the usual big dryfall. The East Fork has a similar look, but according to Byron Lemay and Herb Taylor, there's a **climbers route** to the rim about halfway upcanyon. To get out, you'll have to stand on someone's shoulders, lean a log up against the wall, or build a pile of rocks, then climb about 4 meters up a steep pitch using **old moki steps**. A rope would have to be used to get everyone up, or down; then the last person down may have to jump or slide the last 3 meters or so (?).

Hike Length & Time Needed The hike up **Explorer** is only about 2 kms from the HWM to the dryfall. The author did this once in 1 1/4 hours round-trip; on his 2nd, 3rd & 4th trips he took about 3 hours; but you'll want more time than that because there's lots of things to see. **Fence Canyon** is only slightly longer, maybe 3 kms to its end. The author got to just below the headwall and returned in 1 1/4 hours. **Cow Canyon** is much longer, the **North Fork** being about 12-13 kms long. To hike this one will take all day. The author walked up the **East Fork** to a point where he could see the dryfall at the end, then returned all in 3 1/4 hours. Later, he hiked all the way up Cow's North Fork and returned in 6 1/3 hours. The time it takes, and walking distance, will depend on lake levels, and how far you can boat.

Boots or Shoes In Cow Canyon consider taking wading shoes. In Fence and Explorer you can avoid wading so any kind of shoes will do.

Water There are year-round streams in each canyon, plus beaver, so try to avoid drinking water from

Zane Grey Arch, located in the upper end of **Explorer Canyon**. In the upper left hand side of this picture, and just out of sight, is the small granary shown on **page 150**.

148

the streams in the lower ends of the canyons. Drink from springs or the upper valley creeks only. One man from Texas wrote the author stating he drank water from the creek in Explorer Canyon and got Giardia. Once his doctor determined the problem, he was well in no time. It was likely spread by beaver. There's a **good spring** with a large flow about 1 km above the HWM in **Cow Canyon** on the left.

Main Attractions Deep Navajo Sandstone canyons, small streams and green valleys, one way out of East Fork of Cow, and an arch, small granary and good petroglyphs in Explorer Canyon.

Hiking Maps USGS or BLM map Navajo Mountain (1:100,000); Stevens Canyon South & Davis Gulch (1:24,000--7 1/2' quads) for hiking; The Rincon (1:62,500) if available; or the Trails Illustrated/ National Geographic map, Canyons of the Escalante (1:70,500).

In **Explorer Canyon**, this is what the author calls the **Magnificent Wall**. The colors shown here are real, and have not been enhanced. Be here about mid-day, so the sunlight bounces off the opposite wall and onto this high-angle alcove. Nearby are some crude Fremont Indian ruins.

149

This is the small **granary** located just above and to the south of **Zane Grey Arch** in the upper end of **Explorer Canyon**. The reason for the deep red colors in this picture is, the sun is just behind the camera and is bouncing light into this recess.

Just north of Zane Grey Arch in upper **Explorer Canyon**, is a small panel of rock art or **petroglyphs**, part of which has been vandalized--no doubt by juveniles (?).

This is the waterfall just below the confluence of **Cow Canyon's North** and **East Forks**. When lake waters are low, as they were in 2007, you couldn't even get close to the mouth of Cow Canyon in a boat. In that situation, you'll have to walk a long ways to reach this place (from a 1988 slide).

In the **Escalante River Inlet** just southwest from the mouth of Explorer Canyon, are these Anasazi structures called the **Three Roof Ruins**. They're high on a southeast-facing wall and the only way there these days is by boat.

Fortymile Gulch, Willow Creek and Bishop Canyon, Escalante River Inlet

Location & Campsites This map features **Willow Creek** and all of its tributaries, which include **Fortymile Gulch, Willow Gulch** (on some maps it's named Sooner Gulch), **North Fork of Willow Creek** (the author's name), and **Bishop Canyon**. All these tributaries empty into the middle part of the Escalante River Inlet from the west side.

There are several campsites in **Willow Creek Inlet**; all small, but all sandy, plus several tie-down places. In **Bishop**, there was only a tie-down place or two as of **8/6/2007-WL1099.34m/3606.73'**. In the main channel there were more campsites & tie-down places with low water than when the lake was higher and near the HWM.

Hiking Routes or Trails Right at the upper end of **Willow Creek Inlet (at HWM)**, you'll see a low bench on the north side. Get up on it and look along the main canyon wall for 2 panels of old petroglyphs. From there walk up **Willow Creek** which has a fairly good sized year-round stream of water. About 1 km from the HWM is a junction. To the left is Willow Gulch. Walk up this drainage a short distance and into some pretty good narrows with a couple of huge undercuts. Not far beyond is the interesting **Broken Bow Arch** on the right. It was so named because someone once found a broken Indian bow beneath it. The arch measures 28 x 30 meters. Beyond, you can walk unobstructed to the Hole-in-the-Rock Road which connects Escalante with the Hole-in-the-Rock Trail to the south.

Back at the junction, if you turn north into **Fortymile Gulch**, you'll be wading in a small stream. There are some springs and narrows all the way through this canyon. There are several places that have deep holes, some deep enough to swim through. But you can get through or around them OK. This canyon is just difficult enough to be interesting. The best part is in the lower end. You can walk all the way up this drainage and exit through **Carcass Wash** to the Hole-in-the-Rock Road.

The inlet leading into the **North Fork** is short; and if the lake level is low, you won't even get close to this canyon in your boat! In the beginning, the walk is up through tall cane-like grass, so it might be best to stay right in the small stream. Further up, it's easier walking without the cane grass. As you walk upcanyon, the Navajo Sandstone walls get higher and higher. At the upper end, there's a junction. If you take the right fork, you'll walk 300 meters into a deep, dark and narrow box ending. The left fork is where the author momentarily trapped 5 deer. At the time, he thought this was another captive deer herd, but they know how to swim and they move from one canyon to another. When the lake level is low they walk in or out to the main canyon.

As of **8/6/2007-WL1099.34m/3606.73'**, the end of boating was about 1 km up Willow Creek from the mouth of Bishop. On that day, the author walked up to North Fork, but there wasn't much to see in that part of Willow Creek.

Bishop Canyon is one of the more spectacular around. In the late 1980's, boating up this narrow inlet was slow because of driftwood; in 2001 & 2007, the upper part was again choked with logs. As you walk up Bishop, the Navajo walls get higher and higher, and its depth compares with Sevenmile and Iceberg Canyons. Along most of the hiking part of the canyon it appears the year-round flowing stream is running on top of the upper Kayenta Formation. In the bottom of the canyon is a groove which has

This picture was taken on **8/6/2007-WL1099.34m/3606'** at the head of **Willow Creek Inlet**. This is typical of the mess you'll find at the end of each inlet, but just a few meters away it's easy walking.

Map 18, Fortymile Gulch, Willow Creek & Bishop Canyon

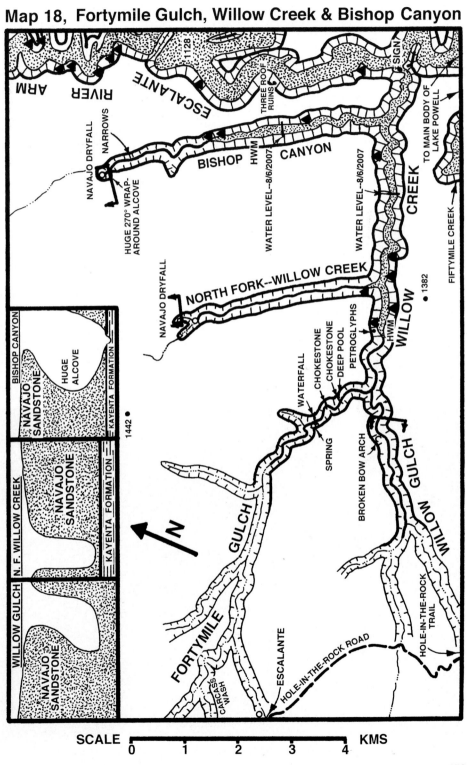

SCALE

0 1 2 3 4 KMS

been cut by raging flood waters. Part of this groove has some vegetation, other parts are bare slickrock. On the author's hike in early April, 2001, he found the slickrock part covered with moss and very slippery. This resulted in 8 falls. One theory for so much moss is, it hadn't seen a raging flood in a while before his hike. Any flashflood should sandblast the slippery moss away.

Near the upper end, there's a short narrow section (in the bottom of the Kayenta groove) so you'll either have to wade, or spread your legs, span the wall, and stem above the stream. It's easy. At the very end of the canyon is a **270° wrap-around alcove** which is the largest feature of its kind the author has ever seen. It's worth the walk to see. Under the Navajo dryfall is the beginning of running water. No sign of beaver in this drainage, but they seem to move from canyon to canyon depending on food.

In recent years, people have installed bolts in the slot above and some have rappelled down the drainage course. It's nearly a 50m drop. Then they jumar back up; or have someone in a boat pick them up at the end of the inlet, and take them around the corner into Willow Creek drainage for the hike out.

Hike Length & Time Needed It's about 10 kms up **Willow Creek & Gulch** to the Hole-in-the-Rock Road. Round-trip will take most people 4-5 hours; it's lots longer if the lake level is low. In **Fortymile Gulch**, you can walk for as long as you like, but it's the lower end that's most interesting. Strong hikers could walk up one, road-walk to the other and return via the other canyon, an all-day hike. The author did this loop once with road access. He went down Fortymile, up Willow, then road-walked back to his car. If the lake is really low, the hike to see the best parts of these 2 canyons will be much longer than if you come to the area by road.

It's 4-5 kms to the end of **North Fork**. The author did this in 1 2/3 hours round-trip, but with high lake levels. You'll probably want 2-3 hours. There's only about 2 kms of walking in Bishop Canyon, and this can be done in a couple of hours, round-trip--depending on lake levels. The author did it with high water in 1 1/2 hours.

Boots or Shoes Use wading boots or shoes in all canyons.

Water No sign of beaver in Bishop, so you can drink water from about any place, but at the source would be safest. North Fork water should be safe higher up, at or near the source. Drink from springs only in Willow and Fortymile Gulches. There may be cattle coming down part way in each of these drainages during the winter season, from about October to June.

Main Attractions Deep, well-watered, narrow canyons, several huge alcoves or undercuts, petroglyphs and Broken Bow Arch.

Hiking Maps USGS or BLM map Navajo Mountain (1:100,000); Davis Gulch & Sooner Bench (1:24.000--7 1/2' quads) for hiking; The Rincon (1:62,500) if available; or the Trails Illustrated/National Geographic map, Canyons of the Escalante (1:70,500).

Boy Scout Tragedy Right where the Hole-in-the-Rock Road crosses Carcass Wash (just off this map) was the scene of one the worst accidents in southern Utah history. That's where 13 boy scouts died on June 10, 1963. A group of scouts and scout masters had made their way from Salt Lake, Ogden and Provo, to Escalante by bus on their way to the Colorado River at the Hole-in-the-Rock Trail. The plan was to board a large open-bed truck and drive the Hole-in-the-Rock Road to where the trail began on the rim of the canyon. Then they were to walk down to the river where they would meet boaters who started at Hite (this was just before the lake began to fill); from there they would float down the Colorado to Lee's Ferry.

As the road crosses Carcass Wash, it dips down, then runs up a steep grade to the rim on the other side. As the truck was climbing the grade the driver apparently tried to shift to a lower gear but missed

Lake Powell boaters trying to climb a waterfall, which in times of low lake levels, is exposed in **Willow Creek** just upcanyon from the mouth of **North Fork** of **Willow Creek**.

and the truck stalled. He tried to use the brakes to prevent it from rolling backwards, but they didn't hold. He then tried to steer the truck back down the steep grade but missed the curve halfway down and it rolled over a 10-meter-high embankment, eventually landing on its side. Since most of the scouts were in the back, many were thrown out and some were crushed as the truck rolled over once. Twelve were dead at the scene, and another died later.

After the accident, 2 boys headed up the road toward Escalante for help. Soon they met a couple of local ranchers mending a fence. One drove to town to sound the alarm. Men from the BLM, Forest Service, and Sheriff's office and several tourists and a number of local towns people joined the rescue. Later, someone drove toward the river, where one of the boaters was a doctor. Eventually several station wagons went to the scene and hauled the injured to the hospital in Panguitch. The nightmare ended when parents and relatives of the dead and injured came to claim their own. So ended one of the worst tragedies in southern Utah history.

In the late 1990's, a memorial monument was erected at the accident site. You can get to it by hiking from the lake but it's a pretty long walk, and not recommended. The easiest way to get there is to drive southeast from the town of Escalante on the main highway, then continue south on the graded Hole-in-the-Rock Road. Any car can make it to the accident site during dry weather conditions.

This scene is at the very upper end of **Bishop Canyon** where you'll find the **270° Alcove**. Here hikers are rappelling from the slot high above. To do this you'll need 2 ropes of 45 & 50 meters to make 2 big rappels--then jumar back up. Or have a boat waiting at the bottom.

Fiftymile Creek, Davis Gulch and Clear & Indian Creek Canyons, Escalante River Inlet

Location & Campsites These 4 canyons, **Fiftymile, Davis, Clear and Indian Creeks**, are all part of the Escalante River system. As you enter the Escalante and boat north these are the first 4 canyons on the left or west (Indian Creek Inlet is not shown but it's just off this map to the right). These waterways or inlets, are some of the narrowest and most fotogenic of all canyons on the lake.

It's in this part of the Escalante River Inlet that flat sandy campsites are the hardest to find. It's all Navajo Sandstone rising vertically out of the water, except for just a few sandy beaches, most of which are found at the head of each inlet. Clear Creek and Indian Creek Inlets have no campsites at all, but Davis and Fiftymile may have about half a dozen small sites each. One was very near **La Gorce Arch**. The number of sites and their size will depend on lake levels. However, with low lake levels as they were on **8/6/2007-WL1099.34m/3606.73'**, there will be a few rocky tie-down places for houseboats.

Hiking Routes or Trails The upper end of **Clear Creek Inlet** is very narrow, but some house boats make it in--just barely. Some have left scratch marks on the walls at one point where their roofs have scraped (this was when the lake was at or near the HWM). Right at the end of the inlet is a cool shaded overhang (regardless of lake levels), then a little narrow place where you get out of your boat to walk upcanyon (this is when the lake water is high). If water levels are low, as they were on 8/6/2007, you'll have to use a rope to get up over one **6 meter waterfall**, then use **moki steps** to get past another 6 meter waterfall. Beyond that there's more moki steps into the upper basin where you'll be stopped by a 20m dryfall. If the water goes below about 1096m/3596', you'll have to rappel over 5 dropoffs from top to bottom.

Before the days of Lake Powell, **Davis Gulch** was one of the most fascinating canyons flowing into the Escalante. Some of the better parts are now **(8/6/2007-WL1099.34m/3606.73')** just emerging from under water. On that day, the author tied-up immediately above **La Gorce Arch**, which is halfway up the long narrow inlet. If the lake is full, you can almost boat through La Gorce Arch. Just beyond the arch and on the right or northwest is a small Fremont Indian structure. At the very end of the inlet, may be a couple of fine campsites, depending on lake levels. Otherwise, on 8/6/2007, there was a great campsite inside an alcove cave just around the bend from La Gorce Arch.

As you hike up Davis, there are **2 little waterfalls** just below the HWM; and about 200 meters above the HWM, you'll see on the right or northwest a sloping ridge coming down to the bottom lands. This is the **first of 2 natural exits** out of the canyon. About 150 meters beyond the first, look to the right again, and next to the hiker-made trail is an old wooden pole corral lying in ruins. Immediately behind this is the **Davis Gulch Stock Trail**. It has steps cut out of the slickrock in the bottom part. As you go up, look for cairns marking the upper part of the trail which in places has more steps cut in slickrock.

The corral at the bottom of this trail was evidently the last camping place of a young naturalist-artist by the name of **Everett Ruess**, who disappeared in 1934 without a trace. His mules and camp were found, but no trace of him. His disappearance has become one of the big legends in southern Utah, not among locales, but by outsiders! There's even been a book written about him.

The **Black Trail** as it dives into the **Escalante River Inlet**. This is located between Clear Creek and Davis Gulch Inlets and right at the end of a narrow promontory. It runs up a natural ramp with steps cut for traction.

Map 19, Fiftymile Creek, Davis Gulch & Clear Creek

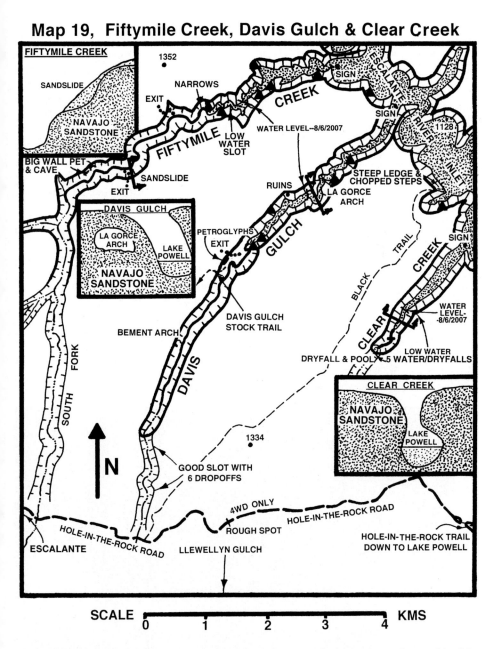

SCALE 0 1 2 3 4 **KMS**

In between these 2 natural exits and on the wall behind the oak brush on the northwest side of the canyon, you'll find a rather long panel of **petroglyphs**. These are likely Fremont etchings, as they often made such panels along important routes or trails.

As you go upcanyon beyond the stock trail, a hiker's path fades and you'll be walking mostly in the shallow stream less than ankle deep. There are active beaver colonies in this part. They burrow under the banks, instead of making dams & ponds. Three kms above the stock trail is **Bement Arch**. Above this arch the canyon narrows and you can walk only about another 2 kms before it constricts to a slot and there are a series of short dropoffs that you can't climb alone. (However, you can hike down the upper slot from the Hole-in-the-Rock Road. It has 6 dropoffs you must chimney down--or jump one or 2 meters. This is for experienced hikers only. For more information on **Upper Davis Gulch**, see the author's other book, *Non-Technical Canyon Hiking Guide to the Colorado Plateau, 5th Ed.* or later.)

As you walk the area near **Bement Arch**, notice the alluvial or soil banks about 6-8 meters high. The erosion or down-cutting began about 1900, likely the result of overgrazing. There are no cattle in the canyon today.

Fiftymile Creek Inlet is another long, narrow and sinuous waterway, with half a dozen small campsites. When the lake is at or near the HWM, there isn't a lot to see in this canyon, but when the lake level is near what it was on **8/6/2007-WL1099.34m/3606.73'**, you can hike up through a nice sculptured narrows. If the lake is at the HWM, you boat right over this neat slot. Not far above this slot, is another fotogenic narrows. Beyond that, the drainage opens a bit and the walking is easy. This canyon has running water in the lower half, but it doesn't have the amount of vegetation as does Davis Gulch. This drainage seems to be more prone to flash flooding than Davis and the creek bed is swept clean of debris and vegetation and is lined with cobble stones.

Less than a km above the HWM in **Fiftymile Canyon**, there's a small drainage coming down from the right. Enter this, then climb over some ledges on the left and you can exit along an old deer trail. About 1 1/2 kms beyond this first exit is a sandslide coming down from the left or south. From either side of this slide you can walk up to the rim. West of this sandslide, the canyon slowly opens and is more shallow. Less than 1 km above the sandslide is a **cave & a big wall** covered with **rock art** (petroglyphs). Just above the rock art site is where the year-round water begins to flow. If you like, you can walk all the way to the Hole-in-the-Rock Road.

Between Clear Creek and Davis Gulch is a short canyon on the southwest side of the Escalante River Inlet. Immediately north of this is a long rounded ridge coming down to the lake. Look carefully and you'll see steps hacked out of the slickrock on the right or north side of the ridge; this trail formerly went down to the lower Escalante River. This appears to be part of the **Black Trail**, which began or ended at the Baker Ranch on Halls Creek. Hoof scratch marks can be seen in places indicating recent horse traffic but how they kept from falling off the sheer cliff is amazing!

In the Escalante River Arm of Lake Powell, most of the canyons have some kind of hiking, but one that doesn't is **Indian Creek**. This canyon is now a short inlet only about 1 km long. Sheer Navajo Sandstone walls rise directly out of the water and it ends in a big alcove where the flood waters drop into the lake during rain storms. There are no campsites in this canyon.

Hike Length & Time Needed When the lake is high, you can only walk up **Clear Creek** about half a km, which will take but a few minutes; in times of low lake levels, there's almost no hiking at all. In **Davis Gulch**, you can walk about 5 kms upstream. About half a day should be enough time to see this one. You can walk for half day or maybe 5-6 hours in **Fiftymile Creek**. It's about 5 kms up to where the water begins to flow.

Boots or Shoes For Fiftymile and Davis, use wading-type shoes. For Clear Creek it doesn't matter.

Water The water comes and goes in **Fiftymile**. Where it first seeps out of the creek bed, it should be good to drink as-is. No sign of beaver or cattle in Fiftymile. In **Davis**, better find a spring to drink from, as there are beaver in the lower parts of the creek. **Clear Creek** flows for a very short distance, but it can be polluted by so much human traffic when the lake is high. With low lake levels, it should be good to drink as-is because no one will be polluting it.

Main Attractions Long, narrow and sinuous waterways, deep narrow canyons, some petroglyphs, 2 historic trails, sandy campsites, and occasionally too many people.

Hiking Maps USGS or BLM map Navajo Mountain (1:100,000); Davis Gulch (1:24,000--7 1/2' quad) for hiking; The Rincon (1:62,500) if available; or the Trails Illustrated/National Geographic map, Canyons of the Escalante (1:70,500).

This picture was taken on **8/6/2007-WL1099.34m/3606.73'**, and the author had just docked at what is the 5th waterfall in **Clear Creek Canyon**. There are 4 more water/dryfalls above this point.

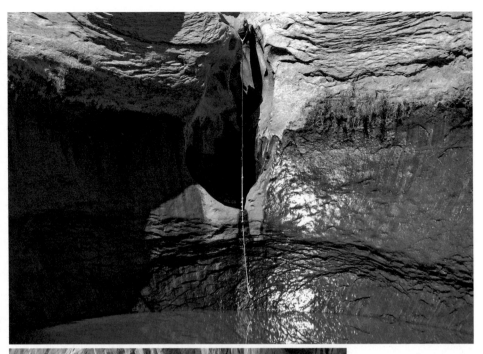

Above This is the 4th waterfall (2nd if going upstream) in **Clear Creek Canyon**. Someone has placed a rope with knots here making it possible to reach the next waterfall. In times of high water, you sail right over this section and up to the 4th waterfall in the canyon (it would be the 2nd if hiking down the drainage).

Left This picture was taken on **8/6/2007-WL1099.34m/3606.73'**, and is about 100 meters below the last or 5th waterfall in **Clear Creek Canyon**. This is a place that never sees the sun.

When the lake levels are high, you boat right over these 2 little waterfalls in **Davis Gulch**, but on **8/6/2007-WL1099.34m/3606.73'**, you had to walk about 750 meters to reach this point.

La Gorce Arch on **8/6/2007-WL1099.34m/3606.73'**. On that day the head of navigation was less than 100 meters above this arch. Notice the HWM right at the bottom of the arch.

This scene is about 200 meters above the end of **Fiftymile Canyon Inlet** as it was on **8/6/2007-WL1099.34m/3606.73'**. The slot shown below is upcanyon about 800 meters from this place.

In the summer of 1988, the author sailed right over this nice little slot in **Fiftymile Canyon**. In the summer of 2007, you had to walk about 1 km from your boat to get here.

Ribbon & Cottonwood Canyons and the Hole-in-the-Rock & Jackass Bench Trails

Location & Campsites There are 4 hikes covered on this map, all within a short distance of each other, and all just downlake from the mouth of the **Escalante River Arm or Inlet**. Near the **Jackass Bench Trail** and **Ribbon Canyon** are buoys numbered M68 (K109) and M67 (K107). In front of **Hole-in-the-Rock Bay** is buoy M66 (K106), while just downlake from the mouth of **Cottonwood Canyon** is buoy M63A (K101).

This used to be a very popular area for camping, but on **8/5/2007-WL1099.38m/3606.85'**, most of the blue ribbon sandy campsites in **Cottonwood Canyon** were left high & dry and full of tamaracks & tumbleweeds. In **Ribbon Canyon** there used to be several small campsites and one large sandy beach, but there were only tie-down places for houseboats in 8/2007. Sandy campsites along the main channel come and go with the rise & fall of lake levels.

Hiking Routes & Trails The **Jackass Bench Trail** was a partly-constructed horse or pack trail running from the rim of Glen Canyon down to Jackass Bench, which is presently partly submerged. Jackass Bench was about 50 meters above the Colorado River and on top of the Kayenta Formation, which is above the Wingate and below the Navajo Sandstone. The bench was used for grazing livestock in 1879-'80 by the Hole-in-the-Rock Party and by subsequent residents at the 'Hole.

C. Gregory Crampton, who studied historic sites in Glen Canyon before Lake Powell times, believes this trail may have been built by the **Hoskaninni Mining Company** as part of the assessment work to keep their claims alive and valid. Apparently, the company had intended to build a road from the mouth of Hole-in-the-Rock Creek, up along Jackass Bench, thence to the rim in the same area as the present trail; but they didn't get that far. This route however proved easier than the old Hole-in-the-Rock Trail.

The Jackass Bench Trail had steps cut out of the Navajo slickrock. It wound its way up to the rim then turned left or west and after 3 kms met the Hole-in-the-Rock Road coming down from Escalante. Parts of this trail are still there today. Steps can be seen coming out of the water (at HWM) about 2 kms northeast or uplake from the mouth of **Hole-in-the-Rock Bay**. There may not be a place to anchor right at the steps, so boat to the northeast about 100 meters to a small inlet. From there, you can walk up on the slickrock parallel to the lake until you see about 4 series of steps. About halfway up, the slope is more gentle and there are only scattered cairns to mark the way. If you can't follow the cairns, just walk up the easiest slope to the west and near the rim, veer to the left. Once on top you'll have excellent views downlake with Navajo Mountain in the background. It's an easy walk from there to the top of the Hole-in-the-Rock Trail.

Ribbon Canyon is a short side-drainage which makes a fun hike. Going upcanyon, you'll be walking along slickrock of the Kayenta Formation. In several places there's running water but it's a small stream. The higher you go, the steeper and more difficult it is to walk. In the upper ends of each of the 2 major forks, there are some large boulders, trees and ledges to slow you down. This is the fourth canyon the author recalls seeing a small deer herd. There is no way out of this box canyon except to swim out through the inlet. The only places deer can swim to would be into Cottonwood Canyon, or to the little canyons northwest of Ribbon. When the lake is low, they may bench-walk to other places.

One of the most daring and difficult journeys ever made during pioneer days of the American West

This sandy campsite is in the upper end of **Iceberg Canyon Inlet** near the end of the navigation. This foto was taken on **8/4/2007-WL1099.42m/3606.97'**. Notice the dead trees on the right.

Map 20, Ribbon & Cottonwood Canyon and the Hole-in-the-Rock & Jackass Bench Trails

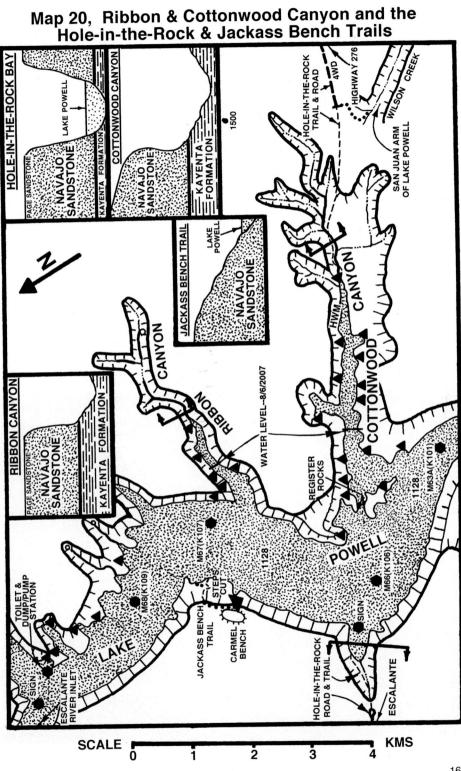

is told in the story of the **Hole-in-the-Rock Party**. Their expedition began in southwest Utah with volunteer Mormons from the Cedar City, Parowan and Paragonah areas. The journey began on October 22, 1879. They were officially called the **San Juan Mission Party**, and were sent to build a settlement on the San Juan River. Their journey took them to Panguitch, Escalante, down what is today known as the **Hole-in-the-Rock Road** to the rim of the Colorado, across the river, up **Cottonwood Canyon** to **Lake Pagahrit**, then northeast to near **Natural Bridges Natural Monument** and southeast to **Comb Wash**, then on to the San Juan River at **Bluff**.

Altogether, there were more than 230 people in about 83 wagons, along with 1000 head of livestock. There had been a scouting party sent out, which had taken an easier but longer route via Lee's Ferry, but they decided to take a short-cut into unknown country. As it turned out, the journey was over 320 kms long, much of which was roadless. The trip was to last 6 weeks or thereabouts, but it took nearly 6 months! Three babies were born along the way. The lead wagons arrived at Bluff on April 6, 1880.

The part of the journey which was most difficult and took the most road building, was the place which we now call **Hole-in-the-Rock**. This is a very steep ravine, cleft, slot or crack in the rim of Glen Canyon. The short canyon was actually created along a minor geologic fault. From the rim to the river was just over a km, but it had a drop of 300 meters. They had to dig and blast out a road wide enough for wagons. The route went straight down the chute in the upper part, then angled to the left part way down. In the upper sections they drilled holes in the sandstone, inserted poles, then laid brush and rocks on top of that. Wagons were taken down one at a time. Wheels were locked, and men on ropes held the wagons back in the steeper parts. The average grade was said to be 25°, while the steepest part was about 45°!

However, not all of what you see there today was made by the Hole-in-the-Rock Party. In 1899-1900, the **Hoskaninni Mining Company** built steps in the upper section which made it easier for men or horses to use. After that time no more wagons were taken down through the Hole-in-the-Rock route. Several large boulders have since fallen into the slot and erosion has taken a toll.

In order to cross the river, the Mormon Church (which sponsored the group) sent **Charles T. Hall** from Escalante to the river to build a ferryboat. Lumber was sent from Escalante and a boat large enough for 2 wagons was built. There was no cable or rope across the river, and only one set of oars was used for power and steering.

When you arrive at Hole-in-the-Rock, tie-down on the right or north side of the bay. From there, you can walk on part of the old road. Near the top you'll likely have to walk or climb on all-4's to get up the steeper parts. Today, one has to wonder how wagons could have been taken down through it.

Much of the wagon road across the Colorado River which took so much time to make, is now under water, but you can pick up the route as it goes between **Register Rocks** on the east side of the river (lake). If the water is at or near the HWM, you can boat between these 2 tall rocks, as shown on the map. From there the party went up **Cottonwood Canyon** which required more road building. In the upper sections near the rim is where they once again had to blast their way through.

When you first start up **Cottonwood Canyon**, you'll likely be walking along a trail on either side of the upper inlet (by 2007, it was easier to walk up the creek bed to avoid tamaracks below the HWM), then just above the HWM will be one main path with posts marking this historic trail. It's now easy to find & follow (hopefully it will continue to be as popular in the 2000's as it was in the 1980's & 1990's,

From the middle of **Hole-in-the-Rock Bay**, looking northwest at the cleft in the wall and the **Hole-in-the-Rock Trail**. This is where they brought wagons down in 1880.

which will keep the trail more visible). After a little more than a km, the old road begins to climb up the hillside on the right or south. There it becomes very visible as it heads up a dugway. For the most part, the old wagon road runs up a kind of hogback or ridge but at the same time runs along the bottom of shallow drainages, until it reaches the top of **Wilson Mesa**.

Along the way and where the road runs across slickrock, you can still see ruts and grooves in the solid sandstone. On top, you'll arrive at the end of the hiking part of the old trail. Beyond is the old road which is presently used by 4WD's only (they start from Highway 276, about halfway between Halls Crossing Marina and Highway 95). At that point are barricades preventing vehicles from going down toward the lake and ruining the most-interesting part of this historic trail. From the end of this 4WD road, you can walk down Wilson Creek into the San Juan River Arm of Lake Powell. More about this on **Map 26**.

Hike Length & Time Needed The hike to the rim along the **Jackass Bench Trail** is about 1 km. Most people can do this round-trip hike in 1-2 hours. In **Ribbon Canyon** you can walk about 3 kms which should take about 2-3 hours, round-trip. The author took about 2 hours.

Up the **Hole-in-the-Rock Trail** on the west side of the lake is less than 1 km, and most people can do this in an hour or so. Some will take longer if they want to rim-walk for better views of the lake. From the HWM to the top of the trail in **Cottonwood Canyon** is about 3 kms one-way. The author did it in about 1 1/2 hours & 2 hours on his 2 trips but some may want 3 hours round-trip.

Boots or Shoes There is no wading in any of these canyons so any boots or shoes will do.

Water The water would likely be good to drink anywhere in Ribbon Canyon although the further up-canyon you go the better the water quality. There's one real good bubbling spring near the head of the main canyon.

There's no water along the Hole-in-the-Rock Trail, so take your own. There's a small year-round stream in Cottonwood Canyon but it's grazed by cattle from October until June, so best to take you own.

Main Attractions Good views of the lake and Navajo Mountain, a box canyon with a sometimes-captive, sometimes-migrating deer herd, and an historic wagon road or trail.

Hiking Maps USGS or BLM map Navajo Mountain (1:100,000); Wilson Creek & Davis Gulch (1:24,000- -7 1/2" quads) for hiking; The Rincon & Navajo Mtn. (1:62,500) if available; or the Trails Illustrated/National Geographic map, Canyons of the Escalante (1:70,500).

Later History For about one year after the Hole-in-the-Rock Party passed through, this was the normal route used between the people at Bluff on the San Juan River and the Mormon settlements to the west. But it was a rough road and Charles T. Hall didn't get much business. So he moved his ferry upstream to Halls Crossing and opened an easier route there in 1881.

Meanwhile, Kumen Jones, the last person of the original Hole-in-the-Rock group to pass through the 'Hole, reported that a William Hyde had set up a trading post on the river to do business with the Utes, Piutes and Navajos, who began to use the trail themselves to reach the Mormon settlements west of the Colorado. Stories tell of outlaws and cattle rustlers using the route as well.

During the Glen Canyon Gold Rush days this route was also a boon to prospectors. In 1888, **J. R. Neilson**, an enterprising miner, with the help of several hired hands, packed several tons of supplies down to the river where he constructed a large **double-decked boat** measuring about 6 x 12 meters. It took 4 men one month to ferry all the supplies down to the river along the trail. The boat was built with living quarters for 4 men and

An aerial view of the **Hole-in-the-Rock Trail** and **Bay**. At the head of this crack is the end of the Hole-in-the-Rock Road which begins in Escalante. In the bay are 2 boats tied-up to shore, and 2 floating signs.

machinery for placer mining, along with a kitchen, and carpenter & blacksmith shop.

In December of 1888, the barge was complete. It had no power and could only float downstream. It was guided by 2 sweeps, one at either end. The first stop for the craft was about 14 kms downstream at a place Crampton believes was near the mouth of Music Temple Canyon. There they began operations. Sand & gravel were screened twice and the fine material placed in a stirring tub. From there it was washed over mercury-coated amalgamators. The amalgam was supposed to collect the fine particles of gold but apparently without success.

The operation was then moved to a point about 16 kms below the mouth of the San Juan River for 2 months, again without success. Finally, it's believed they sailed on down to Lee's Ferry where the boat was presumably abandoned.

It was the **Hoskaninni Company** which spent the most time and money in the area of the Hole-in-the-Rock. In 1898, the company sent **Robert B. Stanton** down Glen Canyon where he staked and reclaimed the entire length of the canyon with 145 claims. But by law, it was necessary to perform assessment work on the claims each year in order to hold them and prevent others from *"claim-jumping"*. Under Stanton, 4 groups of men were sent out into Glen Canyon to build trails and roads and prepare various locations for future mining work.

One group was sent to the Hole-in-the-Rock, so **Nathaniel Galloway** took 26 men to the 'Hole and established camp in the fall of 1899. They lugged 3800 kgs of supplies down the 'Hole Trail to the river on the backs of men. To do that they modified the trail by cutting steps to make it easier for men to walk down. During this same period of time, which was from October, 1899, until January, 1900, they built a better trail from Jackass Bench up to the canyon rim.

They also started a road up on Jackass Bench as well as a trail downstream along the river on the west bank for about 1 1/2 kms. All in all, they made many minor trails along the river from just below the mouth of the San Juan, to nearly the mouth of the Escalante River in the north. Galloway's men may also have built several stone structures at the bottom of the trail. But all this work was for nothing because when it was learned that Stanton's Dredge up in the Bullfrog Creek region, couldn't separate the fine gold dust from the sand, the company folded. That was sometime in May of 1901. The dredge and all the equipment were eventually sold to J. T. Raleigh for $200.

After the Hoskaninni Company left the 'Hole, 2 fellows named **Henry Newell Cowles** and **Joseph T. Hall** (no relation to Charles T. Hall) opened a **trading post** at the mouth of Hole-in-the-Rock Creek next to the Colorado. They built a small stone cabin at the end of the little creek and referred to it as **Fort Hall**, or **Halls Trading Post**. They used the creek water for drinking and irrigating a small garden.

Hall and Cowles had a good business with the Indians from about mid-1900 until mid-1902. They hired 2 helpers, one Navajo and one Piute, to help ferry customers across the river and to lug down supplies from the newly built Jackass Bench Trail. The Indians, who were Utes, Piutes and Navajos, would trade sheep & goat hides, wool, and hand-woven blankets; for sugar, meat, tobacco, yardage, knives, hardware and livestock.

After these traders left, the route was used only sporadically throughout the years by Navajos who occasionally traded with the Mormon settlements to the west. Since the early part of the 1900's, not much was going on there, but with the tourist boom after the building of Glen Canyon Dam, the place is visited daily by dozens of boaters, and people who drive 4WD's down the Hole-in-the-Rock Road from Escalante.

Part of the **Hole-in-the-Rock Trail**. Notice the steps cut in the sandstone in the lower left-hand corner. It's believed these were cut by the **Hoskaninni Mining Company** in 1899 or 1900.

Above From the air looking down on **Register Rocks**. The route the San Juan Party used begins in the middle of this picture, and angles up to the right. There are many signatures of migrants on the wall next to the green brush and below the HWM.

Left Looking down on the lake from the top of the **Hole-in-the-Rock Trail**. On the far side in the background are **Register Rocks & Cottonwood Canyon**. Surely, the pioneers who took wagons down this crack, improved it to a point that was much better than it is today. It's hard to imagine taking anything down this cleft today!

Just above the HWM of the lake are these steps cut in the Navajo Sandstone. This is part of the **Jackass Bench Trail** believed to have been made by the **Hoskaninni Mining Company.**

The **Hole-in-the-Rock Trail**; but these steps were surely cut by the **Hoskaninni Mining Company** in the years of 1899 or 1900, so they could take supplies down to the Colorado more easily.

This is what you'll see looking south from the top of the **Jackass Bench Trail**. In the distance is **Navajo Mountain**; closer, and just out of sight to the left are **Signature Rocks**; on the far right and just out of sight is the **Hole-in-the-Rock Trail**. This picture from an old slide was taken in 1988 when the water level was high and near the HWM.

This campsite, completely under an alcove-type cave, is about 300 meters south from **La Gorce Arch** in **Davis Canyon**. On this day, **8/6/2007-WL1099.34m/3606.73'**, it was one of the best campsites around; with no tumbleweeds, cheat grass or tamaracks (tamarisks).

Llewellyn & Cottonwood Gulches, and Reflection, Hidden Passage & Music Temple Canyons

Location & Campsites All these canyons are located near the lower end of the **San Juan River Arm** of Lake Powell. **Llewellyn Gulch** is north of the confluence near buoy M63 (K101), while the mouth of **Cottonwood Gulch** is near buoyM57 (K91). On the Navajo Mountain metric map & Nasja Mesa 7 1/2' quad, **Reflection Canyon** is shown as a south fork of **Cottonwood Gulch**. The San Juan River Arm runs east from near buoy M57 (K91). Both **Hidden Passage** and **Music Temple Canyons** are just below or south of the mouth of the San Juan River Arm.

This is one of the few places in the main channel of Lake Powell where some good campsites exist, at least during times of high lake levels. Most of the campsites are located between Llewellyn and Cottonwood Gulches and on both sides of the channel. The reason for these campsites is, the rocks have been raised to the point that some of the Kayenta benches are exposed. This, and the weathering Navajo Sandstone cliffs nearby, combine to create a number of sandy beaches.

Llewellyn Gulch may have some sandy campsites in the middle and upper end, and lots of tie-down places for houseboats. This is a fairly popular destination. **Cottonwood Gulch Inlet** is another Navajo Sandstone canyon with walls rising directly out of the water. There are a couple of small campsites in the middle of the inlet and at the end of each channel there are usually some good sandy sites. Near the upper end is one almost continuous beach for nearly 300 meters when the lake is high; but in times of low water **(7/24/2007-WL1099.78m/3608.18')**, sites are smaller and usually with some tamaracks. **Reflection Canyon** has no good campsites, but a few tie-down places in the upper end.

Hidden Passage has no sites, in either high or low water; **Music Temple** has a couple of high water sites, but maybe only one during times of low water **(7/24/2007-WL1099.78m/3608.18')**.

Hiking Routes or Trails To hike up **Llewellyn Gulch**, start by getting upon of the Kayenta bench to the north which is partially covered with tamaracks. Walk upcanyon along a well-used trail. Near the big rockfall, veer right or west and continue to the top of a prominent bench. Once on this high point, which is just above the HWM, continue west along a good trail. Not far above the HWM, and along the bottom of the Navajo cliff on the right, is an **old cowboy camp** with a little stone box for food storage. About 300 meters above that, and seen only from the bench on the right, will be the first of **3 panels of petroglyphs** in the canyon. Immediately around the corner from the first panel, and on the left or south side of the drainage, is a **sandslide**. Climb up this slide and near the top you'll find the remains of an **old cattle trail**. This is the first of **2 livestock trails** entering/exiting the canyon on the south side.

From the first trail, continue along the bench on the north side of the stream. You can use hiker-made paths. After 300 meters or so you'll come to a **2nd panel of petroglyphs**. After that, and perhaps another 300 meters further upcanyon, is a **3rd rock art panel**, again on the right or north side facing south. Just beyond this last panel and on the left or south side and at a tight bend of the canyon is the **2nd cattle trail**. This one has steps chopped in the Navajo Sandstone slickrock.

Above this trail, the canyon constricts and after another km it begins to be very narrow. This is where the stream first begins to flow. The water runs year-round in this drainage and it can be a fair sized stream. On his first trip, the author continued up these very good narrows for 2-3 kms, but simply got tired of walking through a slot canyon. He never did reach the end, even on another trip with his car when he drove down the **Hole-in-the-Rock Road** and walked in from a point about 5 kms from the road's end.

There are at least 3 good panels of rock art, all petroglyphs, in the middle part of **Llewellyn Gulch**.

Map 21, Llewellyn & Cottonwood Gulches, and Reflection, Hidden Passage & Music Temple Canyons

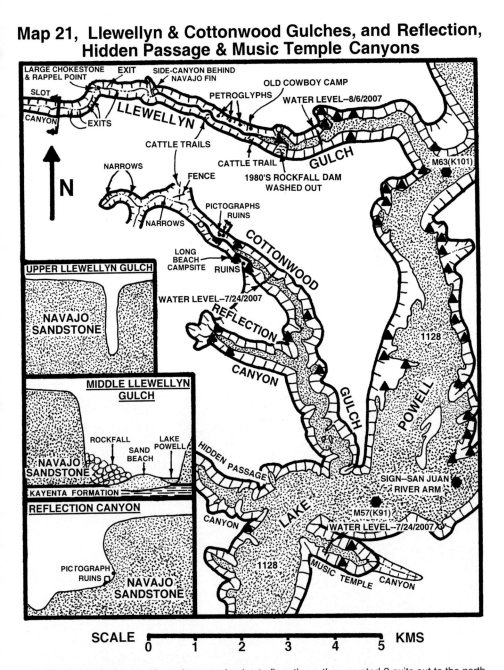

In the upper part, above where the water begins to flow, the author counted 2 exits out to the north or right hand side (the first of which has steps cut, perhaps by a stockman or miner), and 5 exits on the south or left side of the canyon. For those who haven't seen a slot canyon, this is a pretty good one.

Higher in the canyon, there is a large chokestone in the narrows as shown on the map. It's possible for an experienced climber to chimney up the wall and get above this chokestone, but getting down alone is a little risky. With 2-3 people, it should be easy to get up, then it might be best to have a short rope to get everybody back down safely. For awhile someone had left a sling around a rock on the south side of that chokestone which can be used for an easy rappel/handline of 3 meters.

Cottonwood Gulch is another place worth visiting. From your boat, walk upcanyon along the small stream. At the upper end of the inlet near the HWM, is a long sandy beach (now with tamaracks). At the beginning of this beach area, look up to the left or south side and high on the wall in a small alcove is an Anasazi or **Fremont granary**. There are moki steps going up the wall to the ruins, but climbing

171

up will be very risky. Coming down is impossible unless you rig up a rappel with a rope. Best to forget about this one unless you're well prepared!

Going upcanyon, you'll be wading in a small stream or walking on a sandy bench on the right or north, made of alluvial fill. Less than half a km above the HWM, and on the right or northeast side of the stream, you'll see more **ruins** up against the wall and under an overhang. This one has been damaged by cattle. Just to the left of that is one of the few **pictographs (rock art paintings)** seen in the Glen Canyon area. At first the author thought it might be a fake, made by a pale-faced moki, but it seems similar to pictographs in other canyons in the region. Someone has shot bullets into part of it.

One km above these ruins, the canyon opens up for a short distance. At that point you can walk out of the dry creek bottom on an **old stock trail** to the right and through a gate in a short barbed wire fence. Just to the left of the fence is a short & shallow slot. You can walk around this slot as there are a couple of chokestones inside making it difficult to get through. Further up and near the end of the canyon is still another slot and blocking dryfall in the Navajo Sandstone.

Hike Length & Time Needed You can walk up **Llewellyn Gulch** about 4-5 kms before coming to the chokestone. To that point and back might take 3-4 hours. If you can get above the chokestone, might as well make it an all-day hike if you want to explore the entire drainage. The author went up to about where the geology cross section is and returned in 3 1/2 hours. You can walk about 4 kms up **Cottonwood Gulch** easily in half a day. The author's visit lasted 2 1/3 hours. There's no hiking in **Music Temple or Hidden Passage Canyons**.

Boots or Shoes There's water in the lower end of both canyons, but you can normally avoid wading in Cottonwood Gulch, unless you want to wade through potholes in the slot parts of the canyon. Best to use wading boots or shoes in Llewellyn.

Water There were no fresh signs of cattle or beaver in **Cottonwood Gulch** in 1988, 1991, 2001 or 2007, so that water should be good to drink, at least where it seeps out of the creek bed higher upcanyon. If you see cattle (winter months only--October to June), beware. There haven't been any cattle in **Llewellyn** for years, it seems, so it should have good water higher in the canyon. There are beaver and beaver dams in the lower end of Llewellyn.

Main Attractions Anasazi or Fremont ruins, pictographs & petroglyphs, and good slot canyons.

Hiking Maps USGS or BLM map Navajo Mountain (1:100,000), Nasja Mesa (1:24,000--7 1/2' quad) for hiking; Navajo Mtn. (1:62,500) if available; or the Trails Illustrated/National Geographic map, Canyons of the Escalante (1:70,500).

J.W. Powell's Report Just south and across the channel from the mouth of Cottonwood Gulch is another drainage entering Glen Canyon from the east. Here's what Powell had to say about it on August 1, 1869: *On entering, we find a little grove of box-elder and cottonwood trees, and turning to the right, we find ourselves in a vast chamber, carved out of the rock. At the upper end there is a clear, deep pool of water, bordered with verdure. Standing by the side of this, we can see the grove at the entrance. The chamber is more than 200 feet [60 meters] high, 500 feet [150 meters] long, and 200 feet [60 meters] wide. Through the ceiling, and on through the rocks for a thousand feet [300 meters] above, there is a narrow, winding skylight; and this is all carved out by a little stream which runs only during the few show-*

These are the first ruins you come to if hiking up **Cottonwood Gulch**. There are moki steps up this wall, but they're well-worn. It's possible to climb up, but not down. The only way to get down safely would be to take a rope up and handline or rappel down from the boulder you see above.

ers that fall now and then in this arid country..... The rock at the ceiling is hard, the rock below, very soft and friable; and having cut through the upper and harder portion down into the lower and softer, the stream has washed out these friable sandstones; and thus the chamber has been excavated.

Here we bring our camp. When "Old Shady" sings us a song at night, we are pleased to find that this hollow in the rock is filled with sweet sounds. It was doubtless made for an academy of music by its storm-born architect; so we name it **Music Temple [Canyon]**.

Music Temple Canyon now is a short but narrow inlet which opens wider (at HWM) in the upper end, to make a couple of campsites. Right at the very end of the inlet the walls come very close together not allowing boats to enter. But the energetic hiker may try swimming this last part.

This little cascade/waterfall & pothole in **Llewellyn Gulch,** is located just upcanyon from the old cowboy camp & the first cattle trail. The stream flow was pretty low on this day--8/6/2007, which was after a long drought.

Mikes & Copper Canyons and Castle Creek & Johnies Hole and the Nokai Dome Hike, San Juan River Arm

Location & Campsites **Mikes Canyon & Castle Creek**, and the hike to the top of **Nokai Dome & Johnies Hole**, are in the upper end of the **San Juan River Arm** of Lake Powell. In the 1980's, the best way into this area was to launch at the **San Juan Marina**, located at the end of **Piute Farms Wash** very near the upper end of the San Juan Arm of the lake. However, that marina was flooded out in 1989 and will not be replaced (presently the Navajos have a new marina at **Antelope Point** just northeast of Page). To get into this area by boat, you'll have to take plenty of fuel from Dangling Rope Marina and sail all the way up the San Juan. However, the upper end of this part of the lake has muddy & shallow water and mud flats even when the lake is at or near the HWM. On **9/9/2007-WL1098.08m/3602.61'**, this entire area was bone dry with just the river flowing through the dusty mud flats. On that day, the lake ended 1 km below **Spencer's Camp** west of **Zahn Bay**. With low water levels, don't even dream of getting to this area by boat.

With high water, there are many good campsites in the inlet to **Mikes Canyon**. Also, in or near the short bay of **Castle Creek** are some good sandy camping beaches. Just south of this mapped area is the mouth of **Copper Canyon**. However, near the lake it has nothing of interest for hikers. Copper Canyon Inlet has several good campsites, but there may be cattle and semi-wild feral donkeys roaming around the shoreline at times. Also, Navajos in 4WD's make it to the lake/river to fish in this region.

Hiking Routes & Trails **Mikes Canyon** is a long drainage which begins just south of Highway 276. It has a main fork and a left or west fork. It seems the left fork would be of most interest to hikers but it's not on any ones list of best hikes. For most of the year this is a dry canyon, so walk right up the dry creek bed. The way is free of obstacles and the walking is generally easy. The geologic strata you'll be walking through is the **Chinle Formation**; as you walk, notice all the petrified wood. Most of the petrified wood you see on the Colorado Plateau comes from this formation.

In places you'll see the faded remains of an old uranium mining exploration track weaving its way up the canyon bottom. Sometimes you can walk on this. When you reach the fork in the canyon walk into the left or west fork. It continues for many kms, becoming entrenched and narrow. Higher up you'll find some water and a pretty good spring and you can get out of the upper end and walk to Highway 276.

The best hike in this area is up **Castle Creek**, another very long drainage. It begins as Steer Pasture Canyon far to the northeast, and north of Highway 276. Only the lower end including a tributary valley called **Johnies Hole** is covered here.

In the lower end of Castle Creek the walking is a little slow in places because of vegetation. There are some boulders, waterfalls, tamaracks & willows in the canyon bottom, as most of the lower canyon has year-round flowing water (depending on the time of year, and how long the drought is!). There may be cattle in the canyon, so there are some cow trails to follow in places. It's the lower end below the first 2 waterfalls which has these minor obstacles. Pass the **1st Waterfall** on the right, then as you approach the **2nd Waterfall**, look up to the left for a trail on the west side of the canyon which takes hikers around this obstacle. Above the 2 waterfalls, the going is easier and the creek bed will be dry at times. In the author's 3 trips to this canyon from the lake, it had running water twice, but the last time it was dry (a 4th trip in 10/2007 was by road from the north).

In the northern end of **Johnies Hole** is this Navajo hogan dating from sometime in the early 1900's. In the background can be seen dead cottonwood trees, a result of a fire, probably in the early 2000's.

Map 22, Mikes Canyon, Castle Creek & Johnies Hole and the Nokai Dome Hike

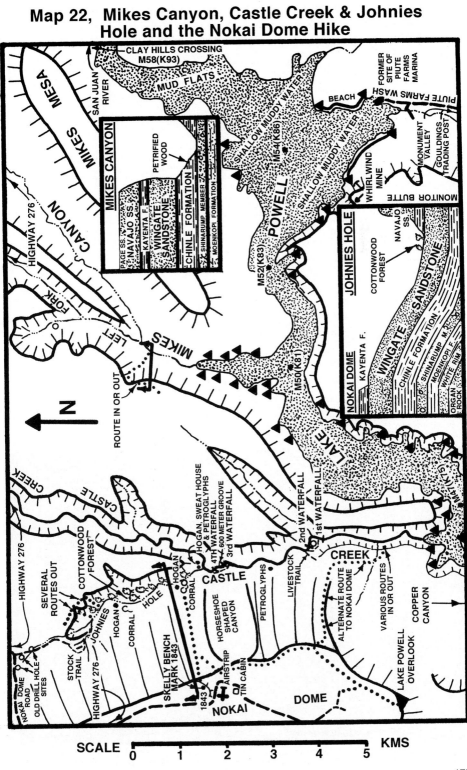

SCALE

0 1 2 3 4 5 KMS

Just above the **2nd Waterfall** is an old livestock trail zig zagging up the slope to the left or west. This short trail provides a way up to a small grazing area on the southeast side of Nokai Dome.

Also, about 1 km above the 2nd Waterfall and on the left is an old Navajo or Piute camp of some kind. On a nearby rock are some recent Navajo etchings. After another km, you'll come to a sizable pond (which used to be a beaver pond, but not in 2007) just below another permanent waterfall. Get out of the willow bottoms on the left and look for cattle trails leading up on a bench. This trail bypasses another 2 Wingate waterfalls just above the pond (**3rd Waterfall**). Or you can climb up to the left of this 3rd Waterfall to enter a **slickrock narrows** in the Wingate. After about 650 meters, and possibly a deep pool or two, you'll come to the **4th Waterfall**, which you can't climb (maybe climb it on the right?).

Just above this **4th Waterfall** is a boulder with a very recent Navajo etching (facing south) reading, *Old Navajo Land*. This is obviously a protest dating from sometime during the 1900's when the BLM ran Navajos out of this canyon and back onto their national lands to the south. In this same area, the valley changes and from there on up, there are good grazing areas, cottonwood trees, and a number of old abandoned Navajo or possibly Piute homes/hogans, sweat houses and corrals.

Right at the junction of Castle Creek and Johnies Hole Valley, and up on a bench, are some log structures; a hogan and sweat house. Behind them on a wall is some rock art. The author went up into Johnies Hole on 2 occasions (came down from his car in 10/2007) instead of up Castle Creek. Far up Castle Creek use some Anasazi ruins next to Highway 276; the road to Halls Crossing Marina.

Johnies Hole is an oasis in the desert. It's a wide little valley with a small forest of mostly cottonwoods, but with some tall gamble oak & cedar trees, and now the ever-present tamaracks. On the author's first and second visits, there was some running water in places. On another trip it was bone dry, except for one minor seep in about the middle of the valley.

In Johnies Hole are several corrals and round log structures, which Stan Jones says were built by Piutes. However, Carl Mahon, a former BLM ranger out of Monticello, Utah, told the author he used to run Navajos and their flocks of sheep & goats out of the area on a regular basis up until the building of the Glen Canyon Dam. So it's likely at least some of these structures were built by Navajo herdsmen. Some appear to date from the early 1900's or perhaps from about World War I. Others are more recent, probably built after World War II.

The late Melvin Dalton of Monticello once told the author there's an **old stock trail** leading down into Johnies Hole from the north. On the author's last trip by car (Chevy Tracker) in 10/2007, he finally found it. At the upper end of Johnies Hole Valley, walk left into a minor drainage with Nokai Dome on the left, and a minor ridge running south on the right. Actually you can climb out of the valley on this little ridge, but look closely for a trail in the drainage, marked with cairns. A little higher up, this trail veers left or west, then heads straight up to the north just left of a small buttress. It's washed out in places, but you can follow it to the rim and out to an old track zig zagging up to the Nokai Dome Road.

An interesting side-trip is to walk from somewhere in Johnies Hole, to the top of **Nokai Dome**. From the lower end of the 'Hole simply start walking west up the sloping slickrock which is likely the top of the Wingate Sandstone. It's an easy walk and the slope isn't too steep. Near the top, route-find up through some ledges. If you go to the top of the little Kayenta bench at 1843 meters, you'll have fine views in all directions.

Once on top, follow the old oil exploration road south and you'll come to an airstrip, a small tin cabin, an old oil drilling site and the cab of a 1940's truck. This road was built by an oil company sometime after World War II. For some good views of the lake, walk about 2 kms south on this same road, then veer left or east, then south again to the end of Nokai Dome. Possibly an easier and shorter route to the rim exists from about where you pass the first 2 waterfalls in lower Castle Creek. The author came down a similar route on his 2001 trip. It's marked as an **alternate route** on the map.

Hike Length & Time Needed You can walk for many kms into either fork of **Mikes Canyon**, but the

Part of a rock art panel on a south-facing wall less than 100 meters east of the sweat house shown on the opposite page. These are located at the junction of **Johnies Hole** & **Castle Creek**.

petrified wood in the lower end might be more interesting than a long hike. It's about 10 kms from the lake to the middle of **Johnies Hole** and another 3 kms to the tin cabin on **Nokai Dome**. To do this hike will take all day. To hike to Johnies Hole and back will be about half a day or 4-6 hours for most hikers; all day for others.

Boots or Shoes There's a stream in **Castle Creek**, but you can avoid getting your feet wet so any kind of shoes are OK. Rugged hiking boots would be best if you plan to hike up to the top of **Nokai Dome**. Mikes Canyon is dry and frankly not very interesting, at least in the lower end.

Water There were some minor seeps in Mikes Canyon upon the author's visit, but they are seasonal. There are springs higher up in the left fork. There are good springs just above and below the second waterfall in lower Castle Creek which would be your best sources. There are cattle in all parts of Castle from October to June, so creek water is suspect.

Main Attractions Petrified wood, waterfalls, beaver ponds, old Piute or Navajo ruins, new & old rock art, and good views from Nokai Dome.

Hiking Maps USGS or BLM map Navajo Mountain (1:100,000); Mikes Mesa, Nokai Dome & No Mans Mesa North (1:24,000--7 1/2' quad) for hiking; or Lake Canyon & Clay Hills (1:62,500) if available.

Historical Sites--Upper San Juan River Arm At the eastern end of the San Juan Arm is **Piute Farms Wash and Bay**. This is the head of navigation for boaters--but only when the lake is at or near the HWM. River runners coming down the San Juan get out on the north side of **Clay Hills Crossing**.

Clay Hills Crossing is where the San Juan River leaves a deep canyon and enters the open main body of the lake at about M58 (K93). This is the river distance in miles & kilometers (kms) from the mouth of the San Juan where it emptied into the Colorado River. The HWM actually extends upcanyon almost to the mouth of Grand Gulch, but it's impossible for boats to get up that far. Rubber rafts can barely float down when the water in the river is high.

Clay Hills Crossing was surely an old Indian route but in more recent times the Navajos used it when they were at war with the United States during the years 1846-1864. An 1860 map by Egloffstein called it **Navajo Crossing**. This would have been a natural route for the Indians if they were heading for the Colorado River via either White or Red Canyons.

The first extensive use of the Clay Hills Crossing by white men undoubtedly came with the **San Juan Gold Rush**, which began in the winter of **1892-93** and lasted for about 10 years. It was in this region that 200 mining claims were staked out between October and December of 1892 by the **Gabel Mining District**. One of the men who created the company was J. P. Williams, the same miner who built the Williams Trail near the mouth of Nokai Canyon (see **Map 23**).

Much later in history, and during the uranium boom days of the 1950's, a better road was built to the crossing. From there, another road was built along the south side of Mikes Mesa to the mouth of Mikes Canyon.

The name **Piute Farms** comes from a broad open area at the mouth of Piute Farms Wash in pre-Lake Powell days. This area was originally settled by Piutes who farmed about 40-60 hectares (100-150 acres). They were living there when the Navajo Nation was at war with the USA. Because of those problems there was a good deal of mixing of the tribes in the San Juan River region.

Just before the waters of Lake Powell covered the farms in the early 1980's, Crampton reported a dozen peach and 3-4 apple trees growing at Piute Farms, but no one lived there permanently. There were also half a dozen hogans, a sweathouse and one new Carter water pump. The pump was used to lift water from the San Juan to the farms when the river was low. It appeared that during the months

What appears to be a Navajo sweat house, is located at the junction of **Johnies Hole** and **Castle Creek**. Just to the right of this is an old log hogan, and on the wall behind, a rock art panel.

177

of May and June they may have used river water to irrigate without using a pump.

On the northeast corner or toe of **Monitor Mesa**, and just above the lake northwest of the now-abandoned San Juan Marina, is the **Whirlwind Mine**. This uranium mine is located in the Shinarump Member of the Chinle Formation. According to Cal Black of Blanding, the ore was discovered in the 1940's but the first uranium was shipped in 1950. It was worked periodically until 1960. Look for this mine high on the cliffs--if you can get uplake that far!

As you head west from the **Piute Farms Bay**, and at about M52 (K83), look south and you'll see the remains of an old hand-built road. This wagon road or trail goes up and down along the shoreline, occasionally rising to just above the HWM. It apparently was built during the San Juan Gold Rush. Crampton believes it was built as part of the assessment work which was required to maintain active claims.

One of the easiest ways to enter the San Juan River Valley from the south before Lake Powell was through **Copper Canyon**. The name undoubtedly comes from the discovery of copper deposits along the upper parts of the canyon and at the base of Hoskaninni Mesa. This is west of Oljeto in Monument Valley. It is quite probable that these deposits gave rise to the legend of the lost **Merrick & Mitchell Silver Mine** that drew prospectors, including **Cass Hite**, into the vicinity in about 1881. Copper and uranium are found in vegetal fossil channel structures in the Chinle Formation.

The legend of the lost Merrick & Mitchell Mine started when 2 prospectors (who may or may not have found the place) by the names of **James Merrick** and **Ernest Mitchell**, were killed by Indians in Monument Valley in March, 1880. When their bodies were later examined, silver samples were found. This led to the belief that Merrick & Mitchell had found the reported Navajo silver mine. This was the single most important event which started the Glen Canyon Gold Rush beginning in 1884, and later the San Juan Gold Rush in 1892-93.

Some time during the San Juan Gold Rush of the 1890's, a road was built from Oljeto Trading Post down Copper Canyon to the San Juan River, a distance of about 35 kms. About 6 kms above the mouth of Copper, the road left the wash and topped out on the east rim of the canyon. It then descended to the river and ended at **Williams Bar**, about 3 kms upstream or east from the mouth of the Copper Canyon. Williams Bar was located at about M49 (K78), while Copper Canyon entered the river at M47 (K75).

Once again, these distances are the mileage (kilomage) from the mouth of the San Juan where it emptied into the Colorado River. There are no buoys in the San Juan Arm of the lake, but the author has put the old river distances on the maps at the mouths of major canyons in this San Juan Arm section of this book.

Williams Bar was one of the major placer gold mining sites along the San Juan River during the gold rush of 1892-93, and later. The site seems to be identified prominently with the name of J. P. Williams, one of the organizers of the Gabel Mining District, who also had many of the claims in the area of Clay Hills Crossing. Williams, in 1884-85 had prospected the Navajo Mountain area looking for the Merrick & Mitchell Mine, during which time his party is reported to have seen Rainbow Bridge. In 1890 he was on the San Juan River.

In 1892, J. P. Williams was trading with the Navajos, presumably at a location on the San Juan River. On file in the Recorder's Office in Blanding, San Juan County, Utah, is the original daybook kept by Williams. It shows entries or transactions with Indians and whites from April 22, 1892 to November in 1893. The same book records the events on Williams Bar. The first official claim recorded in the

The **3rd waterfall**, and large pool, as shown on the map. You can walk around this and enter the lower part of the fotogenic **600 meter groove**, part of which is shown on the opposite page.

Williams Mining District was the Plum Bob. At one time, Williams had a steam boiler, evidently to run a pump, which was fixed to a barge. All this was at a place he called **Williamsburg**.

In 1960 when Crampton visited this place, he found a stone house about 300 meters from the river. It was built up against a cliff which formed one wall. The house measured about 4 x 6 meters and had a fireplace and one door. Less than 1 km upstream was the foundation of another stone house measuring about 6 x 7 meters. Some sources believe it was built by **Charles H. Spencer** before 1908. If this is true, it was the first of at least 4 different sites this mining engineer developed in the Glen Canyon region in a 7-8 year period. This may have been Spencer's first of 4 total failures at gold mining.

From the mouth of Copper Canyon another road headed west. It stayed well above the river and on top the Shinarump bench all the way to Nokai Canyon (see **Map 23**). This road is occasionally used by Navajos today driving 4WD pickups. From the bay at the mouth of Nokai, one track was called **Spencer's Road** and it ran west to end at **Spencer's Camp**. Another road ran to **Zahn's Camp**. Read more about these places under **Map 23**.

This is part of the **600 meter groove** or shallow narrows located between the 3rd & 4th waterfalls just below where **Castle Creek** and **Johnies Hole** meet. See the map. Just downcanyon from this scene is the waterfall & pool seen on the opposite page.

Spencer's Road & Williams Trail and Nokai Canyon & Piute Mesa, San Juan River Arm

Location & Campsites The old road and trail covered on this map are located south of **Zahn Bay**, which is in about the middle of the **San Juan River Arm** of Lake Powell. There are no buoys in the San Juan Arm so the old river mileage (kilomage) is used here to show relative distances. The mouth of **Nokai Canyon** is M44 (K70); and Spencer's Camp at about M38 (K61) from the mouth of the San Juan where it used to empty into the Colorado River. These places are the beginning points of the 2 hikes in this area. **Please note:** all land south of the lake is part of the **Navajo Nation**.

In this region are a number of good campsites, but how many will depend on the level of the lake. Due to drought conditions in the early 2000's, you couldn't even get to these places; on **9/9/2007-WL1098.08m/3602.61'**, the author could only get his boat to within 1 km of Spencer's Camp. So if or when the water level rises and you can get into this area, the best campsites will be in the bay or inlet to **Nokai Canyon**. These are sandy, but in places the water can be shallow leading to the shoreline. Right where the dry Nokai Creek enters, is normally a big sandy delta with lots of tamaracks. Be aware, there may be semi-wild Navajo donkeys around this bay and they can be noisy as hell at night, especially if one of the females is in heat, as was the case on one of the author's visits.

On the south side of Zahn Bay are a number of sites, but some are clay beds rather than sandy beaches. The islands in the bay may also provide good campsites and there are places at the western end of **Spencer's Road** for a camp. Another **word of caution** if camping at the mouth of Nokai Canyon where Spencer's Road enters the lake; with lots of donkeys and other livestock in these 2 areas, and all the manure lying around, expect to see a lot more bothersome bush flies than in other areas.

Hiking Routes or Trails As you boat into **Nokai Canyon Inlet**, look southwest at the inclined slope made of the Shinarump Member of the Chinle Formation. High above, you can see an old wagon road zig zagging up toward the cliffs beyond. This is **Spencer's Road**. To walk it, tie-down your boat somewhere along the southwest shore of the bay. You may have to look around for the beginning of this road, but the further up you go, the easier it will be to find it. Wild Navajo donkeys and cattle use this old track regularly. In areas where the road itself has faded, the livestock have usually created their own trail in its place.

About 2 kms along Spencer's Road from the HWM in Nokai Bay, you'll see on the left and running south, the beginning of an old trail built by a miner named **J. P. Williams**. More on this below. At about that point Spencer's Road is running due west and still climbing. Not far above this junction, the road runs atop landslide debris which came from the big walls to the south, which are made up mostly of Wingate Sandstone. Up to that point the road runs on top of the Shinarump Member of the Chinle Formation, and there is a lot of petrified wood around.

From the highest point, the road runs west and northwest and for the most part along the rim of the Shinarump bench. From the halfway point, the road gradually descends. In some places it's hard to see but there will always be livestock trails to mark the way. The northwest end of the road gradually merges into the lake at about M39 (K62). You can start at either end of this track and walk toward the middle, as did the author. The part of the road most interesting to visit is near Nokai Bay. It's the highest part and it affords the best views of the lake and country side, including the exposed geology of the south side of **Nokai Dome** which is part of the **Waterpocket Fold**.

The **Williams Trail** takes off from Spencer's Road about 2 kms above the southwest side of Nokai

Part of the **Williams Trail** as it zig zags up through the Wingate Sandstone cliffs of **Piute Mesa**. Looking at the way this trail was constructed, it's easy to see it was built by hardrock miners.

Map 23, Spencer's Road & Williams Trail and Nokai Canyon & Piute Mesa

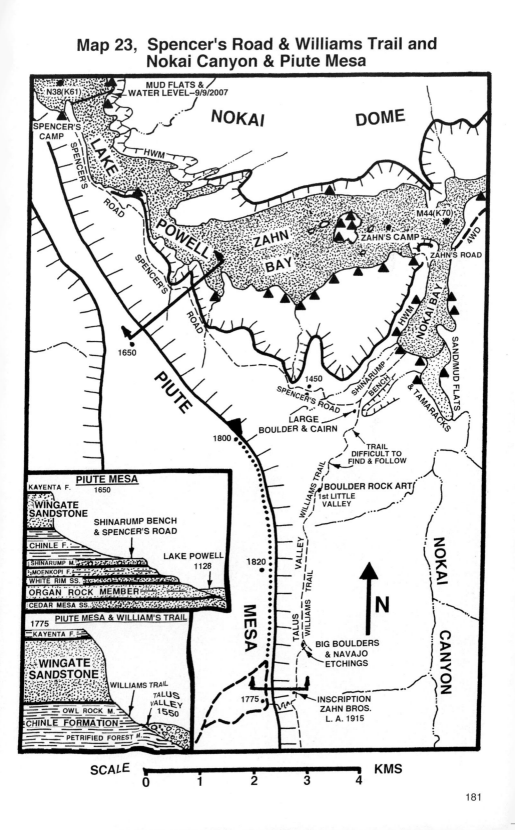

181

Canyon Bay. As you walk up Spencer's Road, look to the left and you should see a shallow canyon or drainage. About 100 meters above the head of this mini-canyon is where the Williams Trail heads south. At that junction are stone cairns. About 100 meters south of the junction, you'll see the trail passing a large red Wingate Sandstone boulder with a cairn on top.

This is a constructed trail, but in places it's hard to find and follow--see the map. The author lost it twice, but managed to stay on it most of the way on his third trip in 2001. The trail zig zags up to the south, southwest and over and around some bluffs made of Chinle clay beds. About 1 km from Spencer's Road, you'll come to a small flat area with some large boulders, one of which has a good panel of petroglyphs facing west. South of that first little flat, you'll gradually climb to a second level which is closer to the big Wingate cliffs of **Piute Mesa**. Finally, the trail runs the San Juan Gold Rush. But the author calls the **Talus Valley**. This little valley is nearly level and used for grazing. You can surely find and follow the trail in that area, but in the sagebrush it's sometimes hard to see.

At the southern end of this long valley, and in an open meadow with several large boulders, the trail veers up to the right, then it's easier to locate and follow. In the part where it begins to steepen, it was dug out with pick & shovel and it's still clearly visible and used by an occasional hiker and livestock. When the trail reaches the bottom of a break in the Wingate cliff, it's clear that hardrock miners built this one. Parts of it have been blasted out of the rock as it zig zags up through the cliffs. It's been said this trail was originally built by a miner named J. P. Williams during the San Juan Gold Rush. But the author believes it's also very likely some work was done on this part of the trail during the Depression days of the 1930's by CCC crews (?).

As you reach the first cliffs you should see on the right or west, an inscription reading, *Zahn Bros, LA, 1915*. A bit further and as the trail starts to zig zag up the face, look to the south and you'll see another trail coming north to meet the one you're on. That trail is apparently connected to the old Wetherill Trail about 12 kms to the south.

When you finally reach the rim of **Piute Mesa** the trail ends. At that point is an old road, which you could follow west to the old now-closed **Navajo Mtn. Trading Post**. From the top of the trail another old vehicle track runs north along the rim for several kms. If you'd like good views of the lake and the exposed geology of the Nokai Dome, rim-walk north about 5 kms. The elevation of the viewpoint shown is about 1800 meters while the lake is 1128 meters at the HWM.

Hike Length & Time Needed The length of Spencer's Road is about 12-13 kms. It would take all day to walk from one end to the other and back, but the recommended hike is from Nokai Bay to a high point in the middle, and return. The Williams Trail runs for about 7-8 kms to the top of Piute Mesa. Add 2 kms along the first part of Spencer's Road, and it's about 10 kms to the top of the mesa and the end of this historic trail. Plan on 5-6 hours or maybe all day to do this hike, round-trip.

Boots or Shoes Any dry weather hiking boots or shoes.

Water There are no springs anywhere near, so take your own water.

Main Attractions Two historic trails, and some great views of the geology of Nokai Dome from Piute

From the southern tip of **Nokai Dome** looking southwest toward **Navajo Mountain**. *This* foto was taken on **10/10/2007-WL1097.76m /3601.53'**, and the lake had receded from this area. *In* the middle part of this picture are the mud flats of **Zahn Bay**. On that day the author drove to Nok*ai* D*o*me for this fotograph. It could be many years before we can boat to and hike, in this ar*ea*.

Mesa.
Hiking Maps USGS or BLM map Navajo Mountain (1:100,000); No Mans Mesa North (1:24,000--7 1/2' quad) for hiking; or No Mans Mesa (1:62,500) if available.
History of Spencer's Road and the Williams Trail This story begins late in 1892 with the San Juan Gold Rush. One of the principal parties who got this one off the ground was **J. P. Williams**. In April of 1892, he was carrying on some kind of trade with the Navajos from a place on the San Juan River. Presumably that location was just east of the mouth of Copper Canyon at about M46 (K73). This was for a time called **Williamsburg**. It was on one of the most productive placer gold mining sites in the canyon, a place called **Williams Bar**.

According to Crampton and Charles H. Spencer, Williams was the man who built this trail from the mouth of Nokai Canyon to the top of Piute Mesa. No explanations were given as to why it was originally built but when Spencer came along, his crews used it to reach the top of the mesa where they cut cedar trees, then threw them over the cliff and used them in his operations at Spencer's Camp. Williams may have done the same thing (?).

Another chapter of San Juan River history was written by the **Zahn brothers** of Los Angeles. The 5 brothers; **Oscar, Otto, Paul, Hector and Oswald** did much of the development work at a place called **Zahn's Camp**. It was actually begun by T. R. Gabel, one of several men who organized the Gabel Mining District in this region in 1892. For many years it was referred to as Gabel Camp, but later the Zahns bought him out along with various other interests in about 1902.

The Zahn brothers, along with their mother, organized the **Zahn & Baldwin Mining Company**. They poured big money into the site which already included a boiler and other machinery. They drove wagon loads of pipe and new equipment from Flagstaff, Arizona, a distance of 300 kms. They also rafted machinery down the San Juan River from Piute Farms (see previous map).

The Zahns operated this placer mining outfit until the end of World War I before pulling out. They never made much profit but one of their most famous accomplishments took place in September of 1915, when they drove a new Franklin automobile from Los Angeles to Zahn's Camp. On the return trip when they were driving out of Nokai Canyon, they broke the transmission, and had to be pulled to Oljeto by John Wetherill and 2 teams of horses.

You can still see part of what remains of Zahn's Road (and, if the lake is really low as it was in 2007, you might hike up along the south side of the river and see part of the camp?). Dock near the mouth of Nokai Bay and walk along the hillside to the west. What remains of this road goes over a little divide and is clearly visible in several places. See the site on the map.

One of the more dynamic figures in the history of both the San Juan River and Glen Canyon was **Charles H. Spencer**. Spencer was a big dreamer and even greater promoter. He originally came to the Glen Canyon-San Juan country in about 1900, but in 1909 built this trail now called **Spencer's Road**. He set up a mining operation on the river near M38 (K61). The road was built with pick and shovel by Navajos and Piutes. It rose from the canyon bottom to a hogsback about 300 meters above the river, then returned to the river with grades up to 25°.

From the southern tip of **Nokai Dome** on **10/10/2007-WL1097.76m/3601.76'**, looking almost due west using a telefoto lens. In the distance is **Fiftymile Mountain**; in the middle left is the area near where Spencer Camp was located. On **9/9/2007-1098.09m/3602.61'**, this area was the head of navigation for the author. On that day it was muddy water and mud flats all around.

183

Spencer's Camp, or **Camp Ibex** as he called it at one time, was set up near the river where great Wingate boulders were in abundance. His dream was to separate gold from the Wingate Sandstone. They used a Sampson crusher, powered by a single cylinder Otto gasoline engine, and installed sorting screens and an amalgamating table. They also used a steam boiler for power and obtained part of their firewood from the top of Piute Mesa. In the area northwest of the viewpoint shown on the map, you may see stumps of trees which, according to Crampton, was the location where they felled the trees and threw them over the cliff (the author never saw any stumps?). They also stretched a cable across the river to catch and haul in driftwood.

Spencer operated his crushing mill using 10 hired men in June, 1909, and again in the winter of 1909-10, but this scheme was a failure. Spencer abandoned Camp Ibex in the spring of 1910 when he heard of gold being discovered in the Chinle clay beds at Lee's Ferry. He was at Lee's Ferry for a couple of years, using up thousands of investors dollars. While there, he devised a scheme to haul coal from Warm Creek to Lee's Ferry in a paddle wheeled steamboat. The coal was to be used to power a steam boiler to help extract the gold from the clay. Things failed there too. He then ended his illustrious career at Pahreah, Utah, in about 1915.

For more information on Charles H. Spencer and his mining operations at Lee's Ferry and old Pahreah in southern Utah, see another book by the author titled, *Hiking and Exploring the Paria River.*

An abandoned Samson Crusher (above) and Otto Gasoline engine. This foto was taken near **Spencer Camp** in about 1960 in the days before Lake Powell began to invade the area. The author wasn't thinking about this place when he was there on **9/9/2007-WL1098.09m/3602.61'**, but there's a good chance you may see some of this old mining equipment if the lake waters remain low, and it hasn't been covered with sediment (Crampton foto).

Spencer Camp in March, 1909. With low lake levels, you might be able to find this site, if it hasn't been covered with mud & sediments (Spencer foto).

Spencer Camp in March of 1909. This foto shows an oxen team with freight, with the **San Juan River** in the background. This was located right where the Shinarump Member of the Chinle Formation comes down to the river's edge. This should be easy to find if you're in the area (Spencer foto).

Great Bend Canyons of the San Juan River Arm, and Neskahi & Piute Canyons

Location & Campsites Shown on this map is a huge gooseneck bend in about the middle of the **San Juan River Arm** of Lake Powell called the **Great Bend**. The author found this section to be fairly popular in the summer months, but there are fewer visitors compared to the canyons between Wahweap & Antelope Marinas, and Rainbow Bridge. The Great Bend has some of the best scenery on the lake but very few boaters go further east up the San Juan Arm. In the future, expect even fewer people to visit the upper end of this long inlet beyond the Great Bend because of silting, and the general lack of inspiring scenery. On **9/9/2007-WL1098.08m/3602.61'**, the author didn't even make it to **Spencer's Camp** (see previous map, number **23**) because of low lake levels.

Campsites are a little scarce in these parts. However, there may be several Kayenta slickrock-type sites on the inside of the bend along the main channel during times of high water. Campsites may exist in the upper end of each side-canyon inlet. Most of those in the little alcoves are sandy and very pleasant. Note the number of springs/seeps on the outside of the bend. Water seeps out from the contact point of the Navajo Sandstone above, and the Kayenta Formation below.

The main channel is rather narrow in this section. On the right-hand side of this map, you'll see the Wingate Sandstone walls rising from water's edge, but they slowly submerge to the northwest and take a dive under **Gray Mesa**. **Neskahi** and **Piute Canyons** are discussed at the end of this section but are not shown on this map. There's little if any hiking in these 2 areas.

Hiking Routes or Trails The longest drainage on this map is called **Navajo Canyon**. Joined to it at the very bottom end is **San Juan Canyon**. The author once camped right at the HWM at the lower end of San Juan Inlet on a sandy beach; one of the best little campsites he had on Lake Powell. However, on **9/9/2007-WL1098.08m/3602.61'** it would have taken a pretty good rock climber to get up above the upper Wingate wall, so when the lake is low it may be difficult to get into these canyons.

If you want to hike into either drainage, you'll have to start at the same place--right at the bottom end of San Juan Canyon. The reason for this is, a dryfall in the lower end of Navajo Canyon just above the HWM (there's even more dropoffs with low lake levels). If the lake level is really low, like it was in 2007, you may have to look for a route up on some of the Wingate & Kayenta ledges along the main channel.

At and just above the HWM in **San Juan Canyon**, the drainage is full of house-size boulders. All this debris covers up dryfalls or dropoffs allowing you to get up through the Wingate Sandstone easily. After perhaps half a km, you leave **boulder alley** and the canyon suddenly opens up. At that point you can walk up either canyon. For the sake of simplicity, this description will take you up Navajo and down San Juan. This is a recommended hike if you're fit and have the time to take an all-day walk.

Once you get to the top of boulder alley in the lower end of San Juan Canyon, make a 180° turn to the left and work your way up along the top of the Kayenta bench. This bench is in both canyons, and you can walk on it from one to the other. This seems the only way into **Navajo Canyon** unless you tie-up out in the main channel somewhere and climb in from there.

Once you've turned the corner and entered the lower end of Navajo, it'll be necessary to stay on the Kayenta bench for 1-2 kms, before the terrain allows you to actually walk in the bottom of the usually-dry creek bed. As you walk along the bottom of the canyon, there will be a number of places where wil-

From the air, looking down on **The Great Bend** of the **San Juan River**. Lower left is **East Alcove Canyon**; then to the right is **Alcove Canyon** with the big alcove; upper right is **Bend Canyon**.

Map 24, Great Bend Canyons of the San Juan River Arm

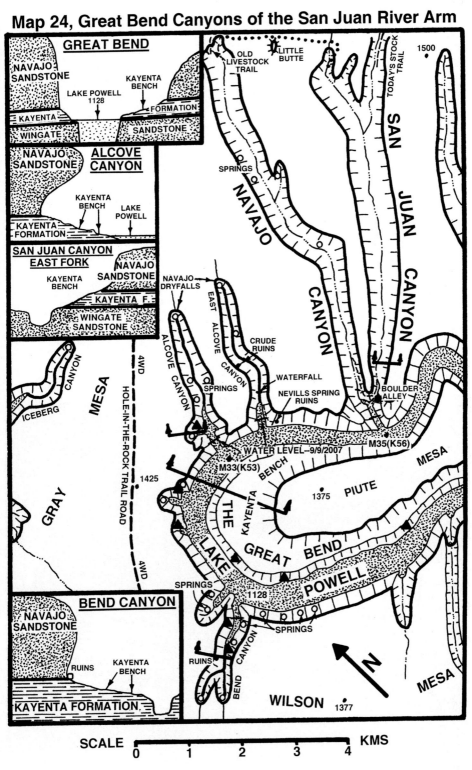

GREAT BEND

NAVAJO SANDSTONE

KAYENTA BENCH

LAKE POWELL 1128

FORMATION

KAYENTA

WINGATE

SANDSTONE

ALCOVE CANYON

NAVAJO SANDSTONE

KAYENTA BENCH

LAKE POWELL

KAYENTA FORMATION

SAN JUAN CANYON EAST FORK

NAVAJO SANDSTONE

KAYENTA BENCH

KAYENTA F.

WINGATE SANDSTONE

OLD LIVESTOCK TRAIL

LITTLE BUTTE

TODAY'S STOCK TRAIL

1500

SAN JUAN CANYON

SPRINGS

NAVAJO CANYON

NAVAJO DRYFALLS

EAST ALCOVE

CRUDE RUINS

WATERFALL

NEVILLS SPRING RUINS

BOULDER ALLEY

ALCOVE CANYON

SPRINGS

ICEBERG

CANYON

MESA

4WD

HOLE-IN-THE-ROCK TRAIL ROAD

1425

WATER LEVEL--9/9/2007

M35(K56)

M33(K53)

MESA

KAYENTA BENCH

1375

PIUTE

GRAY

4WD

THE LAKE

GREAT BEND

POWELL

SPRINGS

1128

SPRINGS

BEND CANYON

NAVAJO SANDSTONE

RUINS

KAYENTA BENCH

RUINS

BEND CANYON

MESA

WILSON

1377

KAYENTA FORMATION

N

SCALE

KMS

0   1   2   3   4

lows, cottonwood trees and other water-loving plants grow. With the author's first visit on October 1, 1988, there was no running water anywhere but he did find springs or seeps in 3-4 places. In wetter times you should find lots more water.

After walking about 10 kms, you'll come to the end of the drainage. It would be a box canyon, but some time in the early days of San Juan County settlement, cattlemen built a **stock trail** down from the Navajo Sandstone rim. To find it, walk right to the upper end of the canyon where you'll find the usual blocking dryfall. On the left or west side, and back downcanyon 300 meters, is a break in the Navajo wall. It's the only place anyone has a chance of getting out and should be easy to locate. It's been blasted out in a place or two and you may see fresh horseshoe scratch marks on the slickrock as this trail is still used occasionally by cowboys today. However, the trail is too steep for cattle so they are taken down into San Juan Canyon, then they make their way into Navajo Canyon via the Kayenta bench just described, according to the late Melvin Dalton of Monticello, Utah. His son Val now grazes cattle in these canyons from October to June, about every other year.

Once you get out of **Navajo Canyon**, look for stone cairns marking the route up along a minor ridge to the northeast. Not far above the constructed trail, the cairns seem to vanish and you're on your own. At that point, turn right 90°, and head southeast past the top of the dryfall which is right at the end of canyon. Continue southeast and to the left of a fairly **prominent little butte** right on the ridge top. Just past this little butte you'll begin to drop down into the upper part of **San Juan Canyon**. You'll then have to route-find south down into the upper shallow drainage, then up the other side while looking for another route over the Navajo Sandstone as shown.

The author actually entered the upper end of San Juan Canyon not far below a big Navajo dropoff, but there is another easier way in if you were to walk further south or southeast. The author didn't take the time to explore every nook and cranny, but there is a walk-in route in the main fork of upper San Juan approximately as shown on the map, according to Melvin Dalton.

From the head of San Juan Canyon, it's about 7 kms back down to boulder alley and the lake. There should be a number of potholes along the upper and middle sections of the drainage which is in the Kayenta slickrock; but don't count on water being there all the time. In wetter times there will be a seep or two. The lower end of San Juan is very dry and sandy with easy walking.

Just to the east of Alcove Canyon is another drainage which could be its twin. The author has named it **East Alcove Canyon** for convenience. Along the main channel and just east of the mouth of East Alcove, is a shallow indentation. Before Lake Powell, river runners called this place **Nevills Spring**, but the main spring is under water when the lake is at or near the HWM. With low lake levels, you'll see water running down a rounded slickrock dropoff, with some greenery above. On a ledge to the left or west is a small **Anasazi granary**. On 9/9/2007, the only way up to the granary, was to walk up East Alcove a ways, then bench-walk south. There's now a pretty good hiker's trail on the bench.

East Alcove has a short inlet and no campsites, whether the lake is high or low (**Note:** If the lake gets much lower than it was on **9/9/2007-WL1098.08m/3602.61'**, then it may be difficult to enter this drainage). Just above the HWM is a **low waterfall** which you can get around easily. As you go up-canyon you'll see a developing hiker's trail in places. The canyon has what appears to be a year-round flowing stream with lots of tall grass and some trees. It's another green oasis in the desert. There are several alcoves in the canyon, each of which seems to have a small seep or spring. One northeast fac-

The northwest wall along **The Great Bend** of the **San Juan River Arm** near point 1425 meters on the map. It's the Kayenta Formation benches at the waterline, then Navajo Sandstone cliffs above that.

ing alcove has some **crude Anasazi ruins**, but they're not much to look at. The author saw no fresh sign of beaver so the water is likely good to drink as is, especially if you get it at the spring source. There are no cattle in the canyon at present but in the past it was used for grazing Navajo livestock.

In Crampton's research of the San Juan River before Lake Powell, he found a man-made stock trail leading out of the main river channel and up through the Wingate Sandstone Formation to the Kayenta bench between Alcove and East Alcove. This allowed cattle to enter either drainage. The Wingate is usually partially covered by water, but when the lake is low, parts of this trail may be visible (?). There was another trail up to the wide Kayenta bench on the inside of the Great Bend curve as well. As of the early 1960's this was also used as a Navajo pasture.

Alcove Canyon is so named because just inside the inlet on the left or west, is one of the biggest **alcoves** around. Actually, there are many large alcoves on the outside curve of the Great Bend so this one isn't as unique as it otherwise might be. Walking up Alcove, you'll see several other alcoves on both sides of the drainage each with a minor spring. It has running water, likely year-round, at least in places, but it could dry up at times. This canyon is green with many water-loving plants. The author saw no sign of beaver, but they seem to come and go into various side-canyons throughout the year. When they finish the food supply in one place they simply swim to another canyon. The only campsite the author saw was at the bottom of the biggest alcove mentioned above (that's when the lake was near the HWM).

The last of the Great Bend canyons has no official name, but the author is calling it simply **Bend Canyon**. It's on the western side of the Bend and is similar in geology and appearance to the twin Alcove Canyons just to the north. This one has 2 upper forks, both of which are box canyons. The inlet to Bend Canyon has several good springs which flow down into the lake (when water levels are high). Early one morning, the author observed a beaver washing itself on the shoreline below one spring. He seemed to ignore the noisy motor boat. Up this canyon there were more sign of beaver indicating a sizable population (on 9/9/2007, they couldn't get into the canyon because of several dropoffs).

As you walk upcanyon, get up on the Kayenta bench to the right or north and scan the walls. There is one fallen-down **cliff dwelling** under an overhanging wall; in 2007, it still had a pile of straight sticks--maybe they were intended to be arrows (?). Along the canyon bottom are several minor waterfalls, a year-round stream, and big alcoves in the Navajo Sandstone at the head of each fork.

Hike Length & Time Needed If you were to walk up either **San Juan or Navajo Canyon** and return the same way, it would likely take 5-6 hours round-trip. But if you make the loop-hike as suggested, plan on a full day's hike. **Alcove and East Alcove** are both about 2 kms long and you can walk up to the end of each and back in 1-2 hours. **Bend Canyon** is slightly shorter, but has more to see, so it's a hike of a couple of hours.

Boots or Shoes What streams there are in these canyons are small and you likely won't get your feet wet so any kind of boots or shoes are OK.

Water Each canyon (with the exception of San Juan) has minor seeps or springs and if you take water directly from a source you shouldn't have any trouble. The author as usual, sampled water from each canyon, and didn't get a belly ache. All water seeping out from the bottom of the Navajo Sandstone is some of the best tasting in the world.

Main Attractions Very high canyon walls in the thickest part of the Navajo Sandstone, short but deep side-canyons, lots of seeps, at least 2 small Anasazi ruins, great scenery and not too many people.

The little granary just to the left or west of the upper part of **Nevills Spring**. With low lake levels, you must walk up **East Alcove Canyon** a ways, then bench-walk back to the spring.

Hiking Maps USGO ui BLM map Navajo Mountain (1:100,000); Alcove Canyon & Deep Canyon North (1:24,000--7 1/2' quads) for hiking; or Lake Canyon & No Mans Mesa (1:62,500) if available.

Other Nearby Canyons Due south of the Great Bend, which is downlake, there's a large open bay, the largest open body of water in the San Juan Arm. Entering this bay from the south are 2 drainages. The first is **Neskahi Wash** which formerly entered the San Juan River at M24 (K38). This is a short drainage, which in its lower parts has lots of landslide debris and the Chinle clay beds exposed at the shoreline. The gentle slope makes some campsites, but there are few sandy beaches. Instead, they're mostly clay-type sites.

Entering this large expanse of water on the southwest corner is **Piute Canyon**. This is a very long tributary which drains all of the eastern slope of Navajo Mountain. It used to enter the river at M21 (K34). It has had several different names throughout the years but whatever may have been the first name applied to this canyon by white men, it marked the practical lower limit of prospecting during the gold rush days. Below Piute Canyon, there were practically no lateral gravel deposits to be seen until Glen Canyon, 34 kms below.

The present-day inlet to Piute Canyon has a gentle slope from the shoreline and a number of good campsites. The Chinle clays are exposed, but there are also some sandy areas. South of this bay, you may see Navajo livestock grazing. There's a 4WD-type road running down to the lake from the old Navajo Mtn. Trading Post. This was likely first built during the 1950's uranium boom when miners were out scratching the Chinle clay beds. Along the shore line is lots of petrified wood from the Chinle Formation. Also, somewhere on the west side of the bay are some large boulders with rock art in the form of petroglyphs (as shown on Stan Jones' map).

In the lower part of **East Alcove Canyon** is this north facing alcove with some crude **Anasazi Ruins**.

This foto was taken on **9/9/2007-WL1098.09m/3602.61'** at the head of the **Bend Canyon Inlet**. On that day you had to get upon the ledge in the upper right, then bench-walk left into the canyon.

The little ruins in **Bend Canyon**. The wood you see, including the sticks which look like they could have been used for making arrows, must be 800-1000 years old (?).

Deep, Desha and Trail Canyons, San Juan River Arm

Location & Campsites The 3 canyons on this map are located in the lower end of the San Juan River Arm and on the **Navajo Nation** immediately north of **Navajo Mountain**. Using old river distances from the Colorado, we find the mouth of **Trail Canyon** is near M13 (K21); **Desha Creek** is at about M15 (K24); and **Deep Canyon** is at about M18 (K29). There are no buoys in the San Juan Arm of the lake.

This is another part of the lake where campsites are scarce but there should be at least one sandy camping place at the head of each inlet. The country these canyons drain is very sandy, so with every storm, more sand is deposited where the flood waters enter the lake. There are several other small sites in the main channel as well, usually on the Chinle bench (just west of Trail Canyon). There are lots of places where houseboats can tie-down, but much of the main channel has Wingate Sandstone walls rising directly out of the water. The number of campsites available will depend on the level of the lake.

Hiking Routes or Trails The inlet to **Deep Canyon** is not long but is moderately narrow. The sheer walls rising from the water are made of Wingate Sandstone. At the end of the inlet where Deep Creek enters, there should always be a sandy beach that's high & dry (?) and hopefully large enough for a tent. There's a stream in this canyon flowing year-round, but it's small enough to avoid wading.

As you walk upcanyon you'll be walking on slickrock, at least that's the way it was on **9/10/2007-WL1098.07m/3602.55'** upon the author's last visit. The walking was easy that day with almost no vegetation, but with running water all the way. Higher up, there are at least 2 trails which allow livestock to enter and exit the canyon. These are located about 3/4's the way up on the right or west side. This drainage is not very deep so hikers can climb out in a number of places without using the trails.

Not far above where the livestock trails are found, there's a major junction in the canyon. The tributary coming from the right or west has a **dryfall** not far above. Below that dropoff is a pool and the start of running water. The main canyon is the one to the left. Not far above the junction is a very good spring coming out of a crack in the wall. This is where the stream begins and where you should be able to safely tank up on water (?). This is where the author stopped. The canyon looks less-interesting above the spring.

Desha Creek or Canyon is one the author has visited 4 times and from both ends. The first time he came down from the Navajo Mtn. Trading Post; the next 3 times were from the lake in a boat. The inlet to Desha is similar to that of Deep Canyon. It has sheer Wingate walls rising from the water, except at its upper end, where there may be several sandy campsites (at or near the HWM only).

Immediately above the HWM and just around the corner may be a beaver pond, then a series of 3 minor waterfalls pouring over Wingate dropoffs. At the bottom of the lower falls is a large pool. To get around this obstacle, regress about 75 meters and look to the east. There's a hiker's route or trail up to the top of a ledge where a side-canyon enters. Climb upon top of the Wingate bench and walk south to a point beyond the waterfalls. Then look for a way down into the slickrock creek bed.

Above the waterfalls and for a distance of about 1 km, the year-round creek flows on top of **Wingate slickrock**. In places it has cut small potholes, ravines and other erosional features in the sandstone. Just above this part is an old wooden fence across the canyon to keep livestock out of the lower end. From this point on, the canyon is less constricted and better suited for grazing. If you walk up from the fence about 4-5 kms, you'll come to an area with a number of **old fruit trees** and **irrigated fields**. Just above the **fruit farm** in the right-hand or western drainage, is where several good springs are located. This is the beginning of Desha Creek and the upper end is heavily grazed by Navajo livestock.

Less than 1 km above the HWM in **Deep Canyon**, is this slickrock section with running water.

Map 25, Deep, Desha and Trail Canyons

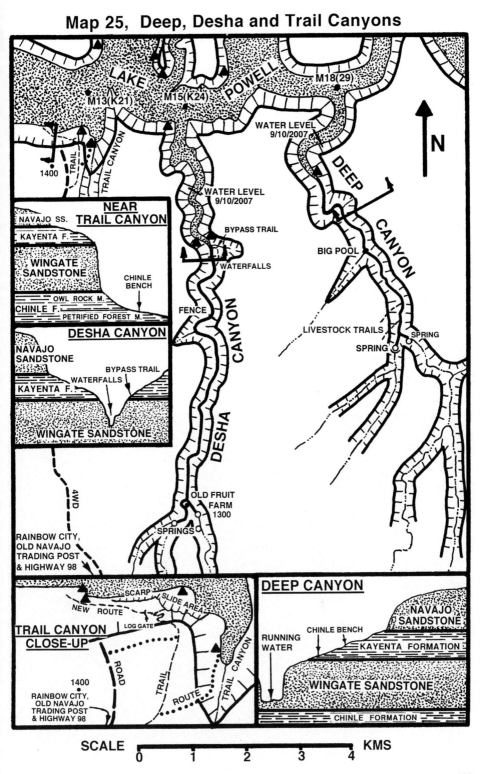

LAKE POWELL

M13(K21)

M15(K24)

M18(29)

WATER LEVEL 9/10/2007

TRAIL CANYON

TRAIL

1400

DEEP CANYON

WATER LEVEL 9/10/2007

BYPASS TRAIL

BIG POOL

WATERFALLS

FENCE

DESHA CANYON

LIVESTOCK TRAILS

SPRING

SPRING

NEAR TRAIL CANYON

NAVAJO SS.

KAYENTA F.

WINGATE SANDSTONE

CHINLE BENCH

OWL ROCK M.

CHINLE F.

PETRIFIED FOREST M.

DESHA CANYON

NAVAJO SANDSTONE

BYPASS TRAIL

WATERFALLS

KAYENTA F.

WINGATE SANDSTONE

4WD

OLD FRUIT FARM 1300

SPRINGS

RAINBOW CITY, OLD NAVAJO TRADING POST & HIGHWAY 98

SCARP

SLIDE AREA

NEW ROUTE

LOG GATE

TRAIL CANYON CLOSE-UP

ROAD

TRAIL

ROUTE

TRAIL CANYON

1400

RAINBOW CITY, OLD NAVAJO TRADING POST & HIGHWAY 98

DEEP CANYON

NAVAJO SANDSTONE

CHINLE BENCH

KAYENTA FORMATION

RUNNING WATER

WINGATE SANDSTONE

CHINLE FORMATION

SCALE

0 1 2 3 4

KMS

The last hike featured here is up an old Anasazi route, and more recently a Navajo livestock trail near **Trail Canyon**. Trail Canyon is very short and has a tiny bay. It has steep terraced walls and large boulders lining the bottom of the dry wash. There will probably be one good campsite in the upper part of the bay. From that campsite you could get to the rim of the canyon by walking up along the right or west side but there's some climbing on all-4's. An interesting route anyone can climb.

The **trail** for which Trail Canyon is named, is actually around the corner to the west and on the north facing wall. This route has been used since Anasazi times but more recently by Navajos. In the years after the Mormons built the Hole-in-the-Rock Trail, Navajos used to go down this trail, ford the San Juan River a km or two above the mouth of Trail Canyon, then went up the trail in Wilson Creek. This would put them at the top of Wilson Mesa and on the Hole-in-the-Rock route to the Colorado. From the Colorado, they went on to the Mormon settlements to trade.

This same trail was used by miners during the **1892-93 San Juan Gold Rush** and later during the **uranium boom** of the **1950's**. In the years prior to Lake Powell, the Navajos used the trail to reach the San Juan River bottoms between Cha and Desha Canyon, where they herded livestock. According to Crampton and his study of the Glen Canyon area before Lake Powell, it was improved by the government **CCC crews** during the Great Depression days of the 1930's. Whoever worked on the trail did a good job as it's almost wide enough for a 4WD vehicle. However, in 1982 (according to Stan Jones) there was a landslide which wiped out the lower half of the trail. It appears the rising lake waters lubricated the clay beds of the Chinle Formation, which allowed the slippage.

Since the landslide, people and horses using the trail have started to develop an alternate route up to the lower part of the cliff face. From a point where Trail Canyon Bay and the main channel meet, boat west about 600-700 meters, then tie-up at a bend in the shoreline (see the small insert map).

Just above the HWM in this immediate area, are several creeping **landslide scarps** which you must avoid. So to start, climb due south but west of the end of these scarps. After about 100 meters, the slope levels out a little, and you should come to one of several minor **horse trails**. Walk east on one of these. After a ways, there's one trail with cairns angling up to the right or south toward the Wingate Sandstone wall. Soon you'll come to a **log gate** which keeps livestock from going up or down. Walk east a few meters until you meet the middle part of the old constructed Trail Canyon Trail. After about 3 switch-backs, you'll go around a corner to the east and head south. About 1 km from that corner, you're be on top. From there continue west to find a road which heads out to **Rainbow City** and a school, and the old now-closed **Navajo Mtn. Trading Post**.

Hike Length & Time Needed It's about 5 kms from the HWM to the large spring in **Deep Canyon**. This round-trip hike can be done in about 3 hours. From the HWM to the old fruit farm in **Desha** is about 8 kms. You'll need at least half a day to do this hike, maybe longer. From the lake to the top of the cliffs beside **Trail Canyon** is about 1 km. Most can do this round-trip in a couple of hours.

Boots or Shoes Normally you can keep your feet dry in Deep or Desha Canyons, but they have year-round flowing water, so consider using wading-type shoes. Use a more rugged hiking boot for the climb up the old trail near Trail Canyon.

Water Because there's lots of livestock in these canyons, drink only water coming directly from springs in Deep or Desha Canyons. Best to always take your own. Trail Canyon is dry.

Main Attractions Waterfalls, old livestock trails, and good views of the lake and Navajo Mountain, all of which is on the Navajo Nation lands.

Hiking Maps USGS or BLM map Navajo Mountain (1:100,000); Wilson Creek, Deep Canyon North,

The first of 2 waterfalls or cascades you'll come to if hiking up **Desha Canyon**. To get around this pool, zig zag up the slope to the east. Above this section is an interesting slickrock canyon.

Navajo Begay & Deep Canyon South (1:24,000--7 1/2' quads) for hiking; or Navajo Mountain & No Mans Mesa (1:62,500) if available.

Above Looking down on part of the trail into **Trail Canyon**. **Below** From the air looking westward: to the right is **Wilson Canyon Inlet**; bottom, **Shoot the Chute Canyon**; lower left, the **San Juan River Arm**; left, the small drainage is **Trail Canyon**; above, then left in the distance, is **Cha Canyon**.

Wilson Creek Canyon, San Juan River Arm

Location & Campsites **Wilson Creek** drains south from BLM lands into the San Juan River Arm of the lake at about M13 (K21). This figure comes from the old river mileage (kilomage). From the lake this canyon heads northwest and ends immediately next to the upper end of **Cottonwood Canyon** right where the 4WD part of the **Hole-in-the-Rock Trail** ends.

There are only about 3 small possible campsites within the Wilson Creek Bay. Upon the author's first visit, when lake levels were high, there was one boat anchored with 2 ropes right at the end of the inlet where the creek flows over a waterfall (see foto below). Nearby is an excellent campsite inside an alcove cave just a few meters from the waterfall (only when the lake is at or near the HWM can you use it). There are 2 likely campsites at the head of **Shoot the Chute Canyon Inlet** below 2 huge dryfalls.

Hiking Routes or Trails If you go to the end of **Wilson Creek Bay,** you'll be confronted with a waterfall. In times of the highest water levels you can climb up next to it then you'll have 500 meters of beaver dams (?), trees and brush until you skirt around a couple of dryfalls to get out of this middle section of the canyon. In April of 2001, and while the water was quite low, the author found a long rope with knots hanging down beside the waterfall. He climbed this and went up Wilson for the second time. On **9/10/2007-WL1098.07m/3602.55'**, the rope was gone, and there were 2 more fotogenic cascades below the above-mentioned waterfall.

However if there's no rope in sight, then you must head back down the inlet to a different place to get above the Wingate Sandstone cliffs. Long before Lake Powell days there was first an **old Indian route**, then later a **cattle trail** into **Wilson Canyon**. Crampton's report states: *Just above the mouth of the canyon a stock trail starts at the river's edge and ascends the irregular walls of Wilson Canyon in switchbacks and steep pitches to top out on a ledge about 400 feet [125 meters] above the San Juan.* Today, that part of the trail is lost under water but you can still see it in places further upcanyon.

The author never did find the exact location where the trail reached the rim but if you tie-down in a little bay on the right or east side, you can walk up through what appears to be the top of the Wingate to the same area where this old trail was located. From there, walk along the bench almost due north. You may or may not see a trail but it doesn't matter; just head upcanyon on the right or northeast side. After less than 1 km there's a stock trail leading down into the entrenched part of the drainage. Or you can get down into the stream bed at a number of locations further upcanyon.

Above the 500 meter middle section, the mostly-dry creek bed is easy to walk in all the way to the top. There are about 4 small seeps which may or may not have water year-round. As you near the upper end of the canyon, the walls close in but are not too high. Right near the end of the canyon, look to the right and you'll see a stock trail ascending a low bench. This takes cattle around a low waterfall (or dryfall). Not far beyond, it opens up and you'll be on top of **Wilson Mesa**. When you reach a point where you can see down to the west, veer right and after another 200 meters, you'll come to the end of the 4WD part of the old **Hole-in-the-Rock Trail**. Here's an idea for the adventurous hiker: walk up Wilson while someone takes your boat around to the end of **Cottonwood Canyon Bay** and meet it there by walking up Wilson and down Cottonwood Canyon along the Hole-in-the-Rock Trail.

Another drainage just east of Wilson is called **Shoot the Chute Canyon**, but you can't get into it from the inlet below because of a big dryfall at the very end.

Hike Length & Time Needed It's only about 5 kms from the lake to the end of the vehicle or 4WD part of the Hole-in-the-Rock Trail. This means about 3-4 hours round-trip for the average hiker. The author did it in 2 2/3 hours.

The waterfall that blocks hikers from proceeding up **Wilson Canyon**. Top of the waterfall is the HWM.

Map 26, Wilson Creek Canyon

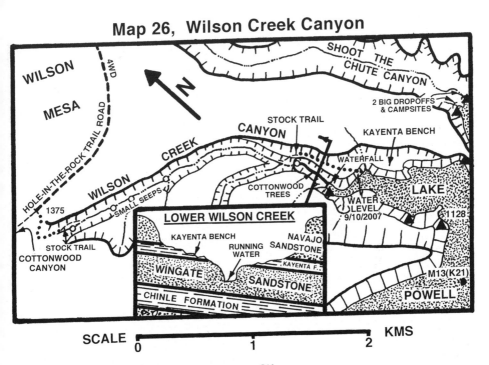

SCALE 0   1   2   KMS

Boots or Shoes Any dry weather boots or shoes are OK.
Water There's a stream in the middle section above the waterfall discussed above, but you may find beaver there (if beavers are there, they are completely cut off from the lake now). There are also cattle in the upper canyon from October to June, so caution should be taken before drinking any of this water. Best to take your own.
Main Attractions An old Indian & cattle trail, a pretty waterfall, and the historic Hole-in-the-Rock Trail.
Hiking Maps USGS or BLM map Navajo Mountain (1:100,000); Wilson Creek (1:24,000--7 1/2' quad) for hiking; or Navajo Mountain (1:62,500) if available.

About 100 meters below the waterfall (opposite page), is this colorful chute with running water.

Nasja, Bald Rock and Cha Canyons, San Juan River Arm

Location & Campsites The 3 canyons **Nasja, Bald Rock and Cha**, drain the north slope of **Navajo Mountain** as they make their way to the lake. All 3 are in the lower end of the San Juan Arm, on the south side of the lake and on **Navajo Nation lands**. The mouth of Nasja, which is shared with Bald Rock Canyon, is located at the old river mileage (kilomage) of M6 (K10), while the mouth of Cha is M11.6 (K18) above the former Colorado River.

There are not many campsites in these parts but right at the end of the inlet to Bald Rock Canyon is a nice sandy place or two under the Kayenta pourover. The same possibilities exist at the very end of Nasja Inlet. There will also be several semi-sandy campsites or houseboat tie-downs near the head of Cha Canyon Bay. Perhaps the best campsite, and one large enough for several boats, is just around the corner west of the mouth of the Nasja-Bald Rock Inlet. It's labeled **good sandy beach** on the map. However, in times of low lake levels, as was the case in all the years after 1991, this beach will be high & dry and difficult, if not impossible, to get to.

Hiking Routes or Trails **Cha Canyon** is likely the most spectacular canyon draining into the San Juan Arm. As you boat into the bay, there will be several campsites on either side in the Chinle clay beds. Hiking upcanyon, you'll find livestock trails on either side of this small stream. The tracks are mostly those of semi-wild horses or donkeys belonging to Navajo herdsmen. About 1 km above the HWM is a fork in the canyon, and a open **flat** place. In that flat are **9-10 boulders** with recent **Navajo etchings**, plus some older **rock art** from **Anasazi days**. Crampton and other researchers have found evidence that this area, as well as areas now covered by Lake Powell, had been used first by Anasazi, then in about 1900 by Piutes and Navajos. Most of the rock art boulders are located east of the main Cha Canyon Creek and north & south of the lower **East Fork** (the boulder with the **triangles** is on a bench facing south, and is just south of lower East Fork). Most boulders on the flat have some rock art.

As you walk upcanyon there will be more livestock trails and cottonwood trees. Soon you'll come to the **1st waterfall** where the creek flows over a limestone layer of the Chinle Formation. Look for a trail on the right or **west side**. Not far above this is the **2nd waterfall** and subsequent pool. Pass this one on the left or **east side**. Above these 2 waterfalls the canyon constricts and the Wingate walls close in. Further along will be large boulders in the canyon bottom and walking is slower. There are old signs of beaver and wild horses, but nothing new or recent, at least on the author's trips. Incidentally, the Navajo word for **beaver is Cha**.

Above the areas with the boulders, the canyon makes a turn to the west and becomes more narrow. There you must get out of the bottom and bench-walk on the left or **east side** above more waterfalls and narrows. Around 2 more turns in the canyon you'll have to wade a bit, then get up on the right or **west side** where an old faded trail has been made up through a talus slope to the Kayenta bench above. This takes you high above some Wingate narrows and still more waterfalls. This trail goes into a side-canyon on the west (with good drinkable water?), then cuts back into the main canyon. From there, the trail is used more and more by livestock until you meet the **North Rainbow Bridge Trail**. This good, well-used trail skirts the north side of Navajo Mountain. If you're coming to this area by road, drive north from the old **Navajo Mtn. Trading Post** and **Rainbow City** on first a good road, then a sandy 4WD road to near

One of the more interesting rock art sites around is located at the confluence of **Cha Canyon** and its **East Fork**. This south-facing boulder, one of many on this flat, is on the south side of a large open area. To the left is Cha Canyon running north, coming in from the right is the East Fork.

Map 27, Nasja, Bald Rock and Cha Canyons

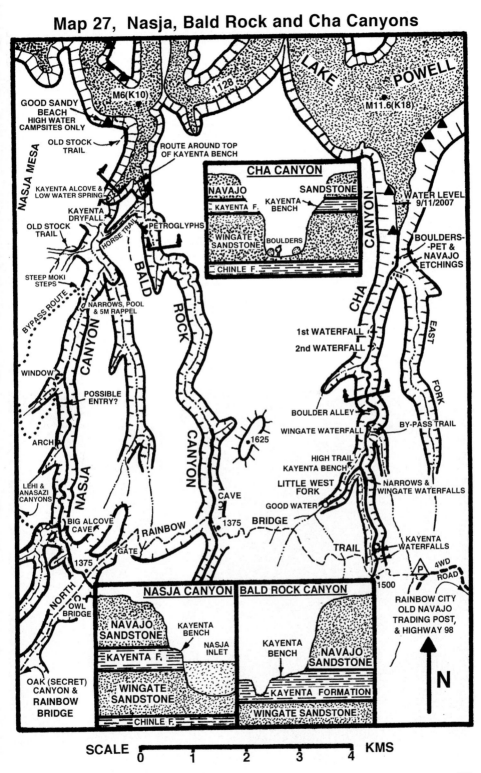

LAKE POWELL

M6(K10)

1128

M11.6(K18)

GOOD SANDY BEACH HIGH WATER CAMPSITES ONLY

OLD STOCK TRAIL

ROUTE AROUND TOP OF KAYENTA BENCH

NASJA MESA

KAYENTA ALCOVE & LOW WATER SPRING

KAYENTA DRYFALL

OLD STOCK TRAIL

HORSE TRAIL

PETROGLYPHS

STEEP MOKI STEPS

BYPASS ROUTE

NARROWS, POOL & 5M RAPPEL

BALD ROCK

WINDOW

POSSIBLE ENTRY?

ARCH

1625

LEHI & ANASAZI CANYONS

NASJA

CANYON

CAVE

BIG ALCOVE CAVE

1375

RAINBOW

GATE

1375

NORTH

OWL BRIDGE

OAK (SECRET) CANYON & RAINBOW BRIDGE

CHA CANYON
NAVAJO SANDSTONE
KAYENTA F.
KAYENTA BENCH
WINGATE SANDSTONE
BOULDERS
CHINLE F.

CHA CANYON

WATER LEVEL 9/11/2007

BOULDERS- -PET & NAVAJO ETCHINGS

EAST FORK

1st WATERFALL
2nd WATERFALL

BOULDER ALLEY
WINGATE WATERFALL
BY-PASS TRAIL

HIGH TRAIL
KAYENTA BENCH
LITTLE WEST FORK
GOOD WATER

BRIDGE

NARROWS & WINGATE WATERFALLS

TRAIL

KAYENTA WATERFALLS

P 4WD ROAD

1500

RAINBOW CITY OLD NAVAJO TRADING POST, & HIGHWAY 98

N

NASJA CANYON
NAVAJO SANDSTONE
KAYENTA BENCH
KAYENTA F.
NASJA INLET
WINGATE SANDSTONE
CHINLE F.

BALD ROCK CANYON
KAYENTA BENCH
KAYENTA BENCH
NAVAJO SANDSTONE
KAYENTA FORMATION
WINGATE SANDSTONE

SCALE 0 1 2 3 4 KMS

the rim of Cha Canyon where the northeastern end of the trail actually begins.

Just before boating into the inlet to **Nasja and Bald Rock Canyons**, you'll have a chance to get upon the rim for some fine views of the lake via an **old stock trail**. To do this, boat to the west side of the **good sandy beach** just west of the mouth of Nasja-Bald Rock Inlet. Tie-down there and walk east along the bench just above the HWM. There are several hiker trails in this area.

As you near the corner, look up to the right for an obvious break in the cliffs. Walk up in that direction and as you near the first set of cliffs you'll see a man-made trail zig zagging up. It rounds the corner and heads south overlooking the inlet. Not far around the corner it seems to disappear as it's heading southwest towards Nasja Mesa. It was probably built at the same time as the one entering the lower part of Nasja Canyon. It may have been built by CCC crews in the mid-1930's (?).

As you near the end of the inlet in **Bald Rock Canyon**, look to the left or **east side** and you'll see a trail & route up through the top of the Kayenta. Once on top of the obvious bench, walk up the mostly-dry creek bed. Along the way, you'll be walking on Kayenta slickrock much of the time.

Around the first major bend going up Bald Rock, look to your right to see some **rock art** on a wall. These petroglyphs indicate this is an old Anasazi trail or route. Further up, you'll be walking inside a shallow section of Kayenta narrows. Before it gets too deep, you'll have to get out and onto a bench on either side as there will be some large potholes and a dryfall further on. In the upper portions of the canyon you'll come to running water. This small stream gets bigger the further up you go. Finally, you'll once again reach the **North Rainbow Bridge Trail**. If you walk up the Rainbow Trail a short distance to the east it ascends a steep dugway in rather spectacular fashion. At the top of that slope you'll have some spectacular views of the upper end of the canyon which is the most beautiful part. This is right under **Navajo Mountain** as it begins its steep rise.

Right at the end of **Nasja Inlet**, is a grotto & dryfall with a spring coming out of the cliff when the lake is low. Also a campsite in times of low water. See the picture on the next page. To get above this, regress about 150 meters to see a break in the top of the Kayenta wall on the east side. Climb up onto the obvious bench (you may find a rope there) and walk back into **Nasja Canyon**. Just inside the canyon you'll come to a low Kayenta dryfall which you can skirt on the left or east side. From there on up you'll be surrounded by high Navajo Sandstone walls.

The lower end of Nasja has some trees but no willows or other greenery and no running water. Big floods roar down this drainage wiping out everything. If you stay in the main channel of Nasja you can only walk about 3 kms before you come to a narrow section and a huge pool & dryfall you cannot climb.

But there are a couple of ways you can get around the pool and reach the North Rainbow Bridge Trail via Nasja Canyon. About 1 km above the Kayenta dryfall look to the right or west and where the canyon walls are low, you can see another **old stock trail** running up through the low bench. It's hard to see because some oak brush has grown up along side the canyon, but once you get above the 3-meter-high bench, it's clearly visible. This trail, marked with several stone cairns runs west inside a shallow drainage then seems to head southwest. The author lost the trail but he continued in the same direction and eventually topped out and could see a route up along the west side of the canyon.

Herb Taylor, Byron Lemay and friends, found another route around the pool as well. On the west side of the canyon about 300 meters below the pool, you can climb up the west side of Nasja and circle

The **1st Waterfall** in **Cha Canyon**. The only way past this is to climb the slopes on the right or west side of the canyon. There you'll use a constructed livestock trail to bypass the falls.

around the Navajo bluffs and eventually drop back down into the main canyon, approximately as shown. Along the way is one steep section of **moki steps**. Don't try this without a good topo map!

But here's a better option for those who enjoy longer all-day hikes without backtracking and who like a little adventure. Tie your boat up at the end of Bald Rock Inlet and hike upcanyon to the North Rainbow Bridge Trail. From there, trail-walk west to Nasja Canyon and head downstream. Along the way you'll pass a **big alcove cave** on the right which is becoming a popular camping place for backpackers. Continue north downcanyon along the stream with cottonwood trees. Further along the canyon narrows and you'll finally come to the pool & dryfall. To get through this short section, **you'll need a rope about 15 meters long**, and a short piece of **webbing or rope** to be tied around a small chokestone to be used as a **sling** (or just take one rope at least 6 meters long, tie it around the chokestone and leave it there). After installing the rope, slide down exactly 5 meters, then walk another 8 meters and slide about 1 1/2 meters into the icy pool and swim 20 meters (**Caution:** If you do this at any time other than June, July, August or early September, you'll need a wet or dry suit for sure as this water will be extremely cold!). From the pool, walk 3 kms back to the lake.

To get back to your boat from near Nasja, walk to the right or eastward along the narrow Kayenta Bench. At one narrow point, you'll have to crawl on your hands & knees. Or a second option would be to locate a little side-canyon running northeast about 750 meters above the head of Nasja Inlet. Along the bottom of this side-canyon is an old partly-constructed **horse trail** which ends (or begins) right at the very bottom end of Bald Rock Canyon. See the map.

Hike Length & Time Needed It seems to be about 10 kms from the HWM to the North Rainbow Bridge Trail in **Cha Canyon**. This isn't far but you'll have to route-find in places, so it's a little slow walking. Plan to take most or all of one day to do this one. The author did it once in just under 5 hours, round-trip.

From the lake to the same North Rainbow Bridge Trail in **Bald Rock Canyon** is about 10 kms. This hike is in an open canyon with easy & fast walking. The author made it to the trail and back in 3 2/3 hours once. You might consider taking a lunch and spend as much as 6-7 hours. You can see lower **Nasja Canyon** and the beginnings of the old stock trails in just a couple of hours; but to reach the North Rainbow Bridge Trail via Bald Rock, then descend Nasja back to your boat, plan on a long all-day hike.

Boots or Shoes In Cha Canyon, better take wading shoes; in Bald Rock take dry weather boots; in Nasja you'll want wading shoes if you expect to explore the upper end of the canyon and swim the pool.

Water Best not to drink the water in Cha Creek, but higher up and in the **little west fork**, there is clear spring water, hopefully without the danger of beaver or cattle to pollute it. There are horses throughout Bald Rock but if you hike up above the North Rainbow Bridge Trail it seems that would be a good place for a drink. The author drank pothole water in lower Nasja Canyon but that was right after a storm. Nasja often has running water in the upper half of the canyon but there are cattle there too.

Main Attractions Cha has good rock art on boulders, and is a wild & woolly canyon with narrows and several waterfalls. The upper end of Bald Rock above the Rainbow Trail is very spectacular, and there is a route-finding experience out of Nasja, or a short handline down and cold swim.

Hiking Maps USGS or BLM map Navajo Mountain (1:100,000); Nasja Mesa, Wilson Mesa, Navajo Begay & Rainbow Bridge (1:24,000--7 1/2' quads) for hiking; or Navajo Mtn. (1:62,500) if available.

The head of **Nasja Canyon Inlet** looking southwest. The bench on the left is where you climb up to from your boat, then walk on into the canyon. Can you see the 2 small boats in the lower right?

Twilight and Anasazi Canyons

Location & Campsites Two canyons are featured here. **Twilight Canyon** is a long narrow drainage but the broad valley through which it runs is called **Navajo Valley**. Before Lake Powell, river runners knew this place as both Twilight and Boulder Canyon. It's located not far southwest of the mouth of the **San Juan River Arm**. Near the mouth of Twilight should be a buoy marked M51 (K82). Nearby and across the channel is **Anasazi Canyon Inlet**.

There aren't many campsites in this part of the main channel of the lake, but there are several sandy beaches inside **Little Oak Canyon** (in times of higher water) and more to the west in **Oak Canyon Bay** just south of some gravel-topped islands in the main channel. There's also a **toilet & dump/pump station** in **Oak Canyon Bay**.

There may be 2 small sites in Anasazi Inlet depending on lake levels. On **7/24/2007-WL1099.79m/3608.18'**, the author saw no campsites in **Twilight Inlet**, but there may be a couple of tie-down places, one near an arch about halfway up the inlet.

Hiking Routes or Trails **Twilight Canyon** is a mostly-narrow, cobblestone-filled drainage with several places to exit on either side. From the end of the inlet you'll be walking up a shallow narrow corridor cut into the Navajo Sandstone. The width of these narrows might average 5 meters.

After hiking about 5 kms above the HWM, you'll come to the head of the narrows where boulders have created a dryfall or dropoff (the author once met some backpackers out hiking for 4 days from the Hole-in-the-Rock Road & Fifty Mile Point; they were rappelling over this 3 meter dropoff). At that point, regress about 300 meters and climb up a crack to the bench on the west side. Once out of the narrows, you'll see a horseshoe shaped circle of cliffs on all sides. To your left or west is **Fiftymile Mountain/Kaiparowits Plateau**. An intermediate level one bench above you is called the **Navajo Bench** (created by the Dakota Sandstone and Tropic Shale Formations). With time and route-finding, you can walk up **Navajo Valley** a ways, then veer west and head up a large talus slope. Once above this you'll again have to route-find up the cliffs of Fiftymile Mtn., but the only route possibility seems at or near the southern end called Navajo Point.

Anasazi Canyon has a long and narrow inlet with Navajo Sandstone walls rising straight out of the water. Near the head of the inlet and to the right is Moepitz Canyon, to the left is Lehi Canyon. On **7/24/2007-WL1099.79m/3608.18'**, there were 2 natural bridges exposed just above water and inside the lower end of **Lehi Inlet**. On that day, there was no chance of climbing up a dryfall into the upper canyon. At the end of **Anasazi Inlet**, was a waterfall of about 8 meters and no chance of climbing up into the main canyon above. **Moepitz** was the same way, there was dropoff and mossy waterfall blocking any up-canyon travel.

There are very good slots in the upper parts of these 3 drainages, but they are out of the scope of this book. However, you can get to these canyons from the Rainbow Bridge Trail. If interested, look for another book by this writer, ***Technical Slot Canyon Guide to the Colorado Plateau***, preferably the ***2nd Edition.*** These hikes are for experienced and tough hiker/climbers only.

Hike Length & Time Needed **Twilight Canyon** above the HWM is about 5 kms long. To hike this and return will take 3-4 hours. The author did it once in 2 1/2 hours. On a second trip he hiked up to the rim of Navajo Valley and back in 6 3/4 hours. See the route symbols. Anasazi, Lehi and Moepitz are basi-

Twilight Canyon just above the HWM on **7/24/2007-WL1099.79m/3608.18'**. Notice all the cobblestones which makes this canyon a little different from most.

Map 28,   Twilight and Anasazi Canyons

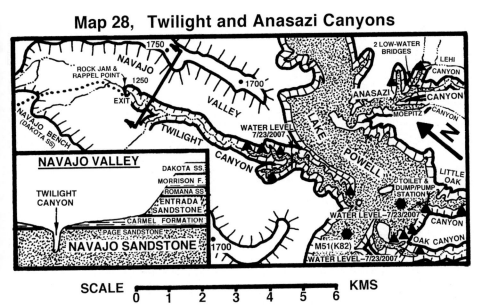

SCALE
0 1 2 3 4 5 6   **KMS**

cally unhikable from the lake.
Boots or Shoes Twilight is a dry canyon so any boots or shoes will do.
Water There are no springs in Twilight so carry your own water.
Main Attractions Twilight is one of the better narrow canyons on the lake, but it does lack the tight meter-wide slot sections.
Hiking Maps USGS or BLM maps Navajo Mountain & Smoky Mountain (1:100,000); Nasja Mesa, Rainbow Bridge & maybe Navajo Point (1:24,000--7 1/2' quad) for hiking; or Navajo Mtn. & Cummings Mesa (1:62,500) if available.

The head of navigation in upper **Anasazi Canyon Inlet** on **7/24/2007-WL1099.79m/3608.18'**. This drop, which is a waterfall at that water level, is about 8 meters.

Oak, Little Oak, Forbidding, Cliff & Rainbow Bridge Canyons

Location & Campsites The canyons on this map are located near the middle part of the lake and not far southwest or downlake from the mouth of the San Juan River Arm. Because of **Rainbow Bridge National Monument**, this is one of the most popular sections of the lake--at least during daytime hours. This is when **tour boats** with tourists, many of whom are from overseas, make their way to the world's 2nd largest natural bridge. Then everyone leaves the area at night (The largest natural bridge or arch in the world is Shipton's Arch or Tushuk Tash in Xinjiang Province of western China soaring to 460 meters. See National Geographic magazine for December, 2000).

This is another part of the lake without many campsites; the exception being **Oak Canyon Bay** and in **Little Oak Canyon** just to the east. Also, right at the upper end of Forbidding Canyon Inlet there may be one possible site. Because of the heavy traffic in Rainbow Bridge Canyon there is no overnight camping allowed; but there are no campsites there anyway.

On some boaters maps, and in previous editions of this book, **Oak Canyon** has been called **Secret Canyon**. However it's called Oak Canyon on the 1:24,000 scale USGS quads (7 1/2'). The apparent reason boaters have called it Secret Canyon is because it's a little difficult to find the actual entrance to this long inlet since the creation of Lake Powell. On those same boater maps they assign the name Oak Canyon to what this writer is now calling **Little Oak Canyon**. On USGS maps this short drainage with big sandy beaches is unnamed. In times of low lake levels, it's impossible to get into this inlet.

Hiking Routes or Trails One of the more popular drainages in this part of the lake is **Little Oak Canyon**. It's popular mainly because of several sandy beaches in the upper end of the inlet which combined are 300-400 meters long (this is only when the lake level is at or near the HWM). The place is very sandy because the surrounding countryside is capped by the Navajo Sandstone. As it weathers, sand is blown down into this canyon by the prevailing southwest winds.

Little Oak Canyon is a very short drainage, less than 1 km long above the HWM. There are hiker-made trails winding along the brushy bottom up to the head of the drainage and to several green & cool alcoves on the south side. This is where water pours off the Navajo bluffs & domes during rainstorms. There is a seep or flowing water coming out of most of these little alcoves as a result. There were some fairly fresh sign of beaver in the lower end of the drainage upon all of the author's visits.

There are **3 hikes or routes** out of this canyon. Two go up steep slickrock ridges on the south side of the inlet. The **first route** you can get to right from your boat--if the lake level is high. Look for moki steps cut in a slickrock ridge right near the HWM. Higher up you'll have fine views of the entire inlet.

The **second slickrock moki trail** begins a little beyond the small waterfall which is just above the HWM. Walk up next to the end of a little ridge coming down from the right or south and look for moki steps cut in the slickrock. These steps have been cut with a sharp metal instrument, perhaps a miner's pick. Head up to the south and you'll run into half a dozen places where moki steps have been cut in the steeper sections. Once out of the canyon, you'll see several stone cairns but they don't seem to lead anywhere. However, you can wander south and southeast and end up in **upper Oak Canyon**, or on the **North Rainbow Bridge Trail**. If you're interested in more extensive hiking in this area, see the author's other books, *Technical Slot Canyon Guide to the Colorado Plateau,* or the *Non-Technical Canyon Guide to the Colorado Plateau.*

One of the deepest and narrowest inlets around is in the upper end of **Oak Canyon**. With high lake levels, the upper end of the inlet is about as tight as regular-sized boats can get through, and the walls

Looking northwest at **Little Oak Canyon Bay** on 6/11/2003. This was when the lake level was similar to what it was in 2007. In the background upper left is Fiftymile Mountain; center is Oak Canyon Bay; right & left just below center are 2 of the little ridges where moki steps are cut.

Map 29, Oak, Little Oak, Forbidding, Cliff and Rainbow Bridge Canyons

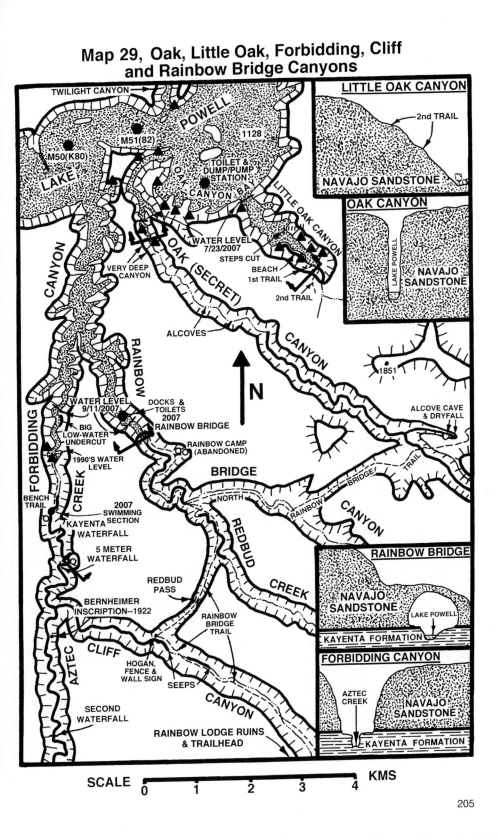

TWILIGHT CANYON

POWELL

M51(82)

1128

M50(K80)

LAKE

TOILET & DUMP/PUMP STATION

OAK CANYON BAY

CANYON

OAK

LITTLE OAK CANYON

WATER LEVEL 7/23/2007

STEPS CUT

VERY DEEP CANYON

BEACH
1st TRAIL

2nd TRAIL

OAK (SECRET)

ALCOVES

CANYON

1851

RAINBOW

N

WATER LEVEL 9/11/2007

DOCKS & TOILETS 2007
RAINBOW BRIDGE

ALCOVE CAVE & DRYFALL

FORBIDDING

BIG LOW-WATER UNDERCUT

RAINBOW CAMP (ABANDONED)

1990'S WATER LEVEL

BRIDGE

BRIDGE TRAIL

BENCH TRAIL

CREEK

NORTH

RAINBOW

CANYON

2007 SWIMMING SECTION

KAYENTA WATERFALL

REDBUD

5 METER WATERFALL

REDBUD PASS

CREEK

RAINBOW BRIDGE

BERNHEIMER INSCRIPTION--1922

RAINBOW BRIDGE TRAIL

NAVAJO SANDSTONE

LAKE POWELL

AZTEC

CLIFF

HOGAN, FENCE & WALL SIGN

SEEPS

CANYON

KAYENTA FORMATION

FORBIDDING CANYON

SECOND WATERFALL

RAINBOW LODGE RUINS & TRAILHEAD

AZTEC CREEK

NAVAJO SANDSTONE

KAYENTA FORMATION

LITTLE OAK CANYON

2nd TRAIL

NAVAJO SANDSTONE

OAK CANYON

LAKE POWELL

NAVAJO SANDSTONE

SCALE

KMS

0   1   2   3   4

are about as high as Navajo Sandstone walls get. There may be one small campsite right at the end of the inlet but only if the lake level is high. More often than not, you'll find quicksand & floating debris (as was found on **7/24/2007-WL1099.78m/3608.18'**). Expect this situation to change with every big flood. As you begin to hike upcanyon you'll pass some extremely high walls and several large alcoves on the right-hand side. Beyond that the canyon gradually opens up and is less interesting.

Semi-wild Navajo horses & donkeys sometimes come down into this lower part of the canyon but there usually isn't any running water in the lower 3-4 kms. Above this dry part you begin to see potholes with water, then running water as you go further upcanyon. The upper end has a nice little year-round flowing stream. After 7-8 kms you'll come to an area with lots of cottonwood trees, gamble oak brush and several campsites. This is where the **North Rainbow Bridge Trail** crosses the creek. It's a heav-ily-used trail especially in the spring months, and is easy to find and follow.

The only times the author felt in danger of having his boat overturned by waves were the times he went to **Rainbow Bridge**. Other boaters were going at warp speed through the narrow channel and those pyramid-type waves don't stop vibrating for 10-15 minutes. Because of this danger, the NPS has now instigated a **no-wake** policy the moment you enter the **Rainbow Bridge Canyon Inlet**!

At the end of the Rainbow Bridge Canyon Inlet there are toilets on floating docks, then everyone must walk about 1 1/2 kms (**when the lake is at or near 7/24/2007-WL1099.78m/3608.18'**) along a floating path, then a road-like trail to the Bridge. Back in 1996, the NPS had blocked off the trail going under the bridge because some Navajos had objected saying it was a sacred place. By 2001, NPS in-terpreters were telling hikers if they wanted to go upcanyon under Rainbow Bridge to walk along the Kayenta slickrock ledges to avoid causing erosion to places with soil. By 2007, you were being asked to volunteer not to go under the Bridge, but you can skirt around the bridge to the north.

From the Bridge, the trail continues upcanyon along the Kayenta bench, then right in the stream bed itself. About 700 meters above the Bridge and on the left under a big overhang, is the **old tourist camp-site**. It was used up until the creation of Lake Powell. Under the alcove is a spring, along with a small cabin, old bed springs and other artifacts of a bygone era. Read more below.

Here's the story of the so-called discovery of Rainbow Bridge. When 2 white discovery parties were searching for the Bridge in August of 1909, one was led by **Nasja Begay**, the other by **Mikes Boy**. Later, the 2 joined forces and allegedly discovered the Bridge together on August 14. About a decade before, Mikes Boy had shown Nasja Begay where the Bridge was after discovering it himself while herd-ing horses. Three quarters of a century later the National Park Service honored the Piute now known as Jim Mike with a ceremony at Rainbow Bridge. In 1977, Jim Mike died at 105 years of age and was buried in Blanding, Utah.

Some of the prominent white men in the group were John Wetherill, Byron Cummings and William B. Douglas. This was reportedly the first time white men had seen Rainbow Bridge, but there are con-flicting stories on that count.

Rainbow Bridge is 88 meters high, 84 meters wide, and at its smallest part only 13 meters thick. On May 30, 1910, President Taft proclaimed Rainbow Bridge a national monument.

From the air, **Rainbow Bridge** center; with **Rainbow Bridge Canyon Inlet** & floating docks/toilets barely visible in the upper left. This foto was taken on **9/25/2007-WL1097.86m/3601.85'**; at that time tourists had to walk about 1 1/2 kms from their boats to the bottom of Rainbow Bridge. When lake waters are high and near the high water mark (HWM), water extends under the bridge and beyond.

In July, 1922, John Wetherill and Charles Bernheimer opened the first trail to Rainbow Bridge. After that, all tourists visiting this national monument came down the Rainbow Bridge Trail which started on the south side of Navajo Mountain at the now-abandoned Rainbow Lodge. The distance is 21 kms.

From the lake, this trail runs up Rainbow Bridge and Redbud Canyons then veers south over Redbud Pass and down into and up Cliff Canyon. It's still a good trail even today. It ends where **Rainbow Lodge** once stood and where only foundations now mark the spot. It burned down in 1965. There's still another trail out of this area called the **North Rainbow Bridge Trail**. It skirts the north side of Navajo Mountain and connects with roads from Rainbow City and the old Navajo Mtn. Trading Post area (see previous map).

A year or so after 1964, the normal route to Rainbow Bridge was from Lake Powell. Today, hundreds, maybe thousands, visit it daily. At the high water mark (HWM), which is 1128 meters (3700 feet), the lake extends under the bridge and up the canyon about 500 meters.

The last drainage covered here is **Forbidding Canyon** through which **Aztec Creek** flows. This is a very long drainage with its beginnings far to the south of Navajo Mountain. The author has been in the upper end and found running water, cottonwood trees and grazing cattle. However, this discussion covers just the lower part, the only section of interest to most boaters. At the very end of the long and winding inlet is a large alcove or overhang near the HWM. But if the water is low as it was on **9/11/2007-WL 1098.03m/3602.42'**, then you'll likely be walking through a **big fotogenic alcove** as shown.

In the area of the HWM, you'll begin to notice a groove down the middle of the drainage. This is where the stream has cut into what appears to be the upper part of the Kayenta Formation. In places this can complicates hiking a little. At times you'll be boxed into an area with waterfalls or large potholes and you'll have to regress a ways and climb upon a bench. Otherwise, the walking is easy and fast with no brush to slow you down. There are trees and waterfalls in some places.

On 9/9/2007, and just above where the **7 1/2' topo maps** show the HWM, the author got to a point where he couldn't bench-walk around a deep swimming section, so he had to swim parts of a 40-meter pool. **This wasn't there, or at least it wasn't a swimmer, in 1989.** Canyons do change with every flood, so be ready to swim in some parts below the **Kayenta** and **5-meter-high waterfalls**. Beyond that, it should be easy walking with no deep pools.

Normally there is running water all the way up Forbidding Canyon, but at times and in some places, it can dry up. About 3 kms or so above the HWM you may find a minor spring on the left. Just beyond this spring is a nice 5-meter-high waterfall and large swimming pool. Get around this minor obstacle on the right side. About 1 km above this waterfall, **Cliff Canyon Creek** enters from the left or east. While you can go up Aztec Creek for many kms, you can also go up Cliff Canyon to the Rainbow Bridge Trail, then walk over Redbud Pass and down to Rainbow Bridge.

Continuing up Forbidding Canyon. Two bends above where Cliff Canyon enters and on the left or east side, will be a large west-facing alcove cave. At the back end is one minor pictograph and an inscription reading, **Bernheimer Exp. 1922**. This inscription must have been put there by Bernheimer, perhaps along with Wetherill, who in that year, first opened a trail to Rainbow Bridge for tourists.

About half a dozen bends above this cave the canyon narrows and finally you'll have to swim through

From just below **Rainbow Bridge** looking east toward **Navajo Mountain**. There are signs below the bridge asking people not to go under it, but you can veer left and walk around the bridge on the left-- or just stay on the slickrock and walk under it to reach Rainbow Camp.

some potholes, then get upon a bench to the right or west side to get past another waterfall about 5 meters high. Or, just before the swimming holes you could stand on a large backpack, a pile of rocks, a short log, or the back of a companion, and get upon the same bench without swimming.

Once on this bench, walk along a steep place until you finally arrive at a pile of cedar trees which Navajos have placed there as a fence. Above that waterfall are no more impediments because livestock will be grazing down to that point. The adventurous hiker could continue upcanyon several more kms, then upon reaching a trail crossing the drainage, could turn right or west and use it to reach the top **Cummings Mesa**. From there you could walk down other sheep & goat trails into **West, Dungeon or Wetherill Canyons** (or a steep route down into **Mountain Sheep Canyon**). See **Area Map 35A, page 241**.

Hike Length & Time Needed You can only walk for a few minutes inside **Little Oak Canyon** then it's a quick and easy walk to the benchland above. Less than an hour is all it will take. It's 7-8 kms from the HWM in **Oak Canyon** to the **North Rainbow Bridge Trail**. This will take most people 6-7 hours round-trip. The author did it in 4 1/2 hours. On another occasion, he walked up Oak Canyon then along the trail to Nasja Canyon, down Nasja to the dropoff & pool, then returned. Total walk-time 11 2/3 hours. You can walk as far and as long as you like up **Rainbow Bridge or Redbud Canyons**. If you walk up **Forbidding Canyon**, it's about 7 kms to the Rainbow Bridge Trail in Cliff Canyon. Most will need 4-5 hours for this round-trip hike. The author did this one in 3 1/3 hours. To hike up **Aztec Creek-Forbidding Canyon** to the second 5-meter-high waterfall and return, will take most people all day--but that will depend on lake levels. The author did this one in just under 5 hours, round-trip (but on that trip, some deep pools were evidently filled with sand; whereas in 2007, he found at least 1 swimming hole!).

Boots or Shoes Best to use wading-type shoes in all canyons except Oak and Little Oak.

Water It will likely be good water in Little Oak Canyon unless you see fresh sign of beaver. Oak Canyon water is suspect unless you hike above the North Rainbow Bridge Trail. There may be cattle in its upper end. The spring at the old tourist camp near Rainbow Bridge probably has good water (?) and cattle can't get to it because the alcove is now fenced off. Treat Aztec Creek water, but water in Cliff Canyon may be good although there are old signs of livestock there too. Water taken from most spring sources should be good to drink as is (?).

Main Attractions The 2nd biggest natural bridge in the world, 2 slickrock trails in Little Oak Canyon, wilderness canyons few people visit and long narrow inlets.

Hiking Maps USGS or BLM map Navajo Mountain (1:100,000); Rainbow Bridge (1:24,000--7 1/2' quad) for hiking; or Navajo Mtn. (1:62,500) if available.

Rainbow Camp. This former tourist campsite is under a big alcove about 1 km above **Rainbow Bridge** (there are other parts of this camp nearby). Before the coming of Lake Powell, this camp was where travelers stayed for at least one night when visiting the monument. At that time all travelers came in from the end of the road and Rainbow Lodge located south of Navajo Mountain. That old lodge burned down in about 1960 (?), and all that's left today is the foundation.

Above This scene is just above where the author tied-up his boat, and just below the *Big Low-Water Undercut*, in the **Forbidding Canyon Inlet**. This foto was taken on **9/11/2007-WL 1098.03m/3602.42'**. With low lake levels, there's lots of sandy places in this part of Forbidding Canyon along Aztec Creek.

Left On the map, this is labeled *Big Low-Water Undercut* in **Forbidding Canyon**. Just above this area, there are more cobble-stones and less sand. This foto was taken on the same day & hike as the one above.

209

Cascade, Driftwood, Balanced Rock & Dangling Rope Canyons and the Klondike Trail

Location & Campsites The 4 canyons and one historic trail on this map are all located just west of the mouth of **Forbidding/Rainbow Bridge Canyon** and on the north side of the lake. They're all short drainages which drain the southern slopes of **Fiftymile Mountain**, which is part of the Kaiparowits Plateau. If you like narrow waterways and tight slot canyons this is the place to go. With all the soaring cliffs, this is one of the most scenic parts of Lake Powell. Also on this map is **Dangling Rope Marina**, the only fuel stop on the lake with boater access only. Read more on the marina below and in the **Introduction** to this book.

This is another area with few campsites. The inlet with the most may be Dangling Rope, followed by Balanced Rock Bay; and sometimes one small campsite at the very end of each of these very narrow inlets. There are also more sites just south of this mapped area on the opposite side of the main channel and in or near Cathedral, Mountain Sheep and Wetherill Canyons. If you don't need a sandy beach to crash on then there are many slickrock anchorages or tie-down places you can use.

Hiking Routes or Trails Cascade Canyon & Inlet is one of the longest & narrowest on the lake, beating anything in the Escalante River system. It's very winding and at the upper end is just wide enough for an average boat to pass through.

Cascade is also one of the narrowest hiking canyons on the lake. You can only walk and climb for about 1 km (above the HWM) before you come to a high dryfall at the end of 2 tributaries. But to get that far, you must climb over some narrow dropoffs and chokestones. To do this it's necessary to use a climbing or canyoneering technique called **spanning**, or **chimneying**. For example, put your back on one wall, and your feet & hands on the other. Or just spread your legs and arms and span your way up. If the walls are just less than a meter apart, this is an easy trick. Best to have knee & elbow pads for these moves. **Beware:** this is not a good canyon to be in if the weather is threatening.

Driftwood Canyon is another extremely deep and narrow slot. The waterway leading into it is winding with high Navajo walls just like in Cascade Canyon. The author once saw a large boat full of tourists having their lunch in the shade at mid-day just inside the left fork near the end of the inlet. Take the right fork as you near the upper end. This upper inlet is 600-700 meters in length and maybe 4 meters wide on average (with water at the HWM). In the extreme upper end it narrows down to 2 or 2 1/2 meters.

Right at the very end of this inlet used to be an area covered with driftwood, thus the name. Depending on lake levels, and if the lake water is rising or falling, you may find an awful looking floating mess right at the end of the inlet (same with all such canyons). Get by this mess by using an oar to push logs out of the way; or get out and wade pulling your boat up to the tiny sandy beach. Wading in the floating debris isn't as bad as it may first appear.

In Driftwood Canyon you can walk very easily for 200 meters (above the HWM) in a slot that's 1-3 meters wide. Then if narrows and you'll have to climb. Some energetic climbers can go further by spanning or chimneying. Above this minor obstruction it should be exciting.

Right at the mouth of Driftwood Canyon on the west side is the beginning of the **Klondike Trail**. This was one of the main routes in or out of one of the major placer gold mining sand bars on the Colorado

When your shoes are dry, this is an easy climb, but when it's muddy....! This is **Driftwood Canyon**; this boulder wasn't there before, but the water level was much lower in 2007, thus exposing more canyon than in 1988.

Map 30, Cascade, Driftwood, Balanced Rock & Dangling Rope Canyons and the Klondike Trail

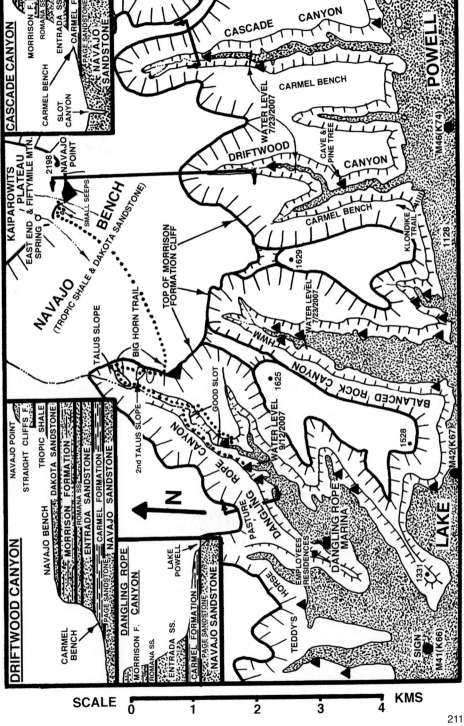

SCALE

0   1   2   3   4   KMS

211

River in the lower Glen Canyon. It was known as the **Klondike Bar** and it extended downstream from the mouth of Driftwood.

The first claims on this placer mining site were filed on December 22, 1897, by Louis M. Chaffin, Seth Laugee and William B. Hay. They named it **Klondike Bar**, because it coincided in time with the Yukon Gold Rush. By 1899, these 3 men had sold their claims and it was mined afterwards as well. When Crampton visited the place in the late 1950's, he saw a considerable amount of mining equipment and debris. There were gravel chutes, ditches, wooden tracks, ore cars, iron scrapers, and sluice flumes.

The Klondike Trail began at the head or east end of the bar. It must have been a spectacular route before Lake Powell covered about 3/4's of it. In those days it wound its way for 250 meters up a steep wall to the top of the Carmel bench. In some places holes were drilled and stakes set in the slickrock wall, with rocks and brush piled on top of poles. In other places, steps were cut in solid sandstone. From the top of the Carmel bench the trail closely followed the 1200 to 1250 meter contour lines. It went eastward into and out of the upper ends of Driftwood and Cascade Canyons, as well as Navajo Valley (Twilight Canyon), then around one more finger of a mesa to Fifty Mile Point. From there it connected with the **Hole-in-the-Rock Road** which led north to Escalante.

To find the beginning of this historic trail, boat to the mouth of Driftwood Canyon and just around the corner to the west side. Look closely in the area just above and below the HWM on a slope facing east. You should see steps coming out of the water. There's no place to dock there so boat around the corner toward Driftwood about 100 meters to a small inlet. Dock there and walk up along the slickrock to the trail. In all, Crampton states there were at least 8 places where steps were cut. You can now see only about 3. In between these steps are several cairns marking the way as the trail runs northwest up to the Carmel bench.

Balanced Rock Canyon has several campsites leading into the far end of its narrow inlet. This is still another very fine slot-type canyon hike but it's a short one. The author walked in only about 250 meters from his boat (at the HWM), but he had to do some climbing to get that far. Put your feet on one wall, and back against the other, to get over one chokestone. Really tough climbers might get further.

Dangling Rope Canyon has a large bay with a sign at the entrance. However, one need not worry about finding this place, as there will be hundreds of boats going that way daily in summer to fuel up at **Dangling Rope Marina**. Originally this marina was located near Rainbow Bridge but traffic there was so heavy and the inlet so narrow, they finally had to move it to its present location in about 1983. Waste disposal was another problem at the Bridge.

Dangling Rope Canyon got it's name because in the days before Lake Powell, river runners found a rope dangling down over a cliff just upcanyon from the river. There were also some old toe holds or steps cut in the wall. These steps originally may have been cut as far back as Anasazi times, but were likely used later by Piutes or Navajos and Glen Canyon gold miners. The rope was put there by white men.

Today the floating marina juts out from a low bench in the middle of the bay. Just behind it on the bench is the employee housing and a field of photovoltaic cells which produces electricity. At this marina you'll find a NPS rangers office--but it's only open intermittently. They have a dock for boat repairs and they sell **regular gasoline** (and Diesel fuel) which was selling for **$4.41 a gallon** on **July 25, 2007**. Bring your own oil for mixing for 2 stroke engines, or buy it there. Gasoline is brought out daily by a large Chevron owned boat. All other supplies arrive in containers on a barge from Wahweap. Garbage is

Next to the mouth of **Dangling Rope Canyon** are these old steps cut in a slickrock bluff called the **Klondike Trail**. The top of these white mineral water deposits (the bathtub ring) is the HWM.

hauled out in container units which are towed to the local dump near Wahweap.

There is water for flushing and drinking, plus garbage bins. The NPS used to hand out free garbage bags--but not in 2007. Please take garbage bags with you and use them. The marina has 2 small stores; one sells items for boats, the other has food, clothes, books, etc, at prices much higher than in land-based supermarkets. You can buy ice cream and ice, both very popular items in summer; and you can eat at a shaded-floating picnic site nearby. They have an information board and a button you can push for the latest weather forecast; it's also posted on the ranger station wall.

Even though this place is in the middle of the wilderness with boater access only, you can still make long distance telefon calls to the outside world via a cellular system. You can send letters or postcards from Dangling Rope, but they'll have a Page, Arizona postmark.

Because all their supplies come from Page and Wahweap, the marina uses **Arizona time, which is not daylight saving time in the summer months**. In summer, you can buy gasoline from 7am until 7pm, Arizona time (If they can fix the electrical & internet problem, you may be able to buy gas with a credit card--but not in 2007). The grocery store has these same hours, but the ice cream shop is open from 8am until 5:30pm (9am to 6:30pm Utah or daylight savings time). Dangling Rope Marina used to be open year-round, but in the early 2000's, they were closing it from November 15 until about March 1. The busy season is from Memorial Day to Labor Day (last weekend in May, and 1st weekend in Sep-tember), and on weekends in the spring (especially at Easter time) and fall.

There may be some campsites in **Dangling Rope Canyon & Inlet**, plus hiking or climbing. In the upper end of the inlet it narrows and if the water is high, you'll pass through a very narrow place then it opens a bit. At that point you can climb out of the narrows and onto the bench to the east or west. If you go directly up the bottom of the canyon you'll be stopped after about 300 meters by a chokestone and dropoff. If you can get above that, there's a pretty good slot beyond.

Or if the water level is low, as it was on **9/12/2007-WL1098.00m/3602.33'**, get out somewhere on the west side of the inlet and route-find north. Soon you'll pass one little side-canyon, then it's an easy walk to the head of the canyon. Higher up, there are a couple of places you can get back down into the drainage; then at a fork where the main dry creek bed veers left or west, you head straight up the obvi-ous **talus slope** which has signs of a big horn sheep trail. The author saw a ewe & lamb in this area on one of his hikes.

As you ascend this easy-to-climb-slope you'll gradually veer to the right or east. Near the top of the talus, scan the slope to the east and south for a route along the benches which are at the top of the En-trada or Romana Sandstone. You must then bench-walk south along **one of two terraces**.

After bench-walking south about 300 meters, turn left or east and climb up the first of **2 visible talus slopes**.

At the top of this, route-find up through one easy ter-race then up through a second cliff band. The big horns make it up some how and so can you, but you'll have to look for the easy way and be climbing on all-4's. Look for **stone cairns** and a developing trail. Once on top of the second rock band, con-tour south to the corner, then make an abrupt 180° turn to the left and walk up through some easy ledges to the north-east. At that point you'll be on top of the **Morri-son Formation cliff** and have a nice view down on Dangling Rope Ma-rina.

Energetic climbers or hikers can continue cross-country northeast toward the southern tip of the **Kaiparowits Plateau/Fiftymile Mountain** and a place called **Navajo Point**. As you walk, be looking for an easy route up through the lowest major cliff band. This will be

This steep little section of **Driftwood Canyon** is just below the HWM. The best parts of this canyon are above this point but can be hard to get to when things are wet.

right below the point that looks to be the highest and between 2 minor drainages. Climb straight up to below the highest cliffs, then veer right or east and bench-walk to the rim. There may be other routes up or down to the east (?). On top, the author once stumbled onto a cliff-face cave with fire wood and corncobs that were put there perhaps 800 years ago (?). There are lots of Fremont Indian sites on top of Fiftymile Mountain.

From Navajo Point you'll have some great views to the south, east and west especially if it's a clear day. Do this one in spring or fall with cooler temperatures if you can. On top it's a lot cooler than at the marina! For more info on trails & ruins on Fiftymile Mtn., see this writer's book, **Non-Technical Canyon Guide to the Colorado Plateau, 5th Edition** (or later).

Hike Length & Time Needed The distance into **Cascade, Driftwood and Balanced Rock Canyons** is very short so in half an hour or an hour you may go as far as you can. You can see everything in a few minutes in the 200 meters of the Klondike Trail. From the lake in **Dangling Rope Canyon** to the top of Fiftymile Mtn. at Navajo Point is a slow hike, so it would be a long all-day affair. It took the author just over 3 hours getting up and 7 1/2 hours round-trip on a warm May day. You can cut the distance in half if you stop at the top of the **Morrison cliffs** which will give you the best view of Dangling Rope Inlet & Marina.

Boots or Shoes In Cascade, Driftwood or Balanced Rock Canyons, any kind of boot or shoe would be OK, but you may have to wade in the upper parts of the inlets to get your boat all the way in. To reach the top of the Kaiparowits you may want some slightly more rugged hiking boots.

Water There are no springs or water on any of these hikes except for some minor seeps just under the top rim of Fiftymile--and they could dry up at times. There is water at the East End Spring on top of the plateau. Take 3-4 liters of water for the Kaiparowits hike if it's a hot summer day!

Main Attractions The narrowest waterways on Lake Powell, some short but very tight slot canyon hikes, a climb to the top of a very high lookout, a chance to see desert big horn sheep, and a place you can buy ice cream on a hot summer day.

Hiking Maps USGS or BLM maps Navajo Mountain & Smoky Mountain (1:100,000); Navajo Point & maybe Cathedral Canyon (1:24,000-- 7 1/2' quads) for hiking; or Navajo Mtn. & Cummings Mesa (1:62,500) if available.

Another part of **Driftwood Canyon**. The narrows in this canyon are about as good as it gets. However, in times of low water, it may be a challenge getting up to this higher section.

The head of navigation in **Cascade Canyon Inlet**. In all of the canyons between Dangling Rope Marina and Rainbow Bridge, you'll have to wade through a driftwood mess like this to get upcanyon.

Dangling Rope Marina (looking southeast) as seen from the top of a nearby hill. Behind the author is the employee housing & photovoltaic solar panels which provides electricity for the complex.

Above These are **photovoltaic panels** which generate almost all the electricity needs for **Dangling Rope Marina** which is only about 300 meters away. They have a propane powered generator as a backup.

Right From the air looking down at **Dangling Rope Marina**, with **Dangling Rope Canyon** and **Fiftymile Mountain** in the background. There's a route up the cliffs in the background, as shown on the map.

From the top of the **Talus Slope**, you can see at least 2 benches you can walk on to reach what is marked as the **2nd Talus Slope** on **Map 30**. From there you can route-find up to the top of the Morrison Cliff and beyond to the top of Fiftymile Mountain and Navajo Point.

Another aerial view of **Dangling Rope Marina**. Employee housing is in the middle right, then the photovoltaic panels, and finally the sewage treatment facility, in lower left with the red pond.

Cathedral and Mountain Sheep Canyons

Location & Campsites These 2 canyons are located south of the main channel and drain part of the north side of **Cummings Mesa**. They are also about halfway between the Dangling Rope Marina and Rainbow Bridge. One buoy marked M46 (K74) is near the mouth of Cathedral Inlet, and another one marked M43 (K69) is near Mountain Sheep Bay. Because they're on the route to Rainbow Bridge there's a lot of traffic in the nearby main channel.

The dominant rock formation at the HWM (and just below) in each inlet is the ever-present Navajo Sandstone (perhaps a little of the very thin Page Sandstone?). This means there's slickrock coming down to the water everywhere. But it also means, because of weathering of this sandstone, you may see, depending on water levels, a number of small sandy campsites. These are never large, but in the back end of some of the little inlets, you'll find some of the cleanest sand on the lake. There are also dozens of small hidden slickrock coves so if you're equipped with the proper ropes and anchors to tie your boat down, you can still have an excellent slickrock campsite. Of the 2 inlets, Mountain Sheep has the most sites. The number of campsites will depend on lake levels.

Hiking Routes or Trails There are few signs of sheep & goat trails in either of these drainages and at first glance both appear to be box canyons. For the most part, **Cathedral Canyon** may not have much hiking. The author boated all the way into the back end of its main channel until the boat was jammed into a slot just over a meter wide. He then swam about 20 meters to get out of the water but was con-fronted by chokestones which were too slippery to get over. If the water level is lower, and/or things are drier, you might have a good hike in the nice slot canyon above. With 2 or more people and a short rope, you'll have a chance to go much further than if you're alone.

Mountain Sheep Canyon on the other hand usually has a slightly wider channel at the end of the inlet which makes one of the better slot canyon hikes in this book. As you head into this upper inlet it may be necessary to get out of your boat and wade or swim upchannel. This is what the author did with his inflatable boat back in 1988 with high water levels. He took it up to a point where it wedged in be-tween the walls and walked a short distance in water. From there he walked for perhaps 1 1/2 kms in sand & rocks. Along the way, there were several small chokestones but they were easy to get around. In 2001 with lower water, he first walked in sand, then found several deep wading pools before he came to a **large chokestone** with water & mud in a pool below. Both times he was stopped there because he was alone without a helping hand. On **7/23/2007-WL1099.78m/3608.39'**, the end of the boating part was wider, but 200m upcanyon was an slippery unclimbable dryfall.

However, Noel Stone wrote the author saying he, a friend and a dog (along with a short rope), man-aged to get above the large chokestone and several others. Later, they left the main slot to the right via a side-canyon. Once out of the slot they managed to climb up to the top of Cummings Mesa.

On the author's 2001 trip, he regressed from the large chokestone and walked up a side-canyon to the west. He came to a large pothole where someone had piled up stones and managed to get out, then left a short sling behind which the author used to climb out. A bit further up, he left the canyon on steep slickrock to the left. Follow his route on the map. From the side-canyon, he headed due south between slots as shown. At times he was on a faint sheep & goat trail. Higher up, he attempted the most-west-

This was the head of **Mtn. Sheep Canyon Inlet** on **7/23/2007-WL1099.78m/3608.39'**. At that time, bigger boats had to wait in line while some adventurous souls swam to where they could walk--but no one was walking very far on that day and that water level.

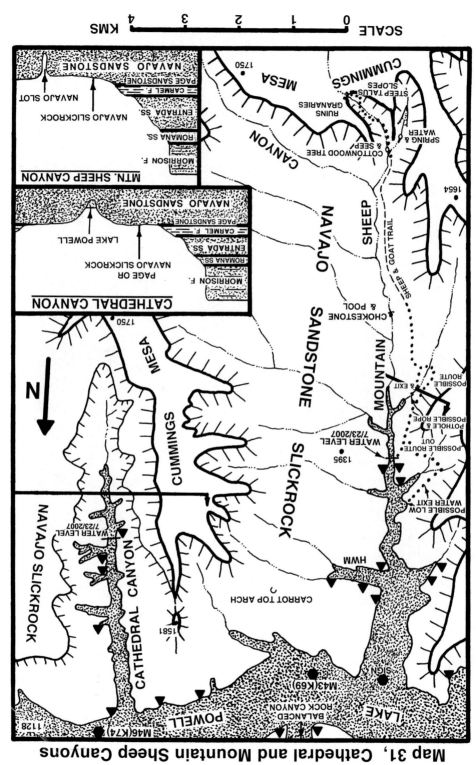

Map 31, Cathedral and Mountain Sheep Canyons

SCALE

KMS 4 3 2 1 0

N

CATHEDRAL CANYON

MTN. SHEEP CANYON

NAVAJO SANDSTONE

PAGE SANDSTONE
CARMEL F.
ENTRADA SS.
ROMANA SS.
MORRISON F.

NAVAJO SLICKROCK

NAVAJO SLOT

NAVAJO SANDSTONE

PAGE SANDSTONE
CARMEL F.
ENTRADA SS.
ROMANA SS.
MORRISON F.

PAGE OR NAVAJO SLICKROCK

LAKE POWELL

1750

CUMMINGS MESA

1750

CUMMINGS MESA

CUMMINGS CANYON

1654

SHEEP CANYON

NAVAJO SANDSTONE

MOUNTAIN

SLICKROCK

STEEP TALUS SLOPES
RUINS GRANARIES
SPRING & WATER
COTTONWOOD TREE & SEEP
SHEEP & GOAT TRAIL

CHOKESTONE & POOL

WATER LEVEL 7/23/2007

1395

POSSIBLE ROUTE & EXIT

POTHOLE & POSSIBLE ROPE

POSSIBLE ROUTE OUT

POSSIBLE LOW WATER EXIT

HWM

CARROT TOP ARCH

NAVAJO SLICKROCK

CATHEDRAL CANYON

WATER LEVEL 7/23/2007

1581

POWELL

LAKE

1128

M46(K74)

BALANCED ROCK CANYON

M43(K69)

SIGN

erly of 2 upper canyons shown but failed in reaching the top. There is a pretty good spring and water in that fork however. From the cottonwood tree and another minor spring, he had a steep walk up the **eastern upper fork** and managed to top out on Cummings Mesa. On top are several **Anasazi grana-ries** under some ledges. His round-trip time was 8 1/2 hours, 2 hours of which was lost in exploring.

Hike Length & Time Needed No one knows what lies ahead for the adventurous hiker in Cathedral, but in Mountain Sheep Canyon and with a friend and short rope you might get around the big choke-stone and end up on top. Or follow the author's route, or use another starting point to the north. Plan on an all-day hike or climb--and stay out of the slot if the weather is threatening.

Boots or Shoes Wading shoes in both canyons but heavier boots if climbing Cummings Mesa.

Water Take plenty of water in warm weather (3-4 liters) if you're heading for the top of Cummings Mesa, in case the springs are dry.

Main Attractions Several little hidden coves for camping, a good slot canyon hike, or a good climb to the top of Cummings Mesa.

Hiking Maps USGS or BLM map Smoky Mountain (1:100,000); Cathedral Canyon (1:24,000--7 1/2' quad) for hiking; or Cummings Mesa (1:62,500) if available.

This short walkable section in **Mtn. Sheep Canyon** was only about 200 meters long. This foto was taken on 7/23/2007-WL1099.78m/3608.39'. On that day the author was stopped by a slippery climb.

This is the narrow inlet to **Mtn. Sheep Canyon**. All the slots between Dangling Rope Marina and Rainbow Bridge, are about like this.

From the air over the main channel looking east toward **Navajo Mountain**. Two of the channels coming in from the right are **Mountain Sheep**, then **Cathedral Canyons**. Just to the left and out of sight is Dangling Rope Canyon and the **Dangling Rope Marina**.

Wetherill and Dungeon Canyons

Location & Campsites On this map are a couple of the more interesting canyon hikes in this book. Together they lie south and southwest of **Dangling Rope Marina** and on the south side of the main channel. A buoy marked M39 (K62) should be in the lake between the mouths of Wetherill & Dungeon Bays.

In this part of the lake the rock formations are dipping slightly to the west. In **Dungeon Bay**, the geologic formation exposed at the shoreline when the lake is at or near the HWM, is the bench-forming Carmel Formation. The Carmel sits atop the Page Sandstone (some still classify it as the top of Navajo Sandstone) which is exposed in Dungeon Bay when the lake level is 20-30 meters below the HWM. Because of these gradual sloping formations, Dungeon Canyon Bay generally has many good sandy campsites. **Wetherill Canyon Inlet** has many little coves with mostly slickrock campsites but some have tiny beaches as well.

Hiking Routes & Trails The upper end of the inlet in **Wetherill Canyon** is long & narrow, similar to the canyons just to the east. The rock exposed is the Page and/or Navajo Sandstone. This has resulted in another very narrow slot-type canyon. You may have to get out of your boat and wade up to the end of the inlet because of shallow water (On **7/23/2007-WL1099.78m/3608.39'**, the inlet was so narrow it was necessary to swim a ways from your boat, or stop in a wider part of the inlet back to the north and walk up slickrock to the west, then head upcanyon to the south on the **Carmel bench**), then it's an easy walk for about a km above the HWM in one of the narrowest slot canyons entering the lake.

If hiking in the slot, and about 500 meters above the HWM, you'll come to a talus slope on the right coming down to the canyon bottom. You can exit there, or continue to the left, staying in the canyon bottom, and walk about another 100 meters into one of the darkest holes anywhere. This section is slanted and overhung so much it's too dark to take good pictures. Just beyond this dark cavern is another exit to the right. This exit is connected with the first one mentioned. The slot at that point really takes a strange twist!

If you were to continue up the slot, you could only walk another 200-300 meters before coming to a small pool and a **chokestone**. You'll need 2 people, or more, and a short rope to get above this obstacle. For some this may be the end of the hike. However with each flashflood, this canyon changes so don't be surprised if it's different when you arrive (Byron Lemay once told the author, he and several other hikers got into this slot in the upper end of the canyon and came down halfway and over several chokestones, before returning the same way. So going up or down this slot is possible, but you'd need several people and several short ropes--maybe more. As far as their trip went, there was nothing in the way of any big rappels, only chimneying/climbing over chokestones).

If you leave the slot at the **twin exits**, you can climb up the Navajo and/or Page slickrock to the west and get upon the **Carmel bench** (top of Carmel Formation) where you'll find an **old sheep trail** heading south upcanyon. Once on this trail it's easy walking. This trail must have been heavily used before the coming of Lake Powell.

For the long distance trekker, here's a good hike. Look at the **Area Map 35A on page 241**. Once on this **Wetherill Canyon Sheep & Goat Trail** head south. The trail is easy to follow and it appears to be used occasionally by Navajos with their sheep & goats. About 6 kms south of the Utah-Arizona line, which is the bottom of this map, is where a reasonably good **constructed trail** winds it's way up to the

Dungeon Canyon and the **fence** across the trail at the base of the talus slope going up **Cummings Mesa**. The trail goes up to the white band, turns to the right, then zig zags up to the rim.

Map 32, Wetherill and Dungeon Canyons

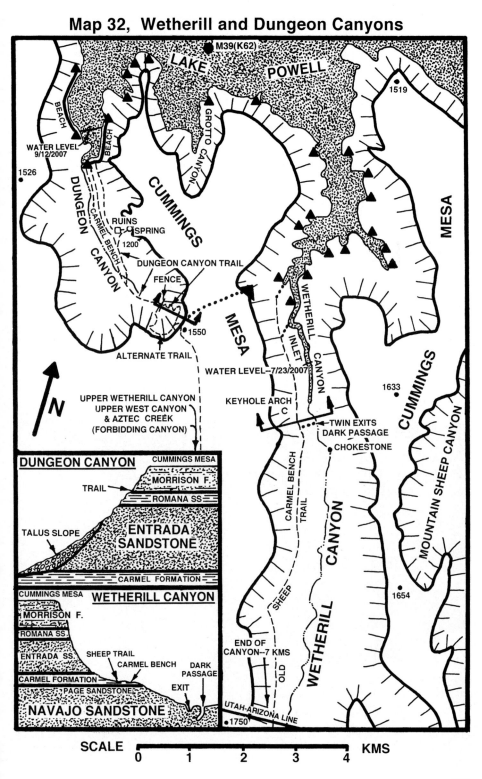

LAKE POWELL

M39(K62)

1519

WATER LEVEL
9/12/2007

BEACH

BEACH

1526

DUNGEON CANYON

CUMMINGS

GROTTO CANYON

MESA

CARMEL BENCH

RUINS
SPRING
1200

DUNGEON CANYON TRAIL

FENCE

1550

WETHERILL

INLET

CANYON

ALTERNATE TRAIL

MESA

WATER LEVEL--7/23/2007

N

UPPER WETHERILL CANYON
UPPER WEST CANYON
& AZTEC CREEK
(FORBIDDING CANYON)

KEYHOLE ARCH
C

1633

CUMMINGS

TWIN EXITS
DARK PASSAGE

CHOKESTONE

MOUNTAIN SHEEP CANYON

DUNGEON CANYON

CUMMINGS MESA

MORRISON F.

TRAIL

ROMANA SS

TALUS SLOPE

ENTRADA
SANDSTONE

CARMEL FORMATION

CARMEL BENCH

TRAIL

CANYON

1654

CUMMINGS MESA

WETHERILL CANYON

MORRISON F.

ROMANA SS.

ENTRADA SS.   SHEEP TRAIL

CARMEL BENCH   DARK
PASSAGE

CARMEL FORMATION

PAGE SANDSTONE

EXIT

NAVAJO SANDSTONE

SHEEP

END OF
CANYON--7 KMS

OLD

WETHERILL

UTAH-ARIZONA LINE

1750

SCALE   0   1   2   3   4   KMS

top of **Cummings Mesa**. At the head of this canyon are 2 short forks. Walk into the **south fork** then turn left and look to the east to locate the beginning of the trail zig zagging up to about the top of the Entrada Sandstone. At a point about halfway up the slope, the trail then heads due north and contours at the same elevation around the corner to the east and into the upper end of the **east fork**. Once there, you'll go down a little to the bottom of the dry creek bed then back up on the east side and finally exit to the top of Cummings Mesa.

From there you could head due south about 2 1/2 kms and use another trail to get down into the upper end of **West Canyon**. You could also head southeast about 2 kms and use still another trail which drops off the mesa and down into **Aztec Creek/Forbidding Canyon**. That trail ends on the south side of Navajo Mountain at a place called **Round Rock**. You could also curl around to the west, then northwest, and after about 15 kms drop down the trail at the head of **Dungeon Canyon**. Lots of great hiking here especially for a cool season trip. Cummings Mesa has lots of hill-top Anasazi Indian ruins & artifacts. The **Area Map, 35A** shows all these trails.

Dungeon Canyon is a little different than Wetherill. This one has no narrow slot canyon to cool off in; instead there's an old **stock trail** to the top of **Cummings Mesa** which makes a different type of hike. From the upper end of the bay, walk south along the left or east side of the drainage. Eventually you'll see several hiker & livestock trails upon the bench to your left. About 1 km above the HWM you will see to your left or east some **old rock corrals** and the **ruins** of an old hogan or some kind of shelter. From there, walk east into a shallow alcove where you'll see some greenery. Up near the cliff you'll see evidence of an old encampment, and just under the cliff a tiny spring with water dripping from the wall. On a hot summer day that water sure tastes good, but be sure sheep or goats haven't polluted it. On **9/12/2007-WL1098.00m/3602.33'**, and after several years of drought, there was wet ground but no dripping water from that spring; so never bet your life on finding water there.

From the spring, head down to the south and to one of several trails, which at that point, are easy to follow. Further to the southeast the best trail is out in the middle of the valley but there are many trails going in the same direction. Still further upcanyon to the southeast, you'll see a fence across the valley floor just as the trail begins to steepen (see foto on **page 222**). This fence has been decorated with old Navajo clothing to mark the scene, and to scare away sheep & goats. Climb over the fence (or go through the gate) and head up the steep talus slope on a single constructed trail.

The trail in this section has been built by the hands of man (but was very much eroded in 2007), very likely during the 1930's when the **CCC crews** built many livestock trails throughout the west and on Navajo Nation lands. It zig zags up the talus slope about 2/3's of the way to the top, then veers right or southwest and contours along one of the terraces. After about 100 meters, this **now-cairned-trail** goes up another level, then cuts back to the northeast. After another 2 switchbacks and climbing a couple of benches, the trail finally tops out on the rim. If you have time, walk northeast about 1 km for a view down into Wetherill Canyon. It's a lot cooler on top than at the lake.

So as not to back-track, you can take another **alternate trail** back to the bottom of the steep upper part. Look this one over from the rim before heading down. When you get back down the trail to the Romana bench (perhaps the top of the Entrada Sandstone?), head southwest instead of northeast, and follow the **alternate trail** as it contours southwest, west and northwest around the perimeter of the huge bowl. As the trail passes one minor ridge, it starts zig zagging down another talus slope. But about

From the rim of **Cummings Mesa** looking northwest down into **Dungeon Canyon**. The sheep & goat trail comes up the middle of the valley and to the lower right-hand side of this foto.

halfway down the trail disappears because of erosion. You can still get down easily but you'll have to route-find either out on the slickrock or down the steep talus slope. This may have been the first trail built up the canyon, but perhaps after a flood, it was rebuilt in the other location.

See **Map 35 of West Canyon** and the **Area Map 35A on page 241** for a broader view and more information on trails to the top of Cummings Mesa

Hike Length & Time Needed If staying in the bottom of **Wetherill,** you can hike only about 1 km (1 hour round-trip), if you're lucky. But if you get out of the slot, walk to the end of the canyon and climb the old sheep & goat trail to the top of Cummings Mesa, you'll walk closer to 12 kms one-way. This would be a long all-day hike. To reach the top of the trail in **Dungeon Canyon,** you'll be walking about 5-6 kms one-way. The author did this several times in less than 3 hours, but you'll likely want 4-5 hours, round-trip. In 2007, with low water levels and a longer hike, the author walked to an overlook of Wetherill and back in 4 1/3 hours.

Boots or Shoes Better use wading shoes in the bottom of Wetherill Canyon, but upon the Carmel bench and in Dungeon Canyon, you can use any kind of hiking boots or shoes.

Water There's no reliable drinking water in either canyon, so take your own from a culinary source.

Main Attractions Good narrows, wild and seldom visited canyons, good campsites, and historic Navajo livestock trails with good views from the top of Cummings Mesa.

Hiking Maps USGS or BLM maps Smoky Mountain & Glen Canyon Dam (1:100,000); Gregory Butte, Cathedral Canyon & maybe West Canyon Creek (1:24,000--7 1/2' quads) for hiking; or Cummings Mesa & Navajo Creek (1:62,500) if available.

From **Cummings Mesa** looking north, northeast toward **Fiftymile Mountain/Kaiparowits Plateau** and the Harveys Fear Cliffs. Below the benches (made of the Carmel Formation) in the middle of this foto is the lighter-colored Navajo Sandstone which makes contact with the lake waters.

Dry Rock Creek and Middle Rock Creek Canyons

Location & Campsites Dry Rock Creek and **Middle Rock Creek Canyons** both drain into **Rock Creek Bay**, which is the first large bay or inlet west of **Dangling Rope Canyon & Marina**. At the mouth of Rock Creek Bay is a buoy marked M35 (K56). Also at the mouth of the bay is a toilet & dump/pump station where you can empty your boat's toilet.

At the entrance of Rock Creek Bay, you'll find the Entrada Sandstone rising abruptly out of the water with few if any campsites around. As you near the upper ends of both inlets, the formations are seen rising and finally the bench-forming Carmel Formation is exposed. There you'll find a number of sandy beaches and campsites under the towering walls of the Entrada, Romana & Morrison Formations.

Hiking Routes or Trails Dry Rock Creek makes one of the better long distance hikes in this book. Boat into the narrow upper part of the inlet which begins to cut into the top of the Page and/or Navajo Sandstone. You'll immediately begin walking in a good shallow narrows or slot section. On **9/12/2007-WL1098.00m/3602.33'**, water was flowing for about 400 meters above the end of the inlet. If it were deeper it would be a nice slot canyon. After 2-3 kms, you can exit left and leave the canyon. Nearby is an interesting **toadstool**, as seen on the map and in the foto on **page 229**. Or after 5-6 kms you'll come to a 3-meter-high dryfall made from the Carmel Formation. Pass this on the left. A short rope at that point could help less-experienced hikers get up or down. The author had no trouble alone.

Just beyond the Carmel dryfall, the main dry creek bed turns west and a minor drainage enters from the northeast. Immediately after this junction turn to the right or north, and walk up the steep **talus slope** in between the 2 dry washes (If you were to continue up the main dry creek bed you would soon find a boulder-filled gorge with a small spring, and not far above that, a blocking dryfall. It was in the area of the spring the author once saw a young big horn ram). As you walk up the talus ridge, it gradually turns to the right or east. In the upper part you'll find a big horn sheep trail and the ridge turns into a **knife-edge.** For about 100 meters it'll be necessary to pay close attention and walk carefully. This is a slightly risky part; and your thoughts may be, *this damn thing could collapse at any moment!*

Above the knife-edge ridge is the broad **Dakota Sandstone bench** covered with landslide debris. The debris covers up the Dakota and Tropic Shale. Walk due east as shown on the map. On this bench you may see **stud piles** (piles of manure from wild stallions) which indicate a herd of feral or semi-wild horses in the area. As you approach the second or final cliff making the top layer of **Fiftymile Mountain**, be looking for the best route up. You will see a small seep and greenery on the left and another on the right in a slightly rounded shallow bowl. Head up slightly to the right near the southerly of the 2 seeps. You won't get water out of this one, but maybe the flow is better at the northern seep (?).

Route-find up through the cliffs. Once on top, rim-walk south. After about 500 meters you'll come to a cattle trail heading down to a small spring just under the first rim rocks. If you're careful, you can build a small mud dam to obtain drinking water just out of reach of the cows. However, this minor seep could dry up at times so don't bet your life on finding water there.

Again walk southeast from this seep and you'll come to the southern exposure of Fiftymile Mtn., a distance of about 5 kms. That place is called **Navajo Point**. This gives you a fine view of the lake and **Dangling Rope Canyon & Marina**. You can also see **Navajo Mtn.** to the east. This hike would be for the fit and adventurous hiker-climber only.

Aerial view of the upper end of **Dry Fork** of **Rock Creek** looking northeast. **Fiftymile Mountain** forms the high country across the skyline. You can hike up one of several talus slopes shown.

Map 33, Dry Rock Creek & Middle Rock Creek Canyons

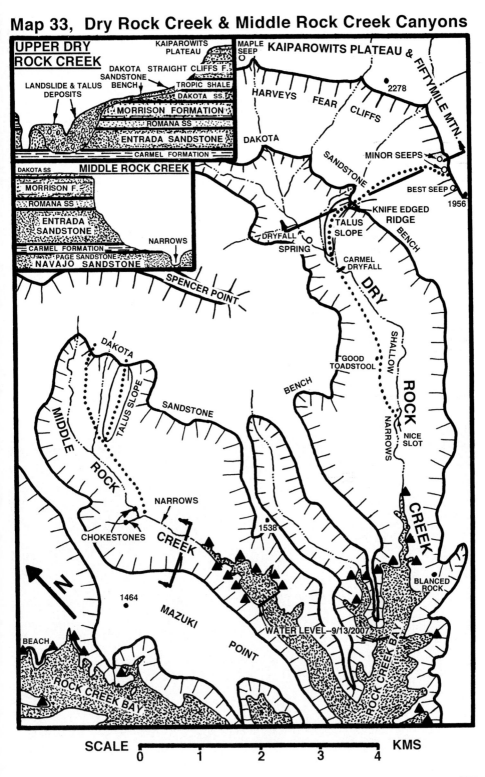

UPPER DRY ROCK CREEK

KAIPAROWITS PLATEAU

DAKOTA STRAIGHT CLIFFS F.
SANDSTONE BENCH
LANDSLIDE & TALUS DEPOSITS
TROPIC SHALE
DAKOTA SS.
MORRISON FORMATION
ROMANA SS
ENTRADA SANDSTONE
CARMEL FORMATION

MIDDLE ROCK CREEK

DAKOTA SS
MORRISON F.
ROMANA SS
ENTRADA SANDSTONE
NARROWS
CARMEL FORMATION
PAGE SANDSTONE
NAVAJO SANDSTONE

MAPLE SEEP
KAIPAROWITS PLATEAU &
FIFTYMILE MTN.
2278
HARVEYS FEAR CLIFFS
DAKOTA
SANDSTONE
MINOR SEEPS
BEST SEEP
1956
KNIFE EDGED RIDGE
TALUS SLOPE
DRYFALL
SPRING
CARMEL DRYFALL
BENCH
DRY
SPENCER POINT
SHALLOW
GOOD TOADSTOOL
ROCK
DAKOTA
TALUS SLOPE
SANDSTONE
NARROWS
NICE SLOT
BENCH
MIDDLE
ROCK
NARROWS
CHOKESTONES
CREEK
1538
CREEK
BLANCED ROCK
1464
MAZUKI
POINT
WATER LEVEL—9/13/2007
ROCK CREEK BAY
BEACH
ROCK CREEK BAY

N

SCALE
0   1   2   3   4   KMS

As you boat into the upper end of **Middle Rock Creek Inlet**, you'll find it to be of the same appearance as Dry Rock Creek. Boat into the narrow end of the drainage which again cuts into the upper part of the Page or Navajo Sandstone Formations. You will again walk up a narrow, shallow canyon. If you stay in the bottom of the drainage you can only walk about 2 kms then there may be chokestones and dryfalls in both tributaries shown. It's easy walking up to that point.

If you want to go further, regress from the junction of the 2 tributaries and climb a steep talus slope to the right, or east (there are actually several exits in the area). This gets you out of the narrow gorge. From there walk north for another 2 kms or so and get onto a big landslide or **talus slope**, as shown in the picture below (there's a 2nd but steeper route to the left of that). This big slide covers the Entrada-Morrison cliffs. The best route is up the landslide to the right where in places remnants of an old cattle trail can be seen. Above this talus slope is the bench just below the final cliffs which form the top of **Fiftymile Mountain**. With some route-finding, you may find a way to the very top but you'll have to go around Spencer Point one way or another to find a place.

Hike Length & Time Needed To walk up the shallow narrows in **Dry Rock Creek** is to walk a few minutes, or an hour or two. But to walk to the top of Fiftymile Mtn. is a long all-day hike for anyone. The author walked the route described in 7 hours round-trip. Some may need 9 or 10 hours, or more. Doing this in cool weather would help.

In **Middle Rock Creek** it'll only take an hour or so to hike up to the chokestone area in the narrows. To get on top of the **Dakota Sandstone bench** will likely take 4-5 hours for a round-trip hike; or much longer if you try to get to the top of Fiftymile.

Boots or Shoes Any shoe will be fine if you stay in the narrow canyon bottoms but to hike to the rim, especially to the top of Fiftymile, you'll want a more rugged, but light-weight, hiking boot.

Water All seeps or springs on this map are small and could dry up at times. So take all the water you'll need--which will be 3-4 liters on a hot summer day--especially if you attempt to reach the top of Fiftymile.

Main Attractions Good but shallow narrows, and some great views from the top of Plateau.

Hiking Maps USGS or BLM map Smoky Mountain (1:100,000); Mazuki Point & Navajo Point (1:24,000--7 1/2' quads) for hiking; or Cummings Mesa (1:62,500) if available.

History According to Crampton's studies of Glen Canyon in the University of Utah *Anthropological Paper #46*, there was an aboriginal route from the Colorado to Fiftymile Mtn. somewhere within the Rock Creek drainage. No mention is made as to which of the 3 forks of Rock Creek was used. But it's this author's opinion there were old Indian routes in and out of all three. In 1931, geologists Gregory & Moore stated there was a stock trail from Fiftymile Mtn. down to Wild Horse Bar at the mouth of Rock Creek on the Colorado River.

The author believes this is probably the present-day stock trail running up **Steer Canyon** to the top of the Kaiparowits not far above or north of **Woolsey Arch** in the upper end of the main **Rock Creek Canyon** (see next map). Steer Canyon is the name shown on the metric 1:100,000 scale Smoky Mountain map. Also, Leo Wilson of Escalante once told the author about a trail in Pleasant Grove Canyon, a short tributary to Steer Canyon. **Pleasant Grove and Pinto Mare Canyons** (another nearby fork) both have springs, alpine-type vegetation & trees, and Anasazi ruins. A much easier way to these places is from Escalante and the Hole-in-the-Rock Road. See the author's book, ***Non-Technical Canyon Guide to the Colorado Plateau, 5th Edition*** for more information.

Before Lake Powell, there was a trail (Indian and miners) from Rock Creek down along the Colorado to the **Ute Ford (Crossing of the Fathers)** located between Cane Creek and Gunsight Canyon.

Aerial view of the upper end of **Middle Rock Creek**. The best route up to the Dakota Sandstone bench/Morrison Formation cliff is via the talus slope in the upper middle part of this foto.

Above Toilet & dump/sump station located at the mouth of **Rock Creek Bay**.

Left The *good toadstool* in **Dry Rock Creek Canyon**, as shown on the map.

Rock Creek & Steer Canyon, and the Woolsey Arch Hike

Location & Campsites The inlet shown on this map is the upper end of the main **Rock Creek Bay**. At the mouth of this bay should be a buoy marked M35 (K56). This means it's 35 miles (56 kilometers) uplake from the Glen Canyon Dam. At the mouth of the bay is a **toilet & dump/pump station**.

As you boat up the bay, you'll find Entrada Sandstone walls rising abruptly out of the water with few campsites, although there are many places to tie-down a houseboat. But as you near the upper end the rocks are uplifted to the north and northeast exposing several sandy beaches. These beaches are on the bench-forming Carmel Formation. Above the Carmel is the Entrada which contributes some of the sand. In times of high lake levels, as you enter the very end of the inlet it becomes narrow and you begin to see the top of the Page/Navajo Sandstone. These formations are exposed in the middle of this large bowl or valley above the water line.

Hiking Routes or Trails Featured here is a hike to **Woolsey Arch**. You could walk up this valley inside the shallow narrows of the dry creek bed, but you can also get out of the drainage to the left or west side, and walk along a **feed-to-water cattle trail**; this is what cows use to get from pastures in the upper basin, down to the lake for water (this is only during the winter season).

Regardless of the lake level, you'll find a small stream seeping out at the sandstone walls, especially when the level is falling. This wet section extends up from the lake about 500m or so. Above that, the canyon is dry. The dry creek bed of **Rock Creek** is shallow and narrow. On average it's only about 10-15 meters deep and there are a number of places you can exit. After about 8 kms of easy walking, you'll come to a minor dryfall made of a conglomerate member of the Carmel Formation. You can by-pass this ledge easily on either side.

Immediately above the dryfall, look to the right or east and you'll see some disturbed ground. Climb a 10-meter-high slope and you'll see a small dam. Then walk north 100 meters to see a 3-meter-high metal pole in the middle of a clearing. This is an **old drill site** which has been capped. The dam was built to handle anything which may have escaped the well.

About 500m northeast of the capped well, **Woolsey Arch** can be seen in an exposed bluff of Entrada Sandstone. It's one of the more interesting arches around. Underneath it is one cowboy etching reading **Burnham Bridge, 7/30/27**. It appears to be genuine and is perhaps the original name for this arch (?). About 250m north of the arch, is a cave in another slickrock bluff. There are moki steps up to the cave, and all kinds of flint chips below. The author found 3 broken arrowheads in front of the cave.

The road leading to the capped well starts at Big Water, which is west of Wahweap near mile post 7 on Highway 89. This is generally called the **Warm Creek Road**. It makes its way across Warm Creek, north of Last Chance Bay, and across **Little Valley Canyon**. From there it heads east to where you see it on this map. It then turns north to the base of Fiftymile Mountain, then south to end at Woolsey Arch. It's no longer usable by vehicles beyond Little Valley Canyon.

Here's a hike the author did on his second trip. From Woolsey Arch, walk north along the abandoned road. At first it drops down into the drainage then you'll pass a corral and a place or two with tamaracks and maybe a little water. Then the road climbs up on the east side of the drainage and heads towards a big talus slope covering the cliffs ahead. It zig zags up a ways then turns west at the same level as **Grand Bench**. Then it heads south toward the **Grand Bench Neck** as shown on this map.

This short, colorful slot is located less than 1 km below **Woolsey Arch** and in a little side-canyon on the west side of the main **Rock Creek** drainage.

Map 34, Rock Creek and Woolsey Arch Hike

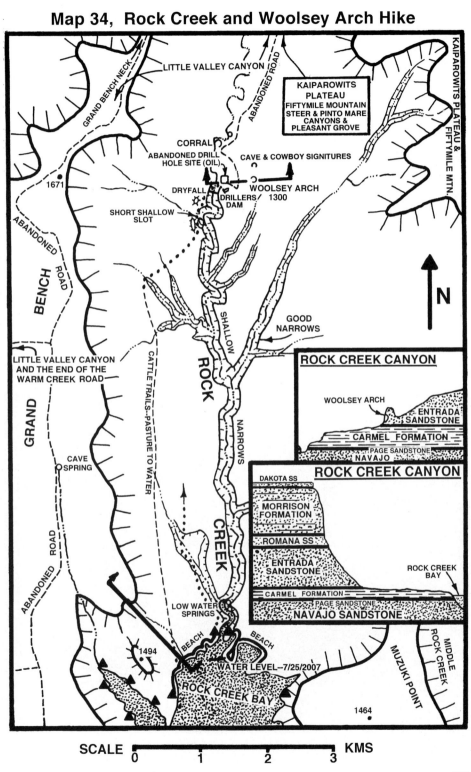

SCALE

0   1   2   3   KMS

From where the old road turns west at the top of the talus slope, you'll see a canyon coming down from the top of Fiftymile Mtn. If you're energetic you can walk due north into what *USGS topo maps* calls **Steer Canyon**. There's the remains of an old **cattle trail** up this short steep drainage (with good springs at the bottom) and into **Pleasant Grove Canyon** (nearby is **Pinto Mare Canyon**) where there's good water and a number of Indian ruins. Not far away is the head of Lake Canyon and small lake and a cabin. See that part in the author's book, *Non-Technical Canyon Hiking Guide to the Colorado Plateau, 5th Edition.*

Hike Length & Time Needed From the HWM to Woolsey Arch is about 8 kms. The author has done this in 4 & 5 2/3 hours round-trip; you may want 5 to 7 hours. If you try the hike up to and through Steer Canyon to the top of Fiftymile, you'll very likely need 2 days with a camp somewhere near the lower springs mentioned above. Really strong hikers might be able to hike from the lake, to the top and back in one very long day, but only in cooler weather. Spring would be the best time to do this long hike.

Boots or Shoes Any dry weather boots or shoes.

Water In the main Rock Creek Inlet, there is normally running water just above the lake level as you find it, but beware of it as there may be cattle in the area in winter. There are several minor springs near Woolsey Arch but they're alkali. And there's good water from springs at the entrance to Steer Canyon.

Main Attractions A long narrow shallow slot canyon, soaring cliffs, Woolsey Arch, and the possibility of reaching the top of Fiftymile Mtn.

Hiking Maps USGS or BLM map Smoky Mountain (1:100,000); Mazuki Point & Blackburn Canyon (1:24,000--7 1/2' quads) for hiking; or Cummings Mesa (1:62,500) if available.

Looking southwest into **Rock Creek** valley from just above **Woolsey Arch**. Behind where the author is standing is a cave on a southwest-facing outcrop that was once a campsite for either Anasazi or Fremont Indians. At that site are many flint chips and lots of charcoal-colored earth.

This etching or signiture is found on the bottom of **Woolsey Arch**. This seems to indicate the original name of this feature. It's not a bridge, because there was never a stream running under it.

From the air looking southwest: far upper left is **Navajo Power Plant & Tower Butte**; just above the middle and to the left a little are **Dominguez & Boundary Buttes**; just left of center is the very prominant **Gregory Butte** (with shadows); and **Last Chance Bay** coming in from the right. The plane was just about over **Friendship Cove** when this foto was taken.

West and Sand Canyons

Location & Campsites These 2 canyons are located on the south side of the lake, and southeast of **Last Chance Bay**, one of the largest open bodies of water on the reservoir. Most of the buoys in this part of the lake have letters instead of numbers. However, one buoy about halfway between the mouths of Face and West Canyons is numbered M24 (K38).

The Utah-Arizona state line cuts across the area about mid-way along **West Canyon Inlet** (during times of high water). When the lake waters are high, this part of the lake will have many sandy camp-sites available. The reason is, the northern parts have the bench-forming rocks of the Carmel Forma-tion exposed along the shoreline. As you head up West Canyon Inlet, the beds will be seen slowly rising from the water and the Page/Navajo Sandstone beds, which underlie the Carmel, will be exposed. This means sheer walls rising abruptly out of the water, with fewer and smaller campsites available.

Hiking Routes or Trails West Canyon offers the most exciting hike in this book. There's a short walk to some good narrows, as well as a longer hike into one of the best slot canyons on the Colorado Plateau. From the end of the inlet, regardless of lake levels, you walk up a very sandy canyon bottom with a small year-round flowing stream. It's so sandy many boaters hike this lower end in bare feet.

As you near the HWM, you'll enter the first slot. In this short section, you may see a log jammed in the walls above. Not far above this you come to a very narrow crack with a group of interconnected pot-holes filled with water year-round. This 40-meter-long **swimming pool** is the source of the water you walked in to arrive at that point. It's always shaded and the water cold, even on hot summer days. You may have to swim through this part depending on whether the previous flood deposited sand or scoured out the potholes. In 7/2007, it was a swimmer.

If you intend to backpack above this swimming pool you'll have to figure out a way to keep your im-portant things safe & dry. Any kind of float device should do, but the best way is to stuff everything into **waterproof drybags** (the kind river runners use), then put those inside your pack and swim through with your pack on, or push it in front of you. An air mattress would also work, but there may be other swim-mers upcanyon, so drybagging is recommended. Most boaters however just swim through this first swimming hole without taking anything with them and return after a short hike.

If you prefer not to swim, you can still get into the canyon above by using a **bypass route**. Regress from the swimming pool about 300 meters and on your left or south will be an embankment with reeds. Make your way up into a very small short drainage, then veer to the right or west and walk up slickrock in a west and northwest direction. There is now a visible trail or stone cairns marking the way. You will soon cross a short drainage with cottonwood trees in an alcove on your left, then walk more slickrock to reach the rim. From the rim follow more cairns in a south, southwest direction toward a cone-shaped rock in the distance and to a point about 2 short bends in the canyon above the swimming pool. At that point you'll see a steep talus-filled ravine heading down to the canyon bottom. Route-find down this and back into West Canyon.

About halfway between the swimming pool and where you reenter the canyon using the bypass route, is a short side-canyon. The author is calling this the **Lower East Fork** on this map. This is a good slot with convoluted potholes and several chokestones you can chimney over. After 400 meters or so you'll come to a dryfall which you can't climb. Adventurous hikers will one day climb around and come

When hiking up **West Canyon**, this is the first narrows you come to in the **Lower Slot**. Sometimes the potholes are filled with sand, other times you have to wade through or around the deep places.

Map 35, West Canyon

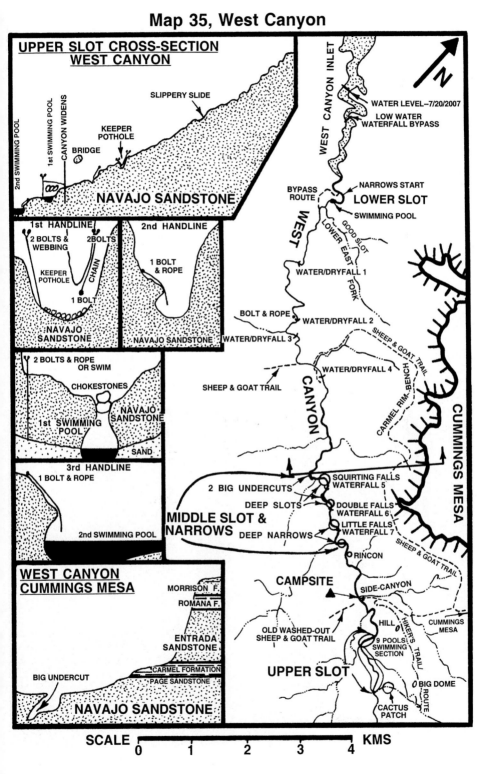

UPPER SLOT CROSS-SECTION
WEST CANYON

SLIPPERY SLIDE

2nd SWIMMING POOL

1st SWIMMING POOL

CANYON WIDENS

KEEPER POTHOLE

BRIDGE

NAVAJO SANDSTONE

1st HANDLINE
2 BOLTS & WEBBING

2 BOLTS

CHAIN

KEEPER POTHOLE

1 BOLT

NAVAJO SANDSTONE

2nd HANDLINE
1 BOLT & ROPE

NAVAJO SANDSTONE

2 BOLTS & ROPE OR SWIM

CHOKESTONES

NAVAJO SANDSTONE

1st SWIMMING POOL

SAND

3rd HANDLINE
1 BOLT & ROPE

2nd SWIMMING POOL

WEST CANYON
CUMMINGS MESA

MORRISON F.

ROMANA F.

ENTRADA SANDSTONE

BIG UNDERCUT

CARMEL FORMATION

PAGE SANDSTONE

NAVAJO SANDSTONE

WEST CANYON INLET

WATER LEVEL–7/20/2007

LOW WATER WATERFALL BYPASS

BYPASS ROUTE

NARROWS START

LOWER SLOT

SWIMMING POOL

WEST

GOOD SLOT

LOWER EAST FORK

WATER/DRYFALL 1

BOLT & ROPE

WATER/DRYFALL 2

WATER/DRYFALL 3

WATER/DRYFALL 4

SHEEP & GOAT TRAIL

CANYON

CARMEL RIM-BENCH

SHEEP & GOAT TRAIL

CUMMINGS MESA

2 BIG UNDERCUTS

DEEP SLOTS

MIDDLE SLOT &
NARROWS

DEEP NARROWS

SQUIRTING FALLS
WATERFALL 5

DOUBLE FALLS
WATERFALL 6

LITTLE FALLS
WATERFALL 7

SHEEP & GOAT TRAIL

RINCON

CAMPSITE

SIDE-CANYON

OLD WASHED-OUT
SHEEP & GOAT TRAIL

HILL

CUMMINGS MESA

9 POOLS
SWIMMING SECTION

HIKER'S TRAIL

BIG DOME

ROUTE

UPPER SLOT

CACTUS PATCH

SCALE | 0 | 1 | 2 | 3 | 4 | KMS

down this canyon using bolts & ropes.

Upcanyon from the **bypass route**, it's usually dry for several kms, then you may find some seeps or even flowing water. In the 5 kms above the swimming pool, you'll pass **3 nice water/dryfalls** (usually dryfalls), the **1st** of which you may want to retreat from, and climb up on a west-side bench to get around it. Just below the **2nd falls** someone has installed a bolt above and left a knotted rope hanging down, so look for this handline. Walk left to bypass the **3rd falls**. Above the 3 water/dryfalls, the canyon opens up some and turns east. This is where a **Navajo log hogan** used to be located before floods in 1998 or '99 took away the bench it sat on. There you'll find a **sheep & goat trail** zig zagging up to the rim to the west. Not far above this is **another old trail** running up a narrow side-canyon to the north, then east. After that is the **4th falls** (bypass on bench to the south), then the canyon narrows and gets deeper.

In the next 2 kms will be moderately good narrows, then comes the **Middle Slot & Narrows**, maybe the best part of West Canyon. In this **2 km section** you'll find **2 overhangs or undercuts** as big as any around, **3 more waterfalls (Squirting, Double and Short Falls)**, **2 very deep, dark & fotogenic slots or narrows** with either deep wading or swimming. In 2007, there were several short pools to swim.

Above the **Middle Slot & Narrows** is another area where the canyon opens up a little with trees and several benches which can be used as campsites, plus a washed-out **sheep & goat trail** coming down from the west rim (it's hard to see from the bottom). You can also climb up a minor drainage and hiker's trail heading northeast and exit to the east-side rim (if backpacking, make **camp** on a bench at the bottom end of this **side-canyon**). A climb for the **adventurous hiker** would be to head for the sheep & goat trail on the south end of **Cummings Mesa**. See the **Area Map 35A**, page 241. Once on the mesa top you could head down another trail into **Aztec Creek/Forbidding Canyon** and eventually reach the south side of Navajo Mtn. Or you can walk north and drop down into upper **Wetherill Canyon** (or upper **Mountain Sheep Canyon** with no trail, just a route up or down), or head northwest and walk down another trail into **Dungeon Canyon**.

If you stay in West Canyon, you'll soon come to more narrows, and a little further up you'll have to do some swimming through 8 very cold pools. It's this part of the canyon which will stop hikers from going further. The only way to get through this upper slot is to exit to the east as shown on **Maps 35 & 35A**, then walk about 1 km upcanyon on the east side. From that upper drainage, you'll head east & southeast, then curl to the south and head southwest across a **cactus patch** and enter the **Upper Slot**. This last part is now a hiker-made trail-of-sorts partly marked with stone cairns. To do this section, you'll need a good topo map & compass.

Upper Slot To do this part successfully, you'll need at least **one 15 meter rope, 1 headlamp each, at least 2 people, and knee & elbow pads**. Also, a **wetsuit**--even in hot summer weather these help a lot! Once in the slot, you'll be climbing in & out of potholes, sometimes sliding and relaying packs. After 20 minutes, is a steep groove called the **Slippery Slide**. Use your headlamp there. After another 20 minutes (?), will be a **4 meter drop** with **2 bolts** above on the left with attached webbing with knots. Handline down this into a **keeper pothole**. There you'll find **2 bolts** high on the right with a chain hanging down. The end of the chain is attached to another **bolt** near the bottom so floods can't flush it out or out of reach to hikers. If that lower bolt (and chain) is gone, you'll have to help each other out!

Not far below the keeper pothole is a **bolt** on the left with a short rope which you can use to get over a short drop (we helped each other down this on our first trip). More potholes, downclimbing and maybe helping each other over drops. Then a wider, very deep narrows, pass under a bridge, then the canyon

On the **West Canyon** map this is called the **Swimming Pool** in the **Lower Slot**. Sometimes after a small flood, sand is deposited and it's a deep wade; but most of the time it's a swim.

opens some. There you can either: **rappel** from **2 bolts** on the far right; handline down from a round boulder in the middle; or put on your wetsuits and downclimb into a slot & swimming pool below some chokestones. Best to start swimming there; which makes 9 swimming pools in the Upper Slot.

Just below this 1st pool, is a 3 meter slide & drop into another swimmer. As of 7/21/2007, there was 1 bolt with a short rope attached; you can either downclimb, then slide with a splash, or handline down and keep your hair dry. This is the beginning of running water and for the next 150 meters or so, you'll swim through another 7 pools. After that, the canyon opens up and you may see the sun. Below that is another easy slot section, then trees and your campsite on the right.

It's recommended you do this in 2 days. Start at Antelope Point Marina in the morning, boat through the inlet and walk up to the campsite. On Day 2, hike up & around and down the Upper Slot. That afternoon, boat back to Antelope arriving in the early evening.

Sand Canyon is very wide-open with nothing of interest in the first several kms. The author observed the upper parts from the air a time or two and saw nothing really good (but a long ways up, there were a couple of short slots that could be interesting).

Hike Length & Time Needed The walk up **West Canyon** to the swimming pool is about 500 meters above the HWM. You can do this in about an hour or less, depending on lake levels. Or you can spend an entire day, or 2 days in the upper drainage. On one of the author's trips, he had 3 people. They boated up the inlet in the evening and camped. Next day it took 5 hours with big packs to reach the campsite. The next day it took about 8 hours to hike up and around and down the Upper Slot then back to the boat. That evening they were at Wahweap. It will take 2 full days from Antelope Point Marina with an average boat, and average hikers.

Boots or Shoes Take wading shoes in West Canyon.

Water You should be able to get a safe drink at the upper end of the swimming hole in the lower West Canyon. All the water in upper West Canyon should be good, unless Navajo sheep & goats are grazing there at the time--which is very unlikely. Running water in the upper slot should be safe to drink.

Main Attractions West Canyon is the best all-around canyon on the Colorado Plateau.

Hiking Maps USGS or BLM maps Smoky Mountain & Glen Canyon Dam (1:100,000); West Canyon Creek (1:24,000--7 1/2' quad) for hiking; or Cummings Mesa & Navajo Creek (1:62,500) if available.

The first of 2 really big & deep undercuts in **West Canyon's Middle Slot & Narrows**. Both undercuts are overhanging the creek by nearly 100 meters, and both are cut out of Navajo Sandstone about 100 meters deep.

Near the end of the **Upper Slot** of **West Canyon**, is a pool & dropoff. To get over it, you can rappel or handline down on the left-- see the rope hanging down? (if coming down-canyon it's on a bench to your right). Or you can handline or jump from the small boulders in the middle. Or you can down-climb into a shallow pool from above, then swim out as we did.

This is **Waterfall 5**, or the **Squirting Falls**. The easiest way up is to climb right up the middle of the waterfall. This fotogenic cascade is in between the 2 biggest & deepest undercuts in the **Middle Slot & Narrows** of **West Canyon**.

This picture shows one of
2 deep narrows in the
Middle Slot & Narrows
of **West Canyon**. They
don't quite qualify as
slots, but they're very
deep & scenic.

On the **Upper Slot
Cross-Section**, this is
called the **Slippery
Slide**. It's about a 5-
meter drop and almost
vertical, but it's easy to
slide down because the
groove is just the width of
the average person's
rear end. It's best for
each person to have a
headlamp here so you
can see what you're
landing on--either a large
cobblestone, or a snake!
This picture was taken
with a flash because it
was so dark.

As you hike up **West Canyon**, this is part of the 2nd of 2 deep narrows you pass in the **Middle Slot & Narrows** section. Not far above this area is a good campsite on the left, which is at the beginning of the side-canyon & trail you use to reach the **Upper Slot**.

Area Map 35A, Sheep & Goat Trails up to
Cummings Mesa from Nearby Canyons

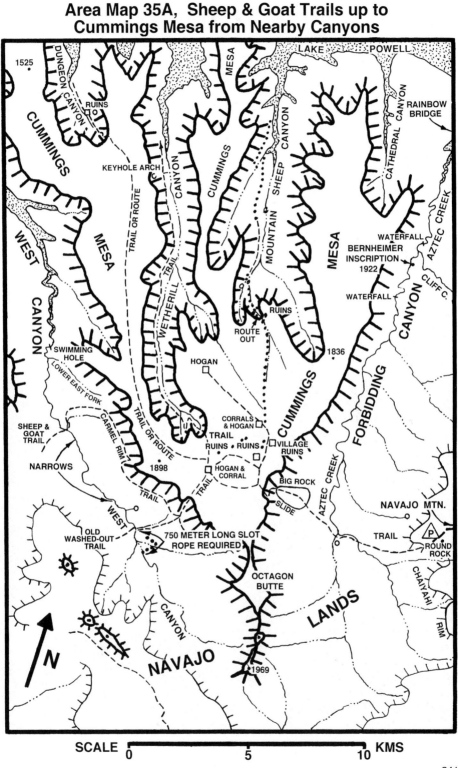

SCALE 0   5   10 KMS

Face and Labyrinth Canyons

Location & Campsites Face and Labyrinth slot canyons are located just west of **West Canyon**, on the south side of the lake, and immediately south of **Padre Bay**. The lower or northern ends of each inlet generally have a lot of campsites, whether the lake level is high or low. Near the mouth of Face Canyon is another **toilet & dump/pump station**.

Hiking Routes or Trails In times of high lake levels, there's not much to see in **Face Canyon**. If the lake ever gets back to or near the HWM, you may find an old trail on the west side just north of a fork in the upper-most inlet. There you'll see an **old stock trail** running up and out of the shallow canyon bottom. Someone chopped or drilled holes in the slickrock, then placed oblong stones in the holes, and finally more stones and sand were placed on those. In other places steps were cut in the slickrock. The trail is only visible for about 30-40 meters then it disappears in the nearly flat sandy and slickrock bench.

However, the **best part** of Face Canyon isn't exposed until the lake gets **below 1100 meters (3608')**. This was the situation in the early 2000's. At that level, you'll boat into a shallow narrow channel. You may have to wade and pull your boat in a ways. From there, and on **7/25/2007-WL1099.74m/3608.56'**, you only had to walk 300 meters or so until you were in a **sculptured slot** very much like **Antelope Canyon** just east of Page. On that day, the author had to wade into the slot, then swim a little, but a big flood will remove the sandy dam and drain the water. See fotos. In the upper end, you may have to do a little climbing, so take knee & elbow pads if you have them. Observe the colors in the foto.

On the author's first trip to **Labyrinth Canyon** in 1988, he went into a side-drainage and found nothing to write about. After that, someone wrote and corrected his silly mistake. In 4/2001 & 7/2007, he got into the right fork and found one of the best slots on the lake.

Immediately **above the HWM,** you'll come to an open area where you can climb out of the canyon on the east side. Staying in the canyon bottom, you'll walk through 500 meters of **convoluted slot**, then a deep pool that one person may not get out of if conditions are right (or wrong)! You might climb out to the west at that point, but it's steep. Or regress and exit to the east near the HWM and walk south along the east side to see several short sections of shallow, but tight narrows above. Some good parts extent to just northeast of **Pinnacle Rock**.

However, the **very best slot** in **Labyrinth** is exposed when the the the **lake level is below about 1100 meters (3608')**. On **7/22/2007-WL1099.90m/3608.56'**, the author boated into the moderately narrow channel and pulled his boat in a little, then walked for 5 minutes. He found an even better slot than what you find above the HWM. This sculptured or **corkscrew slot** has colors equal to Antelope Canyon. Be there when the sun shines down into parts of the slot, but not right in your picture. That way, with lots of light bouncing around, the colors really come out.

Hike Length & Time Needed The best parts of both canyon slots are just a few minutes from your boat. Ask someone at a marina what the lake lever is; that will give an indication of how far you'll have to walk, and if the best slots will be above water when you arrive.

Boots or Shoes Any kind will do, but better have waders.

Water Take your own water from a culinary source.

Hiking Maps USGS or BLM map Glen Canyon Dam (1:000,000); or Face Canyon & Wild Horse Mesa

This was the upper end of the inlet to **Labyrinth Canyon** on **7/22/2007-WL1099.90m/3608.56'**. Not far above this narrow boating section was the 1st of 2 really nice fotogenic slots.

Map 36, Face and Labyrinth Canyons

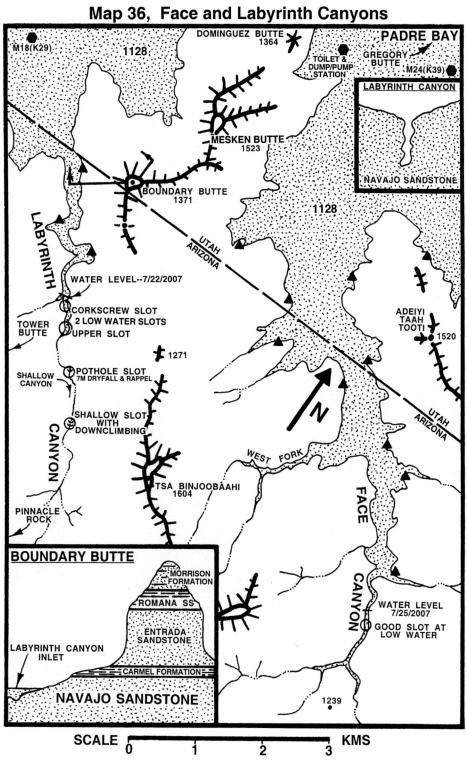

DOMINGUEZ BUTTE
1364

PADRE BAY

M18(K29)

1128

TOILET &
DUMP/PUMP
STATION

GREGORY
BUTTE
M24(K39)

LABYRINTH CANYON

NAVAJO SANDSTONE

MESKEN BUTTE
1523

BOUNDARY BUTTE
1371

1128

LABYRINTH

UTAH
ARIZONA

WATER LEVEL--7/22/2007

CORKSCREW SLOT
2 LOW WATER SLOTS
UPPER SLOT

TOWER
BUTTE

ADEIYI
TAAH
TOOTI
1520

1271

SHALLOW
CANYON

POTHOLE SLOT
7M DRYFALL & RAPPEL

SHALLOW SLOT
WITH
DOWNCLIMBING

CANYON

N

PINNACLE
ROCK

TSA BINJOOBÁAHI
1604

WEST FORK

UTAH
ARIZONA

FACE

BOUNDARY BUTTE

MORRISON
FORMATION

ROMANA SS

CANYON

WATER LEVEL
7/25/2007
GOOD SLOT AT
LOW WATER

ENTRADA
SANDSTONE

LABYRINTH CANYON
INLET

CARMEL FORMATION

NAVAJO SANDSTONE

1239

SCALE   0   1   2   3   KMS

243

(1;24,000--7 1/2' quads) for hiking.

History During the Glen Canyon Gold Rush days which lasted from about 1884 until 1900, there was considerable activity along the river in this section. Most of the action was north of the San Juan River, but there were a number of gravel bars prospected in this lower half of Glen Canyon as well. One of those places was **Mesken Bar** located 2-3 kms upstream from **Face Canyon** on the south side of the river.

Crampton states the bar was named after a German prospector and trapper from Denver, Colorado named Edward Mesken. He located a placer claim there on September 18, 1889. Mesken was one of the earliest prospectors to work the lower Glen Canyon. He stayed there for many years. He would travel up & down the canyon in a small boat, accompanied by a dog, while trapping and prospecting. Apparently he made this bar his home but no one mentions anything about any house or cabin.

The last claim locations were filed in 1932 during the Great Depression. Just before Lake Powell came to be, Crampton reported many signs of mining activity on the bar, including sorting screens, a shaking machine, a wheelbarrow and camp debris. There were signs of horses grazing there and a trail from the head of the bar up to the bench above and evidently on up to the canyon rim to the south.

A small part of the **Upper Slot** in **Labyrinth Canyon**. Lots of colors and erosional features in this section of the slot.

This is part of what's labeled **Upper Slot** on the map and in **Labyrinth Canyon**. The embedded pebbles in these wall are similar to xenocrysts, but they're in sandstone, not igneous (volcanic) rock.

244

Labyrinth Canyon. This is what's labeled **Corkscrew Slot** on the map.   This was less than 500 meters from the author's boat on **7/22/2007-WL1099.90m/3608.56'**, so it's easy to walk.

This is what the **Face Canyon Slot** looked like on **7/25/2007-WL1099.74m/3608.56'**. This was only a day after a flood, and the lake was only about 300 meters away, so it will surely be dry when you arrive--if the drought continues, and the lake level stays low.

This is commonly called **Boundary Butte** (looking south from Padre Bay) but on USGS quads or maps at 7 1/2' or 1:24,000 scale, it's labeled **Mesken Butte** (the higher flat part), after the old German miner who lived nearby.

Part of the slot in **Face Canyon** on **7/25/2007-WL1099.74m/3608.56'**. Don't worry, the next big flood after that day would have removed the sand dam at the bottom of the slot. So it should be dry when you arrive--if the lake levels remain low as they were in 2007.

Last Chance, Croton, Little Valley & Friendship Cove Canyons and Last Chance Bay

Location & Campsites The 3 short canyons on this map are all at the upper or northern end of **Last Chance Bay**. Last Chance Bay is located between **Padre Bay** and **Dangling Rope Marina**. Buoy number M23 (K37) is found near the mouth, as is the unmistakable **Gregory Butte**. Last Chance is one of the longest and largest bays or inlets on Lake Powell. **Friendship Cove**, located due east of Last Chance Bay, is not on this map but is discussed below.

There are not many campsites in Last Chance Bay. The reason is, in the lower or southern end of the inlet, the Entrada Sandstone walls rise abruptly from the water and there are simply no beaches or talus slopes around. However, if you like to tie-up on slickrock there's lots of that. But as you head up the bay, the geologic strata are gradually dipping to the north and the walls aren't as high. At a point about 2/3's the way up the bay, things change and the top of the Entrada is right at the shoreline. This is also where the Romana Sandstone is exposed. At that point a minor bench is formed thus some campsites might be found, at least when lake levels are high. Most of the campsites in Last Chance Bay, and when lake levels are high, are found in the **Twitchell Canyon Inlet** as shown on the map. South of this section of the lake there are very few places to pitch a tent.

The author once drove his VW Rabbit from Big Water on Highway 89 up along the Warm Creek Road. It's a good road especially in the beginning, but the further you go, the rougher it gets. Most cars driven with care, can make it to **Croton Canyon** crossing, but the last part of the road to the corral at the rim of **Little Valley Canyon,** is for high clearance vehicles only.

Hiking Routes or Trails Probably the most interesting place on this map for hikers (in all honesty this area is not a very interesting place to hike!) is **Little Valley Canyon**. It begins on the western slopes of the Kaiparowits Plateau and drains into the upper right-hand fork of Last Chance Bay. There should always be some kind of campsite at the upper end of the inlet regardless of lake levels.

As you start upcanyon you're going to find lots of tamaracks so stay in the dry wash bottom until you're above the HWM. As you walk along, all the rocks visible in the walls will be part of the Morrison Formation. It's a rather confined canyon in the lower end, but higher up, it opens into the broad Little Valley. In the lower end are several small seeps or springs. The one furthest upcanyon will be the best to get a safe drink from (?). The canyon is grazed by cattle beginning in October, then they're taken out by June 15 each year and put onto summer range.

About 5 kms upcanyon from the HWM you'll come to an old abandoned road. This used to be an extension of the **Warm Creek Road** which begins at Big Water on Highway 89 west of Wahweap (very near mile post 7). It's usable up to the corral on the west side of the canyon, then it's been blocked off and the rest now serves as a cow trail. This is the same road you see dead-ending at the **drill hole site** next to **Woolsey Arch** near the head of **Rock Creek** (see Map 34). It was built and used by an oil company in about 1960, and again in 1973 when the drill hole site mentioned above was used. You can use this road to get out of the canyon bottom on either side.

Last Chance Bay from the air looking northwest toward the high ground known as the **Kaiparowits Plateau**. This is a long bay with few sandy beaches, but lots of places to tie-down a houseboat. Throughout this part of the lake, the rock at the shoreline is the Entrada Sandstone.

Map 37, Last Chance Creek, Croton & Little Valley Canyons

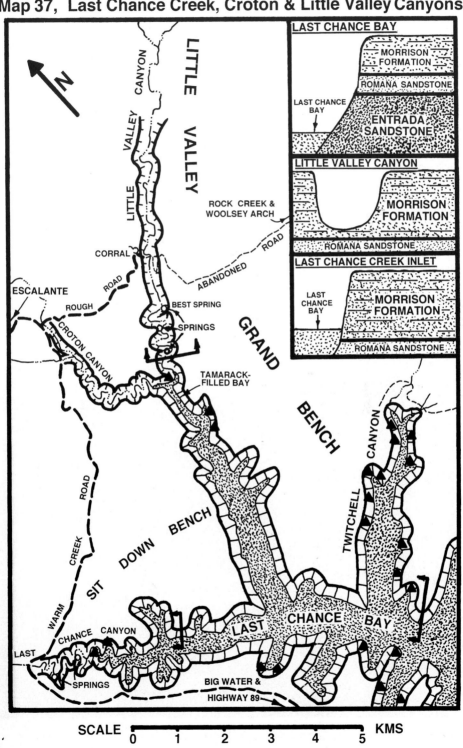

LAST CHANCE BAY

MORRISON FORMATION

ROMANA SANDSTONE

LAST CHANCE BAY

ENTRADA SANDSTONE

LITTLE VALLEY CANYON

MORRISON FORMATION

ROMANA SANDSTONE

LAST CHANCE CREEK INLET

LAST CHANCE BAY

MORRISON FORMATION

ROMANA SANDSTONE

LITTLE VALLEY CANYON

LITTLE VALLEY

VALLEY

LITTLE

ROCK CREEK & WOOLSEY ARCH

CORRAL

ROAD

ABANDONED

ROAD

ESCALANTE

ROUGH

ROAD

CROTON CANYON

BEST SPRING

SPRINGS

GRAND

TAMARACK-FILLED BAY

BENCH

TWITCHELL CANYON

ROAD

CREEK

WARM

SIT DOWN BENCH

CHANCE CANYON

LAST CHANCE BAY

LAST

SPRINGS

BIG WATER & HIGHWAY 89

SCALE 0 1 2 3 4 5 KMS

249

Where you begin hiking up Little Valley Canyon, you can also hike up another drainage to the north called **Croton Canyon**. The author went halfway up to the road but turned back because it's not interesting at all.

The last hike included here is up from the end of the inlet in **Last Chance Canyon**. This is the shortest hike of the 3 (when the lake has high water levels) and is in the same geologic formations so it looks the same. There should always be some kind of campsite at the end of navigation in the inlet. As you walk upcanyon there may be running water part of the time in the main drainage. Part of this stream comes from a side-canyon. If you head up this short drainage there will be a short jump-up or ledge which keeps cows out. Above the little waterfall, the water looked safe to drink.

Continuing upcanyon the walls become lower and lower until they become a low bench. After about 3 kms of walking (above the HWM) you'll come to the **Warm Creek Road**. At that point you'll be in a wide open valley. You can continue up this very long drainage to the northwest but it doesn't look interesting for hikers. Further upcanyon there must be more running water because the author saw several pieces of wood in the lower canyon which had been cut by beaver for dam construction.

Hike Length & Time Needed It's about 5 kms to the old road in Little Valley Canyon, and a round-trip hike there will take 3-4 hours (more when lake levels are low). It's about the same distance to the road up Croton Canyon, but may take a little less time. There's only about 3 kms of walking up Last Chance Creek or Canyon to the Warm Creek Road which will take only a couple of hours round-trip.

Boots or Shoes While there's some water in each canyon there will be no wading, so any kind of boots or shoes will be OK.

Water From the highest spring in Little Valley Canyon, or from the side-canyon along Last Chance Creek. Be careful though, there are cattle in the area from October 1 until June 15 each year.

Main Attraction Short hikes in unknown canyons and solitude.

Hiking Maps USGS or BLM map Smoky Mountain (1:100,000); Sit Down Bench (1:24,000--7 1/2' quad) for hiking; or Gunsight Butte (1:62,500) if available.

Other Nearby Canyons In between the inlets of Rock Creek and Last Chance is another minor drainage called **Friendship Cove**. This is a rather short and open bay with slickrock walls of the Entrada Sandstone rising out of the water. However, the author plotted 5 campsites on his map of the bay, the best of which are at the very end. On **7/25/2007-WL1099.74m/3608.04'**, there were lots of boats and campers in this bay. This is a box-type canyon with no exit at the upper end, nor is there any long drainage associated with the canyon. There's no hiking opportunities either.

The west side of **Gregory Butte** from the air looking north, northeast toward **Fiftymile Mountain** in the upper left background. On **10/7/2007-WL1097.80m/3601.52'**, there were several nice sandy beach campsites on the west side.

Machine for shaking gold-bearing gravels in the mining operation at **Mesken Bar** before it was inundated by Lake Powell (Crampton foto).

From the air looking south, southwest at: **Pinnacle Rock**, far left; **Leche-e Rock** far away just left of center; **Tower Butte**, background near center right; nearest is **Dominguez Butte**; and behind that is **Mesken Butte** (big flat top center) hiding **Boundary Butte** just beyond.

Gunsight Canyon, and Padre Bay & Crossing of the Fathers

Location & Campsites **Gunsight Canyon** drains from the north into what is known today as **Padre Bay**. Padre Bay is located about halfway between **Wahweap and Dangling Rope Marinas**. The buoy closest to Gunsight Canyon in the main channel is numbered M19 (K29). Gunsight Canyon is the most westerly of 5 canyons or inlets on the northern side of Padre Bay, perhaps the largest body of water on the lake. For a better look at the area, see **Map 38A** titled, **Padre Bay and Crossing of the Fathers**, page 255.

The inlet to Gunsight Canyon has some very fine campsites--unless they're overgrown with tamaracks! There is one beach about 200-300 meters long, plus several other smaller sites. The number of sites will depend on the level of the lake. The shoreline formation at the HWM is the Entrada Sandstone. In the upper end of Gunsight Bay it forms a low bench, thus the many sandy beaches. Further out in Padre Bay, the Carmel Formation is exposed with even more sandy beaches. On each of the author's visits, it was a very busy, noisy and popular place for camping, water skiing and use of PWC.

Hiking Routes or Trails As you enter the upper part of **Gunsight Canyon Inlet** it will become moderately narrow. As you hike upcanyon the walking is easy--but when the lake level is low, stay right in the dry stream channel to avoid tamaracks. Above the HWM, there is no running water; thus no willows, brush or trees. Nor are there any boulders or other obstructions to speak of. After 5-6 kms of easy walking, the walls begin to close in and the canyon becomes more confined. At about that point, you'll come to 3 minor dryfalls in a distance of about 50 meters. The author had no trouble climbing up these on the left side (but for some it might be best to take a short rope to help less-experienced hikers up). From the top of the 3-tiered dryfall, walk another 300 meters or so to where the canyon forks; then straight ahead 150 meters to the northeast is Gunsight Spring under a dryfall.

Gunsight Spring is a tiny green **hanging garden** in the middle of the desert. This spring has been cemented-up at the bottom of a dripping wall to form a drinking trough for cattle, but it appears cattle haven't been there for years. The water is clear & cool and should be safe to drink. Nearby is an old metal tank that hasn't been used recently either. This is a fine place to cool off in the shade.

If you head back downcanyon from the spring about 250 meters, and look to the right or northwest, you'll see faintly visible, the beginning of an old **cattle trail** marked with stone cairns. It runs along a bench at the same elevation as Gunsight Spring. This trail is man-made and under one ledge are 2 shovels left behind by some rancher. This trail runs for about 1 km on the same bench and finally goes around a bend to the right or west. Then it heads out a shallow drainage to the mesa top called **Alstrom Point**, and to an old road near the head of the canyon. From that point it's 34 kms (21.1 miles), mostly along the Warm Creek Road, to Big Water, Utah on Highway 89. Cars can make it to this trailhead.

Hike Length & Time Needed From the HWM to Gunsight Spring is about 6-7 kms. The old cattle trail is about 1 1/2 kms long. The author hiked to the spring, and to the end of the road, and back to his boat in 4 hours. You may need 5 hours to reach the spring and return (depending on lake levels).

Boots or Shoes Any dry weather boots or shoes will do.

Water At Gunsight Spring, one of the best around.

Main Attractions The upper canyon is interesting with the spring and old cattle trail. Nothing is left to see, but under Padre Bay is the **Crossing of the Fathers**, an historic location worth mentioning. Read

Gunsight Spring. It's under an overhang with a hanging garden above. It's been cemented-up at the bottom to hold water for cows, but apparently cattle haven't been here for many years.

Map 38, Gunsight Canyon

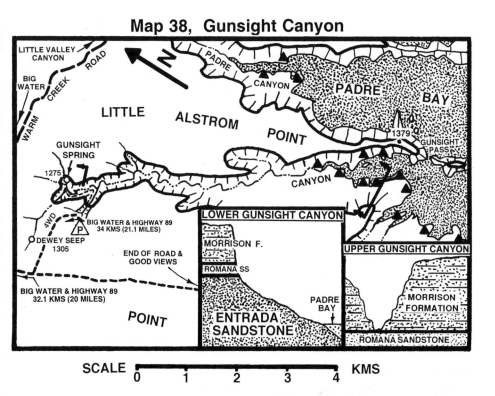

LITTLE VALLEY CANYON

BIG WATER

ROAD

WARM CREEK

PADRE CANYON

PADRE BAY

LITTLE ALSTROM

POINT

1379

GUNSIGHT PASS

GUNSIGHT SPRING

1275

4WD

CANYON

LOWER GUNSIGHT CANYON

DEWEY SEEP
1305

P BIG WATER & HIGHWAY 89
34 KMS (21.1 MILES)

END OF ROAD &
GOOD VIEWS

BIG WATER & HIGHWAY 89
32.1 KMS (20 MILES)

POINT

MORRISON F.

ROMANA SS

ENTRADA
SANDSTONE

PADRE
BAY

UPPER GUNSIGHT CANYON

MORRISON
FORMATION

ROMANA SANDSTONE

SCALE 0   1   2   3   4 KMS

Not far below **Gunsight Spring**, **Gunsight Canyon** drops quickly in a 50 meter section. It may look a bit scarry to some, but it's easier that it first appears.

its history below.

Hiking Maps USGS or BLM map Smoky Mountain (1:100,000); Gunsight Butte (1:24,000--7 1/2' quad) for hiking; or Gunsight Butte (1:62,500) if available.

History of Padre Bay and the Crossing of the Fathers Below the waters of Padre Bay is one of the most famous historic sites associated with Lake Powell--or at least with the former Glen Canyon. This place was known as the **Crossing of the Fathers**. It was at that location on the Colorado River where the expedition known as the **Dominguez & Escalante Party** crossed on their return journey to Santa Fe, New Mexico, in **November of 1776**.

The story of their journey in this part of the country begins on the Colorado at the mouth of the Paria River. That's the place we now call **Lee's Ferry**. They had camped on the lower Paria from October 26 through November 1, 1776, while looking for a way to cross. On November 2, they left the Paria River about 5 kms upstream from the Colorado and made their way up the eastern canyon wall to the mesa top. That pass is still called **Dominguez Pass** (for more details, see the author's other book, *Hiking and Exploring the Paria River*).

From there they headed north and down into **Wahweap Creek** at a location which is now under water. This was likely in the area due north of Wahweap Marina. The next morning they headed southeast down Wahweap Creek on a bench 150 meters above the river. They then followed the river gorge upstream in the area that is now the south shore of Antelope Island. They ended up making one camp just about opposite the mouth of **Navajo Canyon**.

During the day of November 4, they looked for a way down to the canyon bottom eventually finding a route, which in 1960, was just a ravine for big horn sheep or deer. Two of their party, Domingo and Muniz, crossed the river and entered Navajo Canyon. After some distance and not finding a route out of that canyon, they returned. Had they continued up Navajo Creek they would have saved themselves a lot of time. They camped the night of the 4th on a sand bar just above the Colorado.

The next morning they returned to the canyon rim via the same ravine then went north to the lower end of Warm Creek. But Warm Creek was entrenched in the lower end and they had to move north on the west side of the narrows. About 1 1/2 kms upcanyon from the river they found a way down into the gorge. About 500 meters further upstream, they made an exit to the east side and got back above the Navajo Sandstone and onto the Carmel Bench.

They camped the night of November 5 near a spring which is now under the eastern part of today's **Warm Creek Bay**. On the morning of the 6th, they headed east around the southern end of **Romana Mesa** on top of what we call today The Sand Hills. There is to this day an old 4WD road on top of this bench. Before the lake came to be, this same road headed around the cliffs and ended near the Kane Creek boat landing site which was once used by river rafters.

From Romana Mesa, they headed northeast into the bottom of **Gunsight Canyon**, then southeast around the south side of **Gunsight Butte**. From there it was again southeast to a point overlooking the river directly above the Crossing of the Fathers. They would have been better off had they used the normal Indian route which crossed through the canyon wall at **Gunsight Pass** rather than go south of Gunsight Butte. From the pass, the normal route went to the northeast side of Padre Canyon, or as it was known then, Navajo Canyon. From there the normal Indian trail went down to the river in several places as shown on **Map 38A, page 255**.

Looking east from near the end of **Alstrom Point**. **Gunsight Bay** is in the center; **Fiftymile Mountain** is in the upper left far background; **Navajo Mountain** is in the distance and upper right; and **Gunsight Butte** is in the upper right just below Navajo Mountain.

Map 38A, Padre Bay and Crossing of the Fathers

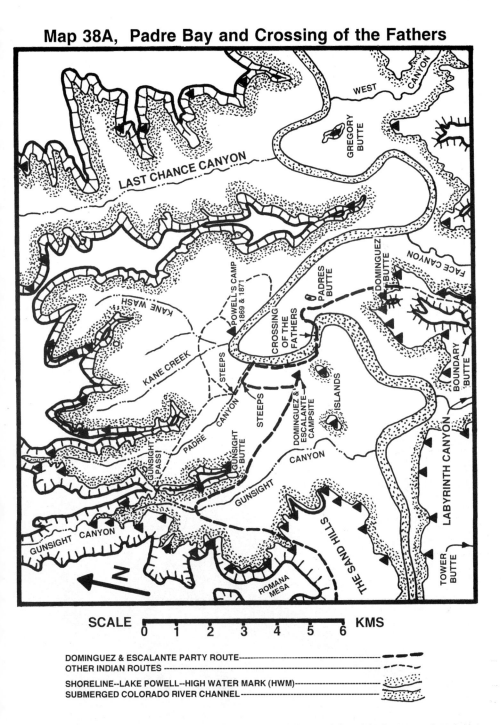

SCALE 0 1 2 3 4 5 6 KMS

DOMINGUEZ & ESCALANTE PARTY ROUTE------------------------------
OTHER INDIAN ROUTES -----------------------------------
SHORELINE--LAKE POWELL--HIGH WATER MARK (HWM)----------------
SUBMERGED COLORADO RIVER CHANNEL-----------------------

On the night of November 6 they camped in the area southeast of Gunsight Butte on a bench just above the river. Because they were south of the mouth of Padre Canyon, instead of north, they had to do some trail work with axes to get their horses down one steep 3-meter-section of slickrock. The next morning, part of the group went down Padre Canyon to the river and to a point just below their camp. Part of their supplies were lowered over the cliff from their camp directly down to the river's edge. Then they crossed in waist-deep water. Everyone made it across to the east side that day where they camped.

That night, **November 7, 1776,** they celebrated and called the ford **La Purisima Concepcion de la Virgen Santisima.**
The next day they began by going north up some steep slickrock then veered to the east and passed along the bench between the river and **Padres Butte.** Today, only the upper part of this butte is showing above the lake. From there, they headed almost due south east of **Dominguez Butte,** then south and over a low divide into the shallow **Labyrinth Canyon** drainage. The part of their old trail above the HWM is still there today (apparently?). From Labyrinth, the well-beaten trail veers southeast then south and finally southwest to where it zig zags down into upper **Navajo Canyon** very near where **Chaol Canyon** enters. **See Maps 38 and 38A.** On those maps, the author calls this part the North Dominguez & Escalante Trail. That part of their trip was on November 11. Just into Chaol Canyon they made an exit up the eastern wall, then headed south to Hopi Land and on to New Mexico.

In early Mormon history and during the 2 river exploration trips of John W. Powell, this crossing was known as the **Ute Ford.** Jacob Hamblin used it several times while preaching to the Indians south and east of the Colorado. This ford was used by Navajos as well, often times with stolen cattle taken from the Mormon settlements to the west.

Dellenbaugh's Diary mentions the events of Powell's second expedition when they landed in the vicinity of Crossing of the Fathers in early October, 1871. Evidently they were very low on supplies as they neared the area, because he states: *The Major contemplated stopping long enough for a climb to the top [of Navajo Mtn.] but on appealing to Andy for information as to the state of the supplies he found we were near the last crust and he decided that we had better pull on as steadily as possible towards El Vado [Crossing of the Fathers] at Music Temple Canyon.*

The next morning: *Friday, October 6th, we got away as quickly as we could and pulled down the river hoping that El Vado was not far ahead and feeling somewhat as Escalante must have felt a century before when he was trying to find it. He had the advantage of having horses which could be eaten from time to time. Of course we knew from the position of the San Juan and of Navajo Mountain, that we could reach El Vado in most two days, but the question was, "would we find any one there with rations?"*

Later on that afternoon they found a place where some brush had been burned and the tracks of shod horses and 2 men. They went on about 5 kms more and: *caught a glimpse of a stick with a white rag dangling from it stuck out from the right bank, and at the same moment heard a shot. On landing and mounting the bank we found Captain Pardyn Dodds and two prospectors, George Riley and John Bonnemort, encamped beside a large pile of rations.*

The party camped at that location for about a week, taking observations, and eating lots of food which they had sent for ahead of time. They were also doing their best to recover from various illnesses. One member named Steward was very ill. On October 13, and as they were contemplating moving on, 2 Navajos arrived in camp. Dellenbaugh stated: *We saw by their dress, so different from the Ute (red turbans, loose unbleached cotton shirts, native woven sashes at the waist, wide unbleached cotton trousers reaching to a little below the knee and there slashed up on the outer side for seven or eight inches [18 to 20 cms], bright woven garters twisted around their red buckskin leggings below the knee, and red moccasins with turned up soles and silver buttons), that they were Navajos.*

An hour later, 7 more Navajos arrived in their camp on their way to the Mormon settlements on a trad-

Tower Butte from the air, looking northeast toward **Fiftymile Mountain** in the far background. In the upper left and down a little is the west side of Gregory Butte.

ing mission. None of the whites spoke Navajo and none of the Navajos spoke English so after a while, and after the rivermen discovered one of the visitors had sticky fingers, they decided to move their camp downriver a ways: *Just below was El Vado de los Padres by which these Navajos had now come across. It was also sometimes called the Ute Ford. The necessary route was indicated by a line of small piles of stones showing above water. It was not an easy crossing, feasible only at low water, and quite impossible for waggons, even had there been a road to it. A shoal was followed up the middle of the river half a mile [800 meters] with deep channels cutting through it, reached from the south over a steep slope of bare sandstone and from the north through a very narrow, small canyon, not over ten feet [3 meters] wide.*

  This crossing was the main route across the Colorado River for about a century or until **January 11, 1873**. That's the day **John D. Lee** made the first trip across the river in his newly built ferry boat. **Lee's Ferry**, at the mouth of the **Paria River**, was then the normal route across the Colorado until **1929**. That's when the **Navajo Bridge** was finished across the upper part of **Marble Canyon**.

  From then on, the Crossing of the Fathers was lost in history with the possible exception of cattlemen and prospectors who roamed the canyon. It was finally rediscovered in 1936 by a prospector named Byron Davies. He told historian Russell G. Frazier about it and in 1938 a party of several people rafted down the Colorado and erected a copper plaque right at the mouth of Padre Canyon commemorating the spot.

This is the lower end of the 50 meter section where **Gunsight Canyon** drops quickly.

Above Double Falls in the **Middle Slot & Narrows** of **West Canyon**. In 2007, the stream flow was much reduced compared to previous years and on previous trips.

Right The last swimming pool in the **Upper Slot** of **West Canyon.** Just behind the author (holding the camera) the canyon opens quickly and it's a relatively easy walk from there on down to the lake.

This is the 2nd of 2 really big, deep undercuts in the **Middle Slot & Narrows** of **West Canyon**. Both of these undercuts are about 100 meters deep and about another 100 meters overhung. It's the opinion of this writer, West Canyon rates No. 1 on the Colorado Plateau.

Navajo Canyon & Creek, Chaol Canyon, and the Dominguez & Escalante Trail

Location & Campsites To get to the hikes on the 2 maps shown, you first have to head for **Navajo Canyon Inlet**, which is the 2nd major drainage east of Glen Canyon Dam, and 1st one east of Antelope Point Marina on the south side of the lake. The inlet begins just east of Antelope Island and about 9 miles or 14 kms above the dam. If there's a buoy around it should be marked M9 (K14). Navajo Canyon Inlet is one of the longer tributaries on Lake Powell, about 25 kms in length. It's a very straight canyon until it forks at the southern end as seen on **Map 39** and **Map 39A**. At that point Navajo Creek heads east for a long distance, while **Chaol Canyon/Kaibito Creek** extends to the south for many kms.

Because of the north-south nature of Navajo Canyon and the prevailing southerly winds, expect to find some **driftwood** in the upper end of this inlet, regardless of water levels. Best to slow down as you enter the driftwood slicks, otherwise some of the floaters can do serious damage. With care and a little more time, you can get through these obstacles without problems. Above the HWM is one of the more interesting canyons for hikers discussed in this book.

There are very few campsites along Navajo Canyon Inlet but several do exist at about the halfway mark. The **best site** is labeled **Sand Dome** on **Map 39-1**. It's right across the bay from the **first old Navajo trails**. You'll also find good campsites just south of the Sand Dome, and on either side of the **Yazzie Trail**.

At the time of the author's first visit, he thought the water level was about 2 meters below the HWM. He camped at the head of the inlet, which at that time was 250 meters downstream from the junction of Navajo and Chaol Canyons. However, the USGS map shows lake water going up Navajo Creek for about 5 more kms! Perhaps a mistake (perhaps it is the boundary of the GCNRA, and not the HWM that is shown), but it does tell you the drainage at the upper end of the lake has a very low gradient and the campsites will likely be in different places than are shown on these maps.

Also, one park employee told the author, Navajo Canyon Inlet is silting up quicker than most others. The reason for this is the entire drainage is very sandy and there are lots of Navajo livestock being grazed year-round upstream. With this constant sedimentation caused by overgrazing, the upper end of the inlet and the campsite locations will change with every big storm and subsequent flashflood.

Hiking Routes or Trails In about the middle of the **Navajo Canyon Inlet** is what the author calls the **First Navajo Trail**. You can find the lower end of it on the south side of a small peninsula just across the water from the **sandslide/Sand Dome** as shown on Map 39-1. At the beginning of the trail you'll see a number of finely cut steps in the slickrock as the trail emerges from the water and zig zags up to the rim on the east side. Most of the cut steps are in the lower parts, while higher up, there are some stone cairns marking the way. Once on the rim you'll have fine views of the entire inlet looking north and south.

This first trail was surely an old Indian route in the beginning, but what you see there today was upgraded by the **Civilian Conservation Corps (CCC's or Triple C's)** during the Great Depression year of 1936. This information comes from the late Navajo patriarch **Owen Yazzie** who lived until 1994 with his family of about four generations just southeast of the butte called Leche-E Rock, which is about 16

From the **Yazzie Trail**, looking southeast along the upper **Navajo Canyon Inlet**. Just above the center of this picture is sand & mud where the lake began/ended on **7/26/2007-WL1099.71m/3607.93'**

Map 39, Navajo Canyon Inlet and Navajo Trails

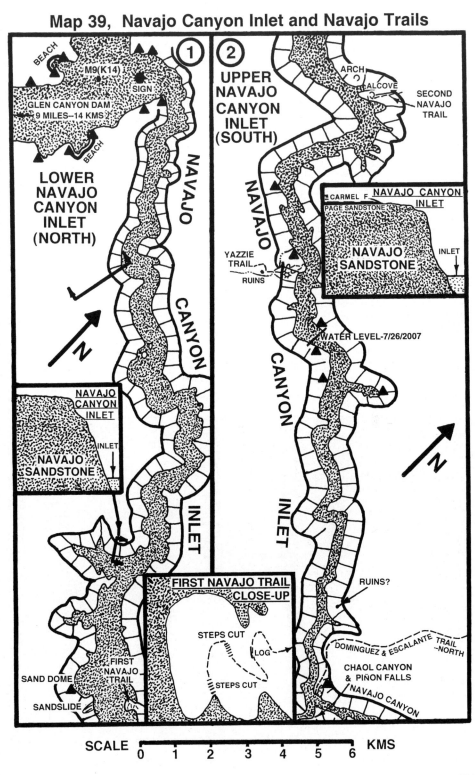

BEACH

M9(K14)

SIGN

GLEN CANYON DAM
9 MILES--14 KMS

BEACH

**LOWER
NAVAJO
CANYON
INLET
(NORTH)**

N

NAVAJO

CANYON

INLET

NAVAJO
CANYON
INLET

NAVAJO
SANDSTONE

INLET

FIRST
NAVAJO
TRAIL

SAND DOME

SANDSLIDE

① ②

**UPPER
NAVAJO
CANYON
INLET
(SOUTH)**

ARCH
ALCOVE

SECOND
NAVAJO
TRAIL

NAVAJO

NAVAJO

CANYON

INLET

CARMEL F.

PAGE SANDSTONE

NAVAJO CANYON
INLET

NAVAJO
SANDSTONE

INLET

YAZZIE
TRAIL

RUINS

WATER LEVEL-7/26/2007

N

RUINS?

**FIRST NAVAJO TRAIL
CLOSE-UP**

STEPS CUT

LOG

STEPS CUT

DOMINGUEZ & ESCALANTE TRAIL
--NORTH

CHAOL CANYON
& PIÑON FALLS

NAVAJO CANYON

SCALE 0   1   2   3   4   5   6   KMS

kms (10 miles) southeast of Page.

Yazzie was born in 1909 in the bottom of Navajo Canyon about halfway between the Colorado River and the lower part of Kaibito Creek. He couldn't place the spot on a map, but his family lived there until the waters of Lake Powell drove them out in about 1964. Their canyon home must have been northeast of Leche-E Rock and close to the Sand Dome. His family were the only people living in that section of the canyon and they had peach, apricot and apple trees, plus a vineyard. They grew corn, squash and all the other vegetables common to this part of the country.

Yazzie had a hard time remembering dates so long ago, but he did recall working at least 2 summer seasons for the CCC trail crews. He said the crews were typically made up of 15-20 men. The tools were almost exclusively picks and shovels, but they did use dynamite in places. They got around mostly on horseback.

The work began in the spring of the year and finished not long before Christmas. There were many crews on the Navajo Nation but he only worked in the area of Navajo Canyon. The one summer he remembered was 1936. They spent the entire warm season building trails in and out of the canyon. There were many trails. At the bottom of one, now under water, he said someone cut the date, 1936, indicating the year it was built.

Now back to boating & hiking. About 1 1/2 kms southeast of the First Navajo trail, you'll see high on the rim to the left or northeast, a small arch. About 300 meters southeast of the arch, and along the eastern shore, you'll see some steps cut in the slickrock. You'll have to look closely; it's on steep slickrock. On **Map 39-2** this is called the **Second Navajo Trail**. These steps are found halfway in between 2 little short inlets. This was surely another project of the CCC's.

Boat south from this second Navajo trail about 5-6 kms, then look to the right or west side of the inlet. On a small terrace at the bottom of a minor ridge, look for a stone cairn right at the HWM; in times of low water as on **7/26/2007-WL1099.71m/3607.93'**, the cairn was on a prominent peninsula pointing northeast. This is the beginning of what the author is calling the **Yazzie Trail**. This is the only trail the author found in the area on the west side fitting the description given to him by Owen Yazzie. This surely was the trail the Yazzie family used when they had to abandon their home in the canyon.

To get on this trail, first boat to the east side of the little peninsula, route-find to the top, then turn left or southwest. From the cairn, the trail heads west on a narrow bench or ledge, then zig zags up to the southwest. This trail is marked with cairns, and if you pay attention, it's easy to follow. Several places have either cut steps, or stones stacked up against a ledge. Higher up, you'll reach the canyon rim, then head south to the right side of a dome-like rock. From there, it runs across a flat area to a point where you can see what appears to be Anasazi ruins, but it's really a **Navajo herdsman's shelter** under a ledge. Just above that, the trail disappears in the more level country to the southwest. This is a constructed trail for people & livestock but it hasn't been used in years.

Right at the junction of Navajo & Chaol Canyons, and on the north side, you'll see a man-made trail zig zagging up to a low bench. See **Map 39A, page 263**. This is another old Indian trail, and as the story goes, it was used by the **Dominguez & Escalante Party** after they crossed the Colorado River on November 7, 1776. At that time they had failed to find a suitable route to California and were low on supplies so they were returning to Santa Fe, New Mexico before winter set in.

From the lake, the north branch of this trail runs along a bench parallel to the inlet for a ways, then it turns northeast and after about 1 1/2 kms tops out on the mesa. The trail you see today is not the same as it was in 1776. It has since been worked over in many places, surely by the CCC crew Owen Yazzie

These are the **ruins** shown on **Map 39-2** along the **Yazzie Trail**. It looks like a Navajo herder's creation, but it could have originally been built by the Anasazi.

Map 39A, Navajo Creek & Chaol Canyon, and the Dominguez & Escalante Trail

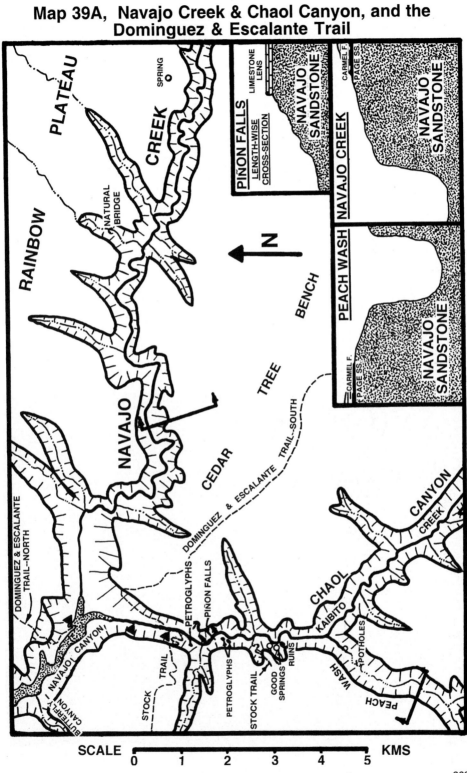

SCALE 0 1 2 3 4 5 KMS

was with in 1936. They used lots of dynamite to build this one and it's still used by Navajo herdsmen.

If you decide to walk up **Navajo Creek**, you'll find a broad open canyon in the lower parts. This is where water covered the bottom during the mid to late 1980's when the lake reached it's HWM for the first and only time. Above the HWM the canyon becomes more narrow. It has a year-round flowing stream which has its beginnings in the area near Inscription House far to the east. This entire drainage is prime grazing country for Navajo livestock. The author found no Anasazi ruins along Navajo Creek, but given the amount of available water, there may be some (?).

If you walk up **Chaol Canyon** about 1 1/2 kms from Navajo Creek, you'll find the second or southern part of the **Dominguez & Escalante Trail**. It will be on your left and heading north northeast as it leaves the canyon bottom on a little minor ridge. It starts just to the side of a little alcove where cattails are growing. Once you get on this trail it's easy to follow as it runs along a little valley to a point overlooking the junction of Navajo & Chaol Canyons. See **Map 39A**. Then it turns southeast and south and heads for Cedar Tree Bench and beyond. Like the northern part of this trail, it tends to disappear on the mesa top. Along some parts, especially as it heads up the slickrock or steeper sections, it has steps cut and stones piled up. But it has not had the heavy blasting and construction as the northern part of the trail.

About 300 meters upcanyon from the South Dominguez & Escalante Trail and on the right or west side is another very well-built **stock trail**. It begins at about the HWM as shown on the USGS maps, and zig zags up to the north. This one is easy to find and follow and the CCC crew spent a lot of time on it. It switchbacks up through the different layers of the Page/Navajo Sandstone until it reaches the mesa top. Of the 3 trails the author found leading down into lower Chaol Canyon, this one sees by far the most hoof traffic. By observing animal tracks it's clear that horses, cattle, sheep, goats and probably donkeys use this trail to gain access to Kaibito Creek and drinking water.

About 200 meters above the stock trail on the right or west, is a panel of **rock art** or **petroglyphs** mostly hidden behind some cattails and brush. Wade through the cattails and you'll see some etchings of big horn sheep both high and low on the southeast facing wall.

Continue up **Kaibito Creek**. It begins many kms to the south and beyond Highway 98, the main link between Page and Kayenta. This is a year-round stream and combined with Navajo Creek is one of the larger of the small creeks entering Lake Powell.

About 1 km above the first petroglyphs is **Piñon Falls**, which is perhaps the most fotogenic waterfall within walking distance of the lake. These falls were created because of a thin limestone (or siltstone?) lens within the Navajo Sandstone. This lens is more resistant to erosion than the surrounding sandstone. The water first cascades over the limestone, then has cut interesting erosional features in the sandstone beneath. The falls, or perhaps it's best to call them cascades, are only about 5 meters high. See the length-wise cross-section on **Map 39A** to get an idea of the shape of Piñon Falls.

Above the waterfall about 300-400 meters, and on the right or west, are 2 panels of very good **petroglyphs**. Most of the figures are big horn sheep. These are among the best preserved the author has seen.

Continuing upcanyon. After another 400 meters or so, and again on the right or west, is another old stock trail. This one is the steepest of all the trails in the Navajo Creek and Chaol Canyon area. This one is also built up in places and is easy to find and follow. It's located just across the canyon from a

Near the center of this picture are steps cut leading up to the notch. This is part of the **First Navajo Trail** as shown on **Map 39-1**.

major drainage coming in from the east.
    Another 400 meters upcanyon from the last stock trail, and within an area of about 100 meters, are 3 springs. Each comes out of a crack in the rock and the water should be safe to drink as is. The third or upper-most spring is interesting. It drains out of a crack about 2 meters above the creek bed and is surrounded by a small **hanging garden**. Upon the author's first visit, there was a log standing against the wall right at this spring. At the top of the log, about 3 meters up, were several very old and eroded moki steps cut in the wall. The author followed these up to **Anasazi ruins** just to the left. A word of **caution:** that log will have been washed away when you arrive but regardless whether it's there or not, it's recommended you forget trying to climb up. The author went up to find nothing of interest at the ruins then was lucky to have gotten back down without falling or being injured. The old steps are about worn out and it's all steep slickrock. Your best view of the ruins is from the creek bed anyway.
    The author went into **Peach Wash** about halfway then returned. Peach Wash is short and deep and is a box canyon (the upper end has a great technical slot). There are several dryfalls to pass in the lower end but they're all easy. If you continue up Kaibito Creek, you'll find a deep, well-watered canyon for several kms. Further up and where the big power lines cross the canyon (see the Glen Canyon Dam metric map), it narrows to just a slot and there's a series of 5 waterfalls which you cannot climb. However, that section is so far from the lake boaters are likely not be interested.
Hike Length & Time Needed Hiking up Navajo Creek could be a short, or longer hike--your choice. The 3 trails in lower Chaol Canyon are all within about 2 kms of where Navajo Creek enters and can all be visited easily in maybe 3 hours (if the lake is high--much longer in time of low lake levels as they were on **7/26/2007-WL1099.71m/3607.93'**). It's about 7 kms up to the 3 springs and the ruins. This trip to see the ruins, petroglyphs, waterfalls and trails in Chaol Canyon will likely take most of a day depending on how fast you walk, and how far you can boat into the inlet at the time. The author considers this to be one of the most interesting hikes in this book--but in times of low lake levels it will be a long walk.
Boots or Shoes Wading boots or shoes in either canyon, but any kind of shoes on the trails leading out of Navajo Canyon Inlet.
Water With all the possible livestock in the canyon, drink only from the springs near the ruins, or further up Kaibito Creek. Peach Wash has a small stream in its lower 300 meters or so and it should be good to drink as is, unless you see sheep & goats in the drainage
Main Attractions Ruins, rock art petroglyphs, old historic stock trails, one of the prettiest waterfalls around, and very few other boaters. You may also meet Navajo children herding flocks of sheep & goats. The driftwood in the upper end of Navajo Canyon Inlet scares away some visitors, but the author has been through it 3 different times, and really had no problems.
Hiking Maps USGS or BLM map Glen Canyon Dam (1:100,000); White Horse Mesa, Leche-E Rock, Cedar Tree Bench, and maybe Face Canyon & Tse-esgizii (1:24,000--7 1/2' quads) for hiking; or Navajo Creek (1:62,500) if available.

The **Sand Dome** camping area in the middle part of the **Navajo Canyon Inlet**. As of **7/26/2007-WL1099.71m/3607.93'**, there were almost no tamaracks (tamarisks) here.

From the air, and on **10/7/2007-WL1097.80m/3601.66'**, looking south toward **Leche-e Rock** in the left background. Closeup is the **Sand Dome** in the middle of the **Navajo Canyon Inlet**.

Again from the air, looking down on the **Sand Dome** in the middle of the **Navajo Canyon Inlet**. This is one of the best campsites on Lake Powell, and as of **10/7/2007**, there were few tamaracks around.

Piñon Falls (some have called this Chaol or Kaibito Falls) in **Chaol Canyon** along **Kaibito Creek**. With low lake levels, as found in the late 1990's & 2000's, this is quite a long hike--but it's one of the most fotogenic scenes anywhere.

This picture of 2 rows of big horn sheep is from along the Colorado River in **Glen Canyon** below the **Glen Canyon Dam**. There are also several **rock art panels** like this in the vicinity of **Piñon Falls** in **Chaol Canyon**.

Warm Creek Bay, Crosby Canyon and the Spencer Coal Mines

Location & Campsites This map shows the upper parts of **Warm Creek Bay** which is located just northeast of Wahweap Bay and where the Wahweap & Stateline Marinas are found. Because it's so close to Wahweap, this is a very popular place in summer both for camping and water skiing. Warm Creek Bay, most of which is shown on this map, probably has more good campsites and beaches per/km than any other section of the lake (when the lake is at or near the HWM). It's almost wall to wall beach. The reason for so many good sandy beaches is that much of the shoreline (at or near the HWM) makes contact with the Carmel Formation which is just below the Entrada Sandstone walls. Little if any of the Carmel is actually exposed as it's covered with eolian deposits--mostly windblown sand from the Entrada Sandstone. Even with low lake levels, as they were on **7/26/2007-WL1099.71m/3607.93'**, there should be plenty of campsites--if they're not covered by tamaracks.

Also featured here are the historic **Spencer Coal Mines**. They're located in a little-known side-drainage entering Warm Creek Bay. The site is in **Crosby Canyon** only about **300 meters** from where the **Warm Creek Road** crosses the dry creek bed. You can drive to these old mines, or you can get there by hiking from the lake. The history of these mines is told below. The walk to these mines is about the only place on this map where hiking is feasible.

Hiking Routes or Trails The easiest way to get to the **Spencer Coal Mines** is to drive east from Highway 89 near mile post 7 at Big Water, Utah, along the **Warm Creek Road**. After 15.6 kms (9.7 miles), turn right or east where the road crosses Crosby Canyon. After 300 meters the mines will be along the wall on your left 20 meters away. However, when it rains part of that clay-based road is impassable even for 4WD's. The other way is 4.7 km (2.8 mile) hike from the lake's HWM.

At the upper end of **Crosby Canyon Inlet**, you may see vehicle tracks. When the lake is high, some people drive there and occasionally launch boats. Tie-down and start walking upcanyon. Once you get above the HWM, you'll be on a road that is graded occasionally by Kane County road crews and which the NPS seems to patrol on a regular basis (this was during the 1980's and early 1990's). This road is along the bottom of the dry creek bed. Floods roar down this canyon on occasions making big changes. But the drainage is short so the road should remain good for long periods of time after grading. This road makes walking fast and easy.

This is what you'll find at the Spencer Coal Mines today. About 300 meters after turning off the Warm Creek Road, look to the north against the south facing 10-meter-high canyon wall and you'll notice a gray horizontal seam. This is the coal bed and is about 1 meter thick. The outside surface, which is exposed to weathering, looks more like gray shale than coal. Inside the tunnels, it looks more like real coal.

Just above the level of the dry creek bed you can see the entrance to 6 tunnels. Of the 6, two are almost completely buried by cave-ins, and a third is barely noticeable. Only 3 short tunnels were clearly visible. Upon inspection in 1988, the author found 2 of the 6 still had the wooden braces in place after so many years (they were mined in 1910 or 1911). In 1988, you could see the end of each tunnel from the entrance--without going inside, but the NPS decided they were too risky. So in the early 1990's, they along with the state and its mine closure program, sealed off the entrances to 3 of the tunnels. All you'll see today (2007) is a cinder block wall about 1 meter inside each tunnel.

Hike Length & Time Needed From the HWM to the mines is about 4.7 kms (2.8 miles) along a road-

This sign is at the junction of the **Warm Creek Road** and the road heading down **Crosby Canyon**--to the right out of sight. About 300 meters from this point are the **Spencer Coal Mines**.

Map 40, Warm Creek Bay, Crosby Canyon and the Spencer Coal Mines

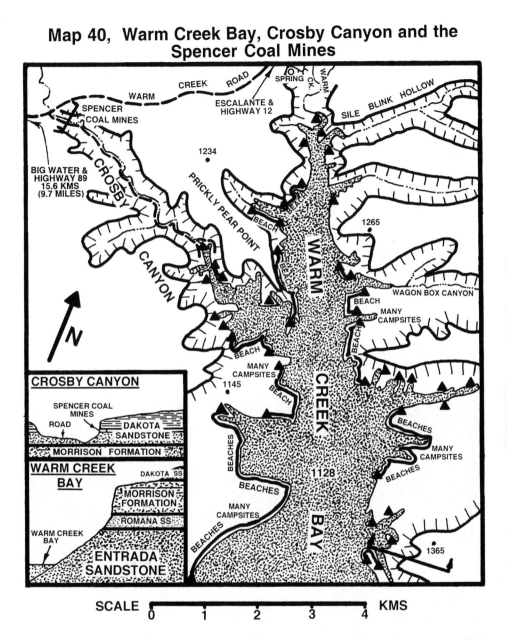

CREEK ROAD
WARM
SPRING CK.
WARM
ESCALANTE & HIGHWAY 12
SPENCER COAL MINES
SILE BLINK HOLLOW
1234
BIG WATER & HIGHWAY 89 15.6 KMS (9.7 MILES)
CROSBY CANYON
PRICKLY PEAR POINT
BEACH
BEACH
BEACH
1265
WARM
BEACH
WAGON BOX CANYON
BEACH
MANY CAMPSITES
N
BEACH
MANY CAMPSITES
CREEK
1145
BEACH
BEACH
BEACHES
CROSBY CANYON
SPENCER COAL MINES
ROAD
DAKOTA SANDSTONE
MORRISON FORMATION
BEACHES
MANY CAMPSITES
1128
BEACHES
WARM CREEK BAY
DAKOTA SS
MORRISON FORMATION
ROMANA SS
BEACHES
MANY CAMPSITES
BAY
1365
WARM CREEK BAY
BEACHES
ENTRADA SANDSTONE

SCALE 0 1 2 3 4 KMS

way or dry creek. The time it will take for most people to see the mines and return to the lake, will be about 3 hours--depending on lake levels. The author once went down this canyon to the lake in his VW Rabbit, then drove back up from the lake to the mines in 8 minutes.

Boots or Shoes Any kind of dry weather boots or shoes will be fine.

Water There are no springs around so take your own water.

Main Attractions Lots of good campsites and some historic coal mines.

Hiking Maps USGS or BLM map Smoky Mountain (1:100,000); Warm Creek Bay & maybe Lone Rock (1:24,000--7 1/2" quads) for hiking; or Gunsight Butte & Nipple Butte (1:62,500) if available.

History of the Spencer Coal Mines In the days before Lake Powell the lower 6-7 kms of **Warm Creek** was deeply entrenched in a Navajo Sandstone canyon. Above that part it opened up into an broad valley, a result of the Carmel Formation being exposed. Even though the lower end of the canyon was narrow and entrenched, it was still wide enough for wagons or even 4WD's, to be driven down to the river. Because of this, Warm Creek was to become famous in the mining history of Glen Canyon.

Just above the entrenched part of Warm Creek and just into the open valley there were, before being covered by the lake, the remains of 8 stone buildings. Their origins dated from about 1910 and were built by the **American Placer Corporation** headed by **Charles H. Spencer**. When Crampton visited the scene in the late 1950's only 2 buildings were still standing. The others had fallen down and were in very bad condition.

Quoting now from Crampton's writings in the *University of Utah Anthropological Papers, #46* he states: *The rock buildings at Warm Creek were built as one part of an extensive mining enterprise at Lee's Ferry undertaken by the American Placer Corporation, a company formed in Chicago. Gold prospects in the Chinle Formation at Lee's Ferry and in the gravels at the mouth of the Paria River, and on the platforms on both sides of Marble Canyon downstream for several miles from there, were located in 1910 and 1911 by officers of the company. The company also staked claims near the town of Paria [Pahreah] on the Paria River [in southern Utah].*

It was planned to begin mining operations at Lee's Ferry. Steam boilers were to be used as a power source to operate pumps to provide water for hydraulicing and placering. In order to operate the boilers at Lee's Ferry, two coal mines were developed in Tibbets Canyon [they are actually in Crosby Canyon], an upper right fork of Warm Creek, and the cluster of rock buildings described here were built about this time to serve as headquarters for the coal mining and transport operation. It is believed that the coal was hauled down to this site by pack train and from there by wagon, probably with ox teams, down Warm Creek Canyon to the mouth and from there to Lee's Ferry by boat. The company operated a few months at Lee's Ferry in 1911 and 1912 before suspending operations after which time the cabins at Warm Creek must have been abandoned.

Spencer first thought coal could be brought directly to Lee's Ferry by mule using an old trail called the **Ute or Dominguez Trail** which was about 5 kms up the Paria River Canyon from the ferry on the Colorado. Because of that extra distance it was decided to make a shortcut route directly above the operation on the Colorado. So in the fall of 1910, Spencer and his men constructed the **Spencer Trail** from the river to the top of the cliffs. From there it was hoped they could head out to the northeast with mules for the Warm Creek Coal Fields. But the trail was never used to bring in coal. Instead it was more of a promotional scheme than anything else.

Once the decision was made to use boats to transport the coal, the next job was to build a wagon road right down the middle of Warm Creek to the Colorado. While some workers were constructing the road, others were building a barge on the banks of the river. This all went well--they brought coal down the canyon, loaded it onto the barge, then floated it down to Lee's Ferry. But then the problem was to get the barge back upstream again.

This problem, it was thought, could be solved by a tugboat of some kind. So with investor's money a 9-meter-long tug boat called the **Violet Louise**, was purchased and brought to Lee's Ferry. As it turned out, it was far too underpowered to push a large barge upstream against the current. The current wasn't that fast but pushing a barge against it wasn't easy.

While Spencer worked on problems at Lee's Ferry, the managers of the Chicago company he worked for, ordered a steam powered boat from San Francisco. The boat was built in 1911, dismantled, and shipped by train to Marysvale, Utah, which was the end of the railway line. It was then put onto large wagons for the rest of the 320 km trip to the mouth of Warm Creek. There it was reassembled in the spring of 1912. It was the biggest thing to sail the Colorado River above the Grand Canyon, with the

A closeup look at 1 of 6 coal mine entrances in the upper end of **Crosby Canyon**. This is where Stanton's men dug coal out of 1-meter-thick seams and transported it down Warm Creek to the Colorado River, thence downstream to Lee's Ferry.

exception of the Stanton Dredge up near Bullfrog. It measured 28 x 8 meters, was powered by a coal boiler, and had a 4-meter-wide stern paddlewheel. Even though this part of the scheme wasn't one of Spencer's big ideas, the boat was named the *Charles H. Spencer* anyway.

The next problem was to find a crew for the boat. This wasn't easy in the middle of the desert, but they found a crew anyway. A fellow by the name of Pete Hanna was at the helm, the only crew member who had any experience with boats. They loaded the deck full of coal for the trial run. But almost immediately they hit a sandbar. Then another. Finally, Hanna turned the boat around and allowed it to sail down the river backwards, which gave it better maneuverability. They spent one night in the canyon, then next morning finished the 45 km run to Lee's Ferry.

They then had to figure out how to get the *'Spencer'* back upstream against the current which was stronger than anyone had expected. Hanna decided to keep most of the coal which had been brought down on board, to insure passage back up to Warm Creek. This was a good move because they barely made it back upstream. They again loaded the boat as full as possible and returned to the Ferry where it sat for a couple of months. While this was happening, the chemists and the miners tried to figure out what to do about separating the gold dust from the Chinle clays.

Finally it was decided to try something different. They ended up towing the original barge upstream with the *Charles H. Spencer*. This worked fine. Next, they loaded up both the barge and the steamer with coal. The barge was then allowed to drift downstream with several workers guiding it around the sandbars with the *Charles H. Spencer* following. This worked fine too and it appeared they had this part of the gold mining problem solved. The only thing left to do was to find a successful way to get the gold out of the clay. This, Spencer was never able to do, and the steamboat had made its last run.

Spencer left Lee's Ferry later in 1912 bound for the nearly-abandoned settlement of **Pahreah**. Meanwhile, the steamship *Charles H. Spencer* sat on the river tied to the bank. In 1915, the combination of high water and piles of driftwood, put the boat on its side and it sank in 1 meter of water. Later, parts were stripped off and taken away and some of the lumber from its deck was used for various other projects. Today, you can just barely see the sunken remains of the boat just upstream from **Lee's Fort** and near the bottom end of the Spencer Trail. Nearby is the boiler and parts of the stern paddlewheel (see this author's other book, *Hiking and Exploring the Paria River* for more details on the things to see at Lee's Ferry and vicinity).

About 5 kms downstream from the mouth of Warm Creek was a sandbar, exposed only at low water. This was called the **Wright Bar**, after 2 brothers L. C. and G. W. Wright. They were the first to file claims to it on November 15, 1892. This site was unique because it was one of the few places in the canyon where placer mining was done on a low-water sand bar. It's not known how extensive the mining operation was but it's likely not too much.

For the most part, Glen Canyon was abandoned by miners after about 1900, with only sporadic prospecting thereafter. But when the American Placer Corporation began to stake out the countryside around Lee's Ferry, there was renewed interest in Glen Canyon. This sparked a mini gold rush. According to Crampton's report, in 1909 there were 4 men from Searchlight, Nevada, seen heading upstream to Wright's Bar which appears to have been the last significant mining site in Glen Canyon above Lee's Ferry.

The steamboat *Charles H. Spencer* as it looked in August of 1915 on the banks of the **Colorado River** at Lee's Ferry. The sunken remains can still be seen there today (E.C. La Rue foto).

Looking north across the dry wash at one of the entrances to the **Stanton Coal Mines** in upper **Crosby Canyon**. At the outer surface of the seams, the coal looks more like shale--that's because it's been weathered so much. Three of the tunnel openings have been sealed for safety reasons.

Crampton's group took this foto of one of the stone buildings in **Warm Creek Canyon** just before the waters of Lake Powell covered it. This building likely housed men working in the coal mines.

This scene is just north of the **Warm Creek Road** between **Wiregrass** & **Crosby Canyons**. All the blue-grey clay beds you see are part of the **Tropic Shale Formation**. The sandstone cliffs above the clays are part of the **Straight Cliffs Formation**--same as the top layer on Fiftymile Mountain.

Antelope Canyon

Location & Campsites   Antelope is the first canyon entering Lake Powell east of the Glen Canyon Dam. Antelope begins many kms to the south and runs north to the lake passing between the new Antelope Point Marina and Page. In recent years this canyon has become famous because of post card fotos showing its convoluted slot--also because 11 people drowned there in a flash flood in 1997. It's the parts of this drainage just north and south of Highway 98 that have become so famous. Those parts are very narrow & twisted, and have very intricate patterns eroded in the Navajo Sandstone. The best parts of this slot canyon are easier to reach and explorer from the highway. Read below.

To get to **lower Antelope by boat**, head south from **Wahweap/Stateline,** then east and into the old Colorado River channel south of Antelope Island. Near buoy M4 (K6) is the beginning of Antelope Inlet. **Or better still**, boat south (downlake) about 1 1/2 kms from the **Antelope Point Marina launch ramp**. Just inside the inlet are a couple of possible campsites--depending on lake levels. There are also some beaches just north of this mapped section in the main channel and just across the water north and west of the Antelope Point launch ramp. Read more about this marina in the introduction to this book.

Hiking Routes or Trails From the end of the inlet walk up **Antelope Canyon**. It's an easy hike in moderately good narrows. About 1/4 of the way between the HWM and Highway 98, and on the left or east, is a side-canyon the author is calling the **East Fork**. Walk up this good slot for about 800 meters to find a dryfall and maybe a rope hanging down. If you can climb above this, there's another dryfall or dropoff just beyond which you likely won't be able to climb--but that's the end of the canyon anyway. That same point is an easy 300 meter walk from the Antelope Point Road.

About 3/4's of the way between the HWM and the highway, you'll come to a blocking dryfall about 6 meters high. This will stop you, but when the author passed that way in the summer of 1988, there was a rope hanging down from a bolt in the wall above. He used it then but by 1991, and again in 2001, the rope was gone. If you want to **exit the canyon**, regress about 300 meters from the dryfall, then walk up a side-canyon to the west.

Here's the latest information regarding the best parts of Antelope Canyon accessible from Highway 98. This seems to change every year, so don't be surprised if things are different when you arrive. From the center of Page follow the signs southeast to Highway 98, the main road linking Page and Kayenta. From the signal light, head east in the direction of the **Navajo Power Plant** not far from town. Between mile posts 299 & 300, and immediately across the highway south from the beginning of the **Antelope Point Road**, you'll see a paved road, gate, a fee station, a couple of small wooden buildings and a parking area. Between 8am & 5pm in summer (9am to 3pm in winter), someone from the **Navajo Tribal Parks** will be there to collect fees. As of 11/2007, Tribal Parks was charging $6 per person for a day-pass which allows you to visit one or both sections of Antelope--on the same day. The **Begay family** was charging $20 to be driven upcanyon or south to **The Crack**. The entire trip usually takes a couple of hours. If you're waiting for the sun and better light, they will likely leave you there as long as you like (one person told the author they had to pay a little more to be left there and wait for the best light).

To visit **The Corkscrew** part of Antelope, drive north from Highway 98 on the paved road heading in the direction of **Antelope Point Marina**. After about 300 meters, turn left or west onto a graveled road and drive down to a parking place at the beginning of The Corkscrew. See the map.

Someone from the **Young family** will be there to collect fees. They were charging $15 per person in 11/2007. Since the big flood of 8/12/1997 (read below) they have bolted several steel ladders in the

Near the entrance to the **Corkscrew** part of **Antelope Canyon** is this memorial to the 11 tourists who lost their lives in a flash flood on August 12, 1997.

Map 41, Antelope Canyon

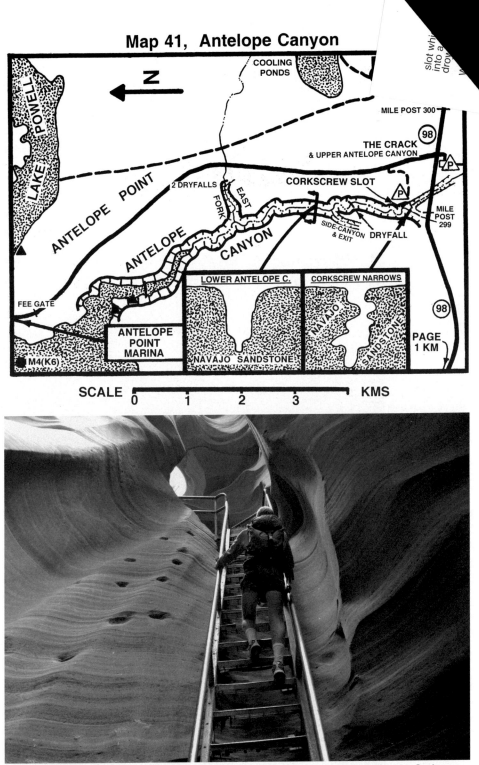

Since the flash flood of 8/12/1997, steel ladders have been erected to help people in the **Corkscrew** part of **Antelope Canyon**. This is now a canyon for tourists & fotographers--not hikers. Notice the moki steps in the wall to the left. These were used my hikers before the ladders were intalled.

ᴊᴎ is immediately west of the parking lot. This makes it easy to get in and out and has made it
ᴀeal tourist trap. Also, between the parking lot and slot is a monument with the names of those
ᴊned in the big flood.

This is probably the most fotogenic slot canyon around (but there are other great slots including
ᴠater Holes, and Face & Labyrinth on the lake--when the lake levels are low as they were in 2007). If
you're a fotographer use a tripod for long exposure settings. It can be dark inside either section, so it's
best to be there sometime in the mid-day period when the sun is shining down into parts of the slot. However, you don't want a streak of sunlight in your picture. Move up or back a little to eliminate the sun;
that way, with plenty of light in the slot, it brings out the colors. If it's really dark, there's no color! Read
about **Fotography in Deep, Dark Canyons**, in the Introduction to this book.

Hike Length & Time Needed It's about 3-4 kms from the HWM to the dryfall in lower Antelope. You
can do this in 3-4 hours or less, round-trip. For **The Crack**, you may need as much as 2-3 hours round-
trip (a walk of only 200 meters), depending on how many pictures you want to take. The **Corkscrew**
can be done in an hour or less, but more if you want the best light, and are taking lots of fotos.

Boots or Shoes Any dry weather boots or shoes, except right after rains, then wading shoes.

Water None around, so always take your own.

Main Attractions One of the most fotogenic narrow slot canyons on the Colorado Plateau.

Hiking Maps USGS or BLM map Glen Canyon Dam (1:100,000); Page (1:24,000--7 1/2' quad) for hiking; or Leche-E Rock (1:62,500) if available.

Flash Flood Tragedy On August 12, 1997, a 3-meter-high wall of water roared down **The Corkscrew**
part of Antelope Canyon and 11 people were washed away and drowned. Only the guide managed to
survive. Seven victims were French, 2 were Americans, and one each from the UK and Sweden. This
made international headlines, even in the South Pacific, where the author was mountain climbing in
Vanuatu at the time.

Since this event, a better warning system has been set up and several rope ladders have been installed on the rim to be lowered so people can climb up the walls if necessary. In addition to the heavy steel ladders inside the slot, they've also constructed a metal staircase up to the rim and out of the slot at the very bottom end. All in all, this 407-meter-long slot, is no longer a hike and certainly no longer an adventure--only a tourist trap. But it's a great fotogenic slot and easy to get to.

Another scene in the **Corkscrew** part of **Antelope Canyon**. This has to be the most fotogenic slot canyon on the planet.

Above The stairs leading out of the lower end of the **Corkscrew** part of **Antelope Canyon** to the rim. In case of a flashflood, this would be your quickest way to safety.

Left Natural bridge in the middle of the **Corkscrew** part of **Antelope Canyon**.

Wiregrass Canyon, Blue Pool Wash and Wahweap Bay

Location & Campsites **Wiregrass Canyon** is located in the upper or west end of **Wahweap Bay**, and drains into the lake just northwest of **Lone Rock**. Until recently this was an unknown canyon but the National Park Service is now promoting it in some of their handouts. The reason is, its 2 bridges are among the newest and most interesting around. More on this below.

Wahweap Bay, which is the open body of water just west of **Wahweap and Stateline Marinas**, is one of the best areas on the lake for camping as much of its shoreline has sandy beaches. The reason for all the beaches is the white Entrada Sandstone cliffs which circle the bay. As they erode, sand is left on or near the shoreline. An interesting observation is, further to the east between Tower Butte and Navajo Mountain, the Entrada Sandstone Formation has a reddish/orange color instead of white.

One of the best camping sites on the lake is **Lone Rock Beach**. You can drive to this one and launch a boat. Leave Highway 89 about 500 meters northwest of the Utah-Arizona state line and drive northeast on a paved road. The beach has about a dozen vault & moveable toilets, plus water & showers at the main brick toilet complex (this is a fee use area). If you intend to launch a boat from this beach, best to have a 4WD vehicle because there's lots of deep sand around. **ATV's & motorcycles are allowed**, so if you're looking for a quiet place to rest, better look elsewhere. This is the only place in the GCNRA where the NPS allows ORV's to be used. Read more about this place under this books introduction.

Hiking Routes or Trails If you're interested in a short and easy hike, boat along the north shore of Wahweap Bay not far northwest of Lone Rock and the Lone Rock Beach. The entrance to **Wiregrass Canyon Inlet** is a little difficult to see, so be observant. The inlet is narrow, now choked with tamaracks, and the white Entrada Sandstone walls aren't too high at that point. As you near the upper end of the inlet, you'll once again have to watch carefully for the first of **2 natural bridges** in the canyon. The **1st bridge** is about 200 meters below the HWM on the left-hand side going up. If the lake is full (very unlikely anytime soon!) you can boat right up to it. In this case, the water would be inside this small 2x5-meter opening. If the lake level is low, you'll be walking up the dry creek bed filled with tamaracks. With low lake levels as they were in 2007, this will likely be a long walk from your boat. See the foto below of the author when he walked downcanyon from the road on 11/7/2007 (if lake levels are low, it will likely be easier to reach both bridges by walking downcanyon from the **Warm Creek Road**).

This 1st bridge has been created in recent geologic time just a few hundred years ago by flood waters which have eroded through one wall of a gooseneck bend and have dropped down and out the other side below. The exit side is lower, thus creating a waterfall when floodwaters come down the drainage. The author was first there with the lake about 2-3 meters below the HWM. He litterally stepped directly from his boat into and through the bridge opening. When there's no water under this natural bridge you can still climb up the 3 meters or so to get through.

As you walk upcanyon from the 1st bridge, the drainage really isn't that interesting. About 3/4's the way up, you'll pass a side-canyon coming in from the right or east. About 300 meters beyond that, and again on the right, will be another hole in the wall. This is the **2nd bridge**. The tributary you just passed, has cut a hole in the wall of the main canyon where they once just came close together. This is a classic example of **stream capture**. There are now no more flood waters in the last 300 meters of the tributary canyon. If you continue up the drainage (you'll have to scramble up a couple of dryfalls--maybe wade into a pothole or two) about another 1 km, you'll come to the **Warm Creek Road** which begins at **Big Water, Utah** near **mile post 7** on Highway 89. If you drive to this canyon (8.3 kms/5.1 miles from

The **1st Natural Bridge** in lower **Wiregrass Canyon**. Flood waters have cut through the wall of a gooseneck bend leaving an abandoned meander high & dry, and a 3-meter dropoff below.

Map 42, Wiregrass Canyon

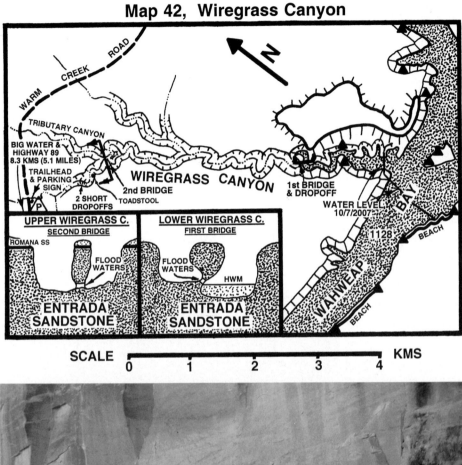

SCALE 0 1 2 3 4 KMS

The **2nd Natural Bridge** in upper **Wiregrass Canyon**. This is the east side of the bridge, and flood waters now flow from this tributary canyon into the main canyon on the other side. This is a good example of *stream capture*.

Big Water & the highway), you'll see a sign and trailhead parking on the right or south side of the road.
For those who would like to explore, you might try another drainage which is almost a twin to Wiregrass. It's called **Lone Rock Canyon** which is due north of **Lone Rock** and just east of Wiregrass (see it on **Map 42A, Wahweap Bay and Blue Pool Wash**). The author walked up nearly to the Warm Creek Road and was stopped by a bunch of tamaracks. It wasn't interesting, but side-canyons might be.

With the low lake levels as they were in the 1990's and 2000's, no one will be interesting in hiking from the lake into the upper part of Wahweap Bay. But there is one interesting slot canyon that may interest some. It's called **Blue Pool Wash**, and the best way to get there is to stop at the bridge on Highway 89 (between mile posts 3 & 4), and either walk in from the top (south of the bridge), or walk north on the east side of the slot. Near the slot's end, scramble down steep slickrock to its mouth then walk updrainage about 500 meters to a dryfall. As of 11/7/2007, there was a thick rope with knots hanging down. If you have strong arms, you can climb up into the middle part of the slot (the author never got there because of a mud hole at the bottom of that rope, and other messy pools upcanyon). If hiking down from Highway 89, there's a 3 meter downclimb into a pool (see foto below), or walk in from the east side just below the chokestone. Below that is another 3 meter downclimb and likely a pool. Below that is the final drop, the author has yet to see--it's not fun swimming potholes on cold November days.

Hike Length & Time Needed In **Wiregrass**, from the 1st bridge or the HWM, to the 2nd bridge, is about 3 kms. From the 2nd bridge to the Warm Creek Road, about another km. Visiting the bridges and going up to the road, will take about 3 hours for the round-trip hike. On 11/7/2007, the author saw both bridges from the road in 2 1/2 hours. To hike **Blue Pool Wash** will take an hour or two, depending on your climbing skills--a rope will be needed for most. In 2007, it was much easier from the highway.

Boots or Shoes Any dry weather boots or shoes will do, but in Blue Pool you may be wading some.

Water These are all dry canyons so take your own water.

Main Attractions Two recently made natural bridges, a nice slot canyon with downclimbing, one great beach you can drive to, and many good beaches and campsites with boater access only.

Hiking Maps USGS or BLM map Smoky Mountain (1:100,000); Lone Rock (1:24,000--7 1/2' quad) for hiking; or Nipple Butte (1:62,500) if available.

Wahweap Bay and History Before Lake Powell came to be, the very first stream to enter the Colorado River above the dam site was **Wahweap Creek**. That distance was only about 2 1/2 kms. The bottom end of this canyon was very much entrenched in the Navajo Sandstone but upstream about 6-7 kms, it opened up dramatically because of the Carmel Formation being exposed.

Dellenbaugh's Diary of 1871 has some interesting statements about what they found at the mouth of Wahweap Creek. It states: *the following morning, October 18th, we had not gone more than a mile [1 1/2 kms] when we came to a singular freak of erosion, a lone sandstone pinnacle on the right, three hundred or four hundred feet [100-125 meters] high, the river running on one side and a beautiful creek eight feet [2 1/2 meters] wide on the other. We named these Sentinel Rock and Sentinel Creek and camped there for Beaman to get some photographs. Prof. and I went up the creek and tried to climb out for observations, but though we made three separate attempts we had to give it up. All this is now covered by about 150 meters of water.*

There seems to have been very little mining activity in or along Wahweap Canyon, but there were some claims staked out 6-7 kms upcanyon along the

Blue Pool Wash just below the Highway 89 bridge. The author rappelled down just below the 1st messy pool, only to find a walk-in route just around the corner. There are at least 4 dryfalls or dropoffs in this short slot--and at least as many pools. This drainage is for expert canyoneers only.

Map 42A, Blue Pool Wash and Wahweap Bay

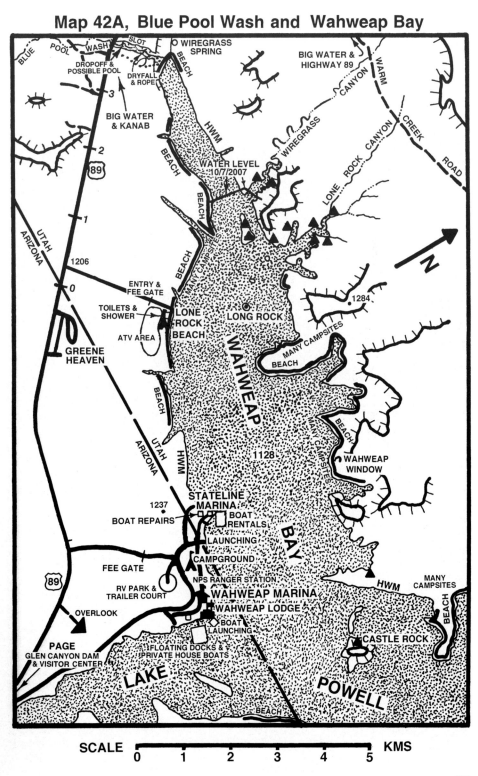

BLUE POOL WASH
SLOT
O WIREGRASS SPRING
BEACH
DROPOFF & POSSIBLE POOL
DRYFALL & ROPE
BIG WATER & HIGHWAY 89
CANYON
WARM
3
BIG WATER & KANAB
HWM
BEACH
WIREGRASS
CANYON
LONE ROCK CANYON
CREEK
ROAD
2
89
WATER LEVEL 10/7/2007
BEACH
1
UTAH
ARIZONA
MANY CAMPSITES
1206
1284
0
ENTRY & FEE GATE
N
TOILETS & SHOWER
LONE ROCK BEACH
LONG ROCK
ATV AREA
MANY CAMPSITES
BEACH
GREENE HEAVEN
WAHWEAP
BEACH
BEACH
ARIZONA
UTAH
HWM
1128
MANY CAMPSITES
WAHWEAP WINDOW
STATELINE MARINA
1237
BOAT REPAIRS
BOAT RENTALS
LAUNCHING
BAY
CAMPGROUND
FEE GATE
NPS RANGER STATION
89
RV PARK & TRAILER COURT
WAHWEAP MARINA
HWM
MANY CAMPSITES
OVERLOOK
WAHWEAP LODGE
BOAT LAUNCHING
PAGE
GLEN CANYON DAM & VISITOR CENTER
FLOATING DOCKS & PRIVATE HOUSE BOATS
CASTLE ROCK
BEACH
LAKE
POWELL
BEACH

SCALE
0   1   2   3   4   5
KMS

281

river. In 1959 Crampton reported seeing an abandoned automobile, perhaps a 1936 model, at the mouth of the canyon. This could only have come down Wahweap Creek.

In the time since the white man has been in this part of the country, this canyon drainage has been known by several names; Sentinel Creek, Sentinel Rock Creek, and Warm Creek. However, Wahweap, which is a Piute word, is likely the best name. Wahweap means something close to alkaline seeps or salt licks, or it may mean little hollows containing stagnant pools of brackish water. With the thick beds of Tropic Shale upcanyon, this certainly is an appropriate name.

Wahweap Bay is one of the largest open bodies of water on Lake Powell. Besides all the good campsites already mentioned, it's a popular water skiing and day-use area as well. There are some scenic sites in the bay too. **Castle Rock** northeast of Wahweap Marina is one of the major landmarks on the lake. **Lone Rock** just north of **Lone Rock Beach** is another site. Almost due north of Wahweap Marina and on the north shore is **Wahweap Window**, an 11 x 13 meter natural arch set in the Entrada Sandstone.

This fotogenic *toadstool* is 5.7 kms (3.5 miles) from **Highway 89** & **Big Water** along the **Warm Creek Road**. It's 100 meters north of the road and easily visible.

Lone Rock Beach & Lone Rock. This foto was taken on **7/19/2007-WL1100.04m/3609.00'**. Regardless of lake levels, there's always a nice beach here--but with lots of noisy ATV's & motorcycles!

From the air, **Glen Canyon Dam** & the Highway 89 bridge looking north. Lower left are the power transformers; just left of dam is the visitor center; to the right and out of sight is the town of Page. Above or north of the dam is Lake Powell; below the dam is the Colorado River and Glen Canyon.

The Colorado River between Glen Canyon Dam & Lee's Ferry

Location & Campsites This part includes the **Colorado River** below **Glen Canyon Dam & Lake Powell**, down to as far as **Lee's Ferry**. This isn't exactly Lake Powell, but it is part of the **Glen Canyon National Recreation Area (GCNRA)**. The distance involved is about 24 kms (15 miles). The water here is always clear & frigid cold and there are no rapids. Because the water is so cold, this is one of the best trout streams in the USA and many people fish here, as well as go sightseeing.

While many tourists get into inflatable rafts just below the dam, float down to Lee's Ferry and are picked up there by bus, all others put their boats in at Lee's Ferry and motor upstream. This is a very popular place for fishing, plus a few people camp. Altogether, there are **6 designated campsites** as shown on the map, which are open on a first come, first served basis. Other sites are for day-use only; these sites offer toilet and/or picnic facilities only. Signs along the river bank will tell you if it's for camping or picnicking/day-use only. New toilets have been installed at each of the 6 official campsites. The nice thing about this trip is, it gives you an idea of what Glen Canyon was like before the dam and lake were built.

Hiking Routes or Trails There's not too many hikes in this gorge, however, there is a **Fisherman's Trail** leading up (or down) from the river to the rim on the west side of the canyon about 2 kms below the dam. Most people doing this hike park somewhere on the rim southwest of the **Carl Hayden Visitor Center** and walk down to the river. This is a steep trail which once had poles and a cable or ropes strung out along the way. Look closely from your boat for the only possible way up the big Navajo Sandstone wall.

Another short hike is to walk about 1 km up the lower end of **Water Holes Canyon**. But there's not a lot to see and there's a big dryfall which blocks your way to the rim.

There's one last hike but it's not along the river. It's to an **overlook or viewpoint** along the canyon rim. Drive south out of Page toward Flagstaff on Highway 89. Between **mile posts 544 & 545**, turn right or west onto a paved road and drive 250 meters to a designated parking place; then walk along an old dirt road to the canyon rim which overlooks the river at what is called **Horseshoe Bend**.

There's also another viewpoint overlooking the river & dam. Drive north from the **GCNRA headquarters** just west of Page and look for a sign pointing out the paved road leading to the overlook.

Hike Length & Time Needed The Fisherman's Trail is about 1 km long and most hikers can climb to the rim in 15-20 minutes--or a half hour or more for some. The walk along the bottom of Water Holes Canyon is about the same length. The hike to Horseshoe Bend Viewpoint is about 1 km and will take 10-15 minutes each way.

Boots or Shoes Any comfortable boots or shoes.

Water While not recommended for drinking, river water has never been tested that bad. On several hikes into the Grand Canyon this writer had to drink river water on several occasions, without treatment, and still lives on. However, river water should only be drank in an emergency--unless treated.

Main Attractions Great scenery, fishing, and one panel of petroglyphs (see the map).

Hiking Maps USGS or BLM map Glen Canyon Dam (1:100,000); Page, Ferry Swale & Lee's Ferry (1:24,000--7 1/2' quads) for hiking; or Leche-E Rock & Lee's Ferry (1:62,500) if available. Or, any Arizona state highway map will show you the way from Page to Lee's Ferry.

Aerial view of **Horseshoe Bend** and **Glen Canyon** looking northeast. Upper right is the town of **Page**, Arizona; upper left are the blue waters of **Lake Powell**.

Map 43, The Colorado River between Glen Canyon Dam and Lee's Ferry

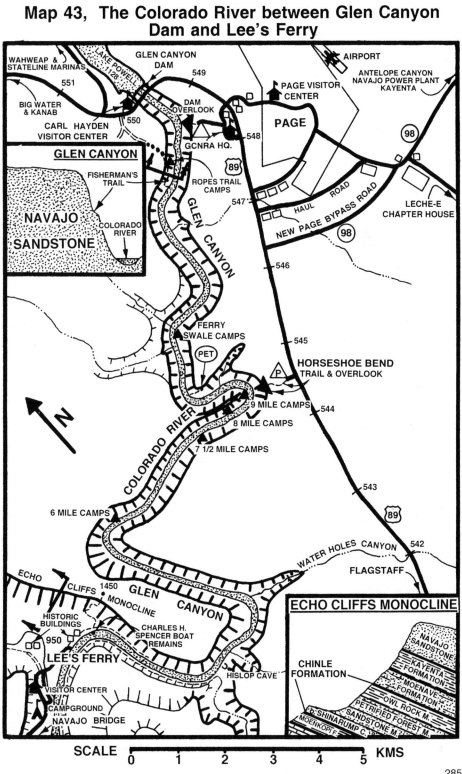

WAHWEAP & STATELINE MARINAS
LAKE POWELL 1128
GLEN CANYON DAM
549
AIRPORT
ANTELOPE CANYON
NAVAJO POWER PLANT
KAYENTA
551
PAGE VISITOR CENTER
BIG WATER & KANAB
DAM OVERLOOK
550
PAGE
98
CARL HAYDEN VISITOR CENTER
548
GCNRA HQ.
GLEN CANYON
89
ROPES TRAIL CAMPS
FISHERMAN'S TRAIL
547
HAUL ROAD
LECHE-E CHAPTER HOUSE
NEW PAGE BYPASS ROAD
NAVAJO SANDSTONE
COLORADO RIVER
GLEN CANYON
98
546
GLEN CANYON
FERRY SWALE CAMPS
545
PET
HORSESHOE BEND TRAIL & OVERLOOK
P
COLORADO RIVER
9 MILE CAMPS
544
8 MILE CAMPS
N
7 1/2 MILE CAMPS
543
89
6 MILE CAMPS
WATER HOLES CANYON
542
ECHO CLIFFS
1450 GLEN CANYON
MONOCLINE
FLAGSTAFF
HISTORIC BUILDINGS
CHARLES H. SPENCER BOAT REMAINS
950
LEE'S FERRY
CHINLE FORMATION
HISLOP CAVE
VISITOR CENTER
CAMPGROUND
NAVAJO BRIDGE

ECHO CLIFFS MONOCLINE
NAVAJO SANDSTONE
KAYENTA FORMATION
MOENAVE FORMATION
OWL ROCK M.
PETRIFIED FOREST M.
SHINARUMP C.
SANDSTONE M.
MOENKOPI F.

SCALE 0 1 2 3 4 5 KMS

Further Reading & Information Sources

History and Archaeology of Glen Canyon Region (some of these publications may be out of print).

A Canyon Voyage, Frederick S. Dellenbaugh, reprinted in 1984, University of Arizona Press, Tucson, Arizona.

Annals of the Carnegie Museum, Special Publication #8, Pittsburgh, 1984, The Pleistocene Dung Blanket of Bechan Cave, Utah (Bowns Canyon), Davis and others.

Anthropological Papers, University of Utah, #104, 1980, Cowboy Cave, Jesse D. Jennings.

Anthropological Papers, University of Utah, #57, 1962, Upper White Canyon and Palmer and Upper Gypsum (Fable Valley) Canyon, Sharrock and others (Carnegie Museum).

Anthropological Papers, University of Utah, #52, 1961, Lake Canyon, Fowler and others.

Anthropological Papers, University of Utah, #49, 1960, The Rincon, Iceberg, Moqui and Forgotten Canyons, Lipe and others.

Anthropological Papers, University of Utah, #73, 1964, Slickrock Canyon, Castle Wash, Steer Pasture Canyons, Sharrock and others.

Anthropological Papers, University of Utah, #63, 1963, Moqui Canyon and Castle Wash, Sharrock and others.

Anthropological Papers, University of Utah, #39, 1959, Kaiparowits Plateau, Fowler and others.

Anthropological Papers, University of Utah, #71, 1964, Kaiparowits Plateau and Glen Canyon Prehistory, Lister.

Anthropological Papers, University of Utah, #42, 1959, Outline History of the Glen Canyon Region, 1776-1922, C. Gregory Crampton.

Anthropological Papers, University of Utah, #72, 1964, Historical Sites in Cataract and Narrow Canyons, and in Glen Canyon to California Bar, C. Gregory Crampton.

Anthropological Papers, University of Utah, #61, 1962, Historical Sites in Glen Canyon--Mouth of Hansen Creek to Mouth of San Juan River, C. Gregory Crampton.

Anthropological Papers, University of Utah, #54, 1961, The Hoskaninni Papers, Mining in Glen Canyon, 1897-1902, Robert B. Stanton.

Anthropological Papers, University of Utah, #70, 1964, The San Juan Canyon Historical Sites, C. Gregory Crampton.

Anthropological Papers, University of Utah, #46, 1960, Historical Sites in Glen Canyon, Mouth of San Juan River to Lee's Ferry, C. Gregory Crampton.

Archaeology of Eastern Utah (Emphasis on the Fremont Culture), J. Eldon Dorman, College of Eastern Utah, Prehistoric Museum, Price, Utah.

Boulder Country and its People, Lenora Hall Lefevre (Boulder, Utah), Art City Publishing, Springville, Utah, 1973.

Desert River Crossing--Historic Lee's Ferry on the Colorado River, W. L. Rusho and C. Gregory Crampton, 1981, Peregrine Smith, Inc. Salt Lake City, Utah.

Ghosts of Glen Canyon--History Beneath Lake Powell, C. Gregory Crampton, Publishers Place, Inc., St. George, Utah.

Glen Canyon Dam and Steel-Arch Bridge, Stan Jones, 1984, Sun Country Publications, Page, Arizona.

Hiking the Escalante, Rudi Lambrechtse, 1985, University of Utah Press.

Hiking and Exploring the Paria River, Including the Story of John D. Lee, Mountain Meadows Massacre and Lee's Ferry, Michael R. Kelsey, Kelsey Publishing, Provo, Utah.

Hiking and Exploring Utah's Henry Mountains and Robbers Roost, Including the Life and Legend of Butch Cassidy, Michael R. Kelsey, Kelsey Publishing, Provo, Utah.

Hiking, Biking & Exploring Canyonlands National Park and Vicinity, Featuring Hiking, Biking, Geology, Archaeology, and Cowboy, Ranching & Trail Building History, Michael R. Kelsey, Kelsey Publishing, Provo, Utah.

History and Settlement of Northern San Juan County, Frank Silvey, unpublished writings.

History of San Juan County, 1879-1917, Albert R. Lyman, unpublished manuscript.

Incredible Passage, Through the Hole-in-the-Rock, Lee Reay, 1980, Meadow Lane Publications, Provo, Utah.

J. A. Scorup: A Utah Cattleman, Stena Scorup, Self Published, Provo, Utah, 1946?

John W. Redd--Oral History, Charles Redd Center/Western Studies, BYU Library, Provo, Utah, 1973.

Lee's Ferry, A Crossing of the Colorado River, Measeles, Pruett Publishing, Denver, Colorado.

Lemuel Hardison Redd, Jr., 1856-1923, Amasa J. Redd, Monticello City Library, Monticello, Utah, 1967.

Museum of Northern Arizona, Bulletin 31, W. Y. and N. K. Adams, Inventory of Prehistoric Sites on the Lower San Juan River, Utah, 1959.

One Man's West, David Lavender, Doubleday & Company, Inc., Garden City, New York, 1956.

Trail on the Water (The Story of river runner Bert Loper), Pearl B. Baker, Pruett Publishing, Boulder, Colorado.

The Outlaw of Navajo Mountain, Albert R. Lyman, Deseret Book Company, Salt Lake City, Utah, 1963.

River Guide to Canyonlands National Park and Vicinity, Michael R. Kelsey, Kelsey Publishing, Provo, Utah, 1991.

San Juan in Controversy: American Livestock Frontier vs. Mormon Cattle Pool, Charles S. Peterson, Charles Redd Monographs of Western History, #3, BYU Library, Provo, Utah, 1974.

Standing Up Country, The Canyonlands of Utah and Arizona, C. Gregory Crampton, Peregrine Smith Books, Salt Lake City, Utah.

The Exploration of the Colorado River and its Canyons, John Wesley Powell, republished by Dover Publications, Inc., New York, 1961.

The Cattle Industry of San Juan County, Utah, 1875-1900, Franklin D. Day, Thesis, Brigham Young University, 1958.

The Quarterly of the Museum of Northern Arizona--Plateau, Stephen C. Jett, Testimony of the Sacredness of Rainbow Natural Bridge to Puebloans, Navajos, and Paiutes, Spring, 1973.

Utah Historical Quarterly, Neal Lambert, Al Scorup, Cattleman of the Canyons, 1964

Geology of Glen Canyon

Glen Canyon Geology (hand out), GCNRA, National Park Service, Page, Arizona.
Geologic History of Utah, Lehi F. Hintze, BYU Geology Studies, Vol. 20, Pt. 3, Provo, Utah.
Geology of Utah's Park and Monuments, Publication 28, 2000, Sprinkel, Chidsey and Anderson (all editors), Utah Geological Association, Salt Lake City, Utah.
Geology Map of Canyonlands National Park and Vicinity, Utah, Huntoon, Billingsley, Breed, Canyon lands Natural History Association and USGS, Moab, Utah.
Geology, Structure, and Uranium Deposits of the Escalante Quadrangle, Utah, and Arizona, Hackman and Wyant, 1973-79, USGS Map I-744.
Geology, Structure, and Uranium Deposits of the Marble Canyon Quadrangle, Arizona, Haynes and Hackman, 1978, USGS Map I-1003.
Geology of the Salina Quadrangle, Utah, Williams and Hackman, 1971-83, USGS Map I-591-A
River Runners Guide to Canyonlands National Park and Vicinity, with Emphasis on Geologic Features (and some history), Felix, E. Mutschler, Powell Society Ltd., Denver, Colorado.

Other Sources

Glen Canyon Camping (handout), National Park Service, 1988
Letter on Lake Powell Water Quality, John O. Lancaster, Superintendent, GCNRA, September, 1988
Stan Jones' Boating and Exploring Map of Lake Powell, Stan Jones, Sun Country Publication, Page, Arizona
Personal Communication, Edith Clinger, Orem, Utah, November 6 & 7, 1988
Personal Communication, Carl Mahon, Monticello, Utah, September 15, 1988
Personal Communication, Clarence Rogers, Blanding, Utah, November 24, 1988
Personal Communication, John Scorup, Monticello, Utah, November 6 & 7, 1988
Personal Communication, Kee B. Tso, Kaibito, Navajo Nation, September 14, 1988
Personal Communication, John Redd, Blanding, Utah, November 22, 1988
Personal Communication, Leo Wilson, Escalante, Utah, September 13, 1988
Personal Communication, Melvin Dalton, Monticello, Utah, October 29, November 6 & 22, 1988
Personal Communication, Owen Yazzie, Leche-e Rock, Navajo Nation, October 1, 1988
Personal Communication, Riter Ekker, Hanksville, Utah, September 12, 1988
Personal Communication, Vernon Griffin, Escalante, Utah, September 13, 1988
Personal Communication, Val Dalton, Monticello, Utah, November 14, 2007
Personal Communication, Robert Redd, Orem, Utah, November 21, 2007

This is **Glen Canyon** at the beginning of **Horseshoe Bend**. These tourists have stopped at the rock art (petroglyph) panel (see fotograph on **page 267**) where there's a sandy beach and toilets. These inflatable boats start immediately below Glen Canyon Dam and float down to Lee's Ferry where the people are picked up and bused back to Page. The boats have motors and they cruise back up to the dock by the dam. This crystal clear water is too cold for swimming, because it comes from the bottom of Lake Powell at 7°C (45°F). It's the same temperature year-round when it leaves the dam.

Other Guidebooks by the Author

Books listed in the order they were first published.
(Prices as of June, 2006. Prices may change without notice)

Climber's and Hiker's Guide to the World's Mountains (4th Edition), Kelsey, 1248 pages, 584 maps, 652 fotos, ISBN 0-944510-18-3. US$36.95 (Mail Orders US$40.00).

Utah Mountaineering Guide (3rd Edition), Kelsey, 208 pages, 143 fotos, 54 hikes, ISBN 0-944510-14-0. US$10.95 (Mail Orders US$13.00).

China on Your Own: and *Guide to China's Nine Sacred Mountains*, Kelsey, **Out of Print.**

Non-Technical Canyon Hiking Guide to the Colorado Plateau (5th Edition-all color), Kelsey, 384 pages, 120+ hiking maps, 285 fotos, ISBN 0-944510-22-2. US $19.95 (Mail Orders US$22.00).

Hiking and Exploring Utah's San Rafael Swell (3rd Edition), Kelsey, 224 pages, 32 mapped hikes, plus History & Geology, 198 fotos, ISBN 0-944510-17-5. US$12.95 (Mail Orders US$15.00).

Hiking and Exploring Utah's Henry Mountains and Robbers Roost, *Including The Life and Legend of Butch Cassidy,* (Revised Edition), Kelsey, 224 pages, 38 hikes or climbs, 158 fotos, ISBN 0-944510-04-3. US$9.95 (Mail Orders US$12.00). **Momentarily Out of Print--Next Edition coming in 2009?**

Hiking and Exploring the Paria River, *Including: The Story of John D. Lee & the Mountain Meadows Massacre,* (4th Edition), Kelsey, 288 pages, 38 mapped hiking areas from Bryce Canyon to Lee's Ferry, 332 fotos, ISBN 0-944510-13-1. US$11.95 (Mail Orders US$15.00).

Hiking and Climbing in the Great Basin National Park--*A Guide to Nevada's Wheeler Peak, Mt. Moriah, and the Snake Range,* Kelsey, **Out of Print.**

Boater's Guide to Lake Powell (4th Edition), *Featuring: Hiking, Camping, Geology, History & Archaeology,* Kelsey, 288 pages, 256 fotos, ISBN 0-944510-10-8. US$13.95 (Mail Orders US$16.00).

Climbing and Exploring Utah's Mt. Timpanogos, Kelsey, 208 pages, 170 fotos, ISBN 0-944510-00-0. US$9.95 (Mail Orders US$12.00).

River Guide to Canyonlands National Park & Vicinity, Kelsey, 256 pages, 151 fotos, ISBN 0-944510-07-8. US$11.95 (Mail Orders US$14.00). **Out of Print**

Hiking, Biking and Exploring Canyonlands National Park & Vicinity, Kelsey, 320 pages, 227 fotos, ISBN 944510-08-6. US$14.95 (Mail Orders US$17.00). **Out of Print**

Life on the Black Rock Desert: A History of Clear Lake, Utah, Venetta B. Kelsey, 192 pages, 123 fotos, ISBN 0-944510-03-5. **Out of Print for a few years.**

The Story of Black Rock, Utah, Kelsey, 160 pages, 142 fotos, ISBN 0-944510-12-4. US$9.95 (Mail Orders US$12.00).

Hiking, Climbing & Exploring Western Utah's Jack Watson's Ibex Country, Kelsey, 272 pages, 224 fotos, ISBN 0-944510-13-2. US$9.95 (Mail Orders US$12.00).

Technical Slot Canyon Guide to the Colorado Plateau, Kelsey, 288 pages, 307 fotos, ISBN 0-944510-20-5. US$13.95 (Mail Orders US$16.00). **2nd Edition coming in Summer of 2008**

Distributors for Kelsey Publishing

Primary Distributor All of Michael R. Kelsey's books are sold by this distributor. A list of Kelsey's titles is in the back of this book.
Brigham Distribution, 156 South, 800 West, Suite D, Brigham City, Utah, 84302, Tele. 435-723-6611, Fax 435-723-6644, Email brigdist@sisna.com.

Most of Kelsey's books are sold by these distributors.
Alpenbooks, 4206 Chennault Beach Road, Suite B1, Mukilteo, Washington, USA, 98275, Website alpenbooks.com, Email cserve@alpenbooks.com, Tele. 425-493-6380, or 800-290-9898.
Books West, 11111 East, 53rd Avenue, Suite A Colorado, USA, 80239-2133, Tele. 303-449-5995, or 800-378-4188, Fax 303-449-5951, Website bookswest.net.
Liberty Mountain, 4375 W. 1980 S., Suite 100, Salt Lake City, Utah, 84104, Tele. 800-578-2705 or 801-954-0701, Fax 801-954-0766, Website libertymountain.com, Email sales@libertymountain.com.
Treasure Chest Books, 451 N. Bonita Avenue, Tucson, Arizona, USA, 85745, Tele. 520-623-9558, or 800-969-9558, Website treasurechestbooks.com, Email info@rionuevo.com.

Some of Kelsey's books are sold by the following distributors.
Anderson News, 1709 North, East Street, Flagstaff, Arizona, USA, 86004, Tele. 928-774-6171, Fax 928-779-1958.
Canyonlands Publications, 4860 North, Ken Morey Drive, Bellemont, Arizona, USA, 86015, Tele. 928-779-3888, or 800-283-1983, Fax 928-779-3778, Email info@clpbooks.net.
High Peak Books, Box 703, Wilson, Wyoming, USA, 83014, Tele. 307-739-0147.
Rincon Publishing, 1913 North Skyline Drive, Orem, Utah, 84097, Tele. 801-377-7657, Fax 801-356-2733, RinconPub@UtahTrails.com.
Recreational Equipment, Inc. (R.E.I.), 1700 45th Street East, Sumner, Washington, USA, 98390, Website rei.com, Mail Orders Tele. 800-426-4840 (or check at any of their local stores).
Online--Internet: amazon.com; adventuroustravelers.com; btol.com (Baker-Taylor); Ingrams.com; Bdaltons.com; borders.com (teamed with amazon.com).

For the **UK and Europe**, and the rest of the world contact: **Cordee,** 3a De Montfort Street, Leicester, England, UK, LE1 7HD, Website cordee.co.uk, Tele. Inter+44-116-254-3579, Fax Inter+44-116-247-1176.
For **Australia** and **New Zealand: Macstyle Media,** 20-22 Station Street, Sandringham, Victoria, Australia, 3191, Website macstyle.com.au, Email macstyle@netspace.net.au, Tele. Inter+61-39-521-6585, Fax Inter+61-39-521-0664.